SPEAKING IN PUBLIC

W9-DFF-761

Sister M. Clare Edward Whalen

SPEAKING IN PUBLIC

Michael Osborn
Memphis State University

Houghton Mifflin Company   Boston
Dallas   Geneva, Illinois   Hopewell, New Jersey
Palo Alto   London

This book is dedicated to Merrill G. Christophersen, mentor and friend, who introduced me to the art of speaking in public.

Chapter-opening photo credits:
Chapter 1 Jonathan Goell © 1980 Chapter 2 Owen Franken/Stock, Boston Chapter 3 Franklin Wing/Stock, Boston Chapter 4 Jeff Albertson/Stock, Boston Chapter 5 Ellis Herwig 1980 Chapter 6 Christopher Johnson/Stock, Boston Chapter 7 Peter Southwick/Stock, Boston Chapter 8 Ellis Herwig 1980 Chapter 9 Owen Franken/ Stock, Boston Chapter 10 Robert A. Isaacs/Photo Researchers Chapter 11 Ellis Herwig 1980 Chapter 12 Elizabeth Hamlin 1976 Chapter 13 Owen Franken/Stock, Boston Chapter 14 Jonathan Goell © 1980 Chapter 15 Jonathan Goell © 1980

Cover photograph by James Scherer

Printed in the U.S.A.

Library of Congress Catalog Card Number: 81-82563

ISBN: 0-395-29692-7

CONTENTS

116 384

Chapter 3
The Art of Listening 57

Chapter 4
The Art of Evaluating Speeches 71

Part II
Preparation for Public Speaking:
The First Steps 99

Chapter 5
Selecting and Analyzing a Speech Topic 101

Chapter 6
Research for Speaking in Public 117

Chapter 15
Conflict Management Through Debate 353

Appendix
Who Shall Guide America?
The Ongoing Political Debate 385

PREFACE

Speaking in Public is intended for the first course in public speaking. The purpose of the text is threefold. First, it offers advice on the preparation and presentation of effective speeches. Second, the text helps students become better communication consumers, for the ability to listen efficiently and to evaluate what one is hearing is essential in today's world of sophisticated media. Finally, the text introduces students to that universe of behavior implicit in symbolic communication. By studying, listening to, and preparing speeches, we can gain perspective on an important dimension of ourselves.

Throughout, the text emphasizes the *humanistic* nature of public speaking. It assumes that the primary value of speech training is not so much preparation for specific communication tasks as it is the general development of the person speaking, enlarging the range of competencies and sensitivities that enhance every aspect of our lives as communicators. The "Overview" develops in detail this humanistic theory of public speaking, which holds that improvement in speech effectiveness creates a desirable multiplier effect throughout the human personality.

Part I, "Orientation to Speaking in Public," describes the rhetorical functions of language and ties each of these to the four fundamental uses of communication as identified by Charles Morris: informative use, valuative use, incitive use, and systemic use. The speech assignments included in the text—the self-introductory speech, the informative speech, the persuasive speech, group discussion, and debate—parallel this model of communication uses. Experiencing them as a sequence in the speech class allows the student to relive the natural process of his or her own communication development and to correct any flaws in that development along the way.

There is, of course, a certain discipline attached to the student's development in public speaking. To that end, the text outlines a comprehensive, systematic Speech Preparation Plan. In Parts II, III, and IV, the student is introduced to the processes of topic selection, analysis, and research as well as audience analysis and adaptation, and to the language, outlining, and presentation skills needed for effective informative and persuasive speeches. Part V applies these skills to group discussion and debate.

There are additional features of this text that deserve mention. The discussion in Chapter 2 of the self-introductory speech in relation to *ethos* is unique. The speech of self-introduction facilitates audience adaptation by allowing class members to get to know one another and by preparing speakers and listeners for the speeches that will be given later in the course. Chapter 2 also provides advice for overcoming speech anxiety. Chapters 3 and 4 discuss critical listening and evaluation with the purpose of improving both speaking and listening skills.

Another novel feature of the text is its approach to an ancient subject, *invention*. Chapter 5 presents a method for discovering and analyzing the rhetorical potential of a speech topic. Chapter 6 examines research sources from the speaker's distinct point of view. Also unique is the approach to audience analysis and adaptation developed in Chapters 7 and 8. Chapter 8, with its emphasis on the symbolic nature of an audience, is especially innovative.

I have both people and places to thank for their help in completing this book. I am grateful to the following people for their helpful suggestions and criticisms of the manuscript: Al R. Weitzel, San Diego State University; Robert S. Adams, University of Oregon; Ray G. Ewing, West Texas State University; Roderick P. Hart, The University of Texas at Austin; George M. Brown, Miami-Dade Community College; and Michael Calvin McGee, University of Iowa. The staff at Houghton Mifflin has been exceptionally dedicated and excessively patient during the five years required for the writing of this book. Working with such professionals is a joy and satisfaction only a writer could appreciate.

Among the friends, colleagues, and students at Memphis State University and in Memphis, Tennessee, who have helped me understand the power of speech in social and political undertakings, I would like to acknowledge especially John Bakke, who has been a companion and wise teacher for many years. A score of librarians and an encouraging administration at Memphis State University have been invaluable aids. I would also like to thank the Memphis State students in section 25, Public Speaking, who studied this book in manuscript during the fall semester, 1980, and who made many helpful suggestions. I am especially indebted to Tim Adams, a grain inspector on the Mississippi River, who turned out to be an even more acute inspector of academic writing.

Finally, I would like to acknowledge Mary Jane, Cecil, Chuck, Susie, Red, Big Marvin, and other friends at Sugar Tree, Tennessee, and the Tennessee River itself, on which or near which a good part of this book has been written. If there is some occasional charm or even beauty in the writing, the Tennessee should get the credit. As Socrates spoke of the pastoral setting in the *Phaedrus,* there are surely gods in the place that one must not offend by deceitful or inaccurate words.

OVERVIEW

The greatest strength we human beings possess may be the power of the word. Words give form to our thinking and provide the connection between ourselves and others. Words are generated by speech, and it follows that the capacity to produce speech is the most essential human trait. It follows further that training in speech must be a significant part of our education.

This book has the important purpose of improving speech as it is used when one person addresses prepared remarks to a group of others. Essentially, its aim is to help you speak more effectively and to listen more intelligently in public communication contexts. It focuses on oral utterance that unites a speaker and an audience with some consequence for the larger community they help to form. We shall build on the philosophical approach of Charles Morris, who suggests that the sharing of information, the building of values, the exercise of persuasion, and the establishment of overall order are the major uses of human speech.[1] They forge the bond that joins speaker and audience. Thus the teacher, the preacher, and the persuader all play vital roles in any society.

Beyond these basic uses, we often exchange speech just for the pure enjoyment of the interaction, for the fun and good fellowship that certain kinds of public speaking can provide. Speech can also perform another important task, that of inspiring the individual and of strengthening the bonds that bring people together in community. Every Fourth of July and Memorial Day, speeches across the land remind us of how valuable and fragile is our ongoing experiment in self-government.

Speech can also be used by group members to probe together for answers to difficult problems and to seek consensus when there is disagreement. Group discussion and debate have emerged as important techniques, especially in societies that pride themselves on free inquiry and individual responsibility. Such societies place great faith in words.

Cicero once described *rhetoric*, the ancient term for the study and practice of public speaking, as "an art made up of five great arts." I have kept the form of that statement, but I have entirely rebuilt its content. The "five great arts of rhetoric," as they will be developed in Chapter 1, make effective the basic communication uses described by Morris. They help us see the world as the speaker sees it, stimulate our

1. Charles Morris, *Signs, Language, and Behavior* (Englewood Cliffs, N.J.: Prentice-Hall, 1946), p. 95.

feelings, forge us together as a social group, impel us toward action, and ensure our long-range survival as a community. Together they constitute an overall human behavior system that I call the rhetorical process. These concepts are perhaps organized in a new way, but the book also includes much traditional wisdom and procedures that ages of public speakers have proved and perfected. Eight basic principles about the meaning and value of public speech have served as a guide.

Speaking in public is a significant use of language. Plato is probably responsible for characterizing public speaking as at best a minor and at worst a debased form of language use. But great speakers, like great poets, cast light on the human condition. Jefferson, Lincoln, Churchill, and Franklin Roosevelt all possessed an eloquence that helped to form the public mind of their own time and of years thereafter. Lincoln's "of the people, by the people, for the people," for example, created a consciousness among Americans that would rebuild the spirit of a torn nation for generations thereafter. The eloquence of Susan B. Anthony, Elizabeth Cady Stanton, and Sojourner Truth rang a liberty bell for women that continues to echo and reverberate to the present day. This potential power of speech leads to the second principle of the meaning of public speaking.

Speaking in public is an important practical art that both deserves critical appreciation and requires sophisticated listening habits on the part of the audience. George Campbell once compared the art of building speeches to the art of architecture. Both arts, he said, combine beauty and usefulness.[2] The comparison is even more apt when it focuses on bridge building, because a great speech can indeed bridge the differences among people and can join them in common interests. When John F. Kennedy spoke eloquently of the unacceptability of thermonuclear war in our time and urged instead an all-out search for peaceful means of world cooperation, a noticeable thaw occurred in Cold War tensions, and the Russian and American people were drawn closer together.[3]

On the other hand, the power of this practical art demands that we develop sound listening habits as well as rhetorical appreciation. Bad listening habits reduce our capacity to learn and make us vulnerable to unprincipled exploiters.

Speaking in public is a serious intellectual enterprise that requires disciplined habits of subject selection, analysis, and research. Years of exposure to bad speaking have given some people the mistaken notion

2. *The Philosophy of Rhetoric,* ed. Lloyd F. Bitzer (Carbondale, Ill.: Southern Illinois University Press, 1963), p. xlvii.
3. "What Kind of Peace Do We Want?," *The Burden and the Glory,* ed. Allan Nevins (New York: Harper & Row, 1964), pp. 53–58.

that public speech is shallow, showy, at worst exploitative, and generally without serious consequence. Speaking ability, they feel, is a trick or a secret shared among the initiated. Such views are ill-informed. Instead, speaking in public tests our capacity for creative thinking, demands rigorous preparation and careful analysis, and requires much practice. Speakers perfect their art by long and often hard experience.

Speaking in public requires rhetorical sensitivity, an in-depth feeling for the needs and wants of an audience. Speaking in public is an adaptive art, because it is shaped by the interplay of speaker, subject, occasion, time, and the particular audience. The speaker must be able to sense how interested audience members are in the subject and how much resistance they have to it. Though largely intuitive, this sensitivity improves with practice. Great speakers are acutely aware of the human possibilities in the speech situation, and they shape not only speeches but audiences. Such people make history move and turn it in certain directions. As the philosopher Hegel has observed, "Speeches from peoples to peoples or to peoples and princes are integral parts of history. . . . In these orations [such as those by the great Greek leader Pericles] these men expressed the maxims of their people, of their own personality, the consciousness of their political situation, and the principles of their moral and spiritual nature, their aims and actions."[4]

The best speaking in public rises out of a passion in the speaker to exchange certain information, to advocate certain values, or to urge a certain program of action. The speech subjects you select should reflect your deepest interests and concerns. The humdrum speech conveys a humdrum person, whether that characterization is deserved or not. Enthusiasm is contagious and so is intense feeling; if you seem excited about your subject, it is easier for your audience to develop interest in what you are saying. Malcolm X and George Wallace both spoke with passionate conviction, and both left an abiding impression on American values and beliefs.

The best speaking in public is deeply humanistic in that it expresses, exercises, and develops a speaker's mind and character, raising a keen awareness of self in society. The Roman rhetorician Quintilian once defined the ideal orator as "a good man skilled in speaking." Thus he focused on the character of the speaker as the key to effectiveness. Our speech expresses us and confesses who we are. But improvement in speaking can also contribute to character development and personal growth. History is filled with examples of shy, repressed children who, by force of inner character, sought development of mind, body, and

---

4. George Wilhelm Friedrich Hegel, *Reason in History: A General Introduction to the Philosophy of History* (New York: Bobbs-Merrill, 1953), pp. 4–5.

speaking ability, and who grew through such development. Theodore Roosevelt was one such person, and Malcolm X has recorded his own growth through public speaking in his autobiography.

Speaking in public is also humanistic in that it engages and creates an audience, helping us discover ourselves and our world, sometimes even opening up new ways of seeing and being. Plato complained that speakers typically flatter their audiences and pander to mass tastes, reinforcing the debased state of the public mind (see his dialogue, entitled *Gorgias*). But the best and most important speaking helps a people to discover themselves. John F. Kennedy's Inaugural Address created a world view for the 1960s, giving Americans a new, vital sense of their global responsibility. The leaders of the women's movement, too, have helped their listeners discover a new self-concept.

The best such speaking is a communion between a speaker and an audience that enhances both and makes possible the growth and continuation of community. The speaker draws power from the encouraging response of listeners; they receive direction and inspiration from the words that fill and bridge the silence. Martin Luther King spoke in Memphis on the night before his death; although the audiotape is faulty, his words capture the passion of that last communion between himself and his listeners.

About a century ago, John Caird, an almost forgotten Scottish intellectual, delivered an address at the University of Glasgow. His words convey this idea of communion with considerable sensitivity:

> *In certain scientific observations you must eliminate what is called the personal equation; but in good speaking, the personality of the speaker, instead of needing to be discounted, is that which lends special value to the result. What reaches the auditor is not thought frozen into abstract form, but thought welling warm and fluent from a living source. In reading a book or report the whole burden of the process is thrown upon the reader. In listening to a spoken address more than half of the burden is borne by the speaker; or rather, activity and receptivity become almost indistinguishable. Charged alike with the electric force of sympathy, the minds of speaker and hearer meet and mingle in a common medium of intelligence and emotion.*[5]

This book is divided into five parts. Part I, "Orientation to Speaking in Public," considers the nature of speaking in public and develops a foundation of theory on which the remainder of the book is con-

5. "The Art of Public Speaking," November 9, 1889. Reprint ed. David J. Brewer, *The World's Best Orations* (Chicago, Ill.: Ferd. P. Kaiser, 1899), pp. 855-863.

structed. Anticipating the initial speech assignment, it discusses the art of effective self-introduction. It suggests techniques for the improvement of listening. It develops nine basic criteria by which speeches can be assessed, so that students may (1) take part more effectively in class evaluations of speeches, (2) construct their own speeches with an eye to satisfying standards of quality, and (3) become in general more discriminating consumers of words. This part also outlines a self-help technique for those who may suffer acutely from speech anxiety.

Part II, "Preparation for Public Speaking," develops a method for selecting speech topics and lays the groundwork of effective preparation for speeches. Speakers draw materials from their own experience and inventiveness, from the expertise of others, and from the needs and nature of their audience.

Part III, "The Informative Speech," talks about processing the materials from these sources into finished informative speeches. The basic arts and options of speech design and organization; the use of facts, figures, and opinions; and effective oral language are relevant at this point. Rehearsal for presentation, including attention to the voice and to body language, is another important consideration. Controlling the perceptual process through verbal and visual aids is also treated.

Part IV, "The Persuasive Speech," deals with the effective communication of values, attitudes, and plans of action. There the challenge and design of persuasive messages and the relationship between argument and persuasion are considered. Because so much depends on the personal power and presence of the speaker, the actual presentation of the speech and the art of delivery receive special attention.

Different points of view often clash in the process of deliberation. Part V, "Public Speaking in the Management of Public Problems," considers the healing and probing art of small-group discussion and the conflict-resolving art of debate. Because formal procedure is often encountered in these various arts, this part includes the various parliamentary motions and how to present them.

I
ORIENTATION TO SPEAKING IN PUBLIC

In the world of business and public affairs, one often hears either wistful statements such as "If I had only studied public speaking" or more positive statements like "That public speaking course I took at the university has helped me more than anything else." Why is training in public speech thought to be so important?

The discussion in Part I should provide some answers to this question. Chapter 1 introduces you to the value of speech training and provides the basic theoretical equipment you will need to perform well in this course. Chapter 2 takes you through the speech of self-introduction and covers the problem of speech anxiety as well as the art of effective narration. Because speech is nothing unless it is heard, Chapter 3 is devoted to improving listening skills. Finally, Chapter 4 introduces the major criteria by which speeches should be assessed. To be an effective speaker you must first become an exacting and perceptive critic of your own speaking.

1

SPEAKING IN PUBLIC: AN OPENING VIEW

A theory of language . . . has to teach us how to
speak and to act in our actual social and
political world.

ERNST CASSIRER, *An Essay on Man*

WHAT TO LOOK FOR IN
THIS CHAPTER

The humanism of public speaking

Personal and social values of speech training

Fundamental uses of human communication

Public speech as an instrument of communication

Human beings have always been known as toolmakers. Even today, archaeologists measure the level of culture among ancient prehuman species by the sophistication of the tools found buried with them. With tools humankind could fashion and shape the environment and not simply be subject to it. Although primitive hatchets and spearheads might indicate a great leap forward in the human adventure, the greatest tools devised by early human beings could not be preserved and cannot now be studied. These tools were words. Words remain our most powerful technology, the greatest shapers of our lives; indeed we live more or less effectively according to how well we use them. Speech is the remarkable ability we human beings possess that enables us to talk about the world around us and the world within us, as those worlds can be represented in language.

THE HUMANISM OF PUBLIC
SPEAKING

Public speaking tends to occur in vital moments when our social and individual selves come together—when we stand before our companions in moments of need, crisis, or important ritual, giving voice to our concerns, dreams, desires, and fears. The occasion may seem small to an outsider; perhaps it concerns only a zoning change in one's neighborhood or a proposed ordinance before the town council. But to those involved the issue may be momentous. Thus training in public speaking is direct preparation for the larger moments of a communication lifetime, when our own vital interests and those of our fellows are often on the line, and a great deal depends on our success or failure to communicate.

This chapter examines the nature and importance of speech and speaking in public. The major theme is that the study and practice of public speech is a *humanistic* activity in that it develops a wide range of skills and knowledge and emphasizes individual creativity. Moreover, such study is humanistic because it makes us more aware of the values that guide us through difficult situations. Those who stand before the zoning commission, fighting against some proposed commercial development nearby, become acutely aware of the values of tranquility, stability, and safety for their children. Those who take the opposite position find that speaking out in favor of the commercial development crystallizes their values of economic growth and full employment. Speech itself is a value-embedded activity; we can hardly open our mouths without projecting and revealing our attitudes toward the worlds around us and within us. Finally, the speech classroom actually becomes a humanistic laboratory as a group of people brought together artificially for the study of speech gradually transforms itself, over the course of the term, into a natural community. Such a community can be very meaningful to its members and can help them develop shared concerns and feelings of mutual support.

Personal Importance

Public speech training, then, is direct preparation for the big moments in a communication lifetime. Further, such training may help people to discover and explore the uncharted selves within themselves, and this adventure is also deeply humanistic. The process of self-discovery through speech training can be so rapid that some people almost feel an identity emerging. Each week in the speech class they experience a growing feeling of mastery. Such positive new feelings readily spread from the classroom into their personal lives.

Beyond such deep personal significance lie surface considerations that are hardly less important. Self-confidence, poise in social settings, and verbal skill that carries over into improved conversational ability are valued by-products of speech training. Social and economic mobility often depends on the kind of flexibility and increased range of communication skills that speech training can provide. In the history of Western civilization, speech training has been most valued when class barriers are breaking down and a rapidly rising under class is asserting itself. For such people effective speech becomes an important means of promoting change in the social hierarchy. In the English

T. C. Fitzgerald

Renaissance, for example, when a wealthy merchant class was rising to challenge the old aristocracy, speech training was especially valued and many speech texts were produced. To be able to articulate one's new sense of power, and to *sound* like a person of gentility when called for, were valued skills indeed.

An important additional benefit of speech training is that it develops one's skills as a critical listener. *Becoming a sophisticated consumer of messages is an essential ability in our rhetoric-ridden culture.* More and more, the general purpose of higher education is to develop citizen-critics who are able to sort the honest from the dishonest, the sincere from the manipulative, in the constant din of messages to which we are subjected. Those who lack this skill are apt to become victims of exploitation, and that goes for societies as well as individuals. In the constant process of putting speeches together and taking them apart during class criticism, speech students gain a feel for the machinery of persuasion. They become alert to the way in which messages are presented outside the classroom.

Finally, a special bonus of the public speaking class is that it can help counteract an unfortunate trend in modern undergraduate education. It is a marvel that so much "liberal" education can be so dehumanizing. In too many cases, the student sits as a passive receptacle for the knowledge poured forth by an instructor. It is not surprising that so many students find the public speaking class so refreshing. Such a class is usually small, and it emphasizes personal interaction between instructor and student. In the constant exchange of information and ideas, the student has an opportunity to participate actively in the ongoing development of knowledge. What is often a stale, impersonal academic atmosphere can be replaced by a vital sense of academic community (it is no accident that the words *communication, commune,* and *community* have such a close and obvious relationship). Your public speaking course should become a positive part of your university life.

Social Importance

To separate social from personal values is not to suggest that society exists "out there" somewhere beyond the barriers of the self. Experience tells us that society helps constitute and complete our sense of ourselves, that it is in us and part of us. The kind of social, economic, and political system we live in goes a long way toward defining our lives and values.

All societies that are governed by elected representatives depend heavily on speech and the flow of public communication. We assume, though perhaps somewhat nervously, that people can be relied on to make responsible decisions when they are exposed to arguments from all sides on an issue. We further assume that people will continue to educate and improve each other in the constant process of communicating. It is no exaggeration to say that our entire political system is built on faith in communication.

Free and open communication is essential to our social lifestyle as well as to our political system. The American lifestyle has been distinguished by its dynamism, by its incessant search for improvement, and by its almost religious faith in progress. Communication that is active, curious, and able is at the heart of our social lifestyle. It is no surprise that society, which like any living system seeks its own continuation, should encourage us in the ways of communicating effectively.

Speech and Individual Development

The study of individual development in speech begins with an overall picture of how language works for us in our everyday lives. An American philosopher, Charles Morris, has identified the major uses of communication systems as follows:

informative use: the exchange of information
valuative use: the exchange of values
incitive use: the exchange of ideas on how to deal with the world

systemic use: the organization of perceptions, values, and actions into coherent and consistent patterns of social behavior.[1]

In Morris's view, any organism that lives successfully in the world must go through the process of informing itself of its environment, deciding what in that environment is good or bad for it, adopting appropriate behavior on the basis of that evaluation, and developing consistent overall patterns of response to its environment. The human organism is different only in that the process of making contact with the world is endlessly more complex. This complexity is due to our unique language ability and to the fact that we not only respond within our environment but also create much of the world in which we live. Indeed, much of our environment is not so much material reality as a symbolic world, a world created largely by words.

Morris's uses of communication systems, or of language, can also be applied to public speaking. For example, a speaker might bring to an audience's attention the facts concerning air and water pollution (*informative use*). The speaker might point out how pollution is increasingly endangering public health (*valuative use*). The speaker might go on to mention several possible solutions to this problem and explain why one of them is the superior solution (*incitive use*). Finally, the speaker might show how such a plan of action would be consistent with previous actions and other goals of the audience, such as preserving wildlife, maintaining ecological balance, and making outdoor recreational activities available to people who need them (*systemic use*).

As you may have concluded from this example, the four basic uses of language identified by Morris build on each other and link together, one making possible the next. Indeed, if it is true that our world views, or overall patterns of expectations, influence strongly *what we see* in our own environment and determine *what information is important* to us, then this chain of language use becomes a circle that circumscribes the world as we know it. See Figure 1.1.

The lessons for the speaker are clear. If you use language well, yours will be an expanding world of greater sensitivity, power, and sharing with others. Within that expanding world, you yourself will grow as a human being. But if you cannot function adequately with respect to the basic uses of language, the walls of your world will harden and eventually close in on you.

Included in this text is a body of speech exercises that can help you increase your capacity for an expanding personal universe. These assign-

1. Charles Morris, *Signs, Language, and Behavior* (Englewood Cliffs, N.J.: Prentice-Hall, 1946), p. 95.

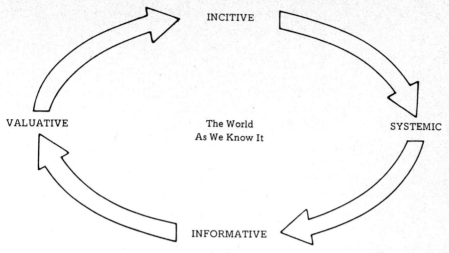

INCITIVE

VALUATIVE

The World
As We Know It

SYSTEMIC

INFORMATIVE

Figure 1.1 THE WORLD AS WE KNOW IT

ments parallel the model of communication uses described by Morris. To experience them *as a sequence* in the speech class is to relive the natural process of your own communication development. Speech training provides a chance to correct any flaws in that development.

The first assignment is the speech of self-introduction, which presents the identity and world views you bring with you to the speech class. Then comes the informative speech, which allows you to exchange perceptions of how the world looks from your own point of view. The informative speech, however, also communicates values, for the very selection of a topic implies priorities. The exchange of values becomes more obvious in the persuasive speech, which frequently aims at inciting the listener to certain actions as well. You may also join other students in group discussion, determining the range of available options in a problem situation and the best alternative for concerted action. Often these discussions succeed in narrowing the number of choices, or they may produce significant disagreement over a possible course of action. Such discussions may even reveal a leadership conflict among several contenders in the group. These situations may call for one of the various kinds of debate, a sophisticated means of managing verbal conflict by converting its energy into a productive test of persons and ideas. Through this sequence of communication exchanges, the many different worlds that students bring to the public speaking class will come together in a larger world of shared experience, which enhances and is enhanced by all who participate.

Speech and the Control of Perceptions

Susanne Langer, a philosopher who has extensively studied symbolic forms, defines *perception* as the basic mental process in which the raw materials of sensation are converted into forms and images that reveal the world to us as it is colored, selected, and distorted by our own needs and feelings.[2] This is why different people often "see" different things when confronted by the same event. Eyewitness accounts in court proceedings are notoriously unreliable, and they frequently conflict with each other. It is not that people are dishonest. Rather, they tend to magnify in importance various aspects of what they see, so that their perceptions make events "fit" the various symbolic worlds of expectation and preconception in which they live.

Speakers have to deal with these private pictures that we form of our world and of ourselves in the world. Thus *the fundamental problem of public speaking is to control perceptions of reality*. The speaker invites his or her listeners to join in the sharing of an image. What all speeches have in common is this search for harmony of perceptions between a speaker and an audience.

As described by Kenneth Boulding,[3] the impact of a message may be to enlarge a certain image, thereby increasing its range. Or a message may bring an image into sharp focus or render it fuzzy and uncertain. For example, a speech on the present state of cancer research may build a picture in your mind where there was little or none before. The successful speaker will bring your previous concept of such research into sharp focus; the less-than-artful speaker may create confusion and bewilderment. The revolutionary message must destroy certain images of reality in order to clear the way for new perceptions. Such is the first item of business for great social and political movements and their orators; witness Castro in Cuba and black and feminist rhetoric in America. Of course a message may also pass by or over an image, leaving it unaffected. Or the listener may reject the message, leaving the image intact and strengthened.

Once we enter the actual arena of public discourse, what we discover are images in conflict over which shall control the public mind. This competition tends to curb the abuse that might occur if one image held unchallenged sway. This is why freedom of speech is such a vital right. The presence of multiple images of reality increases our options and makes possible more intelligent public decision making.

2. Susanne Langer, *Philosophy in a New Key* (New York: Mentor, 1942), p. 45.
3. Kenneth Boulding, *The Image: Knowledge in Life and Society* (Ann Arbor, Mich.: The University of Michigan Press, 1956), pp. 7–10.

Webster-Hayne Debate by George Peter Alexander Healy.
City of Boston Art Commission

Although competing images are normal in everyday communication, there is a level in healthy and stable societies at which the babble of disagreement ceases. Every system, even an "open" society such as our own, tries to maintain itself and is not very tolerant of rhetoric that it interprets as a threat. This basic intolerance becomes severe in times of crisis, especially during war. The deep division and internal strife generated by protest during the Vietnam war were signs of such harsh intolerance. Under these circumstances, protesters run the risk of severe punishment.

It is clearly in the interest of a ruling social and political system to train us from an early age in how we shall encounter and interpret experience. Heroes and villains can be concocted; history can be converted into myth. Indeed, says Boulding, "One of the main purposes of rational education is to distort the image of time and space in the interests of the nation."[4] Such control can be reinforced on television and in the newspapers—on the front page and in the situation comedy as well as on the editorial page and in the frankly partisan documentary. Even mindless game shows help us indulge our fantasies of sudden wealth in a consumer-oriented society. It is simply in the interests of an ongoing social system to influence the most basic processes of

4. *The Image*, p. 68.

perception among its people. Its rhetoric encourages us to see certain things and not others and to value them in certain ways. The public speaking class, which provides an introduction to the theory and practice of rhetoric, can help us understand how such rhetorical impulses can work their quiet but powerful ways in a society. To become aware of such a persuasive force is to develop a healthy resistance that can protect one's individuality.

The role of the rhetorical process in shaping perception is not a dominant theme in the traditional lore of rhetoric. Nevertheless, appreciation of a rhetoric working at the very roots of perception can be traced throughout the long history of thought about communication. The Roman author Longinus, who lived some time during the first several centuries A.D., gave much attention to the image in his *On the Sublime.* Francis Bacon argued in *The Advancement of Learning* (1605) that imagination and reason must work together to control human willfulness through rhetoric. One must be able to "see," he said, the distant and abstract goals and values offered by the orator. George Campbell in *The Philosophy of Rhetoric* (1776) advanced a notion of the "lively idea" as crucial to the rhetorical enterprise, arguing that a concept must be animated and picturesque to hold our attention. And in this century, Kenneth Burke has defined the essential rhetorical function as "a symbolic means of inducing cooperation in beings that by nature respond to symbols."[5] At the heart of his theory is the idea that we live our lives as though we were characters in a drama and that the symbols we use in communication help us plot the play and our roles within it. Such symbols help us *see* our world as a certain kind of stage.

THE RHETORICAL FUNCTIONS OF SPEECH

We have been using the word *rhetoric* in a manner that may seem strange. You may have heard the term used in a negative way. For example, the statement "I am telling the truth, while my opponent offers you nothing but empty rhetoric" is commonly heard during political campaigns. For our purposes, however, rhetoric is viewed as a normal and inevitable behavior. *Rhetoric* is the process in which we influence each other by exchanging ideas, sentiments, feelings, and possible programs of action through the artful use of verbal and nonverbal symbols. As long as we choose to interact with other people, this mutual influence is unavoidable, for the only alternatives to rhetoric

5. *A Rhetoric of Motives* (1950; reprint New York: Meridian, 1962), p. 567.

"And as the ant said to the grasshopper . . ."

Drawing by Richter; © 1981 The New Yorker Magazine, Inc.

are withdrawal from society or submission to the language of force and command. Rhetoric, then, is actually a positive process that allows for flexible, peaceful, and beneficial human interaction. Deceptive or dishonest rhetorical behavior lies not in the nature of rhetoric itself but in the motives of people who use it.

Rhetoric is, of course, closely connected with the art of public speaking. The public speech applies on a grand scale the informative, valuative, incitive, and systemic uses of communication described by Morris. The public speaker uses five special arts to accomplish these uses.

Depiction

First, what Morris identified as the informative use is exemplified in public speaking through the art of *depiction*, the way we reveal to others the world as we see it. In effective depiction, the speaker communicates an image of his or her subject that is *colorful*, because vivid description captures and holds the audience's attention. The image should convey the *active* aspects of the speaker's subject in order to bring it to life for the audience. In addition, the image should be well arranged and *coherent*, because members of an audience are more inclined to understand and accept an orderly picture of the world that "makes sense" to them. Further, the speaker's image should be *strategic*, or selected to achieve the speaker's purpose in addressing that particular audience. Finally, the image should seem *authentic* and *credible*. That is, the depiction must be supported by valid evidence and presented by a speaker the audience is willing to trust.

The weaker any one of these factors is in a depiction, the stronger the others must be. For example, speakers might compensate for a less authentic or believable image by stressing color, action, and coherence in their presentations. But speakers who wish to share their image of a subject with their audiences will work to develop all the skills necessary for effective depiction.

Arousal

It is not enough, however, for an audience to see the world as you see it; they must also share your feelings and value judgments about what they see. This valuative use of language is accomplished through the art of *arousal* (described by the ancient writers as *pathos*). If you understand arousal, you can begin to understand the power possessed by effective public speakers. They become larger than life as their own perceptions and emotions are projected onto others.

At various times in the cultural history of the Western world, emotion has been considered suspect because it is so difficult to analyze or control. Such judgments try to separate feeling from thought, emotional from rational appeal. However, feeling animates thought and moves us to action. Reason is our guide, pointing out the way we ought to go, but feeling generates the energy to move in that direction. There is little doubt that nothing of lasting value is accomplished until feeling and reason are joined together.

Group Identification

A third great art of public speaking, *group identification,* is the power to form many persons into a single action group, ready to move toward a shared goal. Group identification serves both the valuative use and the incitive use of communication, in that it defines group values and provides the potential for mass action. Such communication draws people together and gives them a common identity. Marxists, for example, appeal to "Workers of the World!"; feminists appeal to the "debased, downtrodden, humiliated woman" with an image of "Woman Triumphant!" Rhetoric has the power to form many persons into a "People" who share the same values, goals, heroes, and villains.[6] This sociological function of public speaking is one of its most interesting and dynamic aspects. Hitler contended that the orator is always behind great movements of "the People."[7] He argued that the spoken word is far superior to the written word as the catalyst for mass action.

In a technical sense, the function of group identification is to amplify the energy generated during arousal and convert it to a powerful, shared group emotion. The power to unify becomes especially important when speech goals are difficult and when the forces in opposition to these goals are powerful.

Implementation

The incitive use of communication is accomplished in rhetoric through the art of *implementation,* the proposing and sustaining of a course of action. Implementation can involve two kinds of rhetorical behavior, *deliberation* and *exhortation. Deliberation* occurs when people evaluate various plans for dealing with their common problems and finally commit themselves—either as individuals or as a group—to a single

---

6. See Michael Calvin McGee's discussion in "In Search of 'The People': A Rhetorical Alternative," *Quarterly Journal of Speech,* 61 (1975), 235–249.
7. Adolf Hitler, "The Struggle of the Early Period—the Significance of the Spoken Word," *Mein Kampf,* trans. Ralph Manheim (Boston: Houghton Mifflin, 1971), pp. 463–479.

course of action. Deliberative speech occurs, for example, in legislative bodies as they debate various options.

Exhortation takes place before or during the execution of a chosen plan. Such speech becomes vital during a prolonged period of trial and crisis, and serves to sharpen and clarify faded depictions, rekindle jaded feelings, and reunite the factions that can develop in a group over time. Prominent examples are Lincoln's Second Inaugural Address, delivered to the battle-weary Union forces during the Civil War, and Martin Luther King's final speech in Memphis, intended to rally support for the strike by sanitation workers. Successful exhortation depends especially on inspired use of the resources of language, or what the ancient writers called *style* (discussed in Chapters *8, 11,* and *13*).

Because implementing a specific action is the normal end of rhetoric, this rhetorical art frequently focuses directly on the purpose of the entire rhetorical process.

Renewal

Finally, the art of renewal serves the systemic purpose of ensuring the survival of a group beyond the event that brought the group into existence. Speeches of renewal, often ceremonial in nature, are rituals of celebrating and remembering traditional heroes and enemies in an effort to strengthen a group's sense of common heritage. Such speeches, often heard on national holidays, inspire the group to stay together and may focus on new problems and challenges. We may be inclined to downgrade speeches of renewal as "just so much rhetoric," but they play an essential role in our group consciousness.

The patriotic parades, songs, poems, and speeches commemorating the American Revolution offer a good example of renewal.[8] The great rhetoricians of early American history managed to transform what had been a revolutionary group organized against the British into a society organized according to positive principles outlined in the Constitution of the United States. The change in consciousness from that evidenced in the Declaration of Independence to that behind the Constitution, developed fifteen years later, indicates the power and importance of rhetorical renewal.

Our group identity, reinforced by renewal, sets a certain agenda of concerns for all of us and alerts us to the environment in certain predisposed ways. A reinforced group identity influences our perceptions, our focus, and the nature of the depictions we exchange with each

8. See Wilcomb E. Washburn, "Great Autumnal Madness: Political Symbolism in Mid-Nineteenth-Century America," *Quarterly Journal of Speech*, 49 (1963), 417–431.

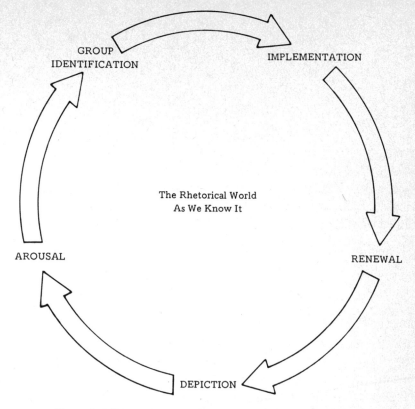

Figure 1.2 THE RHETORICAL WORLD AS WE KNOW IT

other. Thus we have come full circle. The world as we know it is defined and energized by the rhetorical process and by the various arts that make up that process. See Figure 1.2.

Summary of Major Ideas

Speech training can help you discover your own individuality and identity and can help you become a more critical consumer of messages.

Speech training is also valuable because free and unrestrained communication is essential to the American lifestyle.

The major uses of communication systems are to exchange information, values, and plans and to reinforce or establish overall systems of social behavior.

Speech training can simulate each phase of speech maturation in a natural process of development.

A public speech is an invitation from a speaker to an audience to share his or her image of reality.

Rhetoric signifies a natural impulse in communication, the effort to influence by symbolic means.

The rhetorical arts that serve the basic uses of communication in public speaking are depiction, arousal, group identification, implementation, and renewal.

An effective depiction must be colorful, active, coherent, strategic, and authentic.

Reason and emotion work together in effective speech.

Effective speech has the tendency to bring its listeners together, to convert the many persons of an audience into a "People."

Implementing a specific goal or plan is the usual aim of rhetoric.

Ceremonial speech renews in us the values and meaning of our society.

Exercises and Discussion Questions

1. The Office of Consumer Affairs is supposed to protect consumers against uscrupulous business practices. Should there be a corresponding "Office for Consumers of Communication" to shield us from communication abuse? Who would operate such an office, and how would they be selected? How could one be sure that such an office would not engage in political or artistic censorship? Would such an office pose a danger to freedom of speech so grave as to outweigh the office's potential usefulness?

2. Do you agree that "liberal" education is too often dehumanizing? If so, what is the cause of this problem, and how might it be remedied?

3. Can you think of contemporary popular songs that are "rhetorical"? What is their message, and what techniques of musical rhetoric do they employ? Bring tapes or recordings to class for group consideration and analysis. (The project phase of this question could provide the basis for a highly pertinent informative speech.)

4. Observe prime-time programming during a typical week's worth of television entertainment. Did you detect any conscious effort toward social control? What symbols of good and evil, heroes and villains, or moral principles were emphasized? What social perceptions might have been affected by such viewing? Present your findings to the class with whatever recommendations you might have for controlling the rhetoric of social control.

5. Attend a public speech and consider which communication uses it served or attempted to serve. What arts and techniques did it use, and to what extend did it succeed or fail? Report to the class or present your findings in a paper. In speeches of national or international import, certain class members can watch on television, others can listen on radio, and a third group can read the text of the speech in the newspaper to determine what (if any) difference the nature of the medium can make in the transmission of rhetoric.

For Further Reading

Aristotle's *Rhetoric,* trans. Lane Cooper (New York: Appleton-Century-Crofts, 1960), was the first major, surviving effort to explain and manage the marvelous power of human speech. So masterful was it, and so long has been its shadow, that rhetorical studies still normally begin here. And most finally return here to confirm or contend, or to add their bit to its account.

In *The Image: Knowledge in Life and Society* (Ann Arbor, Mich.: The University of Michigan Press, 1956) Kenneth Boulding ventured out of his field of economics to write a provocative essay on how people establish themselves in their worlds and how they affect each other.

Ernest Cassirer's *An Essay on Man: An Introduction to a Philosophy of Human Culture* (New Haven, Conn.: Yale University Press, 1944) summarizes his far-reaching philosophic work on symbolic forms and how they generate meaning.

Susanne Langer's *Philosophy in a New Key* (New York: Mentor, 1942) emphasizes the artistic side of symbolic production.

Richard Weaver's *Language is Sermonic: Richard M. Weaver on the Nature of Rhetoric,* ed. Richard F. Johannesen, Rennard Strickland, and Ralph T. Eubanks (Baton Rouge, La.: Louisiana State University Press, 1970) is a collection of essays that introduces the thought of one of the most stimulating intellectuals of our time on the subject of rhetoric. Weaver's overriding concern is ethical and humanistic problems, essentially what people are doing with and to each other through communication.

2
SPEECHES OF SELF-INTRODUCTION: THE FIRST DEPICTION

Go far; come near;
You still must be
The center of your own small mystery.

WALTER DE LA MARE, "Go Far; Come Near"

THE FUNCTIONS OF THE FIRST
SPEECH ASSIGNMENT

Before the first speeches are delivered, the people gathered for a speech class remain a group of individuals who are largely strangers to each other. To stimulate the transformation of the class into a communication community, speeches of self-introduction are an appropriate first assignment. Such speeches can have a number of other functions. The assignment can serve as an ice-breaker and help relieve the strain and tension that students often experience in a new class. Such speeches can minimize the uneasiness that many feel in a strange group. As class members get to know each other better, the problem of fine-tuning a speech to the needs and interests of one's hearers becomes that much simpler for later speeches.

As a first assignment, the introductory speech is also appropriate in the sense that it replicates the first phase of consciousness in speech maturation, the awakening to a sense of self. As you tell your fellow students about the "I" that is you, you can once again experience self-discovery. Finally, the assignment can help prepare listeners for the speeches you will give throughout the course. Your speech of self-introduction can help establish your character. It can tell us not only where you are coming from but where we might expect you to lead us. And it can incline us to want to go with you.

This final function is probably the one with the most long-range importance. As we have said, the most basic rhetorical function is a sharing of images through the art of depiction. But what makes an audience prefer one image to another? One image, of course, may seem more inherently vivid, colorful, and appealing. Or it may seem more valid in that the speaker can support it with factual data and logically sound reasoning. But a third reason why an audience may select one depiction over another, when images come in conflict, is that it prefers certain speakers to others. Listeners may feel more at home with such speakers. They trust them as sincere, good people who have the listeners' interests at heart. Or they respect them as having expert knowledge and special insight into the problem at hand. Or they simply find them appealing in some way: attractive or possessed of a good sense of humor. Or perhaps they just want to surrender to the strength of character that good speakers exhibit; hearers may take some pleasure in pleasing them by agreeing with their interpretations of reality.

Scholars have long recognized the importance of speakers themselves in the success or failure of speeches. Aristotle identified the personal influence of the speaker as *ethos* and classified it among the three major forms of proof.[1] He thus placed it on a footing with *pathos*, the appeal to motive and feeling, and *logos*, the appeal to reason through fact and argument. All these sources of rhetorical power remain as important today as they were over 2000 years ago, but *ethos* has emerged as especially critical to a speaker's success or failure.

It is important to establish from the beginning an image of oneself as an interesting, competent, attractive, trustworthy, and strong person. *The introduction of self is therefore an important first depiction, which may influence the success or failure of all later speeches.* Take the time to complete this assignment carefully and well.

This chapter describes some techniques you may find useful in developing successful introductions of the self. Because effective story-telling is often essential to such speeches, the middle section of the chapter is devoted to the art of oral narration. Finally, some advice is offered on controlling initial speech anxiety.

PLANNING THE SPEECH OF SELF-INTRODUCTION

While planning your speech of introduction, you may find it beneficial to take up, in turn, three major considerations: (1) your goals in the speech, (2) the approach you should take to reach your goals, and (3) how you should develop your speech.

---

1. See Chapter 2 in Book I of his *Rhetoric.*

What Are Your Goals in This Speech?

Remember that your speech must meet two primary criteria: (1) It must be complete in itself, an artistic whole. (2) It must prepare the way for other speeches you will make by establishing a satisfactory *ethos*. With respect to this second need, you should try to help yourself by making one or a number of favorable impressions. Specifically, in a self-introduction, you:

should seem interesting. As the result of your speech, we should want to know you better.

may be established as having expert knowledge in one or several areas. Here you should try to anticipate future speeches. If later on you will be informing us about the hazards of nuclear waste disposal and persuading us of the advantages of solar energy, your speech of introduction might establish your personal connections with such issues through work, family, or experience.

should seem a person of good will, well balanced and dependable. It is not enough to *say* these things; indeed, they may sound somewhat phony if asserted directly and without support. Rather, you should let an example or a story serve to establish such qualities implicitly and by suggestion.

should seem to possess strength of character, inner power, and assurance. Here again, examples and stories should carry the main burden of suggesting these qualities.

should seem to be someone we might easily identify with in a warm and sympathetic way. If you can talk engagingly and candidly about your small faults, for example, you will often seem—strangely enough—a a larger person.

should seem to be someone whose judgment we could trust and whose advice we might seriously consider. Here stories describing positions of responsibility you have filled successfully should help establish the *ethos* of a person of substance, experience, and sound judgment.

should seem someone whose personal values are in harmony with the public values of society—at least those values presumably embraced by the audience. Unless speaker and listeners respect the same persons, principles, and goals, there will be little ground established for the fruitful exchange of information, feeling, conviction, and ideas for action during later speeches.

Obviously, not every person will qualify on all these possible points of favorable *ethos*. Your job as speaker is to choose which you can emphasize. Then, of course, you must determine how to build these selected impressions into a composite image. Your aim will be an attractive, coherent, believable depiction of yourself.

What Approach Should You Take?

And how can you define your most essential characteristics? Actually there are a limited number of ways to approach a speech of introduction. To consider each of them as you plan your speech requires extensive self-analysis.

1. It could be that the most decisive thing in shaping your character was *environmental*—where you grew up. Tell us about some colorful people in your home town and how you think they may have affected your outlook.

2. The decisive thing in shaping you may have been one particular *person,* perhaps a friend, family member, or childhood hero. The basic question on everyone's mind will be *why* this person had so much influence on you. If the life of some person has been an inspiration to you, this speech may provide an opportunity to honor her or him, reveal an important truth to us, and at the same time give us insight into your values.

3. The thing about you that is exceptional may be some unusual *experience* that has left its indelible impact. What was it about this experience that made it so critical? What does this tell us about you? Through surviving some dangerous situation, for example, one may become a different person.

4. The most decisive thing about you may be some *activity* in which you find special pleasure and meaning. The trouble with this approach is that you can get sidetracked by the activity itself and forget that it is actually a person—you—who is the subject of the speech. Football, knitting, chess, and rock concerts do not interest us nearly so much as *why* these activities fascinate you. Pinpoint specific elements in these activities that are related directly to your personality, needs, and dreams. At the end, we should have an interesting composite of you as revealed in the activity.

5. The thing that may say the most about you is your *goal* or *purpose in life* (or lack of same). What interests an audience especially about a purpose-oriented person is the underlying sense of compulsion and commitment. Again, the danger of such an approach is that you yourself can slip easily into the background while you describe the goal. We are interested more in the *why* of your preoccupation. We will be asking ourselves whether this is an attainable goal or an "impossible

dream." Do you have perspective on your goal and its possible consequences? Commitment is such a rare thing that the person who possesses it, and who is possessed by it, should prove inherently interesting.

6. The most definitive thing about you may be that you try to live your life according to some *value* or *principle*. You have a strong sense of personal morality. This speech lends itself especially well to the rhetorical technique of *contrast*. That is, in order to define and illustrate the importance of your principle, you portray a world in which there are no such principles. Then compare this image with a vision of an ideal world in which your principle is truly realized and fulfilled. For example, would you want to live in a world devoid of caring and appreciation for individuals and their worth? On the other hand what would the world be like if all of us cared for each other and looked constantly for each other's positive qualities? Be careful! This approach can arouse resentment if you seem to be proclaiming how moral you are. Your attitude must be that you are no better than your audience; you simply have discovered a value that might help them too.

These possibilities for self-introduction suggest that you should think in terms of environment, people, experiences, activities, goals, and principles. Such advice to guide the analytical process would have been classified by the ancient writers on rhetoric as *invention*. Inventional methods were meant to assure that speakers would think through their subjects thoroughly, and modern speakers must respond to the same need. Invention is the key to developing substance in a speech, which is critical to the art of speaking in public. Of course, one can not give recipes for thinking, and your own consideration of the topics discussed here may result in a unique blend of themes or still another approach to the speech of introduction.

How Should You Develop Your Speech?

Speeches are not prepared in a vacuum, and they are never pure intellectual constructions. Rather, they are always formed in anticipation of an audience and in light of the speaker's intention and limitations. They are constrained by considerations of time and place. Thus a speech and the underlying structure it expresses represent an adjustment, a compromise, that takes into account audience, speaker, time, and place as well as the substance of the speech.

The speech of introduction is normally brief, confined to several minutes. The overall design must therefore be very simple, but this simplicity can be deceptive. It does not mean, for example, that the period of preparation will necessarily be simple and brief. It does mean that every word has to count and that the structure of the speech has to move quickly to the point, develop it engagingly and well, and make a graceful, effective exit.

The first thing you must do is develop an introduction for your speech. An introduction opens the speech and will often establish a thematic statement, which indicates what the speech is about. Because a speech of self-introduction is most often light-hearted and intended to build a bridge for future good relationships between a speaker and an audience, the *opening* may seek to establish common ground between speaker and audience on which such a bridge can be built. Effective openings may use humor and are often action-oriented; their purpose is to arouse interest in the speech and the speaker.

"Last summer I almost died three times" might be a fine way to begin a speech in which you tell about outdoor work you do for the family business. That business, and its influence on you, could be the real subject of the speech. "Did you ever spend the summer drinking ice-cold water from a spring?" might open a speech in which you tell about your rural upbringing and how it has shaped your values.

The opening is normally followed by a *thematic statement*, which announces what and who the speech is about. For example:

James Johnson knows the loveliest, most sparkling springs in Fentres County. James has lived his whole life—all eighty-four years of it—in Fentres County, which is also my home. To me he is the living history of that county. He represents its heart and soul. James is in my earliest memories, and he taught me the most important things I know: why the mist rises on a lake at night, how to make the best blackberry wine you've ever tasted, and how to take care of baby wild rabbits that have been abandoned. James has a Ph.D. in living, and today I want to tell you more about him—and about myself through him.

The thematic statment is followed by a *development* section. Such development might proceed according to key incidents in time or space. For example, you might talk about major moments in James's life, or you might follow his development over time (James at 16, 30, and 55 years of age). Or again you could build a speech on space contrasts, what James found most different and difficult when he took his one great trip to the city. Obviously, you might combine several approaches. However you choose to develop the speech, don't forget that the audience is most interested in concrete details, stories, and the direct words of people involved in the speech. Provide living dialogue and direct quotations if you would have the people in your speech come to life.

As you complete your speech, look for some graceful way to sum up your message. "Finally, there's a story about James that tells a lot about him." Such a transition suggests to the audience that you are ending and focuses attention nicely on the *conclusion*. Moreover, you are letting the story suggest the character of James and his meaning to you, rather than depending on bald (and perhaps unconvincing) assertion.

As you develop the different phases of your speech, you should be building an effective outline from which to work as you practice your speech for final presentation. The outline also gives you an overview of the structure of your speech and helps you spot opportunities for improvement. The speech outline consists of sentences and clauses that trace the flow of ideas, the techniques you will use to develop these ideas, and the internal logic that unites these ideas into a coherent whole, establishing which lines of thought are dominant and which are subordinate.

Here is an example of a speech outline that might be used for the hypothetical speech we have been discussing. The outline includes bracketed discussions of the strategy underlying each major section. Your instructor may ask you to provide such outlines for each of your own speeches.

I. Introduction: Me and my friend James Johnson.
 A. Opening: "Did you ever spend the summer drinking ice-cold water from a spring?"
 B. Thematic statement: "James Johnson knows the loveliest, most sparkling springs in Fentres County. James has lived his whole life—all eighty-four years of it—in Fentres County, which is also my home. To me he is the living history of that county. He represents its heart and soul. James is in my earliest memories, and he taught me the most important things I know: why the mist rises on a lake at night, how to make the best blackberry wine you've ever tasted, and how to take care of baby wild rabbits that have been abandoned. James has a Ph.D. in living, and today I want to tell you more about him—and about myself through him."

[Strategy: I will gain attention by my opening rhetorical question and also establish the pastoral setting and tone of my speech. I will use striking, concrete language and a vivid word-picture to arouse curiosity and create interest in James. This language will also reveal my values, projected in the virtues I find in James. Because the

language is so vital at this point in the speech, I have written the sentences out and will commit them to memory.]

II. Development: The values James represents.
  A. Simplicity: A typical day in James's life.
    1. Seeing that the birds get fed.
    2. Seeing that the flowers get noticed and smelled.
    3. Taking time for the important things of life.
  B. Caring: James remembers important dates.
    1. When Martha Brown lost her husband—James brings her wildflowers on that day each year.
    2. Birthdays: Typical gifts might be the dogwood slingshot he gave me when I was ten or the cornhusk doll he gave my sister when she was eight.
    3. Each day is important for everyone he meets.
  C. Tradition: James delights in the changelessness of things.
    1. James celebrates what is—all around him.
    2. James is gentle with the faults of others and accepts those flaws as the price of their virtues.
    3. The adventure and ritual of today, with all its chance for fun and goodness, means everything to him. Tomorrow is an adventure yet to come.

[Strategy: The main line of development is from simplicity to complexity, concreteness to abstraction. I present the simple and concrete first, so that my listeners can continue to be introduced to James through everyday activities. Gradually I show him in more ethical depth. I anticipate surprising some of my listeners, who might not expect to find complexity of character in such a child of nature.]

III. Conclusion: "Finally, there's a story about James that tells a lot about him."
  A. The preacher who wanted to save James's soul.
  B. "If I ever manage to grow a soul like the one that lives in James Johnson, God and I both will be very happy."

[Strategy: This final story returns the speech to a concrete level and presents a situation in which a preacher tries to "save" what is already an angelic soul. The irony of this story should make listeners realize even more clearly that James is a rare and beautiful person. To be sure my conclusion ends smoothly, I will memorize much of this final section.]

PRINCIPLES OF EFFECTIVE NARRATION

At the heart of the introductory speech, essential to many of its approaches and necessary to its impact is the story well told: the effective oral narrative. The story well told helps to establish the authenticity of a depiction, so the art of storytelling is basic to speaking in public. However, the story should not just be entertaining and engrossing. It should illustrate an important truth about the speaker or the topic.

Language

The language of an oral narrative must be colorful, concrete, and active. Dizzy Dean may have been ungrammatical as a radio and television announcer, but when he said of a ballplayer, "He *slud* into home," the action leaped before one's eyes. How much more concrete was such a verb than the more abstract and general "He *ran* home." And such an active verb form is much to be preferred, in most narratives, to passive forms such as "home was stolen by the ballplayer." Such a construction is an awkward, drab description of the action. Practice getting the same colorful, concrete, active qualities into your own, more grammatical storytelling. Remember to show the incident; don't just talk about it. If the story is less concrete and interesting than your listeners' immediate surroundings, their attention will drift to those surroundings or to their own daydreams. Your public thoughts must be more interesting than their private ones.

Dialogue

Closely related is a second principle: *An effective storyteller prefers dialogue to paraphrase.* A narrative should seem graphic and alive, and it should involve the listeners in the action. Paraphrase kills these qualities. Storytellers paraphrase when they recast what actually was said into their own language. The paraphrase is a device more appropriate to the compact reporting of events, when one wishes a digest of what was said. For example, a reporter might say, in a space-limited news account, "The suspect shouted that he would never come out alive." Such a concentrated account of an action gives you its essence but no sense of its living reality. Consider how a storyteller using actual dialogue might recount such an action:

Jim Synder

The night was filled with eerie light from the spotlights trained on the house. The police were all behind squad cars and in the shadows of nearby buildings, and it was as though the rest of us were the audience for a piece of theatre gone wild, out of human control.

"Throw out your weapons and come out walking slowly with your hands high over your head," commanded a megaphone with flat precision.

"Hell, no, John Law!" screamed the voice from within the house. "I'd rather die right here than go back." And a shot rang out, shattering one of the trembling spotlights but reducing the centerstage glare hardly at all.

Such a narrative *sounds* alive, and the speech that contains it should be absorbing. It has a sense of immediacy largely because of its use of graphic dialogue, which itself is a major part of the action it describes. Incorporate such dialogue into your narratives whenever appropriate.

But should you make up conversations, inventing dialogue when you were not actually present? It is better to simply report what actually was said, even when the truth is less exciting than fiction. But if you were not actually present, or if the event happened long ago beyond exact recall, or if the actual events did not develop coherently and clearly within a single action, then you can sometimes justify making up dialogue that accurately and fairly represents persons, attitudes, and actions. Ironically, such fiction can help to illustrate truth.

Here we might invoke the literary principle of *verisimilitude*, which holds that the action one describes and the words one quotes must seem true to the moment, must be events that might well have happened, or must constitute dialogue that could appropriately have been spoken. What you are actually offering is your reanimation of an event that can no longer be described confidently by anyone in exact detail. However, verisimilitude is no defense for quoting falsely or out of context when the actual language and situation are accessible to the speaker. The matter becomes serious when the issue itself is of vital concern to the audience and when the words chosen might create false expectations or cause the audience to have an unfair reaction to the person being "quoted." Such pseudo-quotation would be an abuse of the rhetorical technique of living dialogue. When in doubt, check with the person you intend to "quote" to be sure that your version accurately describes his or her feelings.

Economy

A third principle of effective narration is economy, which means that *nothing ought to be in the story except what must be in the story.* A good story gathers a certain momentum in the telling. It creates, as one writer has observed of effective form in discourse, an appetite that must be satisfied.[2] The audience will resent any distracting thought that delays the movement toward resolution and satisfaction. A classic example that may show both excellence and abuse of the principle of economy is a famous section from "The Nabob of Arcot's Debts," a speech delivered in the House of Commons in the late eighteenth century by the orator and statesman Edmund Burke. The speech was a scathing attack on British colonial policy in India. In the passage at hand, Burke was trying to dramatize the devastation wrought by Hyder Ali Khan, a provincial ruler who had been provoked by the colonial authorities into a terrible attack.

When at length Hyder Ali found that he had to do with men who either would sign no convention, or whom no treaty and no signature could bind, and who were the determined enemies of human intercourse itself, he decreed to make the country possessed by these incorrigible and predestinated criminals a memorable example to mankind. He resolved, in the gloomy recesses of a mind capacious of such things, to leave the whole Carnatic an everlasting monument of vengeance, and to put perpetual desolation as a barrier between

2. Kenneth Burke, *Counter-Statement* (Los Altos, Calif.; Hermes, 1931), p. 31.

him and those against whom the faith which holds the moral elements of the world together was no protection.

Burke grinds on in this tedious way until his prose suddenly comes to life:

. . . compounding all the materials of fury, havoc, and desolation into one black cloud, he hung for a while on the declivities of the mountains. While the authors of all these evils were idly and stupidly gazing on this menacing meteor, which blackened all their horizon, it suddenly burst, and poured down the whole of its contents upon the plains of the Carnatic. Then ensued a scene of woe, the like of which no eye had seen, no heart conceived, and which no tongue can adequately tell. All the horrors of war before known or heard of were mercy to that new havoc. A storm of universal fire blasted every field, consumed every house, destroyed every temple. The miserable inhabitants, flying from their flaming villages, in part were slaughtered; others, without regard to sex, to age, to the respect of rank, or sacredness of function, fathers torn from children, husbands from wives, enveloped in a whirlwind of cavalry, and, amid the goading spears of drivers and the trampling of pursuing horses, were swept into captivity, in an unknown and hostile land. Those who were able to evade this tempest fled to the walled cities, but, escaping from fire, sword, and exile, they fell into the jaws of famine.[3]

What is so remarkable about this episode is that its first half should be so tedious and its second half so brilliant as examples of rhetorical narration. In the first part Burke gets bogged down in a maze of intertwining clauses. Especially deadly are the parasitic dependent clauses, which suck the life out of his story line. When he finally discovers his storm cloud image, the description suddenly gathers energy and momentum.

Form

Closely related to economy is the sense of *form*, and out of this consideration grows a fourth principle of effective narration. *An effective story is well plotted, following a plan of development that makes sense in terms of both its own requirements and audience appeal.* A story within a speech is itself a speech in miniature. For one thing, it must begin effectively by gaining attention and establishing a setting

3. *Select British Eloquence,* ed. Chauncey A. Goodrich (1852; reprint New York: Bobbs-Merrill, 1963), p. 346.

and situation. This beginning normally creates suspense and a certain expectation in the audience (called *foreshadowing*). "I never knew how much I loved my town until that summer night when a killer tornado almost blew it—and me—completely away. This is the way it happened. . . ."

As it proceeds along its plan of development, the good story makes use of living dialogue, and its language is colorful, active, and vivid. "'James!' called my mother. 'Here I am, Ma,' I shouted, but the roar of the wind swallowed my words and she couldn't hear me."

The story should follow the principle of economy and not dally by the way. Its ending should be prepared with special care, for the story must conclude well. "So that's how we lived through that nightmare of a night, and the next morning we found that the falling tree had missed me by three feet. Just an extra gust of wind, and you would never have heard this story, because I wouldn't be here to tell it." The punch line, if there is one, must not lose its punch as the speaker rambles on, looking for a better exit. The dribbled-out ending is a common fault of beginning speakers, who either have not prepared their entrances and exits well or lack confidence in how well their conclusions will go over. "At least I think so, but you never know. Do you? Well, I hope you enjoyed my story because it's all true, etc., etc." Such uncertainty may communicate itself to the audience and create a problem where none existed before.

So plan well, and execute the plan unless some real opportunity for productive improvisation presents itself. Even if the conclusion seems flat, it may well have registered better than you imagine. At any rate, you will only make matters worse by groping for something better.

Though what we have just described is the most common narrative form (which traces in a linear and connected manner some real or hypothetical event), there is another, perhaps more sophisticated but occasionally very effective form of narration. We shall call it a *montage* form. Unlike the linear narrative, the montage chooses several scenes and events, connected not by time sequence but by their sharing of a common theme. For example, in a linear narrative you might describe a particularly exciting float trip you took down the Chattooga River. That story in itself might tell a good deal about you or at least your self-concept as adventurer. But if you wanted to make a larger statement, you might choose the montage format and focus first on some sensational moments from the Chattooga trip, then describe a similar trip the late Robert Kennedy took down the Colorado River, and finally turn to some quiet and lovely passages from Mark Twain, describing in Huckleberry Finn's language the adventure of floating down the Mississippi on a raft. All of us are riders to the sea, might be the poetic message of your montage, and you might not even spell it out in words. You might just leave it for your audience to discover for themselves.

Perhaps not all your listeners would derive that message. Those who do understand should perceive you as someone they will look forward to hearing from throughout the semester. And *they* would be precisely the people to whom you would wish to speak. Thus an introductory speech can be a time for finding one's true audience and for those listeners to find their speaker. Such mutual discovery can be gratifying in itself while it prepares a rhetorical setting for future speech interactions.

Insight

A fifth principle of effective narration is that *it ought to lead its audience to some valuable discovery.* A good story gives us insight. In this sense, it functions very much like evidence. What it typically demonstrates is that some abstract moral principle has real human consequence. If you wish to praise courage, wisdom, or love, you must tell stories in which these virtues come to life in the form of people acting and interacting. For example, the moral story (or *parable,* as it is often called) is the chief rhetorical and educational technique of the Bible. As a living exhibition of an important truth, the effective story engrosses its audience and lingers in their minds. How many of us remember important truths from the Bible or other vital documents in abstract form? Most of us were taught Biblical concepts and other crucial ideas in the form of stories (such as the Greek myths or Aesop's fables), and it is the stories that stick with us.

Stories also have a social currency value: People tend to exchange them with each other in conversation. As they are exchanged, they broaden the audience for the principle they embody. Thus a good story can achieve its own mass media effect, and the speaker's ideas may be sown far wider than he or she knows.

Presentation

A sixth principle of effective narration is that *it requires special presentational efforts.* Storytelling is an individual art that cannot be exactly prescribed. But it is clear that effective narration depends heavily on good will between the speaker and the audience. Good storytellers must seem likable and must immediately establish a *confidante* relationship between themselves and their audiences. With very few preliminaries, speaker and listeners must reach a rapport, as if they shared some "inside joke" or some inner truth in an easy, intimate way. Will Rogers and Mark Twain were consummate storytellers in the American tradition, and both had this gift for establishing instant familiarity with an audience.

Good storytellers must enter into the spirit of their stories. A good story usually calls for a lively manner, with gesturing and movement. As you practice, try to develop the kind of dramatic or humorous manner that will put your story across most effectively.

Humor

Thus we are reminded of a final principle of effective narration, that *a good story often depends on humor.* Humor can relieve the pressure that often surrounds speech situations. A classic example was provided when a young Atlanta editor, Henry W. Grady, appeared before the New England Society of New York City on December 22, 1886, to deliver a speech called "The New South." The situation was, to say the least, tense. The audience had just heard a rousing speech by General W. T. Sherman, who had devastated much Southern territory during the Civil War in his "march to the sea." At the conclusion of Sherman's speech the audience had risen to sing "Marching Through Georgia," hardly an auspicious prelude to Grady's effort. When Grady stood to speak, he acknowledged Sherman with graceful and gentle humor and transformed the celebration of past destruction into a vision of future construction. "I want to say to General Sherman—who is considered an able man in our parts, though some people think he is a kind of careless man about fire—that from the ashes he left us in 1864 we have raised a brave and beautiful city; that somehow or other we have caught the sunshine in the bricks and mortar of our homes. . . ."[4]

Grady's humor is based on understatement and irony, which results when everyone knows that the actual verbal statement is not really what the speaker means or what the situation warrants. The audience delights in recognizing the incongruity, and the real meaning of the situation is highlighted. Speaker and audience enjoy an especially close relationship as they share this "insider's" knowledge.[5]

4. *American Speeches,* ed. Wayland Maxfield Parrish and Marie Hochmuth (New York: Longmans, Green, 1954), p. 455.
5. For a more detailed discussion of the rhetorical and communicative values of irony, see Wayne C. Booth, "The Pleasures and Pitfalls of Irony: Or, Why Don't You Say What You Mean?" in *Rhetoric, Philosophy, and Literature: An Explanation,* ed. Don. M. Burks (West Lafayette, Ind.: Purdue University Press, 1978), pp. 1-13.

Jan Lukas/Photo Researchers, Inc.

It is clear from this example why speakers frequently work humorous stories into their opening remarks to relax both themselves and their listeners and to create good feeling. Another kind of pressure can be released when the angry mood of a dispute is cleared away by shared laughter. But the speaker must consider whether humor is really appropriate. If your listeners find your witticisms out of place and forced, they may take their feelings out on you! Clearly, humor can backfire in the face of a speaker who lacks taste, timing, and decorum.

Finally, humor can relieve the pressure of some sensitive issue. Being able to laugh at a troublesome situation can suggest that you have gained some perspective on an issue, some new wisdom and maturity. Such humor invites its audience to share this wisdom. Mark Twain, for example, clearly had a pet peeve: the advice offered with "senile rapture" by older people on how to reach a ripe old age. In a speech in New York City celebrating his seventieth birthday, Twain offered his own life as model. "I have made it a rule never to smoke more than one cigar at a time. . . . As an example to others, and not that I care for moderation myself, it has always been my rule never to smoke when asleep, and never to refrain when awake."[6] Such mockery or burlesque of the behavior of self and others is another important form of humor.

Humor is indeed a fascinating human experience, and many have tried to explore its mysteries. Because it poses important ethical ques-

6. *The Complete Essays of Mark Twain,* ed. Charles Neider (Garden City, N.Y.: Doubleday, 1963), pp. 471–472.

tions as well as rhetorical possibilities for the speaker, let's briefly examine several views of its nature.

SUPERIORITY   The Renaissance intellectual, Thomas Hobbes, who held a rather grim view of humanity, thought that people laugh at the expense of others for the sake of personal gratification. Such laughter occurs at "the apprehension of some deformed thing in another, by comparison whereof they suddenly applaud themselves."[7] The pleasure of such laughter would arise from the sense of *superiority* over another. Those who laugh at others proclaim themselves higher than those others on some scale of value. Winston Churchill's ridicule of Hitler during the Second World War would seem to have been that kind of humor.

Hobbes, however, thought such laughter a sign of weakness and insecurity. What he failed to see was its possible exploitation as a technique of maintaining social order. Because they reinforce feelings of superiority and inferiority, jokes based on race, sexual differences, and profession can strengthen and stabilize the status quo in a society. They can be used, consciously or unconsciously, to keep people "in their places" within a social hierarchy. Thus the king laughs at the peasant to remind himself of his kingship (and the peasant of his servile state). Humor is also used by the downtrodden. The peasant may laugh at the king (behind his back, of course, and *very carefully*) to reassure himself that, material status aside, the peasant enjoys moral superiority. Thus laughter can make a lowly state more bearable. It can even be revolutionary. "If the king is low enough to be laughed at, and if I am high enough and bold enough to do the laughing, then there's no reason for him to rule over me." The joke, Sigmund Freud agrees, can function as a form of rebellion when it makes "aggressiveness or criticism possible against persons in exalted positions who claim to exercise authority."[8]

PUNISHMENT   Freud indeed appears to have had some considerable grasp of the darker social role of laughter. Through mocking, brutal laughter, he observed, we can dehumanize and reduce other people. "By making our enemy small, inferior, despicable or comic, we achieve in a roundabout way the enjoyment of overcoming him—to which the third person, who has made no efforts, bears witness by his laughter." Much political satire would appear to have this function. Via other forms of such aggressive laughter, we can criticize social institutions or—it would seem from Freud's line of thought—regulate social

7. *Leviathan* (Chicago, Ill.: Great Books Foundation, 1949), I, 43–44.
8. Sigmund Freud, *Jokes and Their Relation to the Unconscious*, trans. James Strachey (1905; reprint New York: Norton, 1960), p. 105.

conduct. We can laugh at people to punish them, especially when they engage in behavior we feel inappropriate to their role. In this way we discourage deviance from social norms and encourage conformity of action. Laughter can even be an implied threat, as when political burlesque laughs at leaders to remind them that they can be removed from their exalted position if they do not exercise power properly.

SOCIAL RITUAL Laughter in the service of social rhetoric need not always be the cackle of superiority or the taunt of ridicule. The French philosopher Henri Bergson, writing near the turn of the twentieth century, saw the regulative, corrective role of laughter very clearly. But the more profound nature of laughter, Bergson observed, is that it is inescapably shared and social. "Laughter appears to stand in need of an echo. . . . Our laughter is always the laughter of a group."[9] Thus Bergson senses a more positive role of laughter as social ritual. Laughter can be joyous. It can be a sharing experience in a group of people, which reminds them that they constitute a community. This would seem to have been the humor of Twain, who made us enjoy more the human company we have on our journey through life—especially the company we keep with ourselves. The humor of sharing can heighten that sense of community that makes effective communication possible.

PRESENTING THE FIRST SPEECH

It is natural and even desirable that speakers be somewhat apprehensive as they prepare for speaking, but anticipating their first speech is often very painful for novices. Such speakers, as they look around them during the first class meeting, may see a group of what seem to be hostile, heartless faces. The instructor may look like a sadist who enjoys dog fights.

The truth is that everyone there (including the instructor) probably has some degree of apprehension at the start of a class, no matter how self-confident or indifferent everyone may *look*. But remember that no one will realize how you feel unless you show it. Unless the signs of fear are overwhelmingly evident, the others will sense only the smallest part of your distress. You should not let the fear that others are going to see your fear add to the problem. Nor should you be upset over the chemical changes in your body as you approach the beginning of your

9. *Laughter: An Essay on the Meaning of the Comic,* trans. Cloudsley Brereton and Fred Rothwell (London: MacMillan, 1911), pp. 5-6.

"*Your Majesty, Mr. President, Your Eminence, Your Royal Highness, Mr. Ambassador, Madam Chairperson, Your Excellency, distinguished clergy, most gracious host, fellow-delegates, loyal supporters, comrades-in-arms, honorable fellows, most generous sponsors, honored patrons, distinguished guests, kind friends, fellow-countrymen, ladies and gentlemen— And now I see my time is up.*"

Drawing by Richter; © 1978 The New Yorker Magazine, Inc.

first speech. Clearly you are confronting an unfamiliar situation in front of strangers, and your personal security and prestige may seem threatened. It would be remarkable if you had no feelings of discomfort. So your body releases into your system a considerable dose of adrenalin.

This chemical surge can freeze you into inaction, or it can push you to a level of performance you had not dreamed possible. If at first it tends to impede and bother you, don't be overly concerned. The strangeness will become more familiar. Your classmates will emerge as other human beings who share your experience. Even the instructor will become more recognizably human. He or she has seen this same personal battle repeated countless times and will know how to help you survive these first encounters. The surge of adrenalin will become more controllable, and you may even come to welcome it, knowing how it can energize your speech. Indeed, you may soon start to worry if you don't feel the fright reaction!

One of the techniques you can plan in advance of your speech to relieve any possible freezing reactions is recourse to a visual aid—a model, chart, or blackboard drawing. Practice how you will *use* this aid, emphasizing body movement, gesture, and action. (Warning: Eye contact with your audience is vital. Don't let the visual aid become an escape and a distraction—for you as well as your listeners!) Such planned movement will overcome the frozen fear reaction and should make you more communicative and effective. Visual materials can also increase the credibility of a speech and sharpen its clarity.

From the first, make it a rule not to talk about fear before you speak. Concentrate instead on the ideas you want to get across and on breathing slowly and deeply. When the moment comes for you to speak, respond quickly and look as confident as you can. Appearance, you will be surprised to discover, often creates reality. As you approach the front of the room, be sure that the blackboard is free from diagrams and writings used by previous speakers. If it is not, stop to erase it before proceeding further. You don't need any competing stimuli! Pause before you begin speaking, and start at a comfortable pace that is not too rapid and just a little more deliberate and careful than your normal manner. Try to be smooth and expressive, and let your face help carry your message to your listeners. Look around the audience, and try to involve all of your listeners in what you are saying. Concentrate on the idea and on responding to your own words. Keep your hands in a position from which they can move and gesture in response to what you are saying. Never lock them behind you or at your sides. Avoid the temptation to hide behind the lectern, especially if you are a short person. Moreover, some people find that just using the lectern imposes a formality that may not be appropriate for casual, personal speeches. You may well want to speak from the side or even from in front of the lectern, perhaps sitting casually on the edge of a table. How a speaker decides to stand or sit is an element of rhetorical artistry, just as blocking and staging belong to the art of the theatre.

Never read or memorize your speech. Exact wording is not nearly so important as the direct audience contact and spontaneity you must sacrifice to achieve it. More often than not, reading a speech is just another form of escape from the eyes you really don't want to see—or a confession that you lack confidence. Such negative behavior nullifies the growth potential of speech training. Memorizing a speech is hardly better; memorized speeches invariably sound artificial.

The only place for memorization in speaking is in a carefully worded introduction, which gets one gracefully into a speech, and a carefully worded conclusion, which gets one out of it. Too many speakers waste time fumbling around trying to get started. And too many good speeches have been ruined by speakers awkwardly groping for an effective conclusion. Entrances and exits are as important in a speech as in a play, although the speaker should feel confident enough to respond to unanticipated needs and opportunities that may arise to adjust his or her plans accordingly. Finally, almost every good speech includes certain key phrases and sentences, which have been polished to a high verbal glow and which embody the heart and substance of the speech. It is these highlights that the speaker hopes will be remembered. Exact wording is often the key to their effectiveness, and the speaker should have them down pat.

Other than these special moments for memorization, you should talk to your audience from the outline of ideas imprinted in your head via thorough practice of the speech. If it makes you more comfortable, take with you a card bearing key words that suggest the sequence of major ideas and images. But try not to use this card, and let your wording of the speech flow spontaneously and naturally at the moment of speaking. Actually, you will establish a pattern for such wording in your practice sessions, but if you do not feel bound by absolute memorization, you will be a more flexible and effective speaker. If you find you need the card, place it high on the slanted face of the lectern to minimize the angle of departure of your eyes from the eyes of your audience when you refer to it. Don't try to hide the card, and don't feel guilty or embarrassed because you need to use it. Your listeners will probably not even notice the card unless you make a big thing of it. Feeling is contagious, and whatever a speaker feels emotionally will evoke a like response in an audience. Such a state of harmonious emotional vibrations, known as *empathy*, will occur unless the audience is very hostile to the speaker's ideas or the feelings expressed are extreme and not properly prepared for within the speech. But be sure to make positive use of empathy. Don't let it distract your hearers from your words, which are the important events of that moment, to your personal feelings of discomfort.

If your mind should go blank at some time during the speech, don't stop and apologize. Instead, go back over the point you have just made. This gives your mind another chance to pick up the trail of ideas and, because repetition is often useful in speaking, your circling back to the previous idea will not be noticeable. It may even serve the worthwhile purpose of amplification. Whatever happens, keep talking through your speech to the conclusion.

When you finish, don't take a huge gulp of air and rush to your seat. Your final words should make a strong impression, and you should pause for a moment to give them a chance to register and fix themselves in your listeners' minds. Then walk calmly back to your seat.

Never shake your head or show disappointment about your performance. It may have been much better than you thought and, as a matter
of principle, you should never downgrade your own effort.

Remember this: Your aim is to harness the surge of adrenalin so that
it works powerfully and creatively in your favor.

COPING WITH ACUTE
SPEECH ANXIETY

Much of what we have said thus far has addressed normal speech
anxiety. The advice we have given should prove sufficient to carry
most speakers through the first experience of standing before others
to communicate. Some people, however, may have more than a normal
affliction. If you are one of these "acutes," remember that fright is a
learned behavior. There are no doubt good (though perhaps forgotten)
reasons for your fear. What is learned, however, can be unlearned; one
acquired pattern of response can be replaced by another.

This section of the chapter is a self-help program by which you can
gradually unlearn and extinguish your painful fear responses. This
program is based on the established therapy techniques of successive
approximations and desensitization.[10] Briefly, *desensitization* is based
on the fact that one can slowly build a tolerance for what has been a
painful or irritationally fearful situation by facing the situation in small,
gradually increased doses. It is the equivalent of how one manages to get
into a hot bath (or a cold lake) by dipping first the toe, then the foot,
then the leg, and so on. In successive approximations, one experiences
a carefully planned sequence of situations that are more and more like
the situation one fears. As one moves through this sequence toward
the fear-arousing situation, one enjoys increasing success and builds
confidence. Obviously these principles and techniques can be applied
profitably to speech fright, and they have been applied with dramatic
results. In one experiment they were 100% effective in bringing acute
speech fright under productive control.[11] There is no reason why they
should not work for you as well.

Your instructor may well take the lead in setting up the self-help
program. If no announcement is made, let the teacher know that you
have an acute problem, and ask him or her to announce that there will

10. See the discussion of these techniques and their underlying principles in "Therapy and
Remediation," *Foundations of Abnormal Psychology*, ed. Perry London and David Rosenhan
(New York: Holt, 1968), pp. 580–587.
11. See the fascinating story of this classic experiment with speech fright in Gordon L. Paul,
Insight vs. Desensitization in Psychotherapy: An Experiment in Anxiety Reduction (Stanford,
Calif.: Stanford University Press, 1966).

be a voluntary meeting of such acutes to set up a self-help therapy program. Better still, make the announcement yourself! You would make a marvelous visual aid for your own subject: "If your tongue ties and your face freezes and your knees shake when you speak, just like mine are doing now, I would like to invite you to a meeting of the Public Speaking Acutes. The PSA will hold its organizational meeting . . . etc., etc."

However humorous or serious the manner of your invitation, let us anticipate a group of from six to eight interested persons. Often the acutes from several sections of public speaking classes may be brought together to form such an action group. The business of the first meeting might be to discuss the upcoming speech assignment and what it will require. With the group sitting in a casual circular arrangement, each person can be invited first to introduce himself or herself and then to discuss his or her ideas (or lack of same) about how to approach the assignment. You convened this self-help group, so you should take the responsibility of seeing that each person has a chance to speak and become involved in the discussion. Especially reticent persons should be encouraged by leading questions. "What are your ideas on this, Mary?" or "If you don't have any ideas, perhaps we can help. Where are you from? What did you like to do there? What do you hope to accomplish here? Why?" The group should be able to help its members a great deal, because you all have a common problem and a common motivation to get the better of it.

These informal discussions are actually distant cousins of the formal public speech, for whenever we initiate a conversation with another and play our part in an ongoing dialogue, the communication consists of a number of brief, informal speeches tied together in a sequence. Your own leadership role and the "other-orientation" of group therapy will strengthen and affirm the first signs of a healthy, emerging communicative attitude.

During the next meeting of the group, which may be scheduled two or three days later, the focus should be on speech design, strategy, and initial research. What you have decided to focus on, how you intend to develop the speech, and often the materials you will use in this development (calling on personal experience, interviews, and library research) are appropriate subjects for discussion. The tone of the discussion should be a little more formal than the casual conversational level of the first meeting. Each person should be the center of attention for a certain amount of time, just as in the later speech. The circular arrangement of chairs should be changed so that one chair stands out clearly at the head of the circle. As the center of attention shifts, each person should speak from this chair. Speakers, however, will remain seated, and each explanation of subject, strategy, speech design, and materials should be followed by an informal critique by other group members that emphasizes the positive and offers suggestions for improvement.

The final meeting of the self-help group should be held right before the speech assignment cycle begins in the class. At this point the finished speech should be practiced and ready for presentation. The seating arrangement of the previous class should be maintained, but now the chair at the head of the circle should be replaced by a speaker's stand. Speakers should stand and speak from this position. Again, criticism should emphasize the positive, with a few final pointers for maximum effectiveness.

Such a cycle of meetings provides not just desensitization therapy but effective speech preparation as well. It approximates not only the threatening speech situation but also the ancient model of speech preparation that extends from creative thinking about a subject (*inventio*) to presentation of the final product (*pronunciatio*). The group members may decide to continue to work together to enhance their preparation or help polish newly acquired speech skills.

A SAMPLE SPEECH OF SELF-INTRODUCTION

In the self-introductory speech that follows, Tom Shaner chose the "important experience" approach to communicate a vital picture of himself and his world. Through his graphic descriptions and the careful structure of his speech, Tom was able to share with other students, most of whom knew little about factory work, what it meant in human terms to have a large plant fail. Using concrete and effective imagery, Tom gave us a sense of participating in the fateful meeting that changed his life. We were there, admitted by his language. He gave us just enough background in his work career for us to understand the impact of the bad news announced at that meeting. But then his speech changed its tone, and he let us share his admiration for the strength of those who would not be defeated, who proved once again the toughness of the human spirit. The speech ends on a note of affirmation and hope that such an ordeal might be spared those who work at the plant where he is presently a manager.

While the speech effectively introduced Tom, his outlook, and his world, it also had a subtle persuasive quality. At the time of the speech, the plant was indeed in crisis over low production and high production costs. Using many of the communication techniques he learned from class discussions and readings, Tom helped promote an understanding that kept the plant open, preserving several thousand jobs. His classmates were proud of him and, through speeches such as this, they felt they had come to know him well.

It was the first day of spring and the sun filtered through the dusty venetian blinds into the factory conference room in Barberton, Ohio. I was the first to arrive, so I sat in a chair near the window where the sun hit my back. It felt good because the room had been closed and the air was cool and damp.

All the managers had been told to report to this 9 A.M. meeting for an announcement. So while I waited, I began thinking what the announcement might be about. Was it going to be the usual lecture about high factory costs or perhaps about the lower production we had been experiencing? Maybe it was going to be about additional layoffs. We had already laid 25% of our people off. Or it might—just might—be that the plant was going to be able to begin the expansion we all were hoping for.

Suddenly my thoughts were interrupted by the entrance of the plant manager. He was a man 63 years old with short-cropped gray hair, blue eyes, and very erect posture. His posture was a by-product of 20 years of military service. However, this day he looked 83. His eyes were dark, his shoulders slumped—not at all his usual positive self.

He walked to a small lectern in the front of the room and put down a packet of papers. He began, "Gentlemen and lady," acknowledging the fact that we had a woman factory manager present. Next he slowly surveyed the room as though making a mental count, and then he looked straight at me. "Well," he said, "I see even Tom Shaner has made it here on time." Everyone laughed, including me, but it was a nervous, tense laugh. He then proceeded, "I have a short announcement to read to you. 'This morning the Firestone Tire and Rubber Company has decided to curtail production permanently at the following plant facilities in the United States: Salinas, California; Pottstown, Pennsylvania; Dayton, Ohio; Los Angeles, California; Akron Synthetic Division, Akron, Ohio; and at its Seiberling Division at Barberton, Ohio.''

Suddenly, hearing these few lines, I felt like a foundering swimmer going under for the third time. My work career with Firestone, all fifteen years of it, passed before me. How easily I remembered the first days with the company as a laboratory technician, chasing around the Pottstown chemical plant collecting samples to be tested for quality. Then I thought of an old gray-haired pipefitter I met in the chemical plant. His name was Joe Tascione. It was he who told me some twelve and a half years ago, "Tom, you're wasting your time on this laboratory job. Firestone is opening an apprenticeship here at the plant. Use your head and try out for it. I know you can do it."

Well, I waited until the last day to sign up. And you know, Joe was right. I did qualify. My next four years were spent training for my trade. This was the most satisfying, self-gratifying time in my life. After completing this program, I was fortunate enough to move into the plant engineering department as a technical assistant. Then my next opportunity was to go to Akron, Ohio. In this corporate engineering job I traveled as far west as Salinas, California, east to Cranberry, New Jersey, north to Juliette, Canada, and south to Orange, Texas. Then, as my next assignment, I transferred as department manager to Barberton, Ohio. All this experience, all this work, time, and effort—and now no job!

I then looked around at the others gathered together in the conference room. On their faces were etched the same pain, disbelief, and bitterness I was feeling. And it didn't matter if you were black or white, man or woman, Christian or Jew, it felt the same. We all felt shortchanged.

Over the next several weeks, however, we all dug our heels in. It was time to stop feeling sorry for ourselves and start looking for work. The company provided Career Development Seminars that helped overcome the hurdle of not knowing how to look for jobs. It was at this time that something happened which was a very uplifting experience. The true grit and sheer intestinal fortitude of Americans that politicians always like to talk about was indeed there. People began treating the closing as an opportunity, not a setback.

Some workers decided to go back to school full time. Some found jobs elsewhere and relocated. Some found jobs locally, and were truly happy to leave the rubber industry and not have to move from Barberton. And one opened up a business in northern Michigan, renting out boats and selling bait to summer fishermen. He told me before he left, "Tom, this is something I have always wanted to do. Now's my chance."

Myself, I was fortunate to have three job offers. One was in Akron, with a recycle energy plant. One was in Oklahoma City with another firm. And the third was with Firestone in Memphis, Tennessee. I'm speaking to you here tonight, so you know which one I took.

The plant here has some of the same problems and challenges facing it that the closed plants had. But I feel it can weather the storm. Indeed, the experience I have gone through has given me the insight necessary to contribute to this plant's success. I want to avoid any other 9 A.M. announcements!

Further Discussion

Tom Shaner's speech is especially noteworthy for the effectiveness of its beginning section, which illustrates a number of the narrative techniques discussed in this chapter. The first paragraph establishes an effective ironic contrast between the setting of the meeting and its content: between the warmth and hope of early spring and the grim news that will be delivered. Tom might have indulged in a bit of fiction, setting the meeting on a cold and rainy day that would have been consistent with its content. Such an opening could have been effective in its own way. The irony created here, however, sets the meeting off by contrast and gives it a certain grotesque quality. The meeting is *felt* to be out of tune with its surroundings and—in a certain sense—unnatural. Thus Tom made a quite defensible choice between these symbolic options.

The second and third paragraphs are effective in building suspense and curiosity and in foreshadowing the bad news that will follow. In the second paragraph, for example, we learn that this plant has had some difficulty, pointed up by phrases such as "high factory costs," "lower production," and the possibility of "additional layoffs." Against this background the third paragraph paints a vivid picture of the plant manager and how he looks as he enters the room. (The manager himself illustrates one of the techniques we have discussed, as he tries to soften his harsh message by beginning with a joke.)

All such narrative techniques, which illustrate the ideas of colorful language, living dialogue, and clear, linear movement, prepare listeners to share the news that will have such an impact on Tom Shaner's life and to participate in his feelings. Tom is building a base of identification that will serve him well in later speeches.

Summary of Major Ideas

The self-introductory speech helps to relieve tension, facilitate audience adaptation, and promote a sense of community.

The introductory speech simulates the first phase of speech maturation, an awakening to the sense of one's self.

The introductory speech is an important first depiction. It helps an audience decide whether the speaker will be credible in later speeches.

To establish favorable *ethos*, the speaker should seem interesting, should appear to have special knowledge in certain areas, and should come across as a well-balanced, pleasant individual.

To establish favorable *ethos,* the speaker should also appear a person of character, someone whose judgment we could respect, and one with whom we would like to identify.

A final condition of favorable *ethos* is that the speaker's values should seem in general harmony with our own.

Speeches of self-introduction can emphasize a person's roots, the influence of another person, or some overwhelming experience.

Introductory speeches can also emphasize activities, goals, and values.

Storytelling is essential to the introductory speech and basic to the art of depiction.

The language of oral narration should be colorful, concrete, and active.

Effective storytelling prefers dialogue and direct quotation to paraphrase.

Verisimilitude results when the storyteller recreates the aura of an event's actually happening.

The effective oral narrative practices economy of words, is well plotted, and leads to some valuable discovery.

A good story often makes use of humor, especially to relieve pressure and to build identification within a communication community.

The central problem of delivering the first speech is to control speech anxiety so that it becomes a positive, constructive force.

Victims of acute speech anxiety may be helped by informal meetings that implement therapy programs based on successive approximations and desensitization techniques.

Exercises and Discussion Questions

1. Often people who are required to take public speaking put it off as long as possible. Should such a class be taken early or late in one's college career? Why is there such anxiety surrounding the speech class?

2. Is there any special reason why *ethos* should be so vital in contemporary communication?

3. Who is the best storyteller you know, and why is she or he effective? Prepare a speech in which you tell a favorite story in the manner of your favorite storyteller.

4. Can you think of examples of the ethical use and the abuse of humor? of humor with a social purpose? Should the government regulate the kind of humor we see and hear on television and radio shows? Prepare a written report in response to one or several of these questions for possible presentation in class.

For Further Reading

Readings on the introductory speech are scant, but much has been written on the art of narration. Most of this literature focuses on the art of writing, but Wallace Hildick's *Thirteen Types of Narrative* (New York: Clarkson N. Potter, 1970) gives practical and helpful advice that is easily applied to oral narration.

Concerning humor and its social rhetorical implications, Freud and Bergson are well worth reading. Wayne Booth develops the conception of the communicative potential of irony in his *A Rhetoric of Irony* (Chicago, Ill.: University of Chicago Press, 1974).

For general works related to desensitization and successive approximations, see J. Wolpe, *Psychotherapy by Reciprocal Inhibition* (Stanford, Calif.: Stanford University Press, 1958) and A. A. Lazarus and S. Rachman, "The Use of Systematic Desensitization in Psychotherapy," in *Behavior Therapy and the Neuroses,* ed. H. J. Eysenck (London: Pergamon, 1960). Articles of special interest are the following:

Marvin R. Goldfriend and Christine S. Frier, "Effectiveness of Relaxation as an Active Coping Skill," *Journal of Abnormal Psychology,* 83 (1974), 348-355. This article deals with general anxiety-coping skills among students who reported experiencing acute speech fright.

Kim Giffin and Kendall Bradley, "Group Counseling for Speech Anxiety: An Approach and a Rationale," *Journal of Communication,* 19 (1969), 22-29. This article suggests treatment for acutes through groups but advocates the presence of trained counselors.

James C. McCroskey, David C. Ralph, and James E. Barrick, "The Effect of Systematic Desensitization on Speech Anxiety," *Speech Teacher,* 19 (1970), 32-36. This study focuses on counseling for acute speech anxiety.

3
THE ART OF LISTENING

The study of man is the study of talk. Human
society is an edifice spun out of the tenuous
webs of conversation.

KENNETH BOULDING, *The Image*

┌───┐
│   │
│   WHAT TO LOOK FOR IN   │
│   THIS CHAPTER   │
│   ─────────────────────────────   │
│   │
│   Public speaking as an art form   │
│   The characteristics of effective listening │
│   │
└───┘

Most of the time you spend in a public speaking class, you will be not speaking but listening. After each speech will come evaluation: Was this effort successful? What made it work or not work? How can this speaker improve? How can we listen more intelligently?

These questions are the business of this chapter and the next. We will discuss critical listening and intelligent evaluation as arts in themselves, which exist in relation to the art of speaking in public. Each day immeasurable confusion results because people do not listen well. And in the age of mass media, we must all become more sophisticated consumers of electronically transmitted communication. Evaluation has emerged as an art of survival.

Beyond these practical applications, listening and evaluating allow us to gauge the quality of our interaction with the world around us. They are arts of observation, which determine whether we are in touch with reality or lost in illusions of our own making. One person hears what is said, evaluates the message, and responds in a way that makes the most of the situation. Another hears what he or she wants to hear, withdraws into a dream world, and lives at the mercy of circumstances.

All the more reason for us to learn the arts of listening and evaluating.

SPEAKING IN PUBLIC AS AN ART

For all their importance, listening and evaluating are secondary arts. That is, they exist in relation to the primary art of public speech itself.

We may view public speech as attempting to cross the spiritual barriers that separate human beings. Public speech begins with the simplest of relationships: someone who wishes to speak, the language in which the message is spoken, the medium through which the message is transmitted, and someone who receives and interprets the message.

Eric A. Roth/The Picture Cube

As simple as these relationships may seem, considerable problems can arise at every point along the way. This is why speaking in public is a complex skill that few truly master. The reassuring thing is that all of us can greatly improve our public speaking with just a modest investment of time and patience.

Major problems complicate the art of speech, and they arise at both ends of the journey of a message. We may want to speak, but speaking in public may at first seem a strange and frightening situation. When we speak honestly and completely what is on our minds, we let our guard down. We become vulnerable and leave ourselves open to criticisms or disagreements that may hurt. On the other hand, we create the possibility of growth and constructive change, give ourselves a chance to influence others, and invite the sharing that becomes possible when others listen and open their feelings and thoughts to us in return. But to overcome that initial fear of self-disclosure and risk taking may require a great deal of courage. Our courage grows as we grow confident of our ability to manage such risk.

Listeners pose another problem. They may choose to hear only what they want to hear or not to hear at all. This is because listening—true listening—is also a form of risk taking. Listeners may learn something, and what they learn may transform the universe in which they live. They may have to change their attitudes and values or face living with a lie. Or they may simply be indifferent to a message, refusing to grant its possible relevance to their lives. Speakers may find it quite frustrating to urge such an audience to hear fairly.

At all points in the communication between speaker and listener, severe challenges arise. Language is difficult to manage, and words that will express the fine shades of our thought and feeling may be hard to find. The room in which we speak may be filled with distracting noises and competing objects of attention. Because the art of public speech is complex, those who master it are deeply admired, and rightly so.

Yet public speech struggles to be recognized as one of the great arts. Perhaps this is because the subject matter for most public speeches is some specific issue of the moment and thus significant only for a brief time. The irony is that successful speeches often resolve the controversies that make them relevant. We may not care now whether the Athens of the Golden Age should have resisted the aggression of Philip of Macedonia. That once vital and bloody issue has turned to the fine dust of history, and all the magnificent words once spoken on either side of it have long since faded. We can still read the speeches of the Greek orator Demosthenes, but it is hard to hear the echo of his voice across twenty-four centuries of time.

As what is therefore an ephemeral art, public speaking bears an unexpected and curious relationship to the performance of the matador as described by Ernest Hemingway:

> ... it is an impermanent art as singing and the dance are, one of those that Leonardo advised men to avoid, and when the performer is gone the art exists only in the memory of those who have seen it and dies with them. ... If it were permanent it could be one of the major arts, but it is not and so it finishes with whoever makes it, while a major art cannot even be judged until the unimportant physical rottenness of whoever made it is well buried.[1]

Hemingway's observation emphasizes permanence and timelessness as qualities of major art. But the impermanent arts may gain intensity—perhaps superior to that of the more lasting arts—from their very fleeting nature. Part of the pleasure Hemingway took in the great performances of the matadors Joselito and Belmonte was, quite possibly, an awareness that these rich but passing moments symbolized the central tragedy of all life. No matter how splendid and excellent its appearance, it is all impermanent.

Public speaking may seem tame in comparison with bullfighting, but it remains an intense form of public artistry that can touch off social change or even revolution. It can fill both audience and speaker with a dramatic new sense of themselves and of their shared humanity and purpose. It can bind them together in striving to achieve some

1. Ernest Hemingway, *Death in the Afternoon* (New York: Scribner, 1932), p. 99.

common goal with, as Edmund Burke once said, "ties which, though light as air, are as strong as links of iron."[2] It is a power that, in our time, has been strong enough to arouse hatred and strong enough to overcome it.

Such an intense art form requires study and what we shall call criticism. *Criticism*, which is no more than enlightened appreciation for the virtues, defects, technique, meaning, and importance of a work of art, implies knowing both how to listen and how to evaluate.

EFFECTIVE LISTENING

The listener is no mere passive participant in the public speaking situation. If true communication occurs, interaction is vital.

Effective listening depends on six essential qualities and skills: culture, motivation, concentration, active listening, objectivity, and interpretation.

Culture

It is said that people who visit a foreign country find there what they bring. It is also true to a considerable extent that listeners find in a speech the cultural background that they bring to it. We might be quite satisfied with a speech introduction such as, "The government is hypocritical when it charges us with militancy," if we had never experienced artful irony and simile (figurative comparison) as they are used, for example, by Emmeline Pankhurst. This British feminist, who had just been released from prison for her activities in the women's movement, opened her speech at Royal Albert Hall in London, October 17, 1912, with the following biting words: "It always seems to me when the anti-suffrage members of the Government criticize militancy in women that it is very like beasts of prey reproaching the gentler animals who turn in desperate resistance when at the point of death. . . ."[3]

Until we know our options as listeners, it is hard to register more than vague satisfaction or dissatisfaction with the speech we are hearing. In short, to be good listeners we have to acquire the background, or *culture*, of a listener. We must listen to speeches whenever we can and consider what it is in them that we like or dislike, what succeeds or fails with us. We must think about the technique of speech, because

2. "On Conciliation with America," *Select British Eloquence*, ed. Chauncey A. Goodrich (1852; reprint New York: Bobbs-Merrill, 1963), p. 290.
3. *Feminism: The Essential Historical Writings*, ed. Miriam Schneir (New York: Random House, 1972), p. 294.

technique alone can influence our thinking and acting, quite apart from the content of the speech.

Along with deliberately seeking exposure to public speech, good listeners can study the *theory* of effective speech, just as we will be examining the criteria of good speaking in the next chapter and throughout the book. We constantly check and correct our listening by referring to the principles established in such a theory. Gradually, we develop a *taste* that warns us when we are listening to a defective speech and awakens in us a keener sense of the excellence of a worthy speech. All our listening occurs against the background of such culture. We find in a speech the greater meaning that our experience enables us to bring to it.

Motivation

So much of effective listening depends on proper, positive motivation. Whenever we listen, it should be to *gain* and *learn*, not to trap the speaker or to confirm our preconceptions. Moreover, we must be strong enough to resist the opinions of those around us who would predispose us for or against a speaker.

It is important in a class situation that we listen encouragingly to others. Even if we disagree with them, we should take pleasure when they speak well. Good listening nurtures good speaking, and all the members of a public speaking class tend to rise or fall together. You owe each other the kind of listening that builds on a speaker's strong points and minimizes any weaknesses.

In addition, a well-motivated listener does not demand that the speaker reduce all choices to simple yes-or-no, black-or-white decisions. The good listener is wary of that kind of rhetorical impulse on the part of speakers. Good listeners are also not afraid to inform the speaker when they have not understood. That may seem a simple virtue, but many people find it difficult to say, "I do not understand" in public situations. Such an admission may make them seem less intelligent and expose them to ridicule, or they may be perceived as challenging the speaker. More than likely, many others share their uncertainty and will appreciate the risk they take in informing the speaker of their confusion. Unless communication is clarified, the directions the speaker offers cannot be followed in any accurate or concerted way, and the problem addressed in the speech is compounded.

You can generate motivation by asking yourself how you can benefit from the speech. If you decide to *listen with a purpose*, you will have made an important commitment to effective listening.

Concentration

A good listener is able to concentrate on the message at hand. Often you may enter the speech classroom concerned about the other events of a busy day or excited by prospects for the weekend. Nevertheless, one can decide to postpone such considerations until after class.

If we view the speech itself as only one possible focal point among a whole set of competing stimuli, the rest of which function as potential distractions, we can see how great the challenge to effective communication is. Of course, speakers must do their part to ease the burden of concentration—*must indeed aim to transform conscious concentration into unconscious pleasure and preoccupation.* But what if speakers, though they have worthwhile messages, are not skilled? And what if speaking conditions are uncomfortable and noisy?

The good listener still goes more than halfway to complete the communication. In the classroom setting, one good reason to cooperate in this manner is the moral debt you owe your classmates to help them become better speakers. A second reason is that your time is committed anyway. You might as well concentrate on effective listening. Your teacher and the speaker will appreciate your effort, especially when you indicate, by your suggestions in the post-speech critique, that you have been listening closely.

Effective concentration does not mean that you should try to dwell on every word the speaker says. That can actually defeat effective listening, for the meaning is not so much in the exact words chosen as in the thoughts they express. You should concentrate on the logical relationships of ideas and weigh the ethical and practical value of what you hear. Keeping the following questions in mind may help you concentrate effectively.

1. What ideas are here?
   A. Are they well developed?
   B. Do they follow each other in sequence?
   C. Is adequate evidence given to support them?
   D. Which among these ideas are most important, and which are least important?
2. How is the content of this speech related to my life?
   A. What are the moral meanings of this speech?
      i. Do I agree with them?
      ii. Why or why not?
   B. What are the practical applications of this speech?
      i. How could I make use of them?
      ii. What benefits might I expect?

Imagine for a moment that you were in the crowd at Royal Albert Hall for the Emmeline Pankhurst speech mentioned earlier in this chapter. Apply the foregoing questions to the speech as it is summarized here. Which ideas would you conclude are most important? What kind of judgment would you make about the moral meanings of the speech?

It always seems to me when the anti-suffrage members of the Government criticize militancy in women that it is very like beasts of prey reproaching the gentler animals who turn in desperate resistance when at the point of death.... Ladies and gentlemen, the only recklessness the militant suffragists have shown about human life has been about their own lives and not about the lives of others, and I say here and now that it never has been and never will be the policy of the Women's Social and Political Union recklessly to endanger human life. We leave that to the enemy. We leave that to the men in their warfare. It is not the method of women.... There is something that governments care far more for than human life, and that is the security of property, and so it is through property that we shall strike the enemy. From henceforward the women who agree with me will say, "We disregard your laws, gentlemen, we set the liberty and the dignity and the welfare of women above all such considerations, and we shall continue this war as we have done in the past; and what sacrifice of property, or what injury to property accrues will not be our fault. It will be the fault of that Government who admits the justice of our demands, but refuses to concede them...."

Be militant each in your own way. Those of you who can express your militancy by going to the House of Commons and refusing to leave without satisfaction, as we did in the early days—do so.... Those of you who can express your militancy by joining us in our anti-Government by-election policy—do so. Those of you who can break windows—break them. Those of you who can still further attack the secret idol of property, so as to make the Government realize that property is as greatly endangered by women's suffrage as it was by the Chartists of old—do so.

And my last word is to the Government: I incite this meeting to rebellion!... Take me, if you dare, but if you dare I tell you this,... you will not keep me in prison.[4]

Using the model outlined here is a good way to begin developing the discipline of effective concentration. Some people find it helpful

4. *Feminism,* pp. 294-295.

to take notes as they listen for the patterns of ideas. Taking notes as you listen can help you probe beneath the words to the thoughts. Moreover, if you keep a notebook throughout the course, you will have a record of classroom observations in which you can trace the growth of your classmates as speakers and, at the same time, preserve what you learn about speech from first-hand observation.

Just as a good speaker comes well prepared to speak, good listeners come ready to listen. Try to sit near the speaker—for psychological as well as physical reasons. When you are near the front of a room, you can hear easily, but more important, you make a commitment to listen closely and well. It is harder to be attentive when you are isolated in the back of a room. (This is why a good moderator for a small group of listeners in a large room first appeals to everyone to come down near the front.) The physical act of sitting together near the speaker facilitates group identification and gives the speaker the kind of responsive listening necessary to healthy communication.

Active Listening

Most of us are conditioned to be passive listeners. "Shut up and listen" is the sort of injunction we too often grow used to as children. That kind of listening means that we are expected to sit and absorb what the adult speaker puts before us. We are not expected to question or to argue.

Obviously, if we are to develop adult listening habits and a healthy defensiveness before speakers who do not necessarily have our best interests at heart, we must overcome such bad childhood training. If we are to apply the critical questions suggested for concentration, we must become active listeners. Our minds, our critical faculties, must become *engaged* with the speech we are hearing.

How would you, as an active listener, respond to this passage from a speech Emmeline Pankhurst delivered in Hartford, Connecticut, on November 13, 1913?

> *Well then, there were the men of pleasure, or the businessmen who were so busy earning money during the week that all they could think of when the week came to an end was recreation, and the great recreation in England today is playing golf. Everywhere on Saturday you see men streaming away into the country for the weekend to play golf. They so monopolize the golf links that they have made a rule that although the ladies may play golf all the week, the golf links are entirely reserved for men on Saturday*

and Sunday. . . . Well, we attacked the golf links . . . all the beautiful greens that had taken years to make, had been cut up or destroyed with an acid or made almost impossible to play upon. . . .[5]

As we develop experience as active listeners, we learn that the question is not an act of personal rebellion that should be discouraged, but is rather an invitation to further learning. Finally, we act on what we have heard—we digest it, transform it, and convert it to use in our own lives.

Objectivity

Many people bring to a speech expectations that warp—and sometimes totally distort—their reception of the message. Is the speaker someone they intensely like or dislike? Either way, they distort the words they hear to fulfill their expectations. Does the speaker represent a political party or religious group they endorse or despise? Again, they will hear and not hear what they expect. Having experienced the rhetoric of Emmeline Pankhurst in this chapter, and having formed positive or negative feelings about her, would you be able to listen objectively if she were to appear again among us?

This kind of subjectivity no doubt afflicts all of us to a certain extent and more so in some situations than in others. But when it does become a significant factor, it raises a barrier to communication. If it is true that the message intended is sometimes not the message actually spoken, it is even more often true that the message spoken is not the message received. Between speaker intention and audience reception lies a large chasm of misunderstanding, the *communication gap.*

To the degree that we are subjective, we lose contact with our surroundings. We lose control over events and understanding of the actions of others. To be objective means to accept the world on its own terms and, where it is unacceptable, to resolve to change it. To cultivate objectivity is to develop an outer orientation as opposed to an inner orientation. Suddenly the world around us becomes interesting on its own terms, and we want to *learn* what is in it rather than *confirm* what is in us. Other people—their perceptions, feelings, and values—become interesting and valuable to us, and we open ourselves to sharing their perspectives and to the growth in personality that such sharing makes possible. We may not always agree with their words, but we will understand more clearly why we reject them.

5. *Feminism,* pp. 301–302.

The most crucial consideration in practicing objectivity is to delay making value judgments about what we hear until speakers have had their say. Try not to respond to words that could inflame your feelings, and look instead for the speaker's purpose. When speakers use symbols like "freedom," "justice," and "equality," words that often trigger an emotional response, consider whether your definitions of such terms are similar to the speaker's. Usually you can tell from the context of the speech what the speaker means by such terms and whether you agree.

Interpretation

The mind is not a net that can catch and hold all of the thoughts, feelings, and nuances of a message. If it were, we would quickly become immobilized by trivia. Instead we are forced to be selective: We look for the major elements in a speech.

Indeed, effective listening depends on a complete, disciplined process of *interpretation*. Immature listening habits give us incomplete and uncertain reflections of fragments of a message. The interpretation process of effective listening involves reception, reflection, and application. During the *reception* of a speech, you should form a mental outline of the major ideas and underscore in your mind the major elements that interest, confuse, or disturb you. You do not have time, however, to take off on mental tangents. As the speaker continues, you must delay contemplating these elements until the speech is over. After the speech is concluded, interpretation enters a phase of *reflection*, in which you have time to consider what you have heard. If there is a time for questions or comments, you can ask for information or clarification of what you have underscored in your mind, or you can present your views for the speaker's reaction. Finally, interpretation enters the phase of *application*. Now is the time to ask yourself several questions. What here is worth keeping, and what can I discard? How can this material be used?

Summary of Major Ideas

Public speaking is an ephemeral art, but intensity and social significance may compensate for the brief importance of a speech.

Criticism is enlightened appreciation of the virtues, defects, technique, meaning, and importance of a work of art.

Acquiring the culture of a good listener means listening to many speeches and learning the technique of effective speaking.

The properly motivated listener comes to gain and not entrap, to learn and not to confirm preconceptions.

A good listener develops the ability to concentrate on a speech.

Good listening is active listening, in which our minds become engaged with what we hear.

In active listening the question becomes a probe and an invitation to further learning.

The distance between speaker intention and audience reception is the communication gap, much of which may be created by factors that interfere with audience objectivity.

To develop listener objectivity, we should want to learn rather than to confirm, and we must cultivate the ability to delay making value judgments.

Effective listening depends on a process of interpretation, which includes phases that we have called reception, reflection, and application.

Exercises and Discussion Questions

1. Visit and observe audience behavior at a speech or lecture outside the public speaking class. What good and what bad listening habits do you observe, and what do you conclude about listening behavior? Interview the speaker or lecturer if you can, and ask whether he or she is aware of listener response and is affected by it.

2. Discuss in class your reactions to the Pankhurst speeches quoted in this chapter. Can your class reach consensus on the major ideas she develops and the morality of her speeches?

3. Some people seem incapable of accurate listening. Perhaps they are too busy bending the speaker's statements to suit their own point of view. Perhaps they are self-conscious rather than focused on the speaker or so busy silently rehearsing questions that they cannot attend to the moment. Whatever the cause, such people suffer from woeful lapses of attention as well as from distorted attention. The

following communication game helps to reveal these problems, and provides some helpful practice in avoiding them.

The game requires three players: a sender, a receiver, and an observer. These people engage in a five minute communication exchange, which begins when the sender initiates a discussion on a topic either drawn from a predetermined list of possible subjects or of the sender's own choosing. After this first statement, the receiver may speak only if he or she can first summarize adequately what the other has just said. No new statement or any further response can be offered until the person who last spoke is satisfied that the other has understood the previous communication. The observer serves as a referee and enforces the rules.

When five minutes have elapsed, the players should review the discussion and answer the following questions:

A. Did you have trouble listening? Why?
B. Did you find yourself wanting to interrupt the other person?
C. Did you decide that the other person was right or wrong before he or she had finished speaking?
D. Were you thrown off the track by emotional or colorful language or by any other especially distracting, difficult, or defective uses of words?
E. What did you learn about your listening ability?

When you complete this analysis, change roles and repeat the game two more times, so that each person has an opportunity to play all three parts.

For Further Reading

One way to approach reading related to the art of public speaking is to start with imaginative literature. Creative writers have been especially sensitive to the power of public speech as an art form. A classic example is William Shakespeare's re-creation of the speeches of Brutus and Marc Antony before the Roman mobs. Shakespeare provides an unforgettable picture of the art of controlling a hostile crowd. You will want to read the whole of *Julius Caesar* to appreciate the rhetorical excellence of the speeches in the second scene of the third act.

Another excellent example is Robert Penn Warren's great novel *All the King's Men* (New York: Harcourt, Brace, 1946). The book traces the meteoric rise in Louisiana politics of Willie Stark, a fictional character inspired by Senator Huey P. Long. Stark discovers "life effectiveness" when he discovers speech effectiveness, and he discovers speech effectiveness when he realizes the deep longing of his rural "hicks and red-necks" for a political identity and for some control over the forces that doom them to a hard life. The novel records the rhetorical power that can be generated when speakers find the audiences meant for them. That mutual discovery tells us that *audience adaptation* in depth is audience-speaker identification.

Another vivid portrait of a Southern orator, this time without the veil of fiction, is William Price Fox's amusing description of a stump speaker in rural Georgia ("Eugene Talmadge and Sears Roebuck Co.," *Southern Fried Plus Six* (New York: Ballantine, 1968), pp. 34-40).

Beyond such reflections in imaginative literature are the great practitioners, those who have mastered the art and written insightfully about it. Mark Twain's "On Speech-making Reform" is itself a witty model of after-dinner speaking and says some wise things about speech preparation and practice and about those who botch up the art. See *The Complete Essays of Mark Twain,* ed. Charles Neider (Garden City, N.Y.: Doubleday, 1963), pp. 640-643. The most extensive writings by a speaker on speaking are those of Cicero, the great Roman orator of classical times. Especially recommended are *Brutus*, which comments with charming candor on the orators of his own day, and *De Oratore*, which addresses itself in prose of exceptional readability to the training, lifestyle, and significance of the speaker. See especially the translations of Cicero's works in the Loeb classical series published at Harvard University, Cambridge, Massachusetts.

4

THE ART OF EVALUATING SPEECHES

To speak, and to speak well, are two things.

BEN JONSON, *Timber; or, Discoveries*

WHAT TO LOOK FOR IN
THIS CHAPTER

Examining substance, commitment, and imagination

Assessing credibility, adaptation, and argument

Judging organization, delivery, and language

Much of effective listening depends on knowing what constitutes a good or a less-than-good speech effort. By what measures do we make such determinations?

This chapter presents nine criteria that are basic to the art of evaluating public speaking. Included with each criterion are specific questions to guide your evaluation. The criteria provide the major points to focus on in classroom discussion, and combine to produce an "evaluation profile" which can indicate where you must improve.

SUBSTANCE

Does this speech have something worthwhile to say? The substance criterion comes first, for without substance a speech offers nothing of value to its listeners. At least two specific questions can be asked about substance:

1. *Has the speaker adequately defined and brought the subject into focus?* One ought to be able to reduce any speech to a single key sentence or proposition that contains a clear and complete statement of its purpose. Sometimes a speech focuses too broadly, especially given its time limitations. One could hardly, for example, hope to talk meaningfully about "Crime in America" in five minutes. With "Schoolyard Crime in Peoria" you might have a better chance!

2. *Does the speech reflect adequate research and preparation?* Speeches that are products of desperate midnight inspiration on the evening before they are given have a telltale way of revealing themselves for what they are. Ideas must go through a cooling and curing process in the head, and the speaker must have time to collect vital information and illustrations through reading, conversation, and reflec-

tion. Good speakers begin their preliminary planning as soon as a speech is assigned.

COMMITMENT

How important does this speech seem to the speaker? The first task of speakers is to find subjects that deserve a commitment of time and effort. Ideally, speakers appear in connection with some important question or cause. Thus a critical question in the art of evaluation is whether a speech conveys this quality of commitment. The impression of commitment in a speaker is necessary before there can be arousal, which you will recall is vital in the rhetorical process. Commitment is the spark in the speaker that touches off fire in the audience.

1. *How intense is the feeling in the speech?* The expression of feeling must be carefully controlled by the speaker. Feeling must seem sincere and natural; an audience will resent shows of emotion it perceives as phony. Often, therefore, a quiet intensity of manner expresses feeling most effectively. When Franklin Delano Roosevelt declared war on Japan, his language was simple and restrained, but the depth of the president's feeling came through clearly in his delivery:

> *Last night Japanese forces attacked Hong Kong.*
> *Last night Japanese forces attacked Guam.*
> *Last night Japanese forces attacked the Philippine Islands.*
> *Last night the Japanese attacked Wake Island.*
> *This morning the Japanese attacked Midway Island.*[1]

Here the simple repetition of words at the beginning of each short sentence underscores the gravity of the situation and builds a sense of outrage.

2. *What is the risk factor in the speech?* Willingness to place one's safety, possessions, or good name on the line for a cause is commonly regarded as proof of commitment. When a novice speaker tackles a difficult subject before an uncertain audience, the risk factor is high, and the speech, even if faulty, should be brave and interesting. To be dull in speech classes is to commit the cardinal rhetorical sin!

IMAGINATION

How original is this speech and the mind it reflects? An imaginative mind helps us to find undiscovered meanings and express those percep-

---

1. "War Message—Hostilities Exist," *American Speeches*, ed. Wayland Maxfield Parrish and Marie Hochmuth (New York: Longmans, Green, 1954), p. 508.

tions in images that are vivid and memorable. Consider, for example, the way the great physicist Sir James Jeans helps us to discover the nature of sunlight, or "why the sky looks blue."

> Imagine that we stand on any ordinary seaside pier, and watch the waves rolling in and striking against the iron columns of the pier. Large waves pay little attention to the columns—they divide right and left and re-unite after passing each column . . . it is almost as though the columns had not been there. But the short waves and ripples find the columns of the pier a much more formidable obstacle. When the short waves impinge on the columns, they are reflected back and spread as new ripples in all directions. To use the technical term, they are "scattered."
>
> We have been watching a sort of working model of the way in which sunlight struggles through the earth's atmosphere. . . . We know that sunlight is a blend of lights of many colours . . . as Nature demonstrates to us when she passes it through the raindrops of a summer shower and produces a rainbow. . . . The mixture of waves which constitutes sunlight has to struggle through the obstacles it meets in the atmosphere, just as the mixture of waves at the seaside has to struggle past the columns of the pier. And these obstacles treat the light-waves much as the columns of the pier treat the sea-waves. The long waves which constitute red light are hardly affected, but the short waves which constitute blue light are scattered in all directions.[2]

The ability to form such striking images is central to the art of depiction. This is why the quality of imagination must rank so high among the criteria for evaluating speeches.

It is also clear that the imagination works largely through analogy, the comparing or relating of different things that are alike in some telling way. The more different the two things, the more clever and "imaginative" the successful analogy seems. The success of an analogy, however, depends on whether it illuminates our thinking on some point vital to the speech. Analogy works for speakers when listeners are familiar with one of the things compared and unfamiliar with the other. The familiar subject builds a bridge of understanding to the unfamiliar subject. In the example given, the success of the analogy depends on audience familiarity with ocean waves. For an audience that had never seen the ocean crashing into a pier, the image would be nearly meaningless.

2. *The Stars in Their Courses* (New York: Macmillan, 1932), pp. 23–24.

CREDIBILITY

Speakers who present competing views on an issue pose a problem for listeners, who must decide which view they will accept. In making this critical decision, listeners will, of course, apply the substance criterion. In addition, listeners should also consider the speakers themselves: how able they are, their reputations, and whether they are free from bias. These considerations come under the criterion of credibility.

In order to understand this criterion more clearly, let us consider its components individually.

Expertise

The expertise factor has to do with whether a speaker is qualified to speak on a particular subject. To evaluate expertise, ask yourself the following questions:

1. *Does the speaker have adequate personal knowledge?* Some subjects seem to require that a speaker have personal experience with the subject. One who has been addicted to drugs will command careful attention when speaking on drug rehabilitation. Someone who has been the victim of crime can speak with special urgency on the reform of criminal law. Clearly, this kind of expertise can also be deceptive. The reformed addict and the outraged victim may have had such close, intense contact with their subject that they lack perspective and overall understanding.

2. *Does the speaker convince us that there has been adequate research preparation?* On most issues one must research the questions involved, find the latest and best information, and survey the most authoritative opinions available. The speech should show the speaker's mastery of such information. Accompanying visual materials such as charts and graphs may bear witness to such knowledge and are somewhat authoritative in themselves. They also clarify and reinforce the content of the speech. People whom audience members respect or authorities whose credentials qualify them as experts should be introduced in the speech. When speakers quote such experts, they are borrowing their credibility.

Research and personal experience have a happy way of correcting each other's weaknesses. Personal experience supplies a sense of vitality and immediacy; research provides comprehensive vision and depth of understanding. It follows that the speech that exhibits both experience and research should be highly credible for most audiences.

3. *Has the speaker narrowed the topic enough to permit a responsible statement, given the time allotted and the nature of the audience?* This question assumes special importance in the college classroom, where time limits on speeches must usually be imposed and enforced. Much depends on the audience and the knowledge about the topic that listeners bring to the speech. The weapons speech that could interest your classmates might fall flat before a group of well-informed military officers. Therefore, a major consideration in evaluation is the good sense demonstrated in selecting and limiting a topic and matching it with the speaker and the audience.

Trustworthiness

Is the speaker someone I can trust? A speaker's trustworthiness quotient (TQ) depends on an often-intuitive judgment formed by the audience. This judgment is so vital to speech success that we should at least understand how it may be formed. TQ arises first from the reputation of the speaker. We trust people who have already proved their ability and good character. The importance of the past in determining TQ is pointed up by effective introductions, which establish or re-establish fresh, favorable images of speakers just as they stand to speak. Speakers who refer to past experiences early in their speeches may also be trying to achieve a favorable TQ.

TQ is further shaped by immediate cues given off in the speech situation. Impressions of inner strength and honesty can enhance this dimension of credibility. The very words speakers use can influence the trust audiences place in them. Speakers should speak the words used by listeners themselves in everyday life. Bad rhetorical grammar may have nothing to do with faulty verb–subject agreement and everything to do with faulty word–audience agreement. Robert Penn Warren's thinly veiled portrait of the rise of Senator Huey P. Long of Louisiana (*All the King's Men*) tells the story of one person who discovers how effective such ungrammatical rhetorical grammar can be. When the central character learns to talk to "my hicks" in their own rough language, his political career begins.

There may even be a kind of credibility courtship involved in the songs and music selected for rallies and ceremonies leading up to speeches or in the way in which the platform used for a speech is arranged and decorated. Music and bunting can evoke symbols of familiarity and trust, stroking us into receptiveness to the speaker. The quadrennial political conventions of the major parties in America provide elaborate examples. The sea of posters, the constant patriotic theme music, the staged mob scenes of support for candidates—all aim to create trust.

Above all, perhaps, we may decide to trust speakers because we perceive that it is in their own best interest to support our interests: Our needs coincide with theirs. If we rise, they rise; if we fall, so do they. Least trustworthy are those who change like the weather, turning with the prevailing winds—those whose images are constantly coming into and going out of focus. For a time such speakers may manage to appear all things to all people, their words inviting almost any sort of meaning one wants to project into them. But it is hard for anyone to maintain a vague and vacillating posture for long in the public eye. And the counterreaction against such a chameleon is apt to be devastating.

Likableness

Is the speaker likable? This innocent-seeming question disguises the very crucial personal magnetism a leader can generate in drawing people together in group identification. Humor, charm, sincerity, and plain-spoken honesty all contribute to the likableness of a speaker.

We have discussed four essential criteria in the art of evaluation. Substance involves the intrinsic worth of the speech, whereas commitment, imagination, and credibility are qualities of the speaker as reflected in the message. But there are also other, more technical considerations by which to measure the worth of a speech.

ADAPTATION

Has the speaker tailored the message to this particular audience? That is, has the speaker met the specific needs of his or her listeners and established identification with the audience? Speakers can never forget the need to adapt everything they say to the specific audience they will confront. A speech must seem to have been crafted lovingly with these specific hearers constantly in mind.

Audience knowledge about a subject can be general, incomplete, or even faulty. When the subject is complex and specialized, speakers may have to provide careful definitions of terms, many simple illustrations, and basic visual materials such as charts and models. Their communication goals may have to be quite modest: perhaps to add just a little more depth to the audience's general understanding or to correct a few misapprehensions.

*"Damn it, will whoever keeps saying 'Pshaw'
please refrain until the treasurer has finished his report?"*

Drawing by H. Martin; © 1967 The New Yorker Magazine, Inc.

Again, the audience may have a certain identity that is crucial. If a speaker has to give a speech on taxation one morning before a group of wealthy landowners and must speak again that afternoon before an audience of welfare recipients, he or she may well have to use different approaches. The substance of the speech is the same (if the speaker is ethical), but the strategy and style must be different in order for the speaker to receive a favorable or at least a fair hearing before each group.

Still another important factor in adaptation is the need to establish identification. When both speaker and audience have clearly established identities that are distant from each other, adaptation can be quite difficult. A member of the Young Socialist League, for example, would have to be quite innovative to establish common ground and a sense of shared identity at the Wednesday luncheon meeting of the Rotary Club. Adding to this difficulty is our tendency to view someone outside our social, economic, or political group as even more distant from us, and even more opposed to our interests, than he or she may actually be.[3] Indeed, this tendency to exaggerate "distance" can discourage from the outset all efforts to establish identification. But a speaker can still look for basic human experiences that he or she shares with the audience and can construct a new and more acceptable self-image on that foundation of shared experience. Audiences can build up such ugly preconceptions that, when confronted by the actual person, they discover to their amazement that he or she is human after all. They *do* have things in common! Experienced speakers know that they can take some of the steam out of opposing listeners by appearing as a friendly and balanced human being, rather than as some creature from the depths of their imaginations.

In other speech situations, identification can become difficult when the speaker's reputation has been damaged by some allegation. So wide a gap can open between speaker and audience that even the passage of time cannot restore lines of identification. Such a speaker is actually exiled in spirit from the audience, as President Nixon discovered in the bitter aftermath of the Watergate disclosures.

Looked at more positively, the personal relationship between speakers and their audiences should be warm, close, and enjoyable. Such techniques as using pronouns of inclusion and identification ("we," "our," "us") and telling stories that emphasize the sharing of common values and experiences may significantly build identification and adaptation.

The final measure of audience adaptation is the sensitivity of the speaker to the ongoing needs of an audience during the course of a speech. Is there a need for clarification here, for humor there? Has the audience been put to sleep by a previous speaker, such that it must be shocked into alert attention? ("By this time next year six of us will be victims of crime.") Is the audience ready for action, prepared from previous arousals to move for change? The speaker sensitized to audience adaptation is constantly alert to these signs and possibilities. Anyone who wants to evaluate a speech must give considerable attention to such sensitivity.

ARGUMENT

Speakers often find themselves confronted with audience indifference or active opposition. The measure of argument in a speech reveals how well they overcome these forces by using proofs and rhetorical tactics.

3. C.I. Hovland, O.J. Harvey, and M. Sherif, "Assimilation and Contrast Effects in Reactions to Communication and Attitude Change," *Journal of Abnormal and Social Psychology*, 55 (1957), 244–252.

Does the speaker overcome indifference? Here we evaluate the speaker's ability to transform audience apathy into interest and even enthusiasm. Consider this example:

While we sit here comfortable and perhaps a little sleepy on this warm spring afternoon, people in another country are sitting, not so comfortable, watching their children die of starvation. It's not such a pretty sight nor such a pleasant thing to endure. You have to get used to a lot of sights and sounds, like hearing your own child moan with hunger and reach for food you do not have, day after pitiful day. You have to watch their little bellies swell and their eyes become glazed. They die slowly, and you have to watch them take their time about it.

This speaker is adjusting to indifference by developing a contrast intended both to shame and to shock his or her listeners. The image grapples with indifference through the vividness of its depiction, the mocking irony of its opening tone, and its appeal to parental and family feelings. The aim is to induce horror and fascination, which will make the audience receptive to the facts and conclusions that the speaker will put before them.

Can the speaker overcome the barriers of opposition and neutrality in listeners? There are so many good reasons *not* to be engaged by a speech. For one thing, most speakers want some commitment, and commitments involve risk. So listeners may take refuge in a kind of determined neutrality that resists taking any stand. Or again, other commitments may get in the way of accepting this speaker's message.

In effective argument, the speaker meets such problems head-on, anticipating audience objections. "You may think you can say, 'That's none of my business,' but starving children are the business of all humanity. Are you a part of humanity?" Moreover, the speaker's presentation of evidence must be compelling: "You say, 'Surely she exaggerates,' but do I? When the United Nations, private agencies, and our own government agree that more than a million children starve each month, do I exaggerate? And besides, can we tolerate *any* starving children?" The more controversial the speaker, and the more her or his position departs from previously accepted belief or common opinion, the greater the need for evidence presented carefully, abundantly, and with proper documentation. An audience that has been startled by a claim will inspect such evidence closely, inquiring into its sources, its objectivity, and its recency.

Academic speakers especially are sometimes bewildered when their elaborate arguments do not come home to people. They are inclined to blame general audiences for a lack of intellectual capacity. The more likely explanation is that the speaker has not yet learned to present the argument in human terms, to translate abstractions into concrete and understandable kinds of expression. Edmund Burke, the great British speaker of the eighteenth century, typically accompanied each of his major arguments with a major image, which set forth his meaning in a dramatic and picturesque way. When he defended his philosophy of public service, for example, he spoke of the legislator's moral duty to constantly build and strengthen the house of government during times of ease and plenty. Then, when the storms of crisis rise and rage across the land, they will not be able to blow down the edifice that protects the liberties and Constitution of the people.[4] As Burke demonstrated time and again, logic and emotion, reason and image, need not be at odds. Brought together, they lend to argument a compelling force.

Are speakers able to contend effectively with opposing, competing persuasions? When opponents are present, the scene is set for a formal debate, which includes set times for presentation of each position, direct cross examination by each speaker of the other, and refutation of the other's position. Debate provides for a healthy "trial by combat" of ideas. It emphasizes the soundness of speech substance and the speaker's grasp of the facts and expert interpretations that surround a controversial issue. It ought to spur speakers on to their finest eloquence and so leave the audience in the best possible position to make wise decisions. Debate can provide argumentation's finest moments.

Less dramatic, but no less tactically important, is the conduct of argument when the opposition is not present. Should the speaker acknowledge that there *are* other positions simply for the sake of refuting them? One may end up confusing an audience, alerting them to other options, or appearing defensive. Yet speakers are well advised most of the time to acknowledge that other positions do exist. For one thing, the audience is going to encounter such positions sooner or later. Sophisticated members of the audience, who are probably its influential opinion leaders, may well be aware of these other positions already. Finally, to acknowledge them gives the speaker a chance to refute them. As you evaluate argument, consider the effectiveness of the speaker's tactics in dealing with opposing positions.

Does the speaker's argument rest on sound analysis of the issue? Much of the time we are concerned with problems that have no

---

4. The image is recurrent in his speech "Previous to the Bristol Election," *Select British Eloquence*, ed. Chauncey A. Goodrich (1852; reprint New York: Bobbs-Merrill, 1963), pp. 292–310.

obvious, immediate, or absolute solutions. Rather, people must weigh degrees of uncertainty on all sides, and any commitment is accompanied by risk. Is this the way to proceed? Is the time right? Are we the people who can make this happen? Such doubts can buzz around our heads as we ponder the options open to us. Argument can become the device people use to chart the uncertain ground before them, testing the authenticity of depictions, the reliability of influence, the credibility of conclusions, and the consequences of decisions.

An argumentative speech shows how a speaker traces the causes, effects, connections, consequences, and proposed resolution of a problem. The argument presents a picture of the speaker's analysis. You in turn accept or reject the argument on the basis of the soundness and completeness of such thinking. Analysis gives argument its rational emphasis. Audiences prefer that a position rest upon more than mere sentiment or tradition, even when they are biased in its favor.

Analysis gains validity from the research that precedes and supports it. Involved in analysis are five phases, which begin with the *definition of the problem*. Often the problem is fairly clear ("Ought we to register for the draft?"). At other times it may seem uncertain, being vaguely though powerfully felt ("What shall we do about the *apathy* in this country?"). The second step in analysis is to *identify the considerations that might enter into a final decision to act*. Take, for example, the question "Ought we to register for the draft?" After some reading on this subject and discussion with local military and academic experts, a speaker might record the following possible areas of consideration:

1. Impact on self
2. Impact on family
3. Consequences for the future
4. Consequences for the country

The third step is to *trace specific implications within each area of consideration*. Self-impact, for example, might yield such questions as the following:

1. Would we be liable under the law if we refused to register?
2. How likely would we be to see combat duty if we were drafted?
3. Would military service interfere with our educational plans?
4. Could we use military service to develop useful skills?
5. Would educational travel be a possible benefit of military service?

Once speakers have traced the implications, they are ready for the fourth phase of the process, *testing these implications*. Here they scan possible positions on these implications, including views that are opposed to each other. Speakers must decide which of the questions are really vital to the problem. These will become the issues on which some resolution and decision must finally depend. To summarize the process thus far, the mind in pre-argumentative analysis is a kind of sensing device that moves across the screen of possibilities relevant to a particular problem. It then selects, lifts from that field of possibilities, and arranges in an order of priority the issues surrounding a given problem area. As evaluator, you must make judgments about the quality and completeness of this operation.

Finally, speakers must *decide on a position* for argument. In their speeches they will indicate how they arrived at this final position and how they justify it. Others can follow this demonstration and decide whether they should accept the same conclusion.

ORGANIZATION

Does the overall pattern of the speech serve the rhetorical function intended by the speaker? Is the speech structurally sound?

Functional Organization

Speeches are organized with a definite end in view—the rhetorical function being served by the speech. In evaluating such *functional organization*, keep in mind the speaker's purpose, and consider the pattern of development in light of this purpose. Speeches that aim toward depiction, whether the speaker's motive is to inform or persuade, must create clear and coherent pictures of their subjects. In the following example, observe how Elizabeth Cady Stanton, a great pioneer of the Women's Movement, brings distinctly into focus the status of women in mid-nineteenth-century America. Speaking to the New York State Legislature on the eve of the Civil War, Stanton uses audience sympathy on behalf of slaves as a lens to bring the plight of American women into focus. Note the care with which she develops the parallel, using hypothetical persons to make the depiction clear, until she is able to claim that women are more degraded than blacks in the South. The speech was a major factor in the passage of the New York State Married Women's Property Act of 1860, which guaranteed women the right to keep their own earnings, the right to equal powers with their husbands as joint guardians of their children, and property rights as widows equal to those enjoyed by widowers.

Allow me just here to call the attention of that party now so much interested in the slave of the Carolinas, to the similarity in his condition and that of the mothers, wives, and daughters of the Empire State. The negro has no name. He is Cuffy Douglas or Cuffy Brooks, just whose Cuffy he may chance to be. The woman has no name. She is Mrs. Richard Roe or Mrs. John Doe, just whose Mrs. she may chance to be. Cuffy has no right to his earnings; he can not buy or sell, or lay up anything that he can call his own. Mrs. Roe has no right to her earnings; she can neither buy nor sell, make contracts, nor lay up anything that she can call her own. Cuffy has no right to his children; they can be sold from him at any time. Mrs. Roe has no right to her children; they may be bound out to cancel a father's debts of honor. The unborn child, even, by the last will of the father, may be placed under the guardianship of a stranger and a foreigner. Cuffy has no legal existence; he is subject to restraint and moderate chastisement. Mrs. Roe has no legal existence; she has not the best right to her own person. The husband has the power to restrain, and administer moderate chastisement. . . .

The negro's skin and the woman's sex are both prima facie evidence that they were intended to be in subjection to the white Saxon man. The few social privileges which the man gives the woman, he makes up to the negro in civil rights. The woman may sit at the same table and eat with the white man; the free negro may hold property and vote. The woman may sit in the same pew with the white man in church; the free negro may enter the pulpit and preach. Now, with the black man's right to suffrage, the right unquestioned, even by Paul, to minister at the altar, it is evident that the prejudice against sex is more deeply rooted and more unreasonably maintained than that against color. . . .[5]

Similarly, the well-organized speech to arouse will gradually build intensity of feeling. For example, the speaker who wishes to arouse admiration may describe his or her subject overcoming adversity to win a coveted honor. The speaker who would then arouse genuine liking must show how these efforts helped the audience as well and reveal the subject as someone who respects people like the audience members and what they represent. To arouse sorrow, the speaker might show this admired and well-liked person being overcome by bad luck or misfortune. And to arouse anger, the speaker would identify this person as the victim of some force or enemy. All these feelings

---

5. "Address to the New York State Legislature, 1860," *Feminism: The Essential Historical Writings,* ed. Miriam Schneir (New York: Random House, 1972), pp. 118–119.

would form a natural chain of emotions. For a model of such well-organized arousal, read Marc Antony's funeral speech for Caesar in Shakespeare's *Julius Caesar*.

The speech that aims primarily at group identification as a step in some grand plan of rhetorical action first refreshes the memories of listeners about the experiences they have shared and the feelings that unite them. Such a speech builds upon and presupposes effective depiction and arousal and creates a sense of shared tradition. We might call this phase of identification the building of a rhetorical history. But the speech goes on to develop this emerging sense of identity, talking about beliefs these listeners have (or should have) in common. Out of shared beliefs comes a sense of shared values, which can serve to make the group identity stable. To this sense of shared tradition and shared beliefs and values in the present the speaker adds a vision of the future, giving the group a common sense of direction and hope. Thus building a group past, present, and future provides a natural pattern of organization for the speech of group identification.

The speech of implementing may take two primary forms, and each suggests a different mode of organization. The speech engaged in persuading the group to select a specific course of action can be called a *deliberative* speech. Its intent is to design the future. Such a speech considers the various options open to the group in light of the problem that brought them together. It typically reduces the options one by one, finding each defective in some vital way, until only one option remains. It then shows how this plan of action can succeed. Deliberative speech finds a natural home in Congress, the Senate, or any group responsible for plotting the course of the future.

The second kind of implementing address occurs in the speech that breathes life into a group trying to execute a plan of action. Such a speech can be called *exhortative* or *sustaining* in that it urges the group to carry on the struggle. Such a speech might first remind all present of the importance of the cause—*what is at stake*. Then the speech may turn to a demeaning picture of the opposition, reminding everyone *who or what is the enemy*. Opponents are usually shown as defective in some way that will ensure their defeat—often this defect is some striking moral inferiority. Because the group addressed is morally superior, it is not surprising that the god or gods honored by speaker and audience will smile on their purpose. "God is on our side!" is a typical reassurance of such exhortative rhetoric. Often the speaker then reviews past successes and victories over this enemy. If the group has defeated the enemy before, the speaker reasons, it can triumph again and again until final victory is won. The speech normally concludes with an appeal for courage, steadfastness, sacrifice—all the great virtues that will be necessary to victory. Occasionally the speech tries to lift listeners spiritually onto a new and higher plane. Such exaltation concludes the final speech of Dr. Martin Luther King, Jr., which offers an elevated vision of the "promised land" that lies beyond the struggle for civil and human rights.

Note the sense of elevation and exaltation in the following speech by Carrie Chapman Catt, who played a major leadership role in securing the right to vote for women in this country. Catt uses a fable from the Far East to dramatize her point. Just as King finds faith in his vision of black progress, Catt draws reassurance from her elevated view of the Women's Movement. The rhetorical view from the mountaintop makes the terrain of the future seem favorably predetermined: Listeners may take heart in the symbolic assurance that the movement will flow inevitably on to success, just as rivers flow on to the sea. This is the kind of sustaining confidence that soldiers of the cause need from a speaker during any long struggle. Catt's speech, delivered in 1911 in Stockholm, Sweden, before a meeting of the International Woman Suffrage Alliance, serves this function admirably.

Long centuries before the birth of Darwin an old-time Hindoo wrote: "I stand on a river's bank. I know not from whence the waters come or whither they go. So deep and silent is its current that I know not whether it flows north or south; all is a mystery to me; but when I climb yon summit the river becomes a silver thread weaving its length in and out among the hills and over the plains. I see it all from its source in yonder mountains to its outlet in yonder sea. There is no more mystery." So these university professors buried in school books, these near-sighted politicians, fail to note the meaning of passing events. To them, the woman movement is an inexplicable mystery, an irritating excrescence upon the harmonious development of society. But to us, standing upon the summit of international union, where we may observe every manifestation of this movement in all parts of the world, there is no mystery. From its source, . . . we clearly trace the course of this movement through the centuries, moving slowly but majestically onward, gathering momentum with each century, each generation; until just before us lies the golden sea of woman's full liberty.[6]

Finally, the speech that aims at renewal follows a certain ritualistic form. Often delivered as part of the celebration of some great event,

6. "The World Movement for Woman Suffrage 1904 to 1911: Is Woman Suffrage Progressing?" *Feminism*, pp. 287-288.

such a speech glorifies the event in terms of the ongoing social life of the group. The speaker aims to strengthen the sense of group belonging and to celebrate the great values the event represents. For example, a speech celebrating the signing of the Declaration of Independence might begin by recalling the historical context in which the document was signed. This "rhetorical history" would focus on the mighty issues of the time, which were later transformed into Constitutional principles. These principles live on as ideas that guide our nation. Next the speaker might focus on the key people who fashioned that document and what they risked by signing it. The personal virtues of these great people remain models for our own lives today. Next the speaker might point to specific forces that now threaten these values. But the speaker finds strength and reassurance in the power of the principles and the models that he or she has described. If we remain loyal and true to these values and models, we can overcome our enemies.

Thus the ritual form of the speech of renewal creates useful *myths* and images of the past, showing their vital relevance to the present, and indicating possible challenges to them and their application in the future. Such speeches are often underestimated as "mere rhetoric," but they can have great importance to the ongoing life of the society in which they are celebrated.

Structural Organization

A second way to test the organization of a speech is to consider the structure of the speech itself. The *structural* evaluation leads to several *organization* questions.

1. *Does the beginning of the speech present a preview of how the rest of the speech will develop?* In a longer speech especially, a preview that contains the blueprint of what will follow helps keep the audience on track. A speaker might present a preview along the following lines: "So today I will show why we *must* conserve energy. I will discuss waste as a national problem for all of us and then as a personal problem for each of us." Such a preview creates expectations that the speaker can proceed to satisfy.

2. *Does the speech contain effective transitions that bind it together and keep it moving?* Such transitions both summarize what has gone before and point the way to what is to come. As he or she moves from one major point to another the speaker might say, "As large as the waste on our highways might seem, it shrinks by comparison when we turn to the waste in government offices and places of business."

Frank Siteman 1980

Transitions can also take the form of questions that rise out of one section of speech and shape the discussion in the next. "But why, you might ask, is there such waste, and how does it affect me?" The advantage of the transitional question is that it can arouse curiosity and hold attention effectively until an answer is provided.

3. *Are the major points within the speech well balanced in terms of development?* If a speaker promises to develop two major points in a five-minute speech and then devotes four and a half minutes to the first point, the speech seems badly out of balance. Of course, the time spent in developing each point should vary with its importance, and the speaker can use the length of time spent on a point as a means of emphasis. Researchers have found it hard to determine whether the most important point should come first or last in a sequence of development.[7] There seems little doubt that it should be placed in one of these positions in order to achieve maximum impact. Less important or weaker points should be placed between the vital first and final positions.

A sense of balance can also be achieved if one begins with the most easily developed point and proceeds gradually—devoting more time to each successive point—to the most complex.

4. *Does the speaker make a proper selection among the modes of organization?* Some speeches by their very nature require a *time*

7. For example, see the inconclusive discussion in Carl I. Hovland, Irving L. Janis, and Harold H. Kelley, *Communication and Persuasion: Psychological Studies of Opinion Change* (New Haven, Conn.: Yale University Press, 1953), pp. 112–120.

pattern, the presentation of events in the chronological order of their occurrence. "How did all this come about?" might be the kind of question that would lead to such a structure.

Other speeches call for a *spatial* division: consideration of the subject in terms of related places such as East and West, or state, national, and international. "What do they think about the draft in California, New York, Texas, and Minnesota?" The selection of states here would create an effective illusion of comprehensive perspective. The spatial division would create a kind of geographic poll that might make some interesting comparisons and contrasts possible.

Still other subjects are most easily discussed in terms of appropriate *categories*. Taxation, for example, might be discussed in terms of local, state, and national issues, because these divisions are suitable to the subject. Or subjects may be discussed in terms of *topics* suggested by the interests people have in them. Taxation, for instance, could be discussed in terms of both practical and moral consequences. "Will higher taxes kill the goose that lays the golden egg? Should the goose be able to keep more of its eggs?" Such topics can provide an effective structure for speeches.

Finally, the *image* can be dramatic as a basic mode of organization. Speakers may describe a situation as dark in one part of their speeches and then balance that description with a promise of light. Or they may use contrasting but related images of storm and calm, disease and cure, sin and redemption, or death and resurrection. Such image combinations can have deep affective power for most audiences. Therefore, they can both provide the form for a speech and create an emotional atmosphere appropriate for transmitting its message.[8]

5. *Has the speaker made a wise decision about whether to approach the subject directly or indirectly?* It is often effective for the speaker to open a speech by allowing the suspense to build before revealing his or her purpose. This strategy of indirection can even be useful for an entire speech, especially when the audience is neutral or even hostile. The speaker develops a line of reasoning that moves gradually toward a conclusion that might have been shocking had it been announced at the beginning, without any preparation. For example, a speech in support of the draft delivered to a hostile college audience might well have to build a solid preparatory case before that purpose was revealed.

Of course, a speaker may decide to begin with a direct statement of purpose. This strategy has the advantage of being clear and simple.

8. See Michael Osborn, "Archetypal Metaphor in Rhetoric: The Light–Dark Family," *Quarterly Journal of Speech*, 53 (1967), 115–126, and Michael Osborn, "The Evolution of the Archetypal Sea in Rhetoric and Poetic," *Quarterly Journal of Speech*, 63 (1977), 347–363.

You are "up front" with your purpose, so there is less chance that your audience will misunderstand. When the subject is not controversial or when it is complex and requires a clear and simple development of ideas, the "up front" strategy is more appropriate.

6. *Does the speech reflect a sound decision on the one-sided versus the multisided approach to persuasion?* Should speakers develop only their own views on a controversial issue, or should they present the other side for the sake of refuting it?[9]

Researchers have found that different strategies, audiences, and situations suggest different answers to this question. If an audience is relatively uneducated and if the speaker wants immediate action, the one-sided approach is more efficient. Such audiences may only be confused or distracted by the more complicated, multisided approach. There can be an ethical problem, of course, especially if speakers suggest that theirs is the only approach. But if opposition speakers are there to present the other side, there is nothing morally wrong with the one-sided approach. Such situations invite rebuttal and refutation anyway.

The multisided approach is not only more effective before more critical audiences, who *anticipate* different sides on almost any issue, but it is also better over the long haul for assuring permanency of persuasion. This improved weathering effect has also been called persuasive "innoculation": exposing an audience to an opposing position for the sake of protecting them against it. Persuasion that does not answer in advance the arguments of the other side, researchers have found, can be highly vulnerable when the opposing view is presented. "I didn't know *that* when I made my earlier commitment," can be the reaction when one is finally exposed to counterarguments.

DELIVERY

The physical, nonverbal dimensions of speech, or delivery, are important to the effective communication of a speakers' ideas. Delivery can be evaluated in terms of body, face, and voice.

Do the expressions of the body—through gesture, posture, and platform movement—add to or detract from the message? Speakers can succeed without a great deal of movement, but they may well defeat their purpose by affected or obviously contrived gestures, which

9. See Hovland, Janis, and Kelley, pp. 105–111. See also two articles by W.J. McGuire: "Resistance to Persuasion Conferred by Active and Passive Prior Refutation of the Same and Alternative Counterarguments," *Journal of Abnormal Social Psychology*, 63 (1961), 326–332, and "The Efficacy of Supportive and Refutational Defenses in Immunizing and Restoring Beliefs Against Persuasion," *Sociometry*, 24 (1961), 184–197.

Former president Richard M. Nixon during a televised press conference, 1971.
Wide World Photos

call attention to themselves and divert it from the meaning of the speech. Hence the delivery of a speech should be practiced until body and word are the natural extensions of each other. What the audience sees should harmonize with what it hears. Gesture must seem spontaneous emphasis, such that a step to the side or forward becomes only the natural expression of a transition or the forward progress of the speech itself.

Do speakers maintain vital eye contact with the audience? When speakers are truly committed to a speech, their faces come alive with intensity. There is a kind of rhetorical hypnotism in effective eye contact. If the eyes are the windows of the soul, speakers who stare over, under, or to the side of their audiences have closed the windows to communication.

Via eye contact, speakers signal to their listeners that they want to communicate. The face that responds to its own utterance also becomes a secondary communication system that can strengthen (or even override, when the intention is irony) the verbal level of meaning. How many times have you heard a speaker say something like "Of course we admire them," while facial expression and tone of voice deny the words even as they are uttered! Such eye contact and facial expression are important considerations in the evaluation of delivery.

Is the voice easy to listen to, and does it avoid monotone? A good voice is as alive and responsive to the speaker's ideas as the expressive gesture. A good voice is reasonably pleasant and has adequate power. It has a good sense of timing and pace. It also possesses variety and range enough to register the subtle meanings of an alert and sensitive mind. Nothing kills a speech more quickly, and communicates a less desirable image of the speaker, than a dull, monotonous voice that seems to drone on interminably (even when the speech is actually brief).

LANGUAGE

Words are a direct and vital point of contact between speaker and audience. Much depends on their possessing certain key qualities.

Is the speaker's language clear and immediately comprehensible? You can't do an instant replay on a speaker who is standing in front of you. And you can't put the speaker "on hold" while you contemplate the meaning of some complex reflection. The speaker's language must be luminously clear the moment it is uttered. The sentence patterns must be simple, direct, and free of complex chains of dependent and interlocking clauses. "We want to be free. We want to be free now. We want to be completely free. You can't dilute freedom or measure it out in stingy doses." This speaker grasps the need for simple, clear sentence structure in oral discourse. Such sentences must seem spontaneous and natural, the product of that moment.

Is the speaker's language interesting and concrete? Nothing helps create concreteness and interest more than one or several dominant images, which rise like genies within a speech. If speakers want to focus attention on General Motors or the AFL-CIO, for instance, they can make these somewhat abstract institutions come to life in an image. Perhaps the rhetorical intention is to depict them as kindly and parental or perhaps as scaly beasts that have emerged from dark economic crevices. Speakers can use images to create either positive or negative associations, but they must be careful. They must justify such images with evidence. Hence the ability to use imagery wisely joins clarity and simplicity as major points in evaluating speeches.

Is the speaker's language vivacious and colorful? Vivacity is liveliness of language, which reflects the liveliness of a speaker's mind. Oral language should be imbued with the speaker's personality. It should reflect the urgency of the message and the excitement of ideas building on each other as they mount to a conclusion. Note how the language marches in this brief passage from Adlai Stevenson's "Eulogy to John Fitzgerald Kennedy."

> *Now he is gone. Today we mourn him. Tomorrow and tomorrow we shall miss him. And so we shall never know how different the world might have been had fate permitted this blazing talent to live and labor longer at man's unfinished agenda for peace and progress for all.*[10]

Does the speaker's choice of language reflect a good command of words? Nothing reveals quality of mind more than a generous repository of words and precision in their use. Speakers should be able to select and combine words with ease and grace. This criterion does not mean that speakers should be constantly trying to show how many sesquipedalian words they can wedge into a sentence! It means that a person with a good vocabulary frames more extensive and more complex ideas and communicates them to the audience. For the speaker, of course, a "good command of words" refers more to the ability to express ideas orally than to sheer size of vocabulary.

Does the speaker make effective use of charismatic language? Certain words are the so-called buzz-words of a group or society. People have

---

10. *Great American Speeches, 1898-1963*, ed. John Graham (New York: Appleton-Century-Crofts, 1970), p. 123.

unusually strong reactions, positive or negative, to their mere utterance. In most colleges, for instance, to label someone's behavior or attitude as "high school" is the ultimate deprecation. No doubt your campus has developed its own set of words that have special meaning for the students involved. Indeed, much of your orientation to college and university life probably consisted in learning this vocabulary.

On a wider scale, certain words seem to embody the values of America—they are the buzz-words of our culture. Americans have long admired "progress," "science," "modern," "efficiency," and "facts." These words seem to express our deep traditional faith in technological and material advancement toward a better future under human control. When used in a speech, these words usually have an authoritative, enhancing effect.[11]

Finally, there are certain words that, when expressed in metaphor and symbol, are the buzz-words of all humankind. Audiences across many cultures have long been moved by images based on light and darkness, sin and redemption, disease and healing, war and peace, mountains and valleys, rivers and the sea. Such images are often thought of as belonging to poetry, but their skillful use in a speech can move us powerfully to sympathy with the speaker's position.[12]

An important final measure we can apply is to determine how effectively the speaker uses such language in a speech.

AN EVALUATION PROFILE

Figure 4.1 summarizes our discussion of speech evaluation. Use it as a handy check list to evaluate fully the efforts of your classmates. Also use it in honest self-appraisal, both at the beginning and at the end of the class. At that point you can measure how far you have come and in what areas you need further development as a speaker in public.

Summary of Major Ideas

Whether a speech has real substance is a central issue in evaluating it.

Commitment, measured in the intensity of a speaker's feeling and the degree of risk he or she assumes, is the great energizer of public speech.

The creative or imaginative component of a speech can make the difference between an excellent and a mediocre effort.

11. See Richard M. Weaver, "Ultimate Terms in Contemporary Rhetoric," *The Ethics of Rhetoric* (Chicago, Ill.: Henry Regnery, 1953), pp. 211–232.
12. See Michael Osborn, *Orientations to Rhetorical Style* (Chicago, Ill.: SRA, 1976), pp. 16–19.

Name: ________________ Speech Assignment: ____________ Date: ________

FACTORS OF EVALUATION	RATING SCALE Poor (1) Average (3) Excellent (5)					SPECIFIC STRENGTHS AND SUGGESTIONS
	1	2	3	4	5	
1. Substance						
2. Commitment						
3. Imagination						
4. Credibility						
5. Adaptation						
6. Argument						
7. Organization						
8. Delivery						
9. Language						
GENERAL ASSESSMENT:						

Figure 4.1 SPEECH EVALUATION PROFILE

The credibility of a speech often depends on the credibility of the speaker.

A speech must be shaped and delivered with a particular audience in mind.

Through adaptation, the speaker seeks to build identification with an audience.

The speaker's argumentation must contend with indifference as well as opposition.

The speaker must learn to present arguments in human terms, conveying facts via images and bringing images together in a powerful depiction.

Argument is the device people use to test the authenticity of depictions, the reliability of inferences, the credibility of conclusions, and the consequences of decisions. Sound argument is based on informed analysis.

A speech must be organized in such a way that it achieves (as appropriate) coherent depiction, intensity of feeling, group identification, conclusiveness and strength in implementation, and enthusiasm in renewal.

The structurally sound speech contains a preview if necessary and provides effective and smooth transitions. It exhibits balance in the development of major points, a pattern of development appropriate to the subject, and a strategy of development appropriate to the audience.

In effective delivery the gesture is supportive of the word so that what an audience sees reinforces what it hears. Delivery must be natural and must not call attention to itself.

Eye contact helps hold audience attention and makes communication more genuine and memorable.

The speaker's language should be clear, concrete, lively, and drawn from a good repository of words.

The speaker must be sensitive to charismatic language and able to use its special resources when appropriate.

Exercises and Discussion Questions

1. Using *Vital Speeches of the Day*, select three prominent speakers of our time. Compare their rhetorical artistry, using the criteria developed in this chapter. A special speech assignment might be class reports on the theme "Rhetorical Artists of Our Time."

2. What (if any) contrasts in rhetorical artistry might distinguish revolutionary from conservative, male from female, Western from Asian, or black from white speakers? Divide the class into study teams, each of which can specialize in one of these paired groups and report to the class.

3. In recent times America is supposed to have suffered from a "credibility gap" between its leadership and the people. What is the nature of this problem, and what were its causes?

4. Outline the structure of an argument you might develop on an important contemporary issue. How would you contend with audience indifference in your class? What objections would you anticipate from listeners, and how would you counter them in your speech? How would you go about refuting opposing positions?

5. Concerning the argument you outlined in Exercise 4, how would you organize a speech on the issue to achieve appropriate coherence, intensity, identification, conclusiveness, and enthusiasm? Outline the organizational structure you would select.

6. As an exercise in self-analysis, describe your own qualities of delivery, first as the speaker you now are and then as the speaker you would like to become.

7. Concerning Exercises 4 and 5, what images would you develop to make your argument more powerful? What charismatic words would you want to use or to avoid?

For Further Reading

The criteria developed in this chapter for evaluating speeches have really evolved over thousands of years in rhetorical theory. Some of the landmark statements about topics addressed in this chapter can be found in the following works.

Aristotle's Rhetoric, trans. Lane Cooper (New York: Appleton, 1932) points the way to the formation of sound speech substance and explores the dynamics of credibility in communication. Aristotle also develops a sensitive appreciation for the role of the audience in communication and the need for adaptation. The third book of the *Rhetoric* is noteworthy for its treatment of the speaker's language. Richard Whately's *Elements of Rhetoric*, ed. Douglas Ehninger (7th ed. rev., 1846; reprint Carbondale, Ill.: Southern Illinois University Press, 1963), laid the foundation for the modern theory of argumentation. This nineteenth-century book is especially useful for the theory of debate.

James Winans's *Public Speaking* (New York: Century, 1915) and A.E. Phillips's *Effective Speaking* (Chicago: Newton, 1908) are turn-of-the century textbooks that helped develop the conversational style of delivery suited to modern tastes. There is much good wisdom and help to be found in their books.

Longinus's great treatise *On the Sublime*, trans. Benedict Einarson, in *The Problem of Style*, ed. J.V. Cunningham (Greenwich, Conn.: Fawcett, 1966), contains a classic statement on the speaker's language and on the role of imagination in communication.

II
PREPARATION
FOR PUBLIC SPEAKING:
THE FIRST STEPS

In preparing a speech the speaker has four major initial tasks to perform.

1. Finding a speech topic (*selection*)
2. Discovering what he or she needs to know in order to develop the topic (*analysis*)
3. Collecting the necessary materials (*research*)
4. Analyzing the limitations and opportunities rising out of the anticipated audience (*adaptation*)

This section of the book concentrates on these four steps. It considers especially how the speaker can prepare effectively by drawing on three resources: his or her own experience, the experience of others, and the dynamics of mind and personality anticipated in the audience. Throughout, the intention is to develop cumulatively a systematic Speech Preparation Plan. This plan can guide you in an orderly way through all phases of preparing a speech.

5
SELECTING AND ANALYZING
A SPEECH TOPIC

I keep six honest serving-men
(They taught me all I knew):
Their names are What and Why and When
And How and Where and Who.
RUDYARD KIPLING, "The Serving-Men"

Finding a good subject for a speech

Thinking a subject through systematically

Testing the value of information and opinion

Recording research discoveries

If substance is the first great criterion on which to judge a speech, then building substance into the speech must be the first concern of the speaker. This process begins with finding the right subject and giving it the right kind of analysis.

FINDING A TOPIC

A good speech topic is one that you want to talk about, that fits the assignment, and that your audience will enjoy and benefit from.

Your Own Wishes

Assume that you have been told to prepare a five-minute informative speech. The subject is yours to choose, so long as it leads to an effective speech. But *that* condition bothers you. How can you use this freedom of choice wisely?

You should already have some clues, of course, to interesting subjects. Your work in preparing for the introductory speech may have crystallized some of your own interests, and that speech itself may have started to build your credibility on a certain subject. If, for example, your defining feature was your mania for chess, you might well go on to develop an informative speech about some aspect of the game, such as the psychological suffering of chess champions during international competition or the combative instinct in humans as revealed in the games they play. The primary caution in developing any such topic is that *you must not talk over the heads of your audience.* You must not, for example, use terms that only chess players would understand.

Another and perhaps more systematic means of finding a topic is to draw two vertical lines down the page of a legal pad so that you have left, middle, and right columns. Ask yourself, "What are the things that interest me?" Let your mind roam easily and indulge in free association. Make your own list of interests in the left column, and don't be satisfied with one or even several entries. Need stimulation? Pick up the morning newspaper and scan the headlines, or glance through the latest *Time* or *Newsweek*. What possible subjects leap to attention? By now your head should be buzzing with possibilities, and the left column should be full.

Audience Preferences

Now turn your attention to your listeners. What subjects seem to interest them on the basis of their self-introductory speeches? List these subjects in the middle column. Now ask yourself, "What ought to interest them?" What is happening right now that affects their security, well-being, and future hopes? Continue making entries in the middle column until it is at least as long as the left column.

Now look at the two columns together. Try to find matching pairs or relationships between the two columns. Cross out all those items that do not seem linked to any entry in the other column. Between related items, draw connecting lines that extend in an arrow to the right column. In this column, phrase exact topics for speeches that grow out of the convergence of your interests and those of your audience. *As you word these topics, it is vital that you consider the length of time you will have to speak and any other conditions your instructor may have imposed.*

For example, assume that in the left column you recorded an interest in "efficient crop production" as a result of your growing up on a farm. Before crossing this off as a drab subject, you notice that pesticide use is again in the news as an environmental hazard; you have recorded this as a natural concern for any contemporary audience. This possible convergence of speaker and audience interests, you conclude, could produce a good speech. Your first reaction may be combative: "They shouldn't put such silly restrictions on the farmer." But considering your assignment, which specifies an informative speech, you decide that such a line of thought is not appropriate. It will lead only to a persuasive or argumentative speech.

So you approach the idea again more cautiously. "Informative" suggests the kind of speech that offers listeners a better understanding of an important self-interest. What is at stake here? Obviously your listeners need to eat, but they also need to eat food that is healthy. On the one hand, the farmer may need to use some pesticides, you reason, in order to grow a crop. However, you are willing to grant, some control must be exerted over such usage. Consumers certainly don't need poisoning, but they don't need an expensive and inadequate choice of foods at the grocery store either.

At this point, your vital speech preparation has actually begun. You decide that the better understanding that you can offer your listeners concerns precisely this delicate balance among farmer, consumer, and environmental needs in modern society. But now you recall that you will have only five minutes to speak. Your subject seems so vast and your time so short! It occurs to you, however, that the largest cash crop in your area is corn and that the entire situation could be discussed strictly as it relates to that food. This strategy not only limits and focuses your subject but also adds local and special interest for this audience of listeners. Thus you make the following entry in the right-hand column: "Is there corn in your future?" Come up with at least two more such entries in this column before you decide which of these topics to develop. At this point, your work sheet would look very much like Figure 5.1, which is the first phase of the Speech Preparation Plan. You should complete such a Topic Selection form for each speech assignment throughout the course.

Remember: The speech topic at this stage of preparation, even before extensive investigation, should be sharply focused and well defined. It should interest you, should fit within the assigned time period of the speech, and should seem a vital subject for your listeners. With these conditions satisfied, and all signs pointing toward a successful speech, you are ready to proceed to the analysis stage of speech preparation.

DEVELOPING A RESEARCH PLAN
THROUGH ANALYSIS

Most students recognize the importance of research in preparing for a speech, but many have little idea how to go about it. Too often they dash to the library, check out the first book they can find that is remotely related to the subject, begin reading the introduction, find the reading tedious and unproductive, and finally grow discouraged and quit. This kind of random investigation rarely produces anything but discouragement.

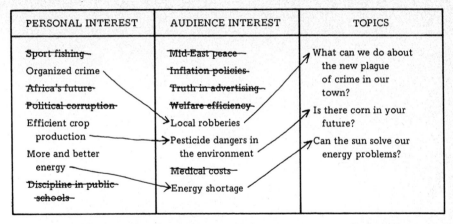

PERSONAL INTEREST	AUDIENCE INTEREST	TOPICS
~~Sport fishing~~	~~Mid-East peace~~	What can we do about the new plague of crime in our town?
Organized crime	~~Inflation policies~~	
~~Africa's future~~	~~Truth in advertising~~	
~~Political corruption~~	~~Welfare efficiency~~	Is there corn in your future?
Efficient crop production	Local robberies	
	Pesticide dangers in the environment	Can the sun solve our energy problems?
More and better energy	~~Medical costs~~	
~~Discipline in public schools~~	Energy shortage	

Figure 5.1 SPEECH PREPARATION PLAN: TOPIC SELECTION

Investigation should begin with a research plan in which you decide how to prepare for your speech. Ask yourself what basic questions you must have answered before you can speak responsibly on this subject for this audience.

This query is an invitation to analysis. The key questions taught to beginning newspaper reporters—which just happen also to be Kipling's "six honest serving-men"—suggest the kind of basic analysis a speaker should pursue. Modified for the purposes of speech research, the so-called five W's and H become

Who is involved in this problem or situation?
What issues or major features of interest characterize this situation?
Why did the problem or situation come about?
Where is this problem or condition happening?
When is it happening?
How is it happening?

For the special purposes of speech research, we add the following questions:

How does the situation *contrast* with other situations (better or worse) or with situations that might come about if we do or do not act?
How much is it happening?
With what consequence is it happening?
What *options* does this audience have in dealing with it?

These tools of analysis or *probe questions*, as we may call them, should prove useful for both informative and persuasive speeches. When applied to a topic, they should suggest specific questions

Frank Siteman/Stock, Boston

for research and even lines of thought and argument for possible development within a speech. For a demonstration of their potential usefulness and to derive some of their most important follow-up questions, let's apply them to our hypothetical topic, "Is there corn in your future?"

"Who is involved?" does not seem very productive at first glance. Obviously farmers and consumers share an especially vital concern with food productivity. On the surface, farmer and consumer may seem opposed, the one wishing to be paid more for produce, the other wishing to pay less. But as we probe deeper, the relationships between these parties seem to change. Farmer and consumer are, after all, necessary to each other. And all of us have an essential interest in the environment. As we consider those who are involved, this matter of relationships among their vital interests seems to emerge as a primary concern. Thus an important follow-up question to the "Who is involved?" probe is *"What are their vital interests?"* If we apply this question in turn to the topic at hand, the specific question for research becomes "What are the vital interests of farmers and consumers in the environment-versus-food-production issue, and how do these interests apply especially to corn?"

Behind this question looms another. Farmers do need to grow as much as possible to serve the national interest and to satisfy their own need for income. Consumers do require the greatest possible abundance of food at a reasonable price. The interests of all citizens demand that the land, air, and water not be contaminated in the process. Linking all these groups are the distributors, marketers, and government agencies, who play managerial and regulatory roles. There is a vast network of real and defensible interests here, and the challenge to public policy is to establish a harmonious balance among them. Only near the surface are unreasonable strains and stresses apparent. Perhaps the real enemies in this dispute (and most disputes) are irrationality and short-sighted self-interest: those certain farmers whose horizons do not extend beyond their 300 acres, extremists who see the farmer only as the enemy of the environment, consumers who forget that they must also consume air and water, and an assortment of other grabbers and grubbers.

Speakers must often address the question of conflict among such narrowly perceived self-interests and the question of rationality versus irrationality, especially when they discuss controversial issues. Whether the intention is to persuade or to inform, such questions can point out barriers and dangers that speakers must either avoid or overcome if they are to achieve their purpose. Thus the follow-up question may be framed *"Who represent the forces of reason and unreason, of public interest and self-interest, in connection with this subject?"* When applied to the topic at hand, the question for research becomes "Who occupy rational and irrational positions in the economic–ecological controversy? Which groups represent the public good, and which defend narrowly defined self-interests?"

The second probe is "What is at the heart of this situation?" This query invites attention to the significant features and central issues of a speech subject. You might decide that most of the important concerns in the subject at hand boil down to a question of the human species in interaction with the environment it is creating. Implied in this question is a deep irony, for people should surely be helped, not hindered, by their increasing ability to control their surroundings. If they are indeed threatened by their own creativity, then the irrational factor in human conduct may be even greater than we suspect. To investigate this grim possibility, you might record for further consideration: "Has the ecology issue revealed that we may be our own worst enemy, possible victims of human creativity run rampant?"

"Why has the situation come about?" invites speakers to consider underlying causes. In addition, you might look for spectacular events that have propelled the subject into the public eye. From your background of general information, you are aware of calamitous events such as fish kills, mercury poisonings, and bird species endangered because eggs will not hatch. You are also aware that environmentalists have been able to attract mass media coverage and capture public attention. You will need to know about these events and activities in precise detail. Thus two follow-up questions that develop this probe are *"What* factors have caused this situation?" and "What events have made this situation prominent in the public eye?" When applied to the topic at hand, these follow-up questions produce the following research problems: "What has caused the conflict between food producers and environmentalists? What events have projected this conflict into public attention?"

"Where is this situation happening?" should remind you that the closer you can relate the subject to the lives of your listeners, the more vital and useful to them your speech will be. A natural follow-up question becomes "What immediate stake do my listeners have in this subject?" Similarly, "When is it happening?" suggests that the subject must be related to the here and now and to the future. Timeliness is the cutting edge of any subject, and the speech that lacks it is apt to be dull. So a follow-up to this probe question is "What immediate and distant-future outcomes of this situation are possible and likely?" When applied to the topic at hand, these questions might suggest the following line of research: "What is the local and immediate impact of the food–environment dilemma, and what does the future hold for us?"

"How is it happening?" might serve again to point you to those organized pressure groups whose conflict has brought the entire question before the public. You will want to determine who leads these groups, how they are financed, and how they attempt to influence public attitude and political policy. You might write down "What agents of conservation and of change are active in this situation, and how do they work?" When applied to the topic at hand, this follow-up question might suggest "Who is actively promoting adversary positions in the food–environment controversy?"

The special topical questions point you precisely to vital aspects of almost all speech subjects. "In contrast with what is it happening?" is a good question to ask, because subjects stand out most clearly and distinctly when viewed in relation to other similar or related subjects that already exist, are remembered from the past, or seem possible in the future. Such a view can even suggest arguments when the speaker's purpose shifts to persuasion. For example, "What would our rivers be like without contamination?" might suggest lines of argument as well as lines of inquiry.

"How much is it happening?" suggests that *magnitude* is an important consideration in rhetoric. Any magnitude is relative and can be communicated most effectively when contrasted with a lesser or greater quantity. A mythical fact will serve to demonstrate this principle. Imagine that the equivalent of 5000 barrels of pesticides is poured into the fresh waters of America each year through waste, seepage, and erosion. That fact may make some impression in itself, but how much more effective it becomes when you say, "In 1950, 2000 barrels of pesticide poison soaked into our lakes and rivers, and if we don't change what we are doing, by 1990 we'll be pumping 10,000 barrels into the water we drink and bathe in. Now let's project what 200 percent of the present level of contamination will do to our natural surroundings and our health." Here you are obviously on your way to a powerful demonstration, having combined both magnitude and timeliness. If you can use magnitude this way, you will touch a vital nerve in your audience. So the follow-up question becomes *"How large is the problem, and is its magnitude likely to change dramatically in the foreseeable future?"* Applied specifically, this follow-up probe might suggest these research questions: "To what extent do pesticide regulations affect the farmer, and how much do pesticides damage the environment? Are these magnitudes likely to change in the future?"

Similarly, "With what consequence is it happening?" invites you to emphasize again the possible impact on those whom you are addressing. Moreover, the probe suggests a follow-up question that completes a correlation with the factors of time and magnitude: *"At what levels of magnitude are certain consequences likely to ensue?* (At what point of contamination, for example, does pesticide poisoning threaten our water supply? Or at what point of pesticide regulation might farming cease to be profitable?) Answering this question will require careful investigation, for the kind of argument we presented to illustrate magnitude is specious unless experts can be found to support it, and expert testimony is often heavily qualified and tentative. Not many scientists are willing to predict the exact consequences of a 100-percent increase in pesticide contamination, but probably most of them would agree that such consequences must be undesirable. But whereas the scientist might stress the uncertain nature of such consequences, your job as speaker is to present these consequences as real possibilities for the future if we do not act to forestall them.

You are prompted by the final probe question to consider the options available to your audience. Follow-up questions include *"Can they change conditions? Or must they adapt to the new conditions? Is there a way to transform what has been a problem into an advantage?"* In a primarily informative speech you describe the various options to your audience, illuminating and broadening their range of choices. In a primarily persuasive speech, you narrow and eliminate options instead. You argue for a certain choice among the options, showing why it should be preferred. Thus, whereas the informative

Drawing by Ziegler; © 1980 The New Yorker Magazine, Inc.

speech *reveals* options, a persuasive speech *evaluates* them and, in so doing, motivates its audience to accept its recommendations.

The mission of this demonstration is now complete. We have proposed that a list of probe questions might indeed be useful in guiding the analysis phase of speech preparation. Such probes and their follow-up questions can reveal vital facets of a subject or issue, suggesting specific questions for investigative research. This discussion is synthesized below in the "Speech Preparation Plan: Topic Analysis." It provides a model to consider after you have completed the Topic Selection form. Following the lines of analysis it indicates should give real purpose and direction to your research preparation.

SPEECH PREPARATION PLAN

Topic Analysis

Speech Topic: _____

_____

1. <u>Who</u> is involved in this problem or situation?
    a. What are their vital interests?
    b. Who represent the forces of reason and unreason, of public interest and self-interest, in connection with this subject?
2. <u>What</u> issues or major features of interest characterize this situation?
3. <u>Why</u> did the problem or situation come about?
    a. What factors have caused this situation?
    b. What events have made this situation prominent in the public mind?
4. <u>Where</u> is this problem or condition happening? What immediate stake do my listeners have in this subject?
5. <u>When</u> is it happening? What immediate and distant-future outcomes of this situation are possible and likely?
6. <u>How</u> is it happening? What agents of conservation and of change are active in this situation, and how do they work?
7. How does the situation <u>contrast</u> with other situations (better or worse) or with situations that might come about if we do or do not act?
8. <u>How much</u> is it happening? How large is the problem, and is its magnitude likely to change dramatically in the foreseeable future?
9. <u>With what consequence</u> is it happening? At what levels of magnitude are certain consequences likely to ensue?

10. What <u>options</u> does this audience have in dealing with it?
    a. Can they change conditions?
    b. Must they adapt to the new conditions?
    c. Is there a way to transform what has been a problem into an advantage?

EQUIPMENT FOR RESEARCH

Chapter 6 discusses four sources of knowledge from which you can draw answers to the questions that emerge during your analysis of the topic. But before you start the actual research phase, you need two kinds of equipment: a system to test the value of whatever information you encounter and a way to record and store the knowledge you decide may prove useful in developing the speech.

Critical Tests of Knowledge

Six tests can help you determine whether the knowledge you encounter is worthwhile.

RELIABILITY Does the knowledge bear the authentic stamp of an expert's own experience, experimentation, and/or learning? For example, a political scientist who has actually worked within the political system in some important capacity, or who may even have been a candidate or elected official, may be more believable when quoted in a speech than an armchair expert.

COMPREHENSIVENESS Is the knowledge drawn from a broad range of experience? Has the source sought to extend this range of experience as much as possible and to qualify its claims according to the limitations of that experience? Any source has its own point of view, of course, but is it aware of its possible bias, does it acknowledge other possible perspectives, and does it temper its claims accordingly? If an elected public official offers broad generalizations about the American political process on the basis of his or her limited experience alone, we might well question the value of the opinion for use in a speech. "Politics is corrupting," offered by a person just convicted of political corruption, may strike us as a rationalization for personal weakness and not as evidence fit to support responsible conclusions in a speech.

TIMELINESS Is the knowledge recent and up-to-date? This consideration is especially vital when supporting data are changing rapidly or even constantly, such as the popularity of a president as indicated in media polls.

IMMEDIACY OF APPLICATION   Does the knowledge fit *this* audience and its immediate surroundings? Information on some subjects can vary strikingly from one locale to another, as can local needs. Economic subjects involving unemployment and cost-of-living figures or taxation rates are especially susceptible to such variation. What is true in Tennessee may not be true in Michigan.

INDEPENDENCE OF VIEW   Has the knowledge been generated by a research effort free from any self-serving interests? Reports on the safety of cigarette smoking sponsored by the tobacco industry must surely be inspected rather closely. The National Association of Manufacturers regularly discovers that labor union wage pressures are the major cause of inflation; labor union publications just as regularly confirm that management's uncontrolled lust for profit is the true cause of our devalued currency. All such "discoveries" should be viewed skeptically and may not be useful in a speech.

CORRECTNESS OF PROCEDURE   Has the source taken all reasonable precautions to see that the knowledge it presents is valid and reliable? If the researcher generalizes from too limited a sample or from a non-representative sample, the conclusion may be quite defective. How would you react to a claim that "college students are suicidal" if support for the statement came from a survey of fifteen students at the health center during final exam week?

Such tests will help you assess the quality of the knowledge you encounter.

Storing Knowledge for Use

Methods of taking notes during research are as personalized as the toothbrush one prefers. Many researchers use index cards to record the data and informed opinions they encounter, simply because such cards are so convenient to handle and to sort according to topics of interest. Index cards lend themselves to the development of a filing system in which the highlights of research can be arranged in orderly and useful ways. Index cards are generally available in 3″ × 5″, 4″ × 6″, and 5″ × 8″ sizes. The larger cards allow one to record extensive quotations on them. However, when quotations are very extensive and important to your research, you may choose to use the copying services that most libraries make available. The more precious and limited your research time, the more useful such services will become. You might think in terms of using two kinds of research cards, the bibliographic card and the evidence card.

THE BIBLIOGRAPHIC CARD   The bibliographic card should perform three major tasks for you. First, it should give you exact information about the source of the research data: *who* said it, *where* it was said, and *when* it was said. For a book, such information typically takes the following form: author, title, place of publication, publisher, and date of publication (1, Figure 5.2). For an article, the bibliographic card lists author, title, name of journal, volume number, date, and pages (2, Figure 5.2).

The second function of the bibliographic card is to list important bits of information about the author or medium of publication that might be useful in the speech (3, Figure 5.2). Such information, often gleaned from the biographical resource books discussed in the next chapter, can help you personalize experts as you introduce them in speeches or aid you in confirming their claims. The third function of the card is to provide a brief summary of what the book or article is about and perhaps an indication of its quality and significance (4, Figure 5.2).

THE EVIDENCE CARD   The evidence card should contain one idea or material relating to one idea, in the form of either exact quotation or paraphrase. The card should contain a *heading*, which explains its relevance for the sake of rapid filing and reference (1, Figure 5.3), an abbreviated *bibliographic notation* (2, Figure 5.3), and the *body* of the card (3, Figure 5.3). Be sure that any statements directly quoted fairly represent the major drift of the article and that you are not "quoting out of context," distorting the author's meaning and position.

Summary of Major Ideas

A good speech topic is one that you want to talk about and that is appropriate to the assignment and the interests of the audience.

An informative speech offers listeners a better understanding of an important self-interest.

The first step in analyzing a topic is to determine what questions you must answer before you can speak responsibly about it.

Timeliness is vital; any speech that lacks it is apt to be dull.

1. Bibliographic information for a book	Wentworth Hollowforth, *The Art of Butterfly Collecting* (Chicago, Ill.: Lavendar Brothers, 1973).
	(or)
2. Bibliographic information for an article	Wentworth Hollowforth, "Stalking the Lepidoptera," *True Adventures*, 36 (May 4, 1976), 88–95.
3. Information on author or medium	"Dr. Hollowforth wields a mean net himself, having captured one summer 39 varieties of butterfly." *Current Biography*, 39 (May 1973), 48. *Note:* the publication of Hollowforth's exploits in *True Adventures* shows that butterfly chasing has arrived as a sport that tests the courage, ability, and stamina of its participants.
4. Summary and evaluation	*Summary:* Hollowforth offers here the ABC's of butterfly collecting from selection of helmet and net to field-dressing the kill. Some terrific adventure stories, including the capture of one rare specimen while hang-gliding over the Brazilian jungles.

Figure 5.2 BIBLIOGRAPHIC CARD

1. Heading	EXCITEMENT OF THE CHASE
2. Bibliographic notation	Hollowforth, p. 89.
3. Body	"What thrill exceeds that of capturing on the wing the glorious lepidoptera? What satisfaction goes deeper than mounting such a wild and fluttering creature in one's own collection?" Dr. Hollowforth attributes this excitement to the hunting instinct in humans and to our eternal quest for elusive beauty.

Figure 5.3 EVIDENCE CARD

An informative speech reveals options; a persuasive speech narrows them, focusing on and advocating a single course of action.

Basic tests of the quality of knowledge include considerations of reliability, comprehensiveness, timeliness, immediacy of application, independence of view, and correctness of procedure.

Using index cards to record information and opinion promotes intelligent selection and imposes a disciplined procedure on the research phase of preparing a speech.

The bibliographic research card gives you information about the source of knowledge, personal information about the author, and a summary and evaluation of the knowledge.

The evidence research card contains one idea or material relating to one idea, in the form of either exact quotation or paraphrase.

Exercises and Discussion Questions

1. Each class member should bring to class at least three appropriate speech topics suggested by headlines and major stories in the morning newspaper. How many potential subjects does the class discover collectively? How valid is the complaint, "I just can't think of anything to talk about?"

2. As a follow-up to Exercise 1, select one of the most promising topics for in-class analysis. Each class member will have ten minutes to write down basic questions for research, using the list of probes suggested in this chapter. Now take ten minutes to compare results. How much variation of analysis results? Which probes were most productive? Repeat the exercise, using another topic.

3. For your next speech assignment, submit in advance a Speech Preparation Plan that includes completed versions of the Topic Selection model and the Analysis model. Also include a brief essay in which you comment on why you chose this subject and on the usefulness of the probe questions for suggesting specific questions for research.

4. For an interesting demonstration of creativity in analysis, three class members should select the same topic and develop speeches on the topic independently of each other. All three speeches should be presented to the class on the same day. What vital differences are there among the speeches? To what variations of analysis might these differences be attributed?

For Further Reading

To deepen your understanding of how to stimulate creativity through analysis, go back to the ancient rhetorical treatises on human invention. See especially Aristotle's elaborate discussion of lines of analysis (topics) in Book I of his *Rhetoric*. Cicero also deals effectively with the subject in his masterpiece, *De Oratore*. Finally, see the classically oriented treatment in John F. Wilson and Carroll C. Arnold, *Public Speaking as a Liberal Art*, 3rd ed. (Boston: Allyn and Bacon, 1974).

6

RESEARCH FOR SPEAKING IN PUBLIC

Learn, compare, collect the facts! . . . In your work
and in your research there must always be passion.

IVAN PETROVICH PAVLOV,
Bequest to the Academic Youth of Soviet Russia

Once you have found a good topic and discovered your basic information needs through systematic analysis, you are ready to embark on the adventure of research. Research provides the substance that gives all the speaker's depictions, pleas, and arguments the solid ring of validity. This chapter considers four sources of knowledge that are valuable to a speaker.

Useful information on a subject will come to you through your own previous experience; through indirect knowledge that you glean from the printed page or electronically via radio, television, or recording; from the experience of others related in a personal interview; and from knowledge that you yourself gather by such means as polling. Each of these sources has its own strengths and weaknesses.

PERSONAL EXPERIENCE

Your own previous experience will provide authentic, fresh knowledge that can be transformed into very personal substance in a speech. Such knowledge can give you a strong justification for speaking as well as high credibility. The weakness of such knowledge is that it may be quite narrow in scope and perhaps even distorted. You might have learned a great deal about growing corn in one area—say, on your father's 300 acres. But your knowledge might not be valid in another part of the state where climate, soil, and pest control differ sharply. Moreover, if there has been any significant time lapse in your experience, your personal knowledge may be out of date. Compounding these difficulties, those who speak from personal knowledge have a tendency to be dogmatic and to overestimate the value of their experience. They think that such experience is enough to qualify them to speak responsibly on a subject, whereas there may actually be large gaps in their knowledge.

Student speakers, however, too often overlook the opportunity of deliberately cultivating personal experience. If you want to deliver an authentic speech on migrant workers, try walking and talking among such people as part of your research preparation. The sights, smells, colors, tones, and tastes—the very atmosphere of the migrant worker's existence—will permeate your speech and mark it as genuine. To arrange to get such experience, you must sometimes be rather bold. For example, if your subject were boredom on the assembly line, you might call your local AFL–CIO public relations representative, ask him or her in what local industries such problems are most pressing, and inquire whether you might tour plants in order to get a first-hand feel for the problem.

When I first wrote the preceding words, I decided on impulse to check the usefulness of their advice. I went to the telephone, called the local Labor Council headquarters, and ended up talking with a prominent local union official. When I asked him about worker boredom, he said that the problem was acute in many industries. I asked whether his office would help student speakers who wished to arrange interviews with workers and to visit local plants. Indeed, he would be happy to cooperate, he said. "Tell the students to call whenever they are ready." His warmth and willingness to help are understandable. Any large private or public organization seeks favorable publicity, and when you call the public relations office of such an organization and identify yourself as a speaker, your power to control a portion of that publicity is not lost on company spokespersons. At no time do you sense the power of speech more vividly than when an organization puts out the red carpet to give you a favorable impression that they hope will surface in your speech.

But how about, say, the police? Surely the police would not assist student speakers. Again I decided to put that assumption to test. Lieutenant Myers works in the public relations division of the local police department (the very existence of the division suggests police are sensitive to their public image). He and a colleague answer telephone calls from "about 50 students a day," he estimates. It is his job to give students all the information he can.

And so it goes. Certainly the representatives of some institutions would be rude and uncooperative. That in itself might be worthy of further investigation. But if personal experience is important to your speech, you will find most such representatives more than happy to help, because it will be in their interest to do so.

LIBRARY SOURCES

Indirect knowledge, while it lacks the immediacy and authenticity of good personal experience, has the advantage of perspective. Books, articles, and documentaries can give you the large view of things, especially when you deliberately seek out several different points of view among the experts. Thus indirect knowledge is often more comprehensive and objective. Books and articles can give you the world's finest, most up-to-date knowledge far more quickly and efficiently than the interview.

If there is any special drawback to such knowledge, it is that indirect authority sources cannot usually answer one's specific questions. And too often we assume that, because something has been printed, it must be true. We may place our faith where it is not deserved. Remember that not every so-called expert deserves the name. Mere titles—Doctor X, Professor Y, and Scientist Z—do not necessarily mean that the person has authoritative knowledge on the specific subject at hand.

The final weakness of indirect knowledge is that it often does not apply specifically to the local setting and the immediate audience one must address. A way around this weakness is often provided by local newspaper files and indexes, as we shall see. One can also compensate by combining indirect knowledge with personal experience and the interview, which can bring the subject closer to home.

The major source of indirect learning is the library, which provides a nerve center of knowledge, a concentration of human discoveries and articulations. Most college and university libraries have the following major research tools: a *card catalog*, which is the key to books and major publications; a *reference room*, which contains up-to-date information on specialized subjects and the key to newspapers, magazines, and journals; *government documents*, which accommodate the vast outpourings from government presses; *nonprint media archives*, films and recordings on many subjects; *special collections*, holdings often pertinent to the immediate geographical area; and the *holdings areas*, wherein are housed all the bound volumes, past and current periodicals, and microfilm collections. And of course one other great resource, the *professional librarian*, often knows his or her area of the library very thoroughly.

© 1960 United Features Syndicate, Inc.

Confronted by such diverse resources, the student may wonder where to begin. The answer often given is that one should begin with the card catalog, which indexes book holdings. But such advice is not always helpful; indeed, the card catalog should sometimes be the last stop in a library search rather than the first. On many subjects of interest, one can encounter as many as 50 or over 500 book titles listed in the catalog. How is one to choose among them?

The problem with such frustrating advice is that it makes no distinction among kinds of researchers. The student preparing a five-minute speech with ten hours to spend on research might just as well be a scholar off on a lifetime quest. So perhaps the first matter to settle is *just what kind of knowledge should reasonably be expected of a student speaker*. The answer may lie in the word "responsibility." You will be expected to have a responsible knowledge of your subject, its main features, the major issues surrounding it, the chief authorities on it, the latest developments concerning it, and how it applies locally. These requirements are suggested, of course, by the list of probe questions developed in Chapter 5. In short, your audience may not expect you to be an expert on your subject, but it will expect you to speak from sound and appropriate knowledge. Your research should result in your knowing a good deal more than the rest of the class about it. The difference between what you and your listeners know measures the information potential of a speech: how much knowledge *could* flow, under optimal conditions, from you to them.

The following review outlines the major library resources in terms of the special requirements of public speaking and the special problems of student speakers, who wish to spend their limited time to best advantage.

The Reference Room

The first visit in preparing most speeches should be to the reference room, which has convenient keys to timely and concentrated sources of knowledge close at hand.

Frank Siteman 1980

ENCYCLOPEDIAS Perhaps the first reference sources to consult, especially when you know little about your subject, are the general encyclopedias. They will help you identify the major topics, divisions, and controversies involved in a subject. Among the prominent general encyclopedias are

Collier's Encyclopedia
Compton's Encyclopedia and Fact Index
Encyclopaedia Brittanica
Encyclopedia Americana
Great Soviet Encyclopedia (compare its perspective with that of the others listed here)
World Book Encyclopedia

SOURCES OF TIMELY FACTS With a general background gained from the encyclopedias, you may now want to learn the latest facts and conditions relevant to your subject. One source of such information is the newspaper index—*The New York Times Index*, for example. Ask your reference librarian to identify the most recent newspaper indexing service available. A quick glance at this index will tell you whether any articles pertaining to your subject have been published during the period of time covered by the index and will reveal exactly where in the newspaper you can find these stories or articles. The major newspaper index offers *abstracts* as well. Reading an abstract gives you a general idea of what a story or article is about and whether you should spend time tracking it down.

The great advantage of the newspaper index is timeliness. You must know the latest developments on your subject; these are precisely the events most likely to be lingering in your listeners' minds. If you seem unaware of such events, your listeners may well lose respect for you, and they will certainly want to have the discussion related to current happenings. For the most recent period not covered by the index, protect yourself by skimming through *Time, Newsweek,* or relevant specialized magazines or journals in the section of the library devoted to current periodicals.

Another source of up-to-date information on current events, housed also in the reference room, is *Facts on File*, which reflects the changing surface of the news by summarizing major stories in major categories. *Facts on File* is not an index; it does not point you specifically to other publications. But it does alert you to what is happening and the time frame in which it is happening, so that you will know what to look for in more detailed publications. Finally, the *Congressional Quarterly Weekly Report* gives you a precise, up-to-date picture of events as they are breaking in the Congress, especially the drift, direction, and probable fate of current legislation. On many issues of public concern, such a survey of ongoing government activity is essential to the timeliness of a speech.

OTHER INDEXES AND ABSTRACTS Other indexes guide you to recent magazine and journal articles that pertain to your subject. If you had only one afternoon to spend researching a speech, you might well start with these indexes. The articles they point to are often almost as timely as the news stories themselves, and they generally represent intelligent responses to concerns of the moment. What they may lose in timeliness they more than make up in depth. Often they interpret and evaluate the news and may even advocate a position, suggesting lines of argument for persuasive speeches. Though deeper than the news story, they are more compact than books, and they often save you valuable research time by reducing complex arguments and situations to the essentials. Finally, by reading a range of such articles, you can discover *which* books and authors you need to know more about. Books that are often cited and authors who are often quoted are the leading authorities the speaker may need to be familiar with to speak responsibly on a subject.

Indexes to periodicals and the abstracts that frequently accompany them range from the highly specialized to the very general. Check the reference catalog or consult the reference librarian in order to determine which specialized indexes and abstracts pertain to your subject. Among the most general and useful are the following:

Book Review Digest. Provides abstracts of reviews indicating the focus, methods, strengths, and weaknesses of recently published books. Can help you approach the card catalog intelligently and selectively.

Business Periodicals Index. Indexes journals across a broad range of economic interests.

Education Index. One among the several general indexes to research on educational matters. Another is *Current Index to Journals in Education.*

Humanities Index. Indexes specialized scholarship in the arts and humanities journals. If you wanted to know the meaning of Ahab's whalebone leg in *Moby Dick* or the reasons for Byron's infatuation with the sea, you might look here. A complementary publication is the *Essay and General Literature Index*, which is the key to such scholarship when it is published in collections of essays. Among the indexes of more narrow scope in this area are *Art Index* and *Film Literature Index.*

Index to Journals in Communication Studies. Of special interest to students of public speaking, this index covers professional journals in speech communication.

Psychological Abstracts. Indexes and abstracts a broad spectrum of research on psychological issues. A publication with similar aims for the field of sociology is *Sociological Abstracts.*

Public Affairs Information Service (PAIS). Ranges across journals, periodicals, pamphlets, and documents to index all subjects connected with public affairs. Often very useful for speakers.

Social Sciences Index. Counterpart of the *Humanities Index*, with which it was once joined. Because they can provide interesting data and statistical trends, the articles it points to can be very useful to the speaker.

If one had to choose a single index or to decide where to begin an index search, one might well go to the *Reader's Guide to Periodical Literature.* The *Reader's Guide* indexes what are usually more general articles in large-subscription, popular periodicals. It is useful for speakers simply because the readers of the publications it covers are much like the audiences for most speeches. More often than not, its articles address large questions that concern the general public rather than the more narrow and specialized topics that are of special interest to the limited audiences of professional journals. Moreover, because these publications pay well and can attract the best writers and experts, the articles are usually of high caliber, providing quality information. Often the magazines themselves have high credibility, such that quoting them enhances the credibility of a speech.

The reference room has so many other tools that we can only begin to mention them here. The reference catalog can point you to some, but the reference librarian may prove your best guide.

ATLASES   Many speech topics may require that you offer your audience some visual projection of a geographical area—a map that locates your subject in space. The atlases area of the reference room should be a great help to you in constructing such a map. You could start with an authoritative general atlas, such as *The Times Atlas of the World*. But if your subject is specialized, look under "atlases" in Eugene P. Sheehy's *Guide to Reference Books,* 9th ed. (Chicago, Ill.: American Library Association, 1976). There you will find a list of topics for special atlases, including commercial, historical, linguistic, religious, and numerous other special atlases. Preparing your own large projection of a map, either by hand copying or by constructing a film slide with the help and advice of the nonprint media resources center at your school, can result in the kind of visual aid that adds distinction and clarity to your speech.

BIOGRAPHICAL RESOURCES   Once you identify who the major authorities on a subject are, it is helpful to know more about them personally so that you can humanize them as you introduce them in your speech. At this point the *Who's Who* series of books, ranging from the general (*Who's Who in America*) to the specific (*Who's Who Among Black Americans*) might tell you much. *Notable American Women, 1607– 1950, Dictionary of American Biography* (noteworthy dead), *Dictionary of National Biography* (United Kingdom, dead), and *Webster's Biographical Dictionary* (famous persons across time) are other important books of this type. They all contain compact pocket biographies that give you salient information about the people they list. Look for a wide variety of such books in the biographical resources section of the reference room.

Of very special interest to speakers (because they are so timely, so detailed, and often more personalized than the *Who's Who* entries) are *Current Biography*, a monthly publication that presents selected articles on people who are prominent in the news, and *Biography Index*, a guide to biographical material appearing in a vast range of periodicals from the highly specialized to the very popular. Be sure to check these two publications first in your biographical prospecting, because whatever you find in them could prove quite useful.

BOOKS OF QUOTATIONS In the reference room you will find books of quotation on almost any subject. Among them is Bartlett's *Familiar Quotations*, which indexes the most striking, witty, and eloquent statements on a variety of subjects. Speakers often find such classic statements useful to begin or to end a speech. Used skillfully, they can place a timely issue within a timeless frame. Among other sources of quotations to drive a point home or enlarge its meaning are H. L. Mencken's *A New Dictionary of Quotations on Historical Principles from Ancient and Modern Sources* and the *Oxford Dictionary of Quotations*. Of special interest to persuasive speakers is Leon Mead and F. Newell Gilbert's *Manual of Forensic Quotations*, which indexes English courtroom eloquence up to the turn of the century. One can also find books of quotations in specialized fields, such as education and religion, and in special categories, such as Oriental literature.

ALMANACS, YEARBOOKS, AND DIRECTORIES As you pursue your research through the periodicals, you will occasionally come across disagreements over fact, questions of fact will become important, or an opportunity for vital comparison will occur to you. At such moments, you should return to the reference room for conveniently concentrated sources of facts: almanacs, yearbooks, and directories. Some especially useful almanacs are

Information Please Almanac
The World Almanac and Book of Facts
Reader's Digest Almanac and Yearbook
Whitaker's Almanac (British)

Such publications present an assortment of information drawn from the entire spectrum of human concerns and interests. Of a similar comprehensive nature are the following:

The Stateman's Year-Book. Looks at the nations of the world in terms of their modes of governing, social organization, and productive capacities as these evolve on a yearly basis.
Statistical Abstract of the United States. Published annually by the U.S. Department of Commerce, this yearbook is *the* authoritative mirror of the factual face of America, from the annual catch of abalone to the yearly production of zinc. It gives you only the raw material of proofs, evidences, and demonstrations, but you can rely on such material as authentic.

As our social structure becomes more complex and bureaucratized, questions of fact often concern organizations, their make-up, and leadership. Thus directories assume increasing importance in research. When such questions concern the make-up of the federal government, consult the *Washington Information Directory*, published by the *Congressional Quarterly*, and the *United States Government Manual*, which "describes the purposes and programs of most Government agencies and lists top personnel." For a larger view of organizations in America, the authoritative source is *Encyclopedia of Associations*, which covers an enormous variety of organized groups in this country. *The Foundation Directory* is also useful in identifying the complex network of foundations and the works they foster and promote via financial grants and encouragement.

VERTICAL FILE Finally, the reference room is often the home of the library's Vertical File, which may have already gathered for you pamphlets, articles, or publications related to your subject. These materials are often locally published and have local application. Therefore, they may be especially useful to the speaker, who needs to bring a subject home to an audience. They may also provide the names of local experts who can be interviewed to lend credibility to a speech. Be sure to ask the reference librarian about this file and where it is housed.

Government Documents

Beyond the reference room lie the other major areas of a research library. Government documents are often segregated in their own section of the library, although they contain important research keys that belong just as logically in the reference collection. Such documents can be very valuable, because they provide in-depth information that extends far beyond the almanacs and handbooks. Moreover, they supplement periodical research at the point of its essential weakness. Whereas the popular article gives you informed opinion, the government document characteristically gives you unformed information, data that have not yet been interpreted. Sometimes you want to penetrate beyond even expert opinion to the foundation of facts on which such opinion is based. Government documents include materials on Congressional hearings, legislation, and proceedings; the proclamations, orders, and statements of the president; and opinions and decisions of the Supreme Court. You will also find mountains of statistical information, including reports from the Bureau of Census and copies of treaties and diplomatic agreements.

Some of the major publications in this area are the following:

House and Senate *Reports*. Deal with proposed legislation or matters under Congressional investigation.

House and Senate *Documents*. Contain all papers ordered printed by the Congress.

Congressional Record. Daily record of the proceedings of Congress. By checking the index to each session of Congress, one can trace the evolution of a piece of legislation.

Statutes at Large. Compilation of federal laws generated during a given session of Congress and published at its conclusion.

Congressional Directory. Contains biographical sketches of the members of Congress.

United States Code. Annual compilation of federal laws in force at the time of publication. Represents a continuing synthesis of the law.

Federal Register. Contains proclamations and orders of the president as well as regulations of the various departments of the executive branch of government.

Treaties in Force. Published annually by the State Department. Lists treaties to which the United States is a party.

United States Reports. Records opinions and decisions of the Supreme Court. *U.S. Supreme Court Records and Briefs* may also be seen on microfiche.

Finding the keys to such publications and the thousands of other documents printed under the auspices of the United States government can be difficult, and you should consult the librarian in this area. The following are some of the keys you should find useful.

Monthly Catalog of United States Government Publications. Required by law to list all government publications except administrative and confidential items, this is the master key to government documents.

American Statistics Index. "Aims to be a master guide and index to the statistical publications of the U.S. Government." (*Statistical Abstract of the United States* is a useful summary of such data).

CIS (Congressional Information Service, Inc.). Provides an index to and abstracts of the wealth of research generated during Congressional hearings on legislation.

Congressional Quarterly Almanac. Reviews the activity (and inactivity) of the Congress in all areas of public concern on a yearly basis. May be used in conjunction with the *CQ Weekly Report*, which adds timeliness to the comprehensiveness of the quarterly review.

Selected Rand Abstracts. Offers a complete guide to the unclassified reports, papers, and books of the Rand Corporation, which conducts studies in the public interest sponsored largely by government and foundation funds. Its authoritative work focuses on the physical, social, and biological sciences.

Undex (United Nations Document Index). Indexes a broad spectrum of documents produced in connection with the many activities of the United Nations.

Other Library Sources

Your research trip to the library might include visits to two other sources. The first should be to *nonprint media* holdings. Check the special catalog of films and recordings for material pertaining to your subject. You may discover that some figure central to your research has recorded an interview on film. If the film is allowed to circulate outside the library, you might even find a way to work it into your speech. You should also visit the *special collections* area, which often contains relevant information of local interest. Using materials that point up local applications for subjects can provide effective adaptation of speech to audience.

The Card Catalog

Having surveyed this wide variety of research materials, you are ready to confront the card catalog, knowing which book or books you will need to develop a responsible speech. If your research puts you in possession of the latest information and best statements on your subject, you have done all you reasonably can in your library preparation for a classroom speech.

THE INTERVIEW

Knowledge gained by interviewing experts has several unique strengths. Whereas gleaning facts from a book makes you a passive recipient of knowledge, interviewing places you in an active role. In an interview you can guide, react to, and follow up on the flow of information. Moreover, a face-to-face encounter with an expert stimulates your interest, an especially important consideration when the subject is abstract and far removed from your actual experience. Such knowledge can have powerful local application and can be very timely. Finally, when you can report in a speech that "Major _____ told me herself," you add much credibility to what you say.

The danger of seeking knowledge via the interview is that one can be awed by an expert into accepting a point of view that is itself con-

Owen Franken/Stock, Boston

troversial and one-sided. This danger could introduce another source of bias into your speech. If you are a novice on your subject, you may have very little basis for evaluating what you hear or determining whether your expert's knowledge is up-to-date. But if you are prepared by previous reading and experience, an interview can add a great deal to your speech. Obviously, much depends on finding the right person to interview and on whether he or she is agreeable.

One way to proceed is to check the file of local newspaper clippings in the reference room of the library. Old news stories should contain the names of local people who are prominently connected with your subject and might have extremely valuable knowledge to enrich your speech. Of course, the newspaper files are themselves a direct source of information. They provide a historical background for your speech, specific questions to ask your experts, and answers to some of the basic questions on your legal pad. Moreover, newspaper stories often dwell on conflict and controversy, so scanning them should give you an idea of the range of expert opinion and the positions of experts with respect to each other. Thus prepared, you are not so likely to assume there is only one legitimate view of the issue—the view endorsed by the expert sitting across from you. Finally, the value of such local files for speech adaptation is undeniable. Even when your subject is abstract and general, such as the role of the United Nations in developing international culture, you must still personalize that subject and bring it home to your own listeners. Statements by local politicians, pundits, and cause-oriented persons, sometimes outrageously funny and other times just outrageous, can relate a faraway topic to local interests. The local newspaper file is too valuable a resource to overlook.

Making Contact by Letter

Having identified your experts, you must now contact them. The procedure suggested here is that you write each expert a letter stating your purpose and convincing them of your seriousness and that you follow this up with a telephone call to fix a time and place for the interview. An example of such a letter follows.

Dear Mr./Ms. _____ :

I am a student at State University, enrolled this fall in a public speaking class. I am presently preparing an informative speech for class presentation. Because of my family farming interest, I would like very much to speak on the future of corn production as it may be affected by government regulations restricting the use of fertilizers and pesticides.

An old family friend, George Stevenson, has suggested you as someone who could tell me a great deal about this situation. I would like very much to interview you at your convenience. I am especially interested in your ideas and opinions about the following questions:

1. Are farmer and consumer both vitally involved with the degree of such regulation, and if so, how?

2. What stake does our community have in this issue, and should students be concerned about it?

3. What could be the long-range impact of this issue upon you and other farmers?

4. Can the public do something about this issue, and if so, what?

5. On August 4, 1973, the News–Sentinel quotes you as having said: "The way things are going, people may have to choose between government and corn, because the government is driving the farmer out of business." Do these words still fairly represent your position?

I look forward to meeting you and will call your home Thursday evening to arrange a suitable time and place. If you wish to contact me earlier, my dormitory telephone number is 834–4922. Thank you for your attention and help.

Sincerely,

Your Name

This letter demonstrates some valuable rhetorical principles. Note that the writer establishes his or her connection to public speaking in the first sentence. For people sensitive to public influence, as no doubt this activist farmer must be, such a connection immediately arouses interest. Here is someone, he or she can infer, who could extend the influence of my point of view. Principle 1: *Show respondents that an interview could be important to them as well as helpful to you.* Quickly the letter moves on to suggest an implicit point of identification between interviewer and respondent, the "family farming interest," and without further ceremony establishes that the writer's specific interest lies precisely within the respondent's area of expertise. Principle 2: *Establish identification with respondents.* Principle 3: *Show respondents the relevance of the interview.*

This letter writer is fortunate enough to have found a respected person known to both parties who serves here as a kind of bridge between student and expert. This "old family friend" functions as a possible reference and as an implicit recommendation. Principle 4: *Provide respondents with references so that they can check your credentials if they wish.* The next few lines contain just enough flattery to please the natural vanity of any public figure without becoming demonstrative and phony. They also lead directly to the key questions the student would like to feature during the interview. Principle 5: *Show respondents that you will respect and value their opinions.* Principle 6: *Establish an agenda for the interview by highlighting in advance your major points of inquiry.*

Listing these questions in your letter accomplishes several things. First, selected as they are from your list of basic questions, they focus the interviewing relationship in advance on the very heart of the issue and cut through frills and peripheral concerns on which the interview might get sidetracked. Second, they suggest you as a businesslike person, as someone who knows something about the problem already and is prepared to acquire some serious professional knowledge about it. Third, they permit respondents to focus their thoughts before the interview and to gather in advance what additional evidence they can make available to you. Finally, the fifth question especially underscores the impression of the serious student who has already done some homework. But it also contains the most subtle and penetrating flattery of all. Who can resist seeing his or her words quoted as an authoritative and enduring statement on an issue?

The final paragraph strives for a gracious exit. It seeks to set the interviewing relationship on a cordial, informal level. Principle 7: *Establish a friendly working relationship with respondents.* It focuses on a follow-up action, the Thursday night telephone call, but also establishes the possibility of an alternative action. If your expert will be out of touch that particular evening, he or she can call you in advance. Principle 8: *Set up clear steps for consummating the interview.*

Note that there is very little verbosity in this letter. As a busy person yourself, you certainly don't want to waste another busy person's time. This is the general message that comes reassuringly through the letter.

Designing and Executing the Interview

Much of the following advice about the actual conduct of an interview is based on common sense: *Be on time, dress appropriately, and establish a friendly, working atmosphere at the outset.* In some interviews, breaking the ice is important in making the whole interview work. As one analyst of communication puts it, "Since we do not know people as individuals, we respond to them initially as stereotyped roles. . . . As the interview progresses, however, each person will begin to recognize the individual characteristics of the other."[1] Casual amenities at the beginning of the interview can be vital if they start to break down stereotypes on both sides and promote the process of individual recognition. Moreover, learn all you can about your experts before interviewing them. Your knowledge of their previous experiences and positions on issues, if it does not permit some beautiful breakthrough, might at least prevent some spectacular blunder. You will be spared exchanges such as the following:

"I'm sure you feel that the government has a vital role in this issue." "I have never felt that, I have never written or said that, and I'm surprised you would come here thinking that."

After the first moments of greeting, ride the interview with a light hand, letting the expert do most of the talking while you concentrate on the neglected art of intelligent listening. Only when you feel the interview drifting or bogging down should you guide it on to another essential question. Of course, all the important ground must be covered in the time available for the interview. Thus you must develop some skill in the art of questioning. The questions you ask should be open and fair, so that your respondent is not put on the defensive by their wording. Normally you should avoid questions that lead the respondent and ask for agreement: "Don't you think . . ." queries. Questions such as "When are you farmers going to stop polluting the environment?"

1. Bonnie McDaniel Johnson, *Communication: The Process of Organizing* (Boston: Allyn and Bacon, 1977), p. 179.

are not only argumentative but ill-mannered. Howard Cosell might get away with them, but don't you try. Ask such questions only if nothing else seems to work and you have nothing more to lose. The kind of angry candor they might provoke could be the only useful statement you come away with. But such unpleasant situations are rare, especially when your expert has consented to the interview freely and without pressure. As a general rule, open-ended questions in the form of "What is the situation as you see it?" or "How do you feel about this?" invite the kind of extended, revealing responses you will find most useful. Such questions should develop from the least to the most sensitive, following the order indicated in your letter, unless there arises a good reason to deviate from the plan.

But main questions are only the most obvious way to guide an interview. Four other techniques that interviewers find useful for developing answers and drawing out an interviewee are probes, mirror questions, verifiers, and reinforcers. *Probes* are follow-up questions that ask the expert to explain, elaborate, provide examples, or extend his or her answer. *Mirror questions* simply restate part of a response to encourage further amplification. The sequence might go as follows:

"... So I told him, 'No dice. I'm not going to cooperate with another fertilizer inquiry.' "
"You told the Senator you wouldn't go along with it?"

The mirror question obviously functions as a kind of conversational link as well as an encourager. It affirms that the listener is comprehending, makes it clear that he or she is interested, and establishes the exact focus of such interest.

The *verifier* is a means of focusing the significance of something that has just been said and verifying an apparent feeling or assumption. Verifiers can take the form of "If I understand you correctly, you're saying that. . . ." Be wary, however, of forcing inferences that cannot be fairly drawn. Respondents may resent your trying to put words in their mouths. Finally, a *reinforcer* is nonverbal behavior that encourages the interviewee. A sympathetic, interested face, for example, that follows the line of thought closely and responds with sensitivity to mood and meaning, can stimulate full and reflective responses to questions.

Of course, guiding an interview means more than developing and encouraging a line of thought. When a response is complete or the interview seems to be drifting into an eddy, the interviewer must change directions by means of a transition. A good transition summarizes what has just been said and moves gracefully by comparison or contrast into a new theme. "I think I understand now how you felt at the time. But was there pressure on you to change your position? If so, why? And who was it coming from?" Transitions both tie the interview together and permit it to move laterally to new subject matter.

Be sure to resist any impulse you might have to argue with your experts. After all, they are doing you a favor: They didn't ask for the honor of this conversation. You are not likely to convince them. You are there to receive their knowledge, whether or not you choose to use it. The interview should be a stimulating and enjoyable experience, and you should come away from it motivated in either opposition or sympathy to prepare a successful speech.

POLLS

Another source of knowledge is the information you gather yourself through administering polls. For example, you might poll a cross-section of students, blue-collar workers, and teachers to determine how a given subject is perceived at a given moment in a given population. The advantage of such knowledge is its timeliness and immediate application to the world of the audience. Moreover, those who bother to conduct any such poll in a responsible way earn the respect of their listeners. Going to the trouble to collect data solely for the speech indicates that you have taken the assignment seriously. The class may be especially interested in prespeech polls you have conducted among them: Your very audience may be the most appropriate population for a poll. The knowledge produced is almost guaranteed to capture and hold the fascinated attention of your listeners.

However, polls can be difficult to conduct in a controlled way. Because arguments based on them gain a great deal of attention, they will be inspected closely for flaws or careless procedure. Another danger is that the speaker may be tempted to create *vox populi* ("voice of the people") arguments that are actually irrelevant to the speech. For example, the fact that 80 percent of a polled sample of teachers endorse the president's program on the environment could be used to argue that the majority of teachers endorse the program. But such a poll would not in itself establish that the program is *right*.

In short, this source lends itself only to the support of certain kinds of claims, those that are factual in nature. When questions involving value judgments or the wisdom of a policy arise, the majority represented in a poll at a given moment may or may not have the answers. If you are preparing a "value" or "policy" speech, you might more profitably spend the time available for research on other sources of knowledge. On the other hand, when the issue is how people feel about some situation or whether they would accept some change, this source of knowledge may be essential.

The poll is obviously a special kind of interview, but it differs in radical ways. In the expert interview, one goes into depth with a few experts; the poll usually requires many subjects and more superficial points of inquiry. Again, the expert interview features open questions that invite extended answers; the poll asks narrow questions and invites simple answers (often just "yes" or "no"). As the name suggests, the expert interview mines a richly informed intelligence for the sake of public benefit; the poll aims simply to monitor the nature and quality of public opinion, no matter how ignorant or how well informed it may be on the subject. Of course, determining the exact state of the public mind on a given issue at a given moment can be very important, especially in measuring the practicality of a proposal. No matter how intrinsically valuable a proposal may seem, if "the people" are dead set against it, it is doomed to remain an idea whose time has not yet come.

When you are starting out to conduct a poll, the first requirement is a *sufficient number of subjects*. Under ideal conditions you would poll everyone within a target population, but for most groups such an exhaustive survey is impossible. Therefore, one must seek a *representative sample* of that population. The concept of representative sample embraces the idea of sufficient number, but it also includes what we may call the *isomorphic ideal*. Isomorphism measures how precisely a model or sample represents the form or structure of its subject. For example, a model airplane might be highly isomorphic to an actual airplane. Guided by the isomorphic ideal, we seek a sample group that is a perfect representation of the wider population it is taken to represent. We call this the isomorphic ideal, because it is rarely if ever totally attained. If you station yourself in front of the Student Union building at noon with the intention of polling student opinion and question the first 50 people who pass by, you may have a sufficient number. But there would still be a considerable chance of error and distortion, simply because some kinds of students might never come to the Union or might not come at that particular time of day. Sophomores might come to the Union more than seniors, single students more than married students, undergraduates more than graduate students, and so on. Perfect knowledge is hard to come by, but we must try to approach the isomorphic ideal as closely as possible in our sampling procedures.

Two especially important factors are *timing* and *place*. If your purpose is to measure norms and general tendencies in people's attitudes, you should avoid polling in the wake of events that may disturb the normal flow of feeling. If, for example, you want to monitor racial attitudes on campus this semester, you would do well to avoid polling the morning after a sensational, polarizing speech by a Ku Klux Klan leader. Likewise, if you select for your poll a sidewalk near the Klan leader's speech, and question students who are leaving, you add bad selection of place to atrocious timing. If you then bring this poll into your speech as representing "general student opinion," you will raise eyebrows among the more intelligent members of your audience.

Finally, remember how questions should be posed during a poll. Even the number and order of questions can be important. For sidewalk, in-front-of-the-Union polls, keep the questions few in number and very simple. You may, for example, decide to ask no more than three questions:

Do you favor the proposed 10-percent average increase in professors' salaries next year?
Would you be willing to pay $50 more in tuition next year to fund such an increase?
What is your university classification?

Such questions go to the heart of the issue and invite simple responses. Your questions should be carefully written out so that they are asked of each subject in the same way. They should be framed as objectively as possible, avoiding adjectives that betray the pollster's bias, and should be asked in a manner that gives no hint of the answer the pollster would like to hear. To avoid wasted time and trouble, show your teacher or a friend whose judgment you respect the questions you have framed. Go through the entire routine of asking the planned sequence of questions while your listener checks to see that your nonverbal manner communicates no telltale bias.

COMPLETING THE RESEARCH PLAN

From this discussion of sources, we can draw one general conclusion. *The greater the quantity and variety of knowledge produced by all these sources, the more likely that the resulting speech will have a sound research base.* It follows that some of the critical decisions you make in speech preparation are which of these sources to use, in what combinations, and with what degree of emphasis. In the hypothetical illustration we have been using, you might decide that your personal experience on a farm will serve only to establish credibility at the beginning of the speech and perhaps to provide an authentic illustration or two. Current articles in national periodicals should give you a comprehensive view and help minimize the risk of distortion that occurs when one relies too heavily on local authorities. But a local expert, as we have noted, might provide some information of immediate interest to your audience. Polling does not seem relevant to the approach you intend to take.

Let us assume you decide that you will need fifteen hours to prepare the speech, ten of which should be devoted to research. You plan to spend eight of these hours in the library, seeking information on the basic questions you have identified. This knowledge should prepare you for an interview with a local expert, to which you allot the other two hours. Seeking indirect knowledge before conducting the interview should give you the background you need to sharpen the questions you ask the expert and to help you detect any bias in the answers you receive.

Of course, all such planning is tentative. You may need more time or less in the library, depending on what you find there. You may have to give up some Saturday night rendezvous and spend it curled up with a book. (Remember that our normal tendency is to underestimate the time required to complete a task.) You may even discover that some of your basic questions are ill conceived. Some environmentalists, for example, claim that the real choice is between pesticides that build up harmful residues and those that do not. The true villain in the piece, so these folk say, is the manufacturer of the less desirable fertilizers and pesticides. In any case, you should be prepared to revise your own first analysis and projections in the light of such discoveries. The important thing is to proceed systematically.

Summary of Major Ideas

Personal experience can add freshness and credibility to a speech. But personal experience can also produce knowledge that is narrow and distorted.

Knowledge derived from print and nonprint media gives one a larger, more objective view of subjects and situations. But indirect knowledge may not apply specifically to the local scene and the immediate requirements of audience adaptation.

The speaker should have a responsible knowledge of his or her subject matter: its main features and the major issues surrounding it, the chief authorities on it, the latest developments concerning it, and how it applies locally.

The difference between what a speaker knows and what his or her listeners know about a subject is a measure of the information potential of a speech. It determines how much knowledge *could* flow, under optimal conditions, from speaker to listener.

One's plan for library research should put one in possession of the latest information and the best statements about a subject.

An interview combines the advantages of both personal and mediated knowledge. It is fresh, authentic, and local in application, but it can also be expert and objective.

Four useful interviewing techniques are probes, which follow up lines of questions; mirror questions, which reflect a particular part of an answer in order to elicit more detail; verifiers, which confirm answers; and reinforcers, the nonverbal general encouragement of respondents.

The poll serves to determine the attitudes and perceptions on a given subject that exist at a given moment in a given population.

A representative sample for a poll includes a sufficient number of subjects who fairly represent a larger population. A perfectly representative sample would be said to achieve the isomorphic ideal.

A good poll is conducted at an opportune time and in an appropriate place.

Exercises and Discussion Questions

1. Take a walking tour of your library, and find the various resources described in this chapter.

2. Write a hypothetical letter requesting an interview with someone prominent in the news. Compare letters in class. Which letters are most persuasive? Why? Evaluate them according to the principles set forth in this chapter.

3. Form two-person mock-interview teams. Members should alternate roles as interviewer and respondent on subjects mutually agreed upon. Look especially for opportunities to practice probes, mirror questions, verifiers, and reinforcers. Practice for five minutes, and then discuss how and why various moments of the interview were or were not successful. Change roles and practice again. To increase the learning value of the exercise, record it on tape for detailed analysis.

For Further Reading

For much more on the use of libraries, see Jean Key Gate's excellent *Guide to the Use of Books and Libraries* (New York: McGraw-Hill, 1974). On the subject of interviewing, see Charles Stewart and William Cash, *Interviewing Principles and Practices* (Dubuque, Iowa: William C. Brown, 1974); Robert Kahn and Charles Cannell, *The Dynamics of Interviewing* (New York: Wiley, 1957); and Bonnie McDaniel Johnson, *Communication: The Process of Organizing* (Boston: Allyn and Bacon, 1977), especially Chapter 5, "Planned Interactions."

7

ADAPTATION TO AN AUDIENCE: SITUATIONAL AND PSYCHOLOGICAL FACTORS

The rhetorician, who teaches his pupil to speak
scientifically, will particularly set forth the
nature of that being to which he addresses
his speeches; and this, I conceive,
to be the soul.

SOCRATES, from Plato's *Phaedrus*

The audience is a great challenge to the speaker and also a great resource. By its specific needs and nature, it creates certain opportunities and raises certain barriers. This chapter and the next will help you develop the sensitivity to recognize these opportunities and barriers.

The speaker's understanding of his or her listeners must be the touchstone of all speech preparation. Identification especially depends on a valid preconception of the audience and a successful adjustment to its nature.

We shall approach analysis of the audience from three directions: (1) the particular requirements and circumstances of the speech situation; (2) the general psychological factors that shape our communication behavior; and (3) in the next chapter, our nature as beings who respond to symbols.

THE SPEECH OCCASION

Every audience has certain special characteristics, and anticipating them can be very important in designing and adapting a speech. At least seven such features, which make up the context or situation in which the speech is given, seem critical.

Time

At what time of day will the speech be presented? The answer to this question can indicate whether the audience will be sleepy or alert and how much lively material you will need at the beginning of your speech. What day will the speech be given? On "blue Monday" a speech may have to be brighter in tone. On Friday the speech may have to be filled with devices to gain and hold attention if you are to prevent people's minds from drifting to the weekend ahead. A related question concerns the time of year. Winter puts an audience in a different frame of mind from the distracting days of April and May. Even weather can be a factor in adaptation. Sunshine and rain affect audience disposition differently. Often a speaker can compensate for such variables by slight adjustments in delivery and technique. For example, a bit more humor and an intensified delivery might enliven an audience on a rainy or somber day.

Place

Is your classroom quiet or noisy? Is it large or small? Are the surroundings pleasant or depressing? Do the acoustics present any problems? Again, you may have to compensate by planning additional brightening and attention-holding material or by making adjustments in delivery, such as speaking louder, slowing the pace, and incorporating more descriptive gestures to clarify and reinforce your meaning.

Medium

For some speeches, especially those planned for radio or television, it may be vital to consider the medium of presentation. A radio speech obviously puts emphasis on vocal adequacy in delivery and on the language of the speech. A television presentation heightens the importance of speaker personality dynamics and appearance, especially as indicated by facial cues. It is said, for example, that the youthful, attractive look of John F. Kennedy (together with the somewhat haggard appearance of Richard Nixon) was an important factor in the Kennedy–Nixon presidential debates of 1960 and in the final result of that campaign. Most of those who heard the debates on radio felt that Nixon had won.[1] Television speakers can never forget that they are addressing not a collective group but a large number of isolated individuals in the sanctuary of their homes. Thus a speech designed for television should usually be more conversational and informal. The speaker's manner is that of a guest speaking to a host in the latter's living room.

Occasionally a speaker designs a speech ostensibly for one audience when he or she actually has another group of listeners in mind. Political speakers often tailor a speech that is to be delivered on some local

1. *The Great Debates: Background–Perspective–Effects,* ed. Sidney Kraus (Bloomington, Ind.: Indiana University Press, 1962). See especially Herbert A. Seltz and Richard D. Yoakam, "Production Diary of the Debates," pp. 73–126.

occasion with an eye to the wider audience they anticipate through newspaper and electronic media distribution. Adaptation to the immediate audience may have to be sacrificed for the sake of adaptation to this larger, remote audience. At a speech I once attended, President John F. Kennedy spoke at commencement exercises of The American University, Washington, D.C., in the late spring of 1963. On that day, during Kennedy's final spring, he delivered what was hailed immediately as a dramatic statement on the nature of peace in our time, a speech that decidedly altered the atmosphere of international relations.[2] The day was hot and muggy, and those wearing the robes of faculty and student graduation regalia suffered directly and without relief under a noon sun. We did not get a great deal from the speech, which was filled with subtle argument. Only later did we realize that we had been ringside spectators at one of the important rhetorical events of our time. But that was it precisely: We were indeed spectators, not members of an actual speech audience.

Context of Recent Speeches

The speeches your class has heard recently, especially those delivered in the class itself, have created a certain rhetorical atmosphere in which you must work. Perhaps that atmosphere is tense and uncertain; if so, you may have to puncture the tension with a humorous story that relates you to your hearers and puts everyone at ease. Perhaps previous speeches have been highly successful or woefully inadequate; if so, you are challenged to do your very best, because you can look either very bad or very good by comparison.

The speech atmosphere on the day of the speech itself can be significant. Unless your instructor assigns an order for speaking in advance of the actual day, you will have to adapt to that variable on the spur of the moment. If you speak first, for example, you have a chance to set the pace for the day. Recognizing the importance of order effects among speeches, teachers often try to "stack the deck" in favor of speech success. If the day begins with a successful speech, a certain positive momentum is established. If the days ends with a fine effort, the class will leave anticipating the next meeting, and speakers for that day will feel challenged to do well. Less successful speech efforts, especially when they occur back-to-back in a class, can create a negative momentum that both class and teacher must work hard to overcome.

---

2. Later printed as "What Kind of Peace Do We Want?" in *The Burden and the Glory*, ed. Allan Nevins (New York: Harper & Row, 1964), pp. 53–58.

As the speeches unfold, observe of how well others have done before you. You can capitalize on previous success. But if the previous effort has been less than adequate, you face a special challenge, especially at the beginning of your speech. Previous speakers may also create an opportunity for you to use *contrast* to advantage. If the previous speaker harangued listeners in a loud voice, they may welcome a quieter approach from you. If the previous speaker lacked vocal variety and lulled listeners into a daze, your voice must be enlivened with changes of pace and pitch. If the previous speech was heavy with seriousness, the audience might appreciate some appropriate lightness from you, especially at the beginning.

The lesson is obvious: Previous speeches prepare a setting for you, to which you must adjust often on the spur of the moment.

Context of Recent Events

As listeners walk into a room on the day of your speech, they bring their memories of recent local, national, and international events. These memories constitute a larger context of audience awareness. You should ask yourself, "what is in the news at the moment? Are these events related to my subject? Might they be associated with my subject in some way?" If you can place your speech in a context of other timely, important events, you can increase interest and attention.

When recent events bear directly on your subject matter, you must acknowledge them in your speech. Not to indicate awareness of them would seriously damage your credibility as researcher. All the more reason to check through such news magazines as *Time, Newsweek,* and *U.S. News and World Report* for the latest information on fast-breaking subjects.

Audience Personality

One should also consider the demographic features of an audience: their age, politics, religious preferences, and level of education. Aristotle once observed that young listeners are apt to be more enthusiastic and older listeners more careful. Better-educated audiences are usually more critical; they require more proof and a full discussion of the options open to them. You should scan all such factors as you design your speech. Moreover, in previous discussions or perhaps in response to a poll, the group may have revealed its likes and dislikes, its heroes and villains, and issues that divide it. You should ask yourself, "Is this group likely to be hostile or receptive to the approach I am taking? How can I get through to them?"

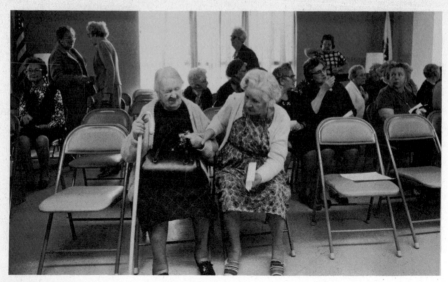

Patricia Hollander Gross

Leader–Follower Dynamics

Has anyone in the group assumed a position of leadership? Your speech might well take into account his or her influence. Political campaigners often concentrate on the opinion leaders, sensing that groups prefer to be coherent and consistent in opinion, and that they often take their cues from such opinion leaders, who become integrating forces. If you can convince these leaders, more than half the battle may be won.

PSYCHOLOGICAL FACTORS

Underlying all the foregoing considerations is the psychology of human nature, the needs and forces that drive us and alert us to messages in certain ways. We shall discuss these needs and forces in terms of five fundamental laws of human communication behavior:

The Law of Priority
The Law of Focus
The Law of Process
The Law of Proof
The Law of Power

It is the speaker's business to make these laws work in favor of the speech by skillfully designing and adapting the message.

The speaker must help us understand the world around us by high-lighting those features that are most important to us.

Human perception is highly selective. We are surrounded by a bewildering confusion of stimuli, all of which we process and place in some order. Art critic Rudolf Arnheim describes this basic encounter with reality in the following way:

> *Far from being a passive mechanism of registration like the photographic camera, our visual apparatus copes with the incoming images in active struggle. It is upset by the intrusion and animated by the stimulation. It seizes upon the regularities of form, which allows comprehension. . . .*[3]

And Gestalt psychologists confirm that "an important determinant of man's behavior is his requirement for an orderly and coherent view of his relations to the world."[4]

All of us, therefore, need communication that helps us form coherent, selective images of reality, such as we discussed in Chapter 1. This is why depiction is the basic function of communication, on which all other functions build. Communication helps us form selective images out of bewildering complexity by highlighting those features of reality that are most important to us. It assigns these features *priority* within our field of awareness. If you wanted to describe the world of the migrant worker, for instance, your first problem as communicator would be to decide which features of that world to select for priority attention. Because your message must compete with the thousand and one other possible stimuli that might distract your audience, you must also determine how the image of migrant life might strike home with maximum impact. Such problems make the art of rhetoric complex and creative.

MOTIVE APPEALS   What alerts us to certain features of our environment as worthy of our attention? One answer to this question involves the concept of motives, the deep desires that generate all action. Maslow has identified five fundamental levels of human need, which he feels motivate our behavior.[5] At the most basic level are the *physiological needs* such as satisfying hunger, thirst, and sex drives. A message that

3. "Gestalt Psychology and Artistic Form," *Aspects of Form: A Symposium on Form in Nature and Art* (Bloomington, Ind.: Indiana University Press, 1951), p. 203.
4. Morton Deutsch and Robert M. Krauss, *Theories in Social Psychology* (New York: Basic Books, 1965), p. 22.
5. Abraham Maslow, "A Theory of Human Motivation," *Psychology Review*, 50 (July 1943), 370-396.

can show that its subject might affect our supply of food and drink or our sexual attractiveness will immediately claim our attention. For this reason, television advertising often strives mightily and beyond all logic to establish a sexual connection between its product and the viewer. True love can be yours if you drink a certain kind of cola.

At the second level, Maslow says, are *safety* needs, including our quest for security, self-preservation, and the maintenance of a stable world. Speech focused on survival-related issues immediately captures our attention. This is why debates over military security and over whether we are poisoning the air, soil, and water around us have a lasting impact.

At the third level is the need for *belongingness and love,* including our need for affection, friendship, and affiliation with groups and currents of feeling within groups we identify with. We look to leaders to help us interpret such movements of group thought and emotion. Most of us don't like to jeopardize the acceptance and respectability we enjoy in the groups vital to us. Therefore, a speaker can highlight a subject by showing how certain of its features can either augment or diminish the effectiveness of a group and/or our standing within the group. It takes a strong person to resist the appeal of group-sanctioned behavior. This is why the bandwagon effect in political advertising can be so powerful. ("Everybody else is endorsing so-and-so. Why don't you?")

Need for esteem, which occupies the fourth level, includes our desires for prestige, self-respect, success, and pride. "If you will only put my plan into effect, you will make yourselves proud" is a common theme among persuasive speakers. Moreover, speakers should show that they respect their auditors and are aware of audience accomplishments. It is easy to praise Athens among Athenians, Aristotle once noted. It is also an advantage for the speaker. Such signs of esteem are especially useful at the beginning of a speech when the speaker is not well known to his or her listeners.

On the other hand, speakers who feel confident of their reception by an audience sometimes take the risk of shaming their listeners, arguing that they do not deserve esteem. Such an approach can be useful when the speaker wishes to goad listeners into some redemptive action. "You've done wrong, but I'm giving you the opportunity to do right" is the pattern here. The technique is obviously dangerous, but it can also shock an audience into action.

The fifth level Maslow identifies consists of *self-actualization needs,* our striving to realize and develop our own potential. We want to grow, excel, experience, become the better person that lies dormant within us. Speeches that tie themselves constructively to this intense drive are listened to very attentively. Much of the appeal of the rhetoric of the Civil Rights movement was directed to this long-stifled impulse among black Americans and to the dream among responsive white Americans of a nation that could realize its promise of equal opportunity.

Historically, the Women's Movement also appealed to this need for self-actualization in a society that no longer constricts a woman's identity on the basis of her sex. Elizabeth Cady Stanton expressed the need for self-actualization through a voyage metaphor: On the rough seas of life each person must sail alone.

> *No matter how much women prefer to lean, to be protected and supported, nor how much men desire to have them do so, they must make the voyage of life alone, and for safety in an emergency they must know something of the laws of navigation. . . .*
>
> *Nothing strengthens the judgment and quickens the conscience like individual responsibility. Nothing adds such dignity to character as the recognition of one's self-sovereignty; the right to an equal place, everywhere conceded; a place earned by personal merit. . . . Seeing, then, that the responsibilities of life rest equally on man and woman, that their destiny is the same, they need the same preparation for time and eternity. The talk of sheltering woman from the fierce storms of life is the sheerest mockery, for they beat on her from every point of the compass, just as they do on man, and with more fatal results, for he has been trained to protect himself, to resist, to conquer.*[6]

Physiological drives, safety, belongingness and love, esteem, and self-actualization—all these needs can act to alert people to certain features of speech subjects. You must relate your speech securely to one or more of these motive appeals. They create that intense and selective interest so essential to the Law of Priority.

PERCEPTUAL TENDENCIES We also interpret reality through the influence of certain perceptual tendencies. One such tendency is that of *proximity:* We respond to a subject if it seems close to us in space or time. If you can show that certain consequences loom just ahead or if you can telescope a subject so that it seems close to the interests of audience members, you will heighten its significance for them. "Here" and "Now" are important words in the vocabulary of public speaking.

6. "Solitude of Self," *Feminism: The Essential Historical Writings,* ed. Miriam Schneir (New York: Random House, 1972), pp. 158–159. See the perceptive discussion in Karlyn Kohrs Campbell, "Stanton's 'The Solitude of Self': A Rationale for Feminism," *Quarterly Journal of Speech,* 66 (October 1980), 304–312.

A second perceptual tendency is that of *contiguity:* We like to recognize connections between things that belong to different classes of objects. We are especially attentive if a speaker can explain an unknown, mysterious thing by connecting it with a known, familiar thing. An image of chromosomes as the "blueprints of ourselves" would establish such a connection figuratively and should make listeners receptive to a longer, technical explanation.

A third important perceptual tendency is that of *magnitude:* In any field of potential stimulation, we notice features that seem large and ignore those that seem small. This tendency explains the effectiveness of what Aristotle identified long ago as the device of magnifying. When we magnify a subject we dwell on it; we turn it this way and that until the minds of listeners are filled with its presence. (This rhetorical art is also called amplification.) Magnification can occur through repetition, as, for example, when a speaker announces a theme and then proceeds to tell a series of stories, each of which repeats and adds to the theme. The idea projects larger and larger in our minds until it dominates our attention. For example, to introduce Susan as a courageous person and then describe three incidents that illustrate Susan's courage is to magnify that virtue in the audience's minds and raise it to a priority position.

Still a fourth perceptual tendency is that of *contrast:* We comprehend more clearly when we juxtapose a subject and its opposite. In a speech based on contrast, you can first establish the contrasting condition or situation and then proceed to describe your subject against such a background. Or you can build a point-by-point contrast gradually to a climax. To make an audience appreciate economic prosperity, a speaker might dwell first on the Great Depression and how Americans lived then. To illustrate the meaning of freedom, a speaker might build a point-by-point parallel image of slavery.

Our attraction to contrast leads directly to our fascination with *conflict,* in which subjects become actively opposed to each other. A speaker who can create a sense of conflict can make us ringside spectators and may even draw us into the symbolic struggle. Clearly, all revolutionary speakers must be skilled in the art of depiction through conflict. Much of the rhetoric of feminism portrays women first in a passive, grim role as victims of male oppression but then invokes a vision of women in active conflict with the oppressor, gradually defeating and overcoming until Woman Militant becomes WomanTriumphant.

In summary, the psychological Law of Priority explains how speakers can use universal human needs and principles of perception to adapt their subjects so that certain features stand out boldly in the audience's minds.

Law of Focus

The speaker must make selected features of reality clear by using vivid examples and the principle of association.

The Law of Focus explains how we bring selected features of reality into sharp, clear form so that they can make a graphic impression during communication. The art of focusing is based on definition. We have to fine-tune a depiction for our listeners by explaining what a subject is and by showing it in its active, living context through vivid examples or audio-visual representations, techniques that are discussed in detail in Chapter 9. If you want to bring the concept of Emerging Woman into sharp focus, you might present Ms. Edna Morton of Dallas, Texas (find or invent a person and locale to fit the context of your speech). Ms. Morton, you might explain, took on the male-dominated business world of this city and blazed a trail for other women into executive employment. It took many years of hard, lonely fighting, but Ms. Morton made it. As you told Ms. Morton's story, you might present photographs showing her (1) in heated argument with some business-man, (2) picketing alone in front of the offending institution, and (3) speaking before a local woman's organization. You would use Ms. Morton as a lens to focus your concept of Woman Triumphant.

Another major focusing technique is to associate a topic with some-thing listeners are already familiar with. The key questions for adaptation are "How can I sharpen and clarify the image of my subject in the minds of these listeners? What examples should I use, what aids might be helpful, and which associations must I establish?" Explorers in the New World brought America into focus by comparing its flora and fauna with European plant and animal life. British parliamentary speakers depicted wrongs perpetrated in eighteenth-century India by describing Indian customs as though they were British values and Indian women as though they were members of the British nobility. Space explorers focused the moonscape by comparing it to Nevada. Whether the motive be persuasive or purely informative, you must bring your subject into focus for those who are listening.

Law of Process

The speaker must help us see subjects in terms of the larger patterns and processes that give order to our world.

We expect all things to have causes, and all causes to have effects. All things begin, grow, flourish, decay, and end, and in every end there is a new beginning. Hence we seek to find patterns of order or perhaps even to impose order on our worlds. In the speech you design, you must satisfy these audience expectations about cause and consequence, action and reaction, endings and beginnings. There are four major features of the Law of Process.

COHERENCE Human beings experience a natural and powerful impulse to seek coherence in the world around them and to sort things into stable patterns. Indeed, we may favor speeches that offer or promise such coherence for that reason alone. We may even go so far as to honor such presentations, saying that they contain "truth."

The urgency of our need for coherence is reflected in how we respond to chaos. When a speaker depicts a scene in disorder, that very image invites listeners to accept a proposal promising organization. President Carter used this pattern effectively in his 1976 campaign when he argued that the federal "bureaucracy" had expanded beyond human control and needed to be tamed by some reasoned plan of political management. Then, in 1980, many American voters sensed that their world was drifting out of control and turned to President Reagan's vision of a more disciplined future.

Coherence is attractive not only in the substance of a speech but in its form. For the speaker, all things in the speech must follow in coherent order. In a speech based on a time sequence, you may begin long ago and work up to the present, or you may begin now and work back to the distant past. Similarly, in a speech exhibiting a spatial pattern, you may begin with your campus and move gradually outward, or you may start with the broad view and pan in on the local and the immediate. In like manner, speeches based on a logical pattern develop a chain of arguments, moving from premise to conclusion, which then becomes the premise leading to a new conclusion, and so on until the chain reaches its argumentative destination: the conclusion that is the point of the speech. For example, you might develop the following chain of reasoning: Because these people are poor, they have no land. Because they have no land, they have no power. Without power they are unable to make the government listen to them. Unless the government listens, it will not make improvements in their lives. But without such improvements, there will be revolution. Will we step in to break the vicious circle before it destroys us?

CAUSE-CONSEQUENCE Because we expect and perhaps even need a coherent universe, all things must seem to have a cause. Thus "how?", "who?", and "why?" become the probes we use for unraveling the often mysterious origins of things. However, the search for causes can have another kind of motive in a political speech built upon the cause-consequence theme. Republicans may depict America as weak and vacillating, unable to solve its problems at home and no longer in control of a chaotic world. Who and what do you think will be indicted as causes for this sorry state of affairs? Similarly, Democrats at the very same time may see an America rich in material abundance, powerful and at peace, holding high the tattered banner of human rights. The only menace to its continuing greatness comes from the possibility of a radical shift in foreign and domestic policy—a danger posed by guess who?

Clearly, the search for causes can be terribly oversimplified and distorted, such that we make hasty, biased, and even faulty judgments. We can be satisfied with discovering *one* cause when there are actually many. When you speak publicly, be sure that your account of causation is complete enough to satisfy even the most demanding listener.

SYMMETRY We tend to seek balance and correct proportion in any pattern or arrangement. We like to see a speech move deliberately from its beginning to its conclusion, without hasty leaps in judgment or flowery, self-conscious dawdling along the way. We like to see points receive just the amount of attention they deserve. The structure of an entire speech must seem pleasing to us, combining strength of reasoning with grace and ease of expression. If you can please our sense of symmetry, we may reward you by taking pleasure in what you say. Study the ancient Greek temples.

CUMULATION In any speech pattern there should be a sense of building toward some final, satisfying conclusion. A speaker must arouse some appetite in the audience, some passion or curiosity, and then proceed to satisfy that appetite as the speech unfolds. There must always be the sense of moving toward some climax, some crescendo. Study the classical symphonic pattern.

Law of Proof

The speaker must overcome the sense of caution that listeners have developed from previous experiences with the power of speech.

Symbolic communication is powerful in its appeal, so most of us develop a protective caution, a skeptical resistance that communication must overcome. This depends somewhat on our degree of trust in the communicator, but we are wary of all communication that seems to have an axe to grind. Specifically, we apply the tests of comprehensiveness, reliability, and authenticity.

"O.K.! Now don't forget the Roosevelt charm, the Eisenhower grin, and the Kennedy magic."

Drawing by Dana Fradon; © 1980 The New Yorker Magazine, Inc.

COMPREHENSIVENESS Does a communication cover the subject adequately? Does the speaker demonstrate a grasp of the situation as a whole in his or her depiction of events? Is concrete and objective evidence offered? When audiences trust a speaker too much, they may forget to apply these tests and become quite gullible. On the other hand, if they mistrust a speaker (especially one who is telling them something they really don't want to hear), they may refuse to accept the truth even when it is solidly based in comprehensive fact and reasoning.

RELIABILITY Can you count on what the speaker says? Is the speech based on stable and recurring fact, or does it depend on random, hearsay, and isolated observations? For example, if a speaker bases a claim that Turkish businessmen are not to be trusted on the reputation of mid-Eastern rug merchants, listeners have good reason to doubt its reliability. On another front, does the speaker draw inferences correctly from evidence? When logical fallacies seem to infest a speech, you are not likely to find its conclusions very reliable.

Therefore, you must test your own speech thoroughly for the soundness and reliability of its evidence and argument. Better still, have a respected friend read through your outline or listen to a practice effort. Ask him or her to subject you to the toughest questions possible. If your speech can stand up to that kind of scrutiny, you should pass the tests of reliability when the speech is actually presented.

AUTHENTICITY   Has the speaker, or at least the authorities presented in support of claims made in the speech, had first-hand knowledge of the situation? As you adapt to your audience, you must show them that the evidence is based on such authentic experience. Do the descriptions offered seem real? Would you believe them and the conclusions drawn from them, if you were a member of the audience? We are in an age that demands reassurance on the question of authenticity.

Law of Power

The speaker must satisfy our need for power over our lives by helping us form an appropriate emotional response to a subject and by encouraging a group identity that will allow us to control the situation.

We all seek to control the forces that govern our lives. Audiences often gather to establish such power collectively, and they look to speeches to help them. Two especially potent factors in the urge to power are emotion and identification.

EMOTION   Since the days of ancient Greece and Rome, speakers have recognized that audience feelings are a source of potential power that can be engaged in a speech to advance a cause. Listeners especially like to sense the human drama of the rhetorical situations in which they find themselves. The next chapter probes this fascinating tendency further, but here we shall simply note that, if a cause can be justified, an audience will wish to be involved through both reason and emotion. Listeners must be angered or sustained by visions of the past and inspired by visions of the future. Feelings of confidence and commitment must surge through the crowd. Speech stripped of all feeling (assuming that were possible) would be not only powerless but dehumanizing as well.

Feelings require an outlet, and in order to be expressed, they require a focus. Moreover, people desire consistency and harmony between their convictions and their emotions. President John F. Kennedy appealed to this need for consistency as he addressed the nation on the racial crisis in America on June 11, 1963. Kennedy wished to point out the inconsistency between the practices of racial prejudice and

David Powers/Stock, Boston

American ideals. His technique was a direct appeal to conscience and to the sense of fairness in his listeners: "... When Americans are sent to Vietnam or West Berlin, we do not ask for whites only."[7] His intent was to arouse sympathy on the basis of identification: "If an American, because his skin is dark, cannot eat lunch in a restaurant open to the public; if he cannot send his children to the best public school available; if he cannot vote for the public officials who represent him; if, in short, he cannot enjoy the full and free life which all of us want, then who among us would be content to have the color of his skin changed and stand in his place?" Those who did not respond to this "moral crisis," Kennedy suggested, invited an inconsistency that was both degrading to them and dangerous to the nation; those who did respond were both moral and practical citizens. As he put it, "Those who do nothing are inviting shame as well as violence. Those who act boldly are recognizing right as well as reality." At stake was the power of the nation in a threatening world.

Remember that appeals to feeling must seem sincere. The audience will not wish to be exploited or manipulated; if your listeners sense that you are deliberately fanning their emotions, they may resent you and react against your cause. The appeal to feelings must be prepared for in advance, either by a situation that clearly calls for a specific emotional reaction or by the art of a speaker who presents evidence

7. John F. Kennedy, "A Moral Imperative," delivered over television and radio, Washington, D.C., June 11, 1963. Reprinted in *Vital Speeches of the Day*, 39 (July 1, 1963), 546–547.

and arguments that justify such a reaction. In the Kennedy example, the strong appeal was prepared for by the situation *and* justified by reasoned argument.

Emotions are engaged by the specific and the concrete. When you have prepared your audience properly, present an example or story in a manner that brings the situation to life and which arouses your listeners. Both your language and your delivery are vital in securing emotional response: you yourself must bear witness to the validity and propriety of the emotion you would invoke, just as Kennedy's earnest manner endorsed the deep feeling of his appeal.

IDENTIFICATION   If we look back to the ancient roots of humanity millions of years ago, we find that we have always been group-oriented beings.[8] We seek and find our identity in terms of some larger collectivity, and in that unity is our strength. Leadership would be meaningless if there were no followers, and those who follow require leaders in order to define themselves. Even rebels see themselves in terms of the group, though they identify not with but against group feeling, custom, or procedure. The lure of group conformity is deeply imprinted in human nature.

The power of identification can explain why the ritual aspect of public speaking can be so appealing. When we come together to declare our common support of certain values (or our common opposition to them), we are actually celebrating our sense of group togetherness. The very language we use reflects the power of group identification. People have died for words like "freedom" and "fatherland" and in reaction to words like "tyranny," "injustice," and "taxation without representation."

Finally, the urge toward identification expresses itself in a tendency to establish larger-than-life leader images. We like to see our leaders as having the heroic virtues we admire. Then we can identify with them and share in these virtues. We also find villains useful and reduce those who fit that role to smaller-than-life caricatures.

The lesson for adaptation seems clear. Our speech, especially when it is persuasive speech, must help people perceive themselves as members of a group, which then serves as a vehicle for collective action. If we are to satisfy the Law of Power, we must satisfy this strong and ancient urge toward group identification and the collective life.

8. See Morris Swadesh, *The Origin and Diversification of Language*, ed. Joel Sherzer (New York: Aldine, 1971); Charles F. Hockett and Robert Ascher, "The Human Revolution," *Current Anthropology*, 5 (1964), 135–168; Richard Leakey and Roger Lewin, *Origins: What New Discoveries Reveal About the Emergence of Our Species and Its Possible Future* (New York: Dutton, 1977); and Michael Osborn, "Our Communication Heritage: The Genetic Tie That Binds," *Southern Speech Communication Journal*, 44 (1979), 147–158.

A MODEL

The discussion of adaptation to an audience given in this chapter is summarized in the "Speech Preparation Plan: Adaptation Model" that follows. This model should prove useful within the overall Speech Preparation Plan.

SPEECH PREPARATION PLAN

Adaptation Model

I. The Particular Circumstances
   1. When will the speech be given?
   2. Where will the speech be given?
   3. What will be the medium of presentation, and who is the actual audience?
   4. What kind of atmosphere have recent speeches created?
   5. What recent events are apt to be fresh in the minds of listeners?
   6. What are the demographic and group personality features of the audience: age, politics, religious profile, level of education, likes and dislikes, heroes and villains, issues on which individuals disagree?
   7. Who are the leaders and who are the followers?
II. Psychological Dynamics
   1. How can I give my subject priority in the minds of listeners?
      a. What universal human motives might it involve?
      b. How might I make use of my hearers' sensitivity to proximity, contiguity, magnitude, contrast, and conflict?
   2. How can I bring my subject most clearly into focus?
   3. Can I develop my subject in a form that satisfies my listeners' need for coherence, causal relationships, symmetry, and the sense of cumulation?
   4. Can I meet the tests of comprehensiveness, reliability, and authenticity of communication?
   5. Can I create and stimulate an urge to power among my listeners? Can I excite them and involve them in a group ready for action?

Summary of Major Ideas

A speech must be adapted to the specific audience and to the specific moment of delivery.

Situational factors to consider in adapting a speech to its audience include time, place, medium, recent class speeches, recent events, demographic and group personality characteristics, and leader–follower dynamics.

We are shaped and driven by psychological forces that influence the design of speeches.

The Law of Priority explains how certain features of the surrounding environment are heightened in our attention while others are diminished. Priority is determined by several universal human motives and by perceptual tendencies such as proximity, contiguity, magnitude, contrast, and conflict.

The Law of Focus explains how we bring selected features of the environment into clear view, especially as we express them to others.

The Law of Process describes our tendency to look for the larger patterns to which features of the environment belong. As we seek to find or to impose patterns and processes, we are influenced by considerations of coherence, causes and consequences, symmetry, and cumulation.

The Law of Proof arises from our concern that the world presented in communication be genuine. We are especially sensitive to questions of comprehensiveness, reliability, and authenticity.

The Law of Power describes our attraction to communication that gives us control over our lives. Two keys to power in communication are effective appeals to feeling and the use of symbols that build a sense of group identity behind a cause.

Exercises and Discussion Questions

1. Assume that you are a speech writer for the president, who wishes to make an important policy speech on an issue of great concern (you choose the issue). Your job is to analyze the national audience the president can expect for that issue at this moment and to suggest adaptations for the speech in light of your analysis. Use the adaptation model presented in this chapter as a guide to analysis. To make this exercise a class project in adaptation strategies, teams of students can study certain state, local, or national issues and recommend adaptation strategies for speeches based on them. These recommendations should be presented and defended in class.

2. Write the script for a three-minute speech, first as you might present it to a live audience of 1000 people, then as a radio presentation, and finally as a television speech. What differences evolve as you adapt the speech to these media?

3. What universal human motives are relevant to the most important issues of the day? Consider how you might make use of this relevancy in speeches on these subjects.

For Further Reading

The often intense relationship between leaders and followers, speakers and audiences, has attracted interest since ancient times. Plato's *Phaedrus* sets forth an ideal ethical vision of this relationship in the mythic terms of love and draws inferences such as that given at the beginning of this chapter. See also Richard Weaver's analysis in "The *Phaedrus* and the Nature of Rhetoric," *The Ethics of Rhetoric* (Chicago, Ill.: Henry Regnery, 1953). Machiavelli's *The Prince*, a more cynical approach to the leader–follower relationship, contains guidelines for exploitation.

For further understanding of the tendencies of communication behavior described in this chapter, study the principles of Gestalt psychology. See, for example, Chapter 2 of Morton Deutsch and Robert M. Krauss, *Theories in Social Psychology* (New York: Basic Books, 1965). Primary sources for many of these concepts can be found in Wolfgang Kohler, *Gestalt Psychology: An Introduction to New Concepts in Modern Psychology* (New York: Liveright, 1970) and Max Wertheimer, *Productive Thinking* (New York: Harper & Row, 1959).

8

ADAPTATION TO AN AUDIENCE: OUR SYMBOLIC NATURE

What the speaker must do is create a plot, which
if properly built, will cause his audience to act in
the probable, or inevitable direction. The rhetor,
therefore, is also a poet, not in the sense of one
who turns a pretty phrase, but in the sense
of a maker-of-plots.

AUGUST W. STAUB,
"Rhetoric and Poetic: The Rhetor as Poet–Plot-Maker"

WHAT TO LOOK FOR IN
THIS CHAPTER

Our tendency to see life in dramatic terms

The charismatic language of our society

Changeless symbols that appeal to human nature

One of the most important themes of philosophy in our time concerns the basic symbolic nature of humankind. Ernst Cassirer has defined human beings as symbol-using animals. Suzanne Langer has argued that we have a biological need for verbal symbols: Our minds, she says, feed on words. Kenneth Burke notes that our symbolic nature makes us see ourselves and the world as though we were all involved in some great living theater. In his view, Shakespeare stated this tendency quite correctly:

> *All the world's a stage,*
> *And all the men and women merely players:*
> *They have their exits and their entrances;*
> *And one man in his time plays many parts. . .*

In the field of speech communication, Ernest Bormann has discussed the importance of social fantasies that give meaning to people's lives, such as the stories we build up about the past and the visions we dream for the future. August Staub has described the speaker as very much like a playwright, designing scripts to catch listeners up in a sustained action. Indeed, asks Staub,

> *Why do people make and why do people listen to speeches? Is it really to communicate and be communicated to? Or, granting the importance of communication, is it not something deeper and more mysterious—the joy, on the one hand, of being a living playwright, and, on the other, of being actual dramatic agents, trapped for a short time within the order of a plot, forced, for the moment, to purify life of all but a single, intense judgment?*[1]

1. "Rhetoric and Poetic: The Rhetor as Poet-Plot-Maker," *Southern Speech Journal*, 26 (1961), 285–290.

If Staub is right, we cannot avoid a sense of drama in our communication with each other.

Obviously these comments about our symbolic nature have important implications for audience adaptation. The speaker must give his or her listeners something more than an interesting and colorful speech that argues convincingly and appeals to important motives. *The speaker must also create a frame of dramatic meaning in which the action suggested by the speech takes its significant place.*

The purpose of this chapter is to examine symbols that can evoke the sense of dramatic participation in listeners. This discussion should help make you more sensitive to the power of these words and how enlisting this power can increase your effectiveness as a speaker. Treated are certain symbols that have unusual local, regional, and national power and other words that seem to appeal to all people and therefore have cross-cultural significance.

THE SYMBOLIC LIFE OF AMERICANS

In college life, athletic competition between certain universities is often intense. There is a certain theater or fantasy here that touches the lives of many people. Knowing that this "theater" exists, a speaker might choose to enhance her or his message by arguing that "If we do this we shall be far ahead of State U., which has yet to move in this direction." Or, even more powerfully, "State U. has already started doing this. Are we going to let them make us look bad?" There is no way to explain the power of such appeals except as they tap the symbolic worlds we build around ourselves.

The charismatic language we first discussed in Chapter 4 draws much of its strength from connection with such folk-drama. Words such as "democracy," "freedom," and "the individual" are given meaning by stories and legends that all of us have heard from our youth, as well as by our actual experiences. The power of such folk-drama obviously depends on many of the laws of communication behavior discussed in Chapter 7. Clearly, our symbolic worlds provide coherence and purpose for living. They provide a sense of larger process, and, as others identify with them and with us through them, they provide a sense of collective power. Even the bumper stickers we display on our cars can indicate the nature of the roles we choose to play and our personal allegiance to sports teams, political candidates, or social and economic movements.

Local Symbols

The appeal of certain words and of certain folk-dramas is quite local. As a cue to such theater, ask yourself "What are the local causes? Who is intensely admired and who is despised in this community? What overriding goals do local people have, and what do they fear?" The response of your audience, as you tie your speech to such drama, will indicate whether you have hit the mark.

Regional Symbols

At the regional and national levels, the folk-drama is a little more patterned and predictable. The American South, for example, has long maintained a fairly distinct culture of its own. Within the South itself, what we might call subcultures differ widely, from the mountain culture of Appalachia to the delta culture of the lower Mississippi Valley. To speak to audiences in areas that exhibit regional identity, the speaker should seem to be of them and from them and to share their sense of participation in a rich fantasy life that belongs alone to them. By all means, consider the regional context in which you are speaking. Often a certain symbolism exists there that you can ethically turn to your advantage.

National Symbols

In his classic study of charismatic language at the national level (which he called "god-terms and devil-terms"), Richard Weaver uncovered a potent American folk-drama of far-reaching importance that still provides valuable resources for audience adaptation.[2] In Weaver's time, the early 1950s, "progress" seemed to be the one word that could give direction to our efforts. Progress and the dramas built upon it called for dedication and even sacrifice. Other potent words related to progress were "science," "modern," and "efficient." The scientist served the cause of progress by making discoveries. Indeed, the scientist became the priest of progress. In a world ruled by progress, the latest is always best, so Weaver's Americans were much moved by the word "modern." Again, a progressive world seeks to get where it is going as quickly and smoothly as possible, so "efficiency" is valued.

The progressive world, however, has little use for the poetic, the speculative, the philosophical, or other endeavors that seek not useful

---

2. See Weaver's discussion in "Ultimate Terms in Contemporary Rhetoric," *The Ethics of Rhetoric* (Chicago, Ill.: Henry Regnery, 1953), pp. 211–232.

President Theodore Roosevelt speaking in New Hampshire, 1902.
The Bettmann Archive

"facts" but mere truth. Devil-terms in Weaver's time included "un-American" and "Communist," which represented forces outside and in opposition to the world of progress. These forces provided the conflict that any good drama needs.

While it is stable and persistent, such folk-drama must also constantly evolve into new plot lines that fit current conditions. In Weaver's time, people obviously regarded the idea of progress as larger than themselves. Perhaps many still do. The American respect for rugged individualism, which was first embodied in the symbol of the pioneer on the frontier, passed on to the image of the cowboy in the wild West, and survives in the new romanticism that has developed around the long-distance trucker. The themes of lonely freedom, of being on the move and not tied down, of being able to go and do just as one wishes and to develop and experience just as one pleases, persist in American popular mythology.

Other Authority Symbols

If "progress" has faded somewhat as a god-term for Americans, other symbols of authority still remain strong. "God" remains powerful for many people. People of democratic political orientation defer to "the majority": "It's the will of the majority," they say, when pressed to explain why they are going along with some action. Others feel obligated by "the law." To them, an ultimate reason for not acting would be that "It's against the law." Finally, many of us defer to particular individuals who represent authority figures for us. Dr. Smith, President Jones, and Dean Sullivan can all intimidate in specific situations by the very authority of their title. Who are the authority figures in your world, and what symbols express them?

FREEDOM "Freedom" is at the center of a cluster of terms that may also be understood in relation to progress. Progress implies movement, and such movement suggests our unfettered ability to advance in whatever direction the future may reveal to us. "Freedom" is the charismatic term that has been connected with our American political experience from its beginnings, and the word continues as a rallying point for social movements redressing ancient and lingering wrongs. Freedom implies the limitation of society's power over us. The attraction of the term suggests the intense appeal of the self-actualizing motive discussed in Chapter 7. Associated words include such negatively charged symbols as "slave," "master," "tyranny," and "totalitarian."

INDIVIDUALITY "Individuality" is another word that resonates with dramatic power. The term is also connected logically with freedom. Freedom implies the sovereignty of the self. We are taught to respect every person's right to his or her own opinion and to his or her own lifestyle. Usually we respect these rights unless they create a problem for us. Individuality is least respected in times of war and crisis, when rhetoric urging conformity and united action becomes intense. At such times we may be asked to surrender individuality for the sake of the whole. Individuality serves as a counterpoise to the deep attraction that group identity has for all of us.

COMMUNITY Functioning as a counterpoise to freedom and individuality is the term "community." The word may represent a yearning for a social system in which people enjoy a sense of togetherness rather than suffering from alienation. "Community" seems to have emerged just recently as a charismatic symbol, pointing perhaps to the strife and division within our society over the past several decades. (Note how Barbara Jordan uses the term in her speech reprinted in the Appendix.) Community expresses the power of our quest for identification with others. Too much freedom or too much individuality cuts us adrift from the nourishing bonds of group togetherness.

GENEROSITY Somewhat similar to the appeal of "community" is that of "generosity," lending others a helping hand. For Americans, this appeal is rooted in frontier experience, which demonstrated the value of people helping each other in times of need. You can still develop effective scripts for your audience by picturing them in warm, generous, helping roles.

AMERICAN Another potent symbol is the term "American," as used in such expressions as "That's the American way." Weaver explains that "American" and "progress" have been closely linked for some time in the consciousness of the Western world. Possibly the appeal of the term has eroded to some extent: one has heard expressions like "the ugly American" (greedy, ostentatious, insensitive) in recent years. But many still respond positively to the term and to associated symbols such as the flag and the national anthem.

SEX ROLES Finally, such national symbolism builds up ideal roles for us to play in our folk-dramas and develops clusters of terms to support such roles. A speech must invite the audience to play parts that are in harmony with these roles, so the speaker must be sensitive to what they require. (Until recently, though there is nothing uniquely masculine about the virtues they embody, the images these roles evoke have been unmistakably male.) The hero of the American tradition must be courageous, honest, and good—someone who honors the deed over the word. Nevertheless, he must be sensitive to the meanings of things and able to articulate them. We also like our hero to be modest and able to laugh at his own expense. We don't like prideful arrogance that places itself above the common people, whose instincts we respect. We admire self-reliance, so we like people to make it on their own and to make it well, even though they must never forget their humble origins. Though distrustful of the government as such, our heroes should respect and be committed to our basic political and social ideals. We also like our heroes to be respectful of sacred things. Finally, it's all right for our heroes to have some little humanizing fault that makes it easier for us to identify with them.

The Women's Movement may well have raised the national consciousness concerning the maleness of such idealized dramatic roles. The American woman of tradition, we observe, is loving, self-effacing, and happy serving her man and children. She is the hub of the family and is content only in that role. Most of the time we think of her as "mother," a security figure that we can always rely on, because we rarely think of her away from the home.

The task of the present movement is to create a new symbolic ideal for women that will not restrict their identity so rigidly. The rhetorical problem is severe. As Leakey has pointed out, a division in symbolic sexual roles is rooted in anthropological prehistory. In the hunter-gatherer bands that roamed the antiquity of our species, man evolved as hunter, woman as gatherer.[3] But we are not frozen by the cultural past, and the transforming power of the symbol is mighty enough to change our role expectations.

CHANGELESS SYMBOLS

One of the most fascinating things about our symbolic nature is that certain symbols seem charismatic—charged with special meaning—across time, space, and societies. People in general seem to be deeply moved by these symbols, which indicates that they are at the very bedrock of our nature. The dramas built into them tell timeless and ageless stories of the human quest for a better life. Incorporating these symbols into speeches lends a ritualistic or ceremonial quality to the utterance. We are taking part in folk theater that has existed for thousands of years and that will continue into the remote future, so long as human nature itself is not radically altered.

What are these symbols, and how do they appeal to us? This is a major question for the speaker, because universal symbols are an important resource for adaptation. As a group, they are suited to crucial subjects that involve the speaker intensely and call for the most powerful expression possible that is appropriate to the situation. *They should never be forced upon subjects and occasions to which they are not suited.*

3. Richard Leakey and Roger Lewin, *Origins: What New Discoveries Reveal About the Emergence of Our Species and Its Possible Future* (New York: Dutton, 1977), pp. 230–237.

The beauty of the sun's rising and setting has long captured the human imagination. And the drama of light escaping and returning is a very powerful symbol for speech uses. Since time beyond memory, we have been conditioned to negative associations with darkness. One is cold in the dark; one cannot see in the dark. Therefore, darkness makes one terribly vulnerable to animal and human predators. The dawn is cheery and life-giving; we learn in the light and things grow in the light. Light warms us and restores our vision and sense of control.

Accordingly, to picture a time of despair as "darkness" imposes a familiar rhetorical pattern on a situation. Normally this symbolic, dramatic frame is provided early in the speech to heighten the sense of audience need. But then comes the light: the speaker's proposal! This rosy and promising future will not be realized, however, unless the audience makes a strong commitment to the speaker's plan. It is up to the listeners to usher in the dawn of a new moral day. Such scenarios can be especially useful in speeches of *deliberation* in which future policy is being decided.

Perhaps the most remarkable instance of such dramatic symbolism in the rhetorical history of deliberative speeches occurred in the British House of Commons on April 2, 1792. On that day William Pitt delivered a speech against the slave trade that has become a classic example of eloquence. In those times it was not unusual for Parliament to sit through the night when matters of great importance were being considered. It happened that Pitt was concluding his speech just as dawn was actually breaking. Apparently inspired by the first light, Pitt urged that members vote down a policy that, he admonished, had prevented civilization from ever dawning in Africa and had kept that continent chained in darkness.[4] Implicit in such rhetoric are powerful symbolic roles for speaker and audience as "bringers of light." This god/sun connection can favorably affect credibility and speaker–audience identification.

If you feel the subject and occasion are right for such a powerful symbol, remember two important rules: (1) the language should be understated and (2) the symbolic use must not seem artificial or obvious. *If the symbol fits, use it—but don't strain to make it fit.*

Fire and *heat and cold* are other powerful symbols that are related to light and can also evoke the sense of dramatic participation in listeners. Such images as the torch of freedom, the smoldering anger of

4. "Speech of Mr. Pitt on the Abolition of the Slave Trade," *Select British Eloquence*, ed. Chauncey A. Goodrich (1852; reprint New York: Bobbs-Merrill, 1963), pp. 591–592.

the oppressed, and the flame of dedication, renewed and enlivened by the speaker, can place the message within a dramatic frame. Note how Lucretia Mott used a fire symbol to express the destructive effect of the ban against women in the clergy, as she addressed a women's rights convention in Philadelphia in 1854:

> There has been a great deal said about sending missionaries over to the East to convert women who are immolating themselves on the funeral pile of the husbands. . . . How many women are here now immolated upon the shrine of superstition and priestcraft, in our very midst, in the assumption that man only has a right to the pulpit. . . .[5]

The *cycle of the seasons* can likewise provide for picturesque expression of long-range views. Such images as the springtime of our hopes and the winter of our discontent tie the brief, momentary concerns of human-kind to the timeless, ageless processes of the natural world and touch our lives with a sense of lasting ritual. Consider, for example, Franklin D. Roosevelt's description of America during the depression years of the early 1930s:

> Values have shrunken to fantastic levels; taxes have risen; our ability to pay has fallen; government of all kinds is faced by serious curtailment of income; the means of exchange are frozen in the currents of trade; the withered leaves of industrial enterprise lie on every side; farmers find no markets for their produce; the savings of many years in thousands of families are gone.[6]

Storm–Calm

This symbolic pattern is best used to depict situations of great social distress. Whereas darkness best expresses a prolonged period of misery, the storm image represents societal turbulence that strikes suddenly in the form of calamitous events. After surveying the wreckage around them, speakers propose a way to restore calm and smooth sailing. This symbol is often combined with images of the sea, as we observed in Elizabeth Cady Stanton's dramatic image of the voyage of life in Chapter 7. More recently, Edward Kennedy described his own personal odyssey, the unsuccessful bid for the presidency, in these terms: "Often

5. "Not Christianity, But Priestcraft," *Feminism: The Essential Historical Writings*, ed. Miriam Schneir (New York: Random House, 1972), p. 101.
6. "First Inaugural Address," *American Speeches*, ed. Wyland Maxfield Parrish and Marie Hochmuth (New York: Longmans, Green, 1954), p. 502.

we sailed against the wind, but always we kept our rudder true."[7] Ronald Reagan used the image in a more critical spirit as he commented somewhat wryly on Jimmy Carter's administration: "You know, there may be a sailor at the helm of the ship of state, but the ship has no rudder."[8] The Reagan example is more in the dramatic tradition of rhetoric, which tends to use the symbol of a storm at sea not to express a personal voyage but to suggest the experience of an entire society. Typically, speakers visualize society as the ship in distress and offer themselves in the dramatic role of the captain who can steer it to a peaceful harbor. The image was applied satirically in political cartoons during the days of Watergate. It became somewhat fashionable for the ship of state to be shown broken or about to be broken on the reefs of that crisis and for the president to be drawn in various absurd poses at the wheel.

A drawback of the storm–sea–ship-of-state scenario is that it casts a romantic glow on the regimented society and on the unchecked authority that a captain enjoys over a crew of sailors in a ship at sea. And it may suggest to some that the ship of state is a vessel of war. Such natural phenomena as floods, hurricanes, and tornadoes are available as alternative symbols to dramatize the old theme of the storm-beset society. An excellent example occurred when Edmund Burke, the great statesman–orator of eighteenth-century Britain, used the storm image to express his view of the mission of the statesman–politician. That mission, Burke thought, was to build, strengthen, and repair the structures of government during times of calm so that they might withstand the storms that occasionally cloud the horizon of any nation.[9]

Storm symbolism can join with the drama of light and darkness to heighten the sense of individual responsibility. We stand at the center of a moral universe. Darkness surrounds us, and it is up to us to make the critical decisions that can light the place we occupy in space and time. In the face of the storm that threatens, our action or inaction determines whether we shall survive or be swept away.

Obviously the storm–calm pattern is picturesque and dramatic. It permits us to give abstract subjects sharp emotional edges and thus serves especially well the Law of Focus.

---

7. "Principles of Democratic Party: Common Hopes for the Future," delivered in New York City at the Democratic convention, August 12, 1980. Reprinted in *Vital Speeches of the Day*, 46 (September 15, 1980), p. 716.
8. "Acceptance Address of Presidential Nomination: Republican National Convention," delivered in Detroit, Michigan, July 17, 1980. Reprinted in *Vital Speeches of the Day*, 46 (August 15, 1980), p. 645.
9. "Speech of Mr. Burke at Bristol, Previous to the Election, Delivered September 6, 1780," *Select British Eloquence*, pp. 292-310. See also Michael Osborn, "Vertical Symbolism in the Speeches of Edmund Burke," *Studies in Burke and His Time*, 10 (1969), 1232-1238.

Disease–Cure

Throughout history public speeches have reflected the human preoccupation with dread disease. Indeed, through such speeches one can trace the evolution of medical science. When a cure is found, the disease tends to drop out of the popular imagination as a dramatic symbol for the crisis that cannot be anticipated and the destruction that cannot be averted. Once people worried constantly about the plague and symbolized their most acute political problems as a visitation of that ruthless illness. Now the predominant disease image is that of cancer; the image is especially popular in ultraconservative rhetoric.[10]

The rhetorical disease–cure pattern typically works in the following way: Having diagnosed the presence of grave illness and graphically charted its symptoms, speakers offer reassurance that the cure lies in their programs of action. Thus the drama can develop powerfully, suggesting roles for speaker and audience as physicians to society's ills. Ernestine Rose used the doctor–patient relationship to dramatize the interaction between women in general and activists in the Women's Movement. Speaking of the campaign in New York state that led finally to the passage of the married women's property bill, Rose observed that women themselves were often unaware of the disease with which they were afflicted. The first job of the physician is often to convince the victim of the existence of her illness:

> We had to adopt the method which physicians sometimes use, when they are called to a patient who is so hopelessly sick that he is unconscious of his pain and suffering. We had to describe to women their own position, to explain to them the burdens that rested so heavily upon them, and through these means, as a wholesome irritant, we roused public opinion on the subject, and through public opinion, we acted upon the Legislature. . . .[11]

When a speaker dwells on the idea that "ours is a *sick* society," as was so frequently done during the 1960s, he or she may be preparing us to endorse, not the reform that cures, but the major surgery of revolution. Thus an even more dramatic scenario can develop out of the pattern. *Caution:* The image of the sick society has probably been overdone recently. If you use it, be specific about the nature of the illness as you see it—violence, greed, apathy, loss of initiative, whatever—but make it clear what the symptoms are and how they threaten us. Be just as precise concerning how your plan of action will heal the alleged illness.

10. See Edwin Black's "The Second Persona," *Quarterly Journal of Speech*, 56 (1970), 109–119.
11. "Petitions Were Circulated," *Feminism*, p. 126.

Anyone who inspected the symbolic appeal of speeches throughout recorded history would have to conclude that human beings are fighting animals. We say that we yearn for peace and that we abhor war, yet our imaginations remain darkly fascinated with the military. The war-peace symbol is especially well suited for aggressive speeches proposing action, for which it supplies a rich vocabulary and all sorts of analogies. Speakers can present their proposals as declarations of war on some dread enemy, can claim peace as their justification, and can urge victory marches or warn against retreats. Speakers can become the generals who will lead us, as we enlist as soldiers in their armies. They can urge compliance and hush criticism, because a time of war demands unquestioned obedience within an army. We find an example of such a scenario in Franklin D. Roosevelt's First Inaugural Address:

> If I read the temper of our people correctly, we now realize as we have never realized before our interdependence on each other; that we cannot merely take but we must give as well; that if we are to go forward, we must move as a trained and loyal army willing to sacrifice for the good of a common discipline, because without such discipline no progress is made, no leadership becomes effective. We are, I know, ready and willing to submit our lives and property to such discipline, because it makes possible a leadership which aims at a larger good. This I propose to offer, pledging that the larger purposes will bind upon us all as a sacred obligation with a unity of duty hitherto evoked only in time of armed strife.
>
> With this pledge taken, I assume unhesitatingly the leadership of this great army of our people dedicated to a disciplined attack upon our common problems.[12]

At the end of every symbolic battle looms bright victory, which justifies all our hard times and our surrender of individuality.

Symbolic Space: Above-Below

We live in a world of space, and the fact that each primary direction has deep symbolic value is impressed on us from our earliest years. We grow upward and we try to avoid falling down. Those who command stand above us, and even the sun warms us from above. Perhaps, then, it is not surprising that the sense of symbolic space often supplies

12. "First Inaugural Address," *American Speeches*, p. 505. For an example of a failed effort to invoke the military image, see Hermann G. Stelzner, "Ford's War on Inflation: A Metaphor That Did Not Cross," *Communication Monographs*, 44 (1977), 284-297.

Martin Luther King, Jr.
Ted Rozumalski/Black Star

dramatic vertical frames. One of the two main issues in the Great Debates between Kennedy and Nixon during the 1960 presidential campaign was: "Is the prestige of America *falling*?"

The vertical symbol can be as flexible as it is rich. The speaker can show the characters in his or her speech scenario as having fallen into a pit, as having hit bottom, as being lost in a valley, as slowly trudging up a hill, as scaling a mountain, or as having arrived at the summit. Each image registers some graphic, rather precise judgment about where they are with respect to where they might be. The overall picture can become a powerful commentary on their lives: If the summit finds them standing at the top of a molehill, perhaps they have lived without meaning.

The kind of society reflected (and perhaps encouraged) by the vertical symbol is strongly authoritarian. The notion of people positioned above and below each other in a social or governmental hierarchy lends credence to the division of humankind into superiors and inferiors. A modern form of the image and its authoritarian vision occurs in those business organizational charts that establish an unmistakable vertical pattern of power and deference, which we sometimes hear euphemistically described as establishing "clear lines of authority."

A more humanistic form of this ancient image is the mountain symbol, especially as it serves those inspired speakers who wish to stand above their listeners to reveal some grand, panoramic vision. Dr. Martin Luther King, Jr. used this symbol when he spoke in Memphis the night before he was assassinated.

Well I don't know what will happen now. We've got some difficult days ahead. But it really doesn't matter now, because I've been to the mountaintop. And I don't mind, like anybody I would like to live a long life, longevity has its place, but I'm not concerned about that now. I just want to do God's will. And he's allowed me to go up to the mountain, and I've looked over, and I've seen the Promised Land. I may not get there with you, but I want you to know tonight that we as a people will get to the Promised Land. And so I'm happy tonight, I'm not worried about anything, I'm not fearin' any man, mine eyes have seen the glory of the coming of the Lord.[13]

Thus the above–below image can set the dramatic scene for spiritual triumph as well as express power relationships.

Symbolic Space: Forward–Back

The other two primary directions to which we become sensitized early in life also carry a rich load of symbolic and dramatic meanings. We learn that it is honorable and right to go *forward* in life. The horizons beckon to us, promising change and fascinating new discoveries. Similarly, it is dishonorable and life-denying to go backwards. Just as "God" stands at the apex of the vertical dimension, "progress" is often the distant beacon that marks the path before us. The second great issue in the Kennedy–Nixon debates was *"How can we get America moving again?"*

As though this powerful dramatic symbol needed any reinforcement, it is often fused with military images, just as the vertical symbol often blends with darkness and light. Thus we may find ourselves marching in columns toward that distant horizon, just as we climb toward the light and try to avoid sinking into darkness. The vertical and horizontal orientations can represent profoundly different styles of thinking. Clearly, if we think of our lives as controlled mainly by forces above us and beyond us—if our world has a *vertical* power orientation—we may not be inclined to pursue our own ambitions. The greater beings that protect and care for us must be respected, feared, deferred to. Authoritarian leaders reinforce this impression of their own elevation, placing themselves far above the people where they can intimidate all who would oppose them. In his Inaugural Address, President Reagan

13. From a transcription of the speech delivered in Memphis, Tennessee, on April 4, 1968.

voiced the resentment and fear people can have when they feel that government is raised above them: "Now, so there will be no misunderstanding, it's not my intention to do away with government. It is rather to make it work—work with us, not over us; to stand by our side, not ride on our back."[14]

If, on the other hand, everything enviable lies before us rather than above us, if we think we can advance toward objects of our desire or escape from threatening forces around us, ours is a more *horizontal* orientation. Whereas the vertical orientation often slights the importance of human actions and the symbolic magnitude of human beings themselves, the horizontal orientation enlarges our sense of ourselves and the importance of our actions. Combined with the aggressive war-peace figure, this horizontal way of seeing things can produce dramatic patterns that invite listeners into action. People can declare war on poverty and disease or, as we saw in the Roosevelt example, on economic depression. They can even do battle with the Devil, as they become—in whatever religion they fancy—the Army of God. Leaders become pictured as those who go before to blaze a trail, visionaries who constantly push back the frontiers of advancing civilization. Following them, people have often launched destructive crusades against other people and other ideas and have even died willingly in the struggle. Such is our hunger for significant action within a significant frame of meaning.

It is impossible to escape the impression that the horizontal perspective is more humanistic and free. Ushered in with the Renaissance, this modern way of emphasizing *this world* in the here and now, rather than some remote world promised or threatened for a later life, has encouraged exploration, research, and discovery. It has enormously increased the human power to create as well as destroy.

While they are profoundly different in these many social, cultural, and therefore rhetorical respects, the two great spatial patterns can be artfully combined. During the darkest days of World War II, Winston Churchill constantly held before the British people the vision of a future that extended both upward and forward. "Their Finest Hour" produced a memorable example of this combination, as he stated: "If we stand up to him (Hitler), all Europe may be free and the life of the world may move forward into broad, sunlit uplands."[15]

If your speech calls for intense value commitments by listeners, by all means consider whether the spatial symbolic patterns might express your message in a natural and forceful way.

14. Reprinted in *Vital Speeches of the Day*, 47 (February 15, 1981), p. 259.

Sin-Redemption

Obviously sin and redemption symbols depend on an intense audience conviction of its own guilt. "You have sinned!" shouts the speaker in one form or another, "and you must redeem yourself. Enact my proposal, and redemption will be yours!"

Hitler used this dramatic pattern in much of his rhetorical approach to the German people. He convinced them—or many of them—that most of their economic and political woes after World War I were the result of betrayal and sin: betrayal by false leadership and, even more profoundly, the sins of the people themselves against their own cultural roots and Aryan traditions. The Serpent in the Garden was the International Jew. Played back in speech after speech, this melodrama first convicted the German people in their own eyes, making them feel shame and humiliation and instilling in them a hunger for atonement and rites of purification. Then this folk-drama offered the demonic myth of Adolph Hitler, Man/God who had come to lead the people through the new, redeeming religion of National Socialism. Finally, Hitler offered them the magnificent redemptive vision of a Reich that would endure a thousand years.

The fact that Hitler used this pattern so effectively should not make us judge the pattern itself too harshly. If you are convinced that your listeners are indeed guilty of some sin of omission or commission, you may find it necessary to use such symbolism. A word of caution: it helps if you can pronounce yourself equally guilty. This minimizes any resentment your audience may feel, and promotes identification as you offer listeners a chance to redeem themselves through action.

Animals

Animal imagery is often used to characterize the players in the rhetorical dramas enacted within speeches. To say that someone has the courage of a lion, the fierceness of a bear at bay, or the power and grace of a panther is to relate the person favorably to the animal kingdom.

Most animal imagery, however, seems to express more negative comparisons. The "coon" epithet of American racism is sadly typical. Malcolm X's transformation of the American "Uncle Sam" image into a "bloody-jawed wolf" was responsive in kind. Similarly, Sojourner Truth characterized the hecklers among an unruly mob she was addressing as "geese" and "snakes."

15. *Blood, Sweat, and Tears,* ed. Randolph S. Churchill (New York, 1941), p. 314.

I see that some of you have got the spirit of a goose, and some have got the spirit of a snake. . . . When she comes to demand 'em, don't you hear how sons hiss their mothers like snakes, because they ask for their rights; and can they ask for anything less? . . . You may hiss as much as you like, but it is comin'.[16]

Elizabeth Cady Stanton used a combination of animal and seasonal symbolism to create a diminished picture of those women who opposed the Movement:

Who are they that we do not now represent? But a small class of the fashionable butterflies, who, through the short summer days, seek the sunshine and the flowers; but the cool breezes of autumn and the hoary frosts of winter will soon chase all these away; then they, too, will need and seek protection, and through other lips demand in their turn justice and equity at your hands.[17]

Such images express arrogance, sometimes anger, and even hatred. In wartime they may be useful to dehumanize the enemy, to prepare soldiers for combat. If we see the Russians, Japanese, or Vietnamese as evil *creatures* rather than as human beings, perhaps we can overcome any such scruples as "thou shalt not kill." When we are ourselves depicted as "running dogs of imperialism," the rhetoric is again a preparatory rite of the kill, a war dance in words.

The temptation to dehumanize fellow beings through animal symbols can be quite powerful. But unless such symbolism is clearly deserved, thoughtful members of the audience will question the practice, and the character of the speaker—that important component of credibility—will itself be diminished.

Family

The family symbol can suggest another kind of relationship among the players in the folk-dramas of public speeches. The image can reinforce loving identification among large groups of people, especially when used in variations on the "Human Family" theme. A favorite expression of idealistic rhetoric, the family image invokes the goal of working together as brothers and sisters to make the world more habitable for us all. On such a symbolic foundation Dr. Martin Luther King, Jr. would have rebuilt the entire system of human relations in the South: "I have a dream that . . . one day right there in Alabama little black

16. "What Time of Night It Is," *Feminism*, pp. 96–97.
17. "Address to the New York State Legislature, 1854," *Feminism*, p. 116.

boys and black girls will be able to join hands with little white boys and girls as sisters and brothers."[18]

As lovely as family imagery is, the metaphor can also be used to generate and sugarcoat scenarios that are exploitive. Thus the pre-Revolutionary War image of Great Britain as the "mother country," in which the colonists were pictured as her "children," did nothing more than place a sweet and amiable mask on imperialism. One of the famed British orators of the day, Lord Chatham, had this to say about the Boston tea party:

> Proceed like a kind and affectionate parent over a child whom he tenderly loves, and, instead of those harsh and severe proceedings, pass an amnesty on all their youthful errors, clasp them once more in your fond and affectionate arms, and I will venture to affirm you will find them children worthy of their sire. But, should their turbulence exist after your proffered terms of forgiveness, which I hope and expect this House will immediately adopt, I will be among the foremost of your Lordships to move for such measures as will effectually prevent a future relapse, and make them feel what it is to provoke a fond and forgiving parent![19]

One of the truly revolutionary actions undertaken by Americans was to break the hold this image had on their own consciousness. Thomas Paine's *Common Sense*, one of the great pieces of revolutionary rhetoric, showed the colonists how to cut the cultural umbilicus. The family for Americans, Paine argued, was the international brotherhood of the oppressed!

Parent–child imagery can be authoritarian, whereas brother–sister imagery is often more egalitarian. Be aware of such rhetorical dynamics if you use family symbols in public speaking.

Structures

The structural image can express dramatically the human power to create and destroy. A sound and well-proportioned building reassures us that we can erect lasting structures to protect ourselves from disorder and mindless change. Politically, therefore, the symbol serves to dramatize the spirit of conservatism. But the symbol can also rally

---

18. "I Have a Dream," *Great American Speeches, 1898–1963*, ed. John Graham (New York: Appleton-Century-Crofts, 1970), p. 120.
19. "Speech of Lord Chatham on the Bill Authorizing the Quartering of British Soldiers on the Inhabitants of Boston, Delivered in the House of Lords, May 27, 1774," *Select British Eloquence*, p. 127.

us for the long-range, cooperative efforts required to make some noble institution or value a reality. For example, the purpose to which President Nixon dedicated his presidency was "to build a generation of peace." Structural images appeal to security motives. Such symbolism invites speaker and audience into cooperative, constructive roles as builders of the future.

A MODEL

All of us daydream, and many of us experience a rather rich fantasy life. Until recently this domain of human behavior seemed the exclusive concern of psychology. But the most effective speakers have always had a sense of submerged worlds of experience in their auditors. Such speakers are able to engage this fantasy life and to create *rhetorical folk-dramas* in support of their causes. These dramas become part of the tradition of a people, vital to their cultural life.

When a speech is adapted to the particular needs and circumstances of an audience, to the psychological forces that drive and shape behavior, and to the dramatic inclinations of our symbolic nature, the impact of that speech is limited only by the scope of its subject matter and by the artistry of the speaker.

The discussion in this chapter can be reduced to a second adaptation model that, when combined with the model on page 158, can provide a complete, systematic approach to the adaptation of any speech. That model appears below.

SPEECH PREPARATION PLAN

Adaptation Model

1. What local concerns and interests engage my listeners in dramatic ways?
   a. In sports?
   b. In politics?
   c. In religion or social issues?
2. What words express this sense of dramatic engagement?
3. To what extent are my listeners influenced by the regional and national cultures to which they belong?
   a. Are there dramas, rituals, and fantasies at these levels that give meaning to their lives?
   b. Is there a charismatic language that expresses this regional and national folk-drama?

c. Could the symbolism of progress be incorporated in my speech?
4. Do any of the changeless symbols of human nature fit my subject, my listeners, myself, and the speech occasion?
   a. Darkness–light?
   b. Fire and the seasons?
   c. Storm–calm?
   d. Disease–cure?
   e. War–peace?
   f. Above–below?
   g. Forward–back?
   h. Sin–redemption?
   i. Animals?
   j. Family?
   k. Structures?
5. Some cautions and goals to remember:
   a. Never force symbolism on a subject.
   b. Symbolic language should be simple and understated.
   c. Symbolic language should never call attention to itself.
   d. Symbolic language is appropriate to expressions of strong feeling that offer value judgments.
   e. Symbolic language should provide dramatic roles favorable to both speaker and listeners.
   f. Symbolic language can provide a sense of overall meaning, purpose, and context for the specific actions proposed in the speech.

Summary of Major Ideas

Speakers must create a sense of drama in their speeches and provide favorable roles for listeners.

Charismatic language draws strength from the folk-dramas that give meaning and direction to people's lives.

Symbolism can have local, regional, or national importance.

The term "progress" functions as a dramatic symbol for many Americans.

Certain symbols endure through time and space and among different peoples. Changeless symbols serve to express intense feeling and give a ritualistic quality to utterance that has strong identification values.

Certain symbols are grounded in nature, such as the drama of light emerging from darkness, or storms on land and sea, and of fire and seasonal change.

Two distinctive symbolic patterns result from our sense of space— heights to scale, depths to avoid, and horizons to explore.

Other basic symbols evolve out of intense human experiences such as the dread of disease, the horror of war, the sense of one's own guilt, family love, and the pride and security of building a sound structure.

Exercises and Discussion Questions

1. Nominate ten words that have special charisma in your community, and bring them to class for discussion. Don't overlook words charged with negative symbolic meaning. A helpful class goal might be to build a lexicon of such words for use in speeches.

2. Analyze a recent political campaign as a clash of competing theaters. Can you account for the outcome of the campaign on this basis?

3. Some twenty-five years after the publication of Richard Weaver's essay on god-terms and devil-terms, a group of students nominated the following as new American charismatic terms:

    a. Positive: natural, communication, liberation, ecology, energy, woman.

    b. Negative: recession, inflation, crisis, politician, pollution, male.
What changes would you make in this list, and why?

4. How would you describe the emerging folk heroes of America? Are there points of conflict among them? Do sex and race still enter into this role formation?

For Further Reading

For additional information on rhetorical symbolism, see the following articles.

Ernest G. Bormann, "Fantasy and Rhetorical Vision: The Rhetorical Criticism of Social Reality," *Quarterly Journal of Speech*, 58 (1972), 396–407.

Michael Osborn and Douglas Ehninger, "The Metaphor in Public Address," *Speech Monographs*, 29 (1962), 223–234.

Michael Osborn, "Archetypal Metaphor in Rhetoric: The Light–Dark Family," *Quarterly Journal of Speech*, 53 (1967), 115–126.

_____ , "The Evolution of the Archetypal Sea in Rhetoric and Poetic," *Quarterly Journal of Speech*, 63 (1977), 347–363.

For a full analysis of Hitler's use of sin–redemption symbolism, see Kenneth Burke's "The Rhetoric of Hitler's 'Battle'," *The Philosophy of Literary Form: Studies in Symbolic Action* (Berkeley, Calif.: University of California Press, 1973), pp. 191–220. Fred L. Casmir, a professional speech teacher who was also a member of the Hitler Youth Movement, writes with unusual authority and sensitivity about Hitler's appeal to his audience. Among his articles, see " The Hitler I Heard," *Quarterly Journal of Speech*, 49 (1963), 8–16; "Hitler and

His Audience," *Central States Speech Journal*, 15 (1964), 133-136; and "Nazi Rhetoric: A Rhetoric of Fear," *Today's Speech*, 16 (1968), 15-18.

Philip Wheelwright develops a generic concept of changeless symbolism in *The Burning Fountain: A Study in the Language of Symbolism* (Bloomington, Ind.: University of Indiana Press, 1954). The Bormann work on fantasy and cultural vision is itself based on Robert Bales, *Personality and Interpersonal Behavior* (New York: Holt, 1970). Kenneth Burke develops the concept of charismatic language further in his difficult but rewarding *A Rhetoric of Motives* (Englewood Cliffs, N.J.: Prentice-Hall, 1950).

III

THE INFORMATIVE SPEECH

Chapter 1 of this book introduced four basic uses of speech: to inform, to exchange values, to urge actions, and to establish overall patterns of behavior. It also introduced five basic arts of rhetoric, which make these uses effective. Controlling perceptions through artful depictions, arousing listeners, building group identity, urging action, and sustaining group identity for the sake of long-term survival—these are the basic arts of rhetoric. Together they form an overall behavior pattern called the rhetorical process.

Two major forms of speaking in public have emerged to exercise these arts, informative speaking and persuasive speaking. Informative speaking is limited to depiction, showing us how things are or how to perform some useful action. It is content to share its "window on the world" with others for the sake of their greater awareness. Persuasive speaking is more complex in that its emphasis may shift among depiction, arousal, group identification, implementation, and renewal.

The next three chapters concentrate on informative speaking, for many of the techniques of communicating information are also basic to persuasion. The speaker's wish to inform his or her listeners affects the entire strategy of the speech, including the use of materials discovered during the research and adaptation phases of speech preparation. The informative impulse can even affect the actual language and delivery of the speech.

THE DESIGN AND DEVELOPMENT OF INFORMATIVE SPEECHES

Seek to delight, that they may mend mankind,
And, while they captivate, inform the mind.

WILLIAM COWPER, "Hope"

┌─────────────────────────────────┐
│   **WHAT TO LOOK FOR IN**   │
│   **THIS CHAPTER**   │
│   │
│   The nature of informative speaking │
│   Designs for informative speeches │
│   Development of the informative speech │
│   The use of verbal and visual aids │
└─────────────────────────────────┘

The impulse to inform others is basic to our nature and essential to our lives as communicating beings. Informative speaking has six primary characteristics.

1. *An informative speech often reveals our options when a choice must be made.* Such speech does not advocate any one choice, nor does it evaluate choices. It simply brings our options into the open.

2. *An informative speech helps to reduce critical areas of ignorance.* The "informative value" of a speech is measured by how much it tells us that we should or must know but did not know before. If a speech simply repeats commonplace knowledge, it is inaccurate to call it informative.

3. *The informative speech rewards the speaker as well as the listener.* Of course we would expect some gain for the speaker; otherwise there would be little motivation to inform. Sometimes informative speech paves the way for later persuasive speaking. But, on another level, there may be an unspoken agreement to exchange information for the sake of mutual betterment. Speakers may offer information with the tacit understanding that audience members will some day return the favor. Or they may give information because they value their subject and feel they can enhance it by sharing their thoughts about it. Or again, they may clarify and enrich their own ideas by communicating them.

Such sharing relates informative speaking to one of the oldest and most vital forms of human behavior. Famed anthropologist Richard Leakey believes that cooperative sharing—of knowledge as well as food—was the definitive characteristic of emerging humankind.

4. *An informative speech gives; it does not ask or take.* Such a speech requires no commitment from the audience to a particular value or course of action. Informative speaking stresses the "is," not the "ought

to be." Therefore, the rhetorical demands of an informative speech are low in tension. Because the speech does not ask for action, there is no psychological inertia to overcome and, because there is no such inertia to overcome, it is not necessary to engage strong feelings.

5. *Informative speaking emphasizes clarity and interest in both language and delivery.* The informative word and gesture are characteristically low-key: if the thought is instantly lucid in the moment of utterance, and if listener interest remains intense throughout, the informative speaker is satisfied.

6. *Informative speaking begins with the speaker's image of a situation, extends to the depiction he or she provides of the situation, and ends with the impact such depiction has on the perceptions of listeners.* This vital linkage is the most fundamental relationship in the communication process.

This chapter and the next treat the special tasks of preparing an informative speech. We assume that the speaker has selected a topic, analyzed its implications, researched it as thoroughly as possible, and considered its adaptation to the intended audience. The next steps are to select an overall principle of design for the speech, develop its content, consider its wording, complete a formal outline, and practice the delivery. Remember that the overall goal is to develop a depiction that is useful, substantial, well structured, credible, and appealing.

ELEMENTS OF THE INFORMATIVE SPEECH

Any depiction must have a clearly defined center, a focal point that expresses its theme. In building an informative speech, you should begin with a clear sense of this central focus: what you want to accomplish and what you will say in order to accomplish it. Only with this basic foundation established can you set out to design the structure of a speech. Purpose and theme suggest what you should include and exclude, and *how* and *how much* to develop critical sections of the speech.

Obviously, the first priority is to define your *purpose* in delivering the speech. In an informative speech you want to share knowledge, but what knowledge, and why, and to what effect? Can this purpose be accomplished in the time available for the speech? To test the clarity of your purpose, see whether you can express it in a simple declarative sentence, such as "I wish to introduce my listeners to the typical structure of a political campaign."

Now consider the message you will frame to realize this purpose: What will be its *theme*? The purpose is an intention within you, whereas the theme must be a center of meaning either stated or implicit in the speech. Again, test the clarity of your theme by stating it in a simple declarative sentence: "Any serious political campaign must control the forces that can elect the candidate." Purpose and theme evolve out of the subject statement produced during topic selection (see Chapter 5). They are that statement as it has emerged through research, analysis, and adaptation. Both *may* appear together in a speech, of course, but when audiences are hostile or subjects controversial, a direct statement of purpose would so alienate listeners that they would never have a chance to evaluate the speaker's message on its own merits.

Another test of the theme is that it should develop easily into a set of primary statements. Each such statement could in turn develop into a vital section of the speech. From the theme in our example, one might derive the following set of primary statements:

The candidate has to be informed: hence the issues and research committee.
The people must be introduced to the informed candidate: hence the publicity and public relations committee.
This favorable impression must be translated into votes on election day: hence the ward and precinct committee.
Timing and organization are the keys to the overall process: hence the campaign manager.
The campaign must be supplied and equipped: hence the headquarters manager.
All of this requires money: hence the finance committee.

As you record and evaluate your purpose, theme, and primary statements, your speech evolves toward its basic design.

DESIGNS FOR INFORMATIVE SPEAKING

To be coherent and clear and to move in a purposeful direction, any depiction must have a basic design, a principle of organization. These principles are rooted in the laws of communication behavior discussed in Chapter 7. There are at least nine such designs from which the speaker can choose at this stage of preparation.

1. The placement of a subject in *time*

2. The placement of a subject in *space*
3. How a subject divides by its nature, resulting in *categories*
4. How a subject is related to our major concerns, thus providing *motivational topics*
5. How a subject is generated, involving *causation* and *consequence*
6. The elaboration and amplification of a subject through *repetition*
7. How a subject is similar to something else in our experience, suggesting *contiguity* and *analogy*
8. How a subject differs from something else in our experience, resulting in *contrast*
9. How the subject answers to some vital *question*

Just as these designs generate structure for informative speeches, they are also useful in persuasive speaking, where they may be absorbed within other forms. And they may be combined in various artful arrangements. For example, one might develop a time/space/contrast view of events leading to the Civil War. "In 1840," you might say, "Northern manufacturers had a boom year, while Southern planters endured hard times and low profits. In 1850 . . . ."

Time

The time or chronological design describes a process or sequence of events, projecting into either the past or the future. There are three major variations in the use of time as a principle of organization.

HISTORICAL   Rhetorical history scans time past and selects just those events that illustrate or prove the point under consideration. Such a view telescopes time into sequences of vital moments that, according to the speaker, account for some truth apparent in the present. Karl Marx, for example, saw history as illustrating the force of economic laws; Thomas Carlyle saw that same history as the stage on which great people worked out their personal destinies. Marx's speeches were patterned on the large flow of economic actions and reactions over the centuries. Carlyle, on the other hand, sought to show how an underlying pattern of significant actions performed by significant persons shaped the consciousness of human societies.

HYPOTHETICAL   The hypothetical time order carries the audience on an imaginary journey through a process from beginning to end. The speech enables listeners to see themselves enacting some role or having some experience the speaker is interested in sharing. "Picture yourself living through the entire process of human evolution within a single, imaginary day. You would awaken to a very dangerous dawn on the African plain. . . ." Because much of our learning comes from vision, this form lends itself to clear informative communication. It can also be useful for persuasion, because visualizing ourselves performing some action makes the action seem easier to accomplish and may make us more likely to undertake it. Moreover, when the action is depicted as enjoyable, the speech becomes an even stronger invitation for us to effect in real life what the speaker has shown in imagination.

PREDICTIVE Predictive time order is futuristic. On the basis of past experience and the present pattern of events, the predictive form projects an imagined future. "What is the future of space travel? By the year 1990, etc. By 2000, etc. By 2010, etc., etc." Speeches based on this design are informative when their only aim is to alert us to probable future developments. They become persuasive when they warn us of some future calamity that we can escape by changing the present course of events. The predictive form can also be useful persuasively when, combined with the hypothetical time pattern, it conveys to the audience some future vision of themselves enacting and enjoying programs the speaker is trying to sell.

Space

Objects and events may seem to belong together in space as well as time. The recurring spatial order may suggest as well an order for speeches. A speech on the solar system, for example, might proceed from the sun outward to the farthest planet.

Speakers may also use spatial perspective, which is the artful arrangement we can give to space. Just as a television camera can zoom in gradually on a subject, so can a speaker consider the same event from international, national, state, and local points of view. Or the speaker could reverse the spatial order, gradually building a larger perspective. Such arrangement can also be based on contrast, such as describing a certain battle through the eyes of a general on the hill and then from the point of view of a foot soldier in the trenches. Finally, such perspective can provide a convenient way of dividing a subject for discussion: "On the one hand . . . on the other hand . . ." or "From the left wing we hear . . . while the right wing maintains. . . ."

Categories

Often subjects have natural divisions that suggest simple, cohesive speech designs. The library, for example, has such divisions (see Chapter 6).

Nevertheless, the categories we think we see in the topic itself may actually express our own habitual ways of seeing things. Sometimes such habits, entrenched in us from an early age, can have real impact on our values. Speakers should consider carefully whether they wish to reinforce such values. An example is the time-honored but dubious habit of dividing women in terms of whether they are married ("Mrs.") or unmarried ("Miss"), a category scheme that seems to be fading in our time.

The controversy that sometimes results when such habits are criticized is negative evidence of the value people place on their favorite categories. Categories represent a way of thinking, a way of relating. Take them away and the world becomes a less familiar, less comfortable place. It follows that when their categories are challenged or attacked, people often react with hostility.

Another interesting aspect of categorical vision is its tendency to cluster in certain numbers, especially the number three. Time and again, speakers discuss "three main issues" as they develop their subjects. Perhaps we are attracted to this number because it suggests an underlying circle or triangle. (Circles and triangles can themselves be satisfying; they exhibit symmetry, balance, and closure.) Or perhaps the number three is best adjusted to the comprehension span of the average person on most novel subjects. Whatever the reasons, trinities seem to arise in an amazing variety of subjects. If you find yourself favoring a design that calls for three categories, be sure that your decision is based on careful inspection of subject matter and sound rhetorical considerations, not just an impulse deriving from habit.

Unless natural divisions of a subject come readily to mind as you consider using the categorical form, some other basic design might be more appropriate. And remember that a subject that splinters into numerous categories is far too complex for most classroom speeches.

Motivation

Within any topic, what directs our attention to certain specific concerns? Chapter 7 revealed that one answer to this question involves the universal human motives. We may focus because of physiological needs, safety considerations, the need for group acceptance and affection, the need to secure esteem, or the impulse toward self-actualization. A speaker can develop a subject informatively by showing, in a point-by-point way, its relevance to all or any of these factors. For example, a speech introducing the class to the recreational possibilities of a nearby river might discuss

1. The importance of self-discovery through appreciation of natural beauty
2. How one can grow in self-esteem (as well as in the eyes of others) by acquiring boating skills and personal resourcefulness on the water
3. The social life possible in parties along the beaches and shores
4. The dangers one must avoid and the respect one must have for safety conditions on the water
5. The value of the river as a release from the strains and tensions of campus life

Such a speech would touch all the major chords in the Maslow hierarchy of motives, moving from the most sophisticated to the most primitive of needs.

When motivational topics are used to alert us to relevant features of a subject, their use is primarily informative; when the pattern pushes us toward specific action, their use becomes predominantly persuasive.

Causation

An informative speech developed on the principle of causation stimulates and then satisfies audience curiosity. It asks "Why?" and provides an answer. The pattern works because we like to track down and understand the phenomena that affect us. The speech that accounts for some event by isolating its causes can illuminate our world of experience. Why do cancer cells develop? Why does cigarette smoking damage the body? Why does sensible exercise prolong life? The informative speech designed on this pattern always begins with a question pinpointing a matter vital to audience interests that the speaker intends to answer in the speech. If it is asked skillfully, such a question can arouse intense curiosity, which sustains interest throughout the speech. However, caution is in order. One of the most common rhetorical blunders is the oversimplified speech of causation, which collapses as soon as an audience member points out a factor that the speaker had overlooked.

A speech built on the causation principle bases its appeal on the Law of Process discussed in Chapter 7. In persuasive speaking causation helps speakers point up the solutions to problems: Once we know how problems are caused, we can determine how to solve and/or prevent them.

Repetition

Kenneth Burke has described repetition as "the consistent maintaining of a principle under new guises." And, illustrating the principle in his own explanation for it, he goes on to describe repetition as "restatement of the same thing in different ways."[1]

The more frequent and varied the presentation of a theme, the more of an impression it makes. This is why advertisers launch expensive campaigns based on sheer repetition of a message. But repetition can occur artfully within a single message, as when the speaker announces his or her theme, provides a definition, and then proceeds to tell a series of stories, each of which illustrates the theme in a different way, repeating old meanings and developing new ones at the same time. In this sense repetition becomes the art of amplification, in which speakers dwell on their meanings by giving a series of examples and illustrations. Very often, repetition invokes the principle of analogy to clarify an otherwise obscure idea. For example, I might explain the persuasive speaker's relationship to an audience first in terms of seller to buyer, then in terms of lover courting the beloved, and yet again in terms of priest and congregation in communion. I would be offering repeated views of the same relationship from the different perspectives offered by the three analogies, arranged in a kind of spiritual progression to accentuate the potential meaningfulness of such an interaction.

This arrangement satisfies our need for both familiarity and novelty in learning. It reverberates the theme again and again as the speech develops. Such a message is likely to stamp itself on our minds. Clearly, the repetitive form can be useful for both informative and persuasive purposes.

Analogy

The foregoing example serves to introduce the depictive powers of analogy, which stands on its own as a basic design for informative speaking. In drawing an analogy, the speaker relates the known to the unknown to make the unknown comprehensible.

In informative speaking, analogy does its most important work when the matter to be communicated is far removed from the actual experience of listeners. They can grasp it only if the speaker can find something in their experience that parallels the subject and to which it can be related. In a point-by-point comparison, the speaker can then draw the new information gradually into the orbit of their understanding. The analogy principle is especially useful for scientific subjects that are remote from popular understanding. For example, the speaker could describe the society of ants by comparing it to our own. Or, drawing on symbolic forms, the speaker could relate the

1. *Counter-Statement* (Berkeley, Calif.: University of California Press, 1968), p. 125.

body's constant battle against infection to a military campaign. Or again, the speaker might describe his or her inner conflict over some problem as a kind of internal warfare, consuming and devastating the mind with its intensity. Consider these three examples. They illustrate that analogy can serve as a telescope to bring the strange and unfamiliar subject closer to us, as a microscope to put the unseen before our eyes, or as a transforming principle to give the abstract subject a concrete form. Analogy can provide enormously useful informative design.

Contrast

Chapter 7 described contrast as a powerful aid to understanding. It is one of the great laws of human understanding that things opposite each other define each other. Informative speeches built on the principle of contrast use a kind of foreground-background approach to create sharply defined depictions. To make you appreciate the virtues of peace, the speaker may depict them against a background of war. To explain the meaning of health, he or she may juxtapose it with images of illness and disease. Opposites may not necessarily attract, but they certainly clarify each other. This principle provides an important design option for the speaker who would inform.

Question-Answer

Designs based on causation suggest the effectiveness of a question-answer procedure. "Why?" can indeed be a vital question for the start of an informative speech. This technique becomes a principle of organization in its own right when a series of questions is used as the backbone of a speech, providing its major structure. "Why does sensible exercise prolong our lives?" could develop into a pattern of questions that actually express key dimensions of the speech. Answering the questions "Who should exercise?," "How should we exercise?," and "Where can we exercise?" could constitute the major divisions of an informative speech. In such a design, the initial question is followed by an answer that suggests another key question, the answer to which yields still another question, which in turn is finally resolved in the conclusion of the speech. This kind of format can give the audience a satisfying sense of closure. It can be used so that questions gradually build in importance, raising audience interest and spotlighting attention on the final portion of the speech. In persuasive speaking this procedure can emphasize the final, action-oriented steps in a pattern of persuasion.

DEVELOPING THE INFORMATIVE SPEECH

Once you have chosen the basic design of your speech, you proceed to develop its content through the three major phases of the speech: introduction, body, and conclusion.

The Introduction

The beginning of your speech must capture attention, establish credibility, clarify your purpose, and motivate the audience to listen. The first words you utter may be the most important; they help your audience decide whether to listen with genuine interest. These words may take the form of a rhetorical question: "Are you marching in the sexual revolution?" A quotation from some leading authority already known and respected by your hearers can build interest and credibility at the same time. Or perhaps a brief story of some exciting adventure might draw your audience into the speech. A speech on local security problems might begin with an account of a recent attack on campus. Whatever your strategy, keep the sentence structure simple: A short punch has more impact. The first question or sentence must show instantly that the audience has much to gain by listening to the speech.

In terms of credibility, it is important to establish early that you are qualified to speak on the subject. Quotations from leading authorities suggest that you have done research and lend a kind of borrowed credibility to your remarks. If the true-life story you tell about campus security problems has *you* as the victim, you not only gain rapt attention but also suggest that you have special qualifications to speak.

Once you have the attention of your listeners, you must tell them what your speech will be about. As you establish your purpose and theme, remember to define any words that may seen strange to your audience. They may not know what a bowline is or how to belay a cleat. Translate such terms into more familiar words, or provide verbal or nonverbal illustrations to help your hearers understand from the outset what you are talking about.

The only time to withhold statements of purpose at the beginning of an informative speech is when you deliberately want to build suspense. In this case your statement of purpose is delayed—sometimes until the end of the speech. Sometimes a speaker *never* announces his or her purpose, leaving it to the audience to discover for themselves. Such strategies of indirection can be artful and effective, but, in using

"Gentlemen, I have good news and bad news."

Henry Martin

them, you run the risk of confusing some members of the audience. They are useful when the subject is familiar and the speaker wishes to take a fresh approach. Simply announcing the subject at the outset might be boring; revealing the subject gradually can be stimulating.

A good speech beginning usually introduces primary statements in the order of their planned development. "First I hope to show how dangerous the situation has become. Second, I will explore what experts feel may be the causes of ineffective security on this campus. Finally, I want to discuss our options: What can we do to re-establish a safe and peaceful campus?" This speaker is giving the audience a program or preview for the speech that will follow. Such blueprints minimize the chance that listeners will get lost or become confused. They know just how much attention the speech will ask of them, and they can adjust their listening so that their minds won't drift or grow fatigued. As long as they are interested, can see where they are going, and can feel that they are getting there, they will listen.

Another function of a good beginning is to create the mood and atmosphere of the speech. The beginning should help the speaker and audience relate to each other and create opportunities for identification. The speaker establishes an image of self and invites the audience to assume a certain role as well. "What happened to me shouldn't happen to you. Let's get angry together. But let's be sure we know *how* to use our anger so that we get results." Here the speaker sets a mood, indicates a self-identity as victim, invites identification, and suggests an audience role favorable to the purpose of the speech.

The Body

The vital work of depiction occurs in the body of an informative speech. The body of a speech fulfills the principle of the design selected and completes its inner logic. Consider, for example, how Thressia Taylor completes the analogy design used in her speech on nutrition (given in Chapter 11). Likening the human body to a fine automobile allows her to develop her subject in a certain way, and she repeatedly returns to this comparison to use all of its resources for expression and to satisfy her listeners by completing the image artistically.

The body of the speech must deliver what is promised in the introduction and reward the interest that was aroused there. It must establish a certain individuality that marks it as a message bringing something new to its auditors, carrying some information of value. Designs themselves are finite and predictable, so this individuality must be established either in the subject matter of the speech or in the peculiar wording and style of its presentation. Ideally, of course, the listener receives both: new and useful data distinctively presented. The best informative speaker functions as a combination of scientist, scholar, and artist.

Because the topics of most speeches extend far beyond what can be expressed by one speaker on one occasion, the major problem is that of selection. What will the speaker include and exclude in the speech? What will the speaker select to represent the subject? And, because we are stressing the importance of depiction in informing, what "mode of vision" will develop in the body of the speech? Mode of vision includes the choice of design, the selection of examples and audio-visual aids, and the use of language.

Beyond its relevance, coherence, and general appeal to listeners, the body of a speech must clearly establish the authenticity and reliability of the image it builds. The skillful use of fact and expert opinion in a speech creates the presumption of authenticity.

Obviously, speakers who have personal knowledge that authenticates their view should make the point known early in the speech. "Last summer I worked as a volunteer in Senator Smith's campaign for re-election, and I had the opportunity to see a first-class political organization in action." Speakers should then buttress such personal observation with the latest and best expert testimony. "Just last month, Dr. Emil Roper, a nationally recognized political scientist who teaches at Harvard, wrote in *Harpers* that 'The Smith campaign of 1978 was a model of efficient and ethical campaigning.'" Note how this expert is introduced with a proper sensitivity to charismatic language, indicated in such words as "Dr." and "Harvard." The recency of the statement and its appearance in a distinguished magazine are also emphasized. Finally, because the expert is quoted directly, he seems almost a witness to the authenticity of the point just made in the speech.

The Conclusion

The conclusion of a successful speech allows us to look back over the speech as a whole. The conclusion should summarize the meaning of the speech and make its lessons explicit for the audience. This statement should be so impressive that the audience will find it difficult to forget the message of the speech. Often the conclusion recalls the beginning. The speaker might say, "So, to the troubled Professor who told us in the beginning that we would be buried in the rubble of our own technology, we can now answer: Have more faith in the creative imagination of humankind. Like modern alchemy, our technology can transform garbage into gold—or at least into energy!"[2] With such an artful ending, the speaker involves the audience itself in providing an answer. The speaker who ties the end of the speech to its beginning creates a satisfying sense of closure for the audience. The circle seems complete.

Still another effective concluding technique is telling a story or parable that captures the message of the speech in dramatic form. Such a story helps express the meaning of the speech in terms that an audience is likely to remember. Finally, the conclusion offers the speaker one last chance to appeal directly to listeners. This technique is more characteristic of persuasion, but even an informative speech can give final instructions. For example, if your speech on the subject of yoga has fascinated several audience members, they will want to know where they can attend yoga classes.

2. Metaphor has been shown to be effective in the conclusions of speeches. See John Waite Bowers and Michael Osborn, "Attitudinal Effects of Selected Types of Concluding Metaphors in Persuasive Speeches," *Speech Monographs*, 33 (1966), 148-155.

THE WORK OF EXAMPLES

Perhaps the technique most critical to the success of informative speaking (or for that matter to communication of any kind) is giving examples. An example is a lens the speaker uses to focus on the subject. Examples represent the subject, so nothing relates an audience more closely to it. "Can you give us an example?" may be a plea for understanding, or it may be a challenge to produce proof. Hence examples can both clarify and authenticate their subjects.

Examples can be vital to a speech, especially an abstract speech, because they ground a subject in the concrete and the familiar. Such grounding can also sharpen our emotional appreciation. This is why fund raisers for charities typically select one or a few individuals to represent the vast multitude of the afflicted. It is hard for the mind to absorb the idea of a million starving children. The horror is simply too enormous to comprehend: It overloads our circuits and produces only numbness. But we *can* relate to the face of one desperate child. Advertisements for charitable organizations often show just such a face, accompanied by a text that may begin, "This is Sheila. . . ." By the time the appeal is over, the reader wants to help all the Sheilas of the world.

If there were only one skill we could give the speaker, it would be that of using examples effectively. In the rhetoric of an able speaker, the example can be quite graphic and pictorial. Consider how Thomas Henry Huxley used example to illustrate the abstract processes of induction and deduction for an audience of British working people during the last century.

> *Suppose you go into a fruiterer's shop, wanting an apple—you take up one, and on biting it, you find it is sour; you look at it, and see that it is hard and green. You take up another one, and that too is hard, green, and sour. The shopman offers you a third; but, before biting it, you examine it, and find that it is hard and green, and you immediately say that you will not have it, as it must be sour, like those that you have already tried. . . . You have, in the first place, established a law by induction, and upon that you have founded a deduction, and reasoned out the special conclusion of the particular case.*[3]

3. "Six Lectures to Working Men 'On Our Knowledge of the Causes of the Phenomena of Organic Nature' (1863)" *Darwiniana: Essays by Thomas Henry Huxley*, Vol. 2 (New York: Greenwood Press, 1968), pp. 365-366.

Examples need not be drawn from the world of reality to be effective. The hypothetical or made-up instance can be a useful fiction, especially when actual examples are hard to come by. Such is the case when we *personify* a subject that is inanimate and abstract. For example, it is hard to exhibit to the senses a current of electricity, and it is difficult for an audience to identify in any way with such a power. Nevertheless, some years ago the electric power interests, wishing to communicate to the public the usefulness of this very real if invisible force, invented a little stick figure whom they named "Reddi Kilowatt." Reddi went about the world making himself useful. He was a cheerful fellow, never lazy, always on the go. Hence he expressed some basic American values, and electric power gradually became patriotic as well as useful. We may yet live to see "Buster Atom" or "Laurie Laser."

Just as intangible forces can be personified in hypothetical examples, so can the abstract, metaphysical sense of community. "Uncle Sam" has become known the world over as the symbol of the United States and its people, government, and culture.

Hypothetical examples should be checked carefully for appropriateness. Clearly, they can have important explanatory and humanizing power in a speech.

Verbal Examples

Because they help us "see" a subject, examples drawn in words function like audio-visual aids. Such verbal "aids" have several advantages.

1. They are much more flexible and convenient than audio-visual aids. One does not have to drag them into a room or set up elaborate equipment to display them. Because they consist of words, they can be woven easily into the texture of a speech. One can use many of them and many different kinds of them in the same speech, because one carries them in the brain rather than on the back.

2. They don't compete with a speaker. They illuminate the speech from within, so they don't set up an awkward situation in which the audience has to decide whether to watch the aid or listen to the speaker. Nor do they linger after a point has been made to distract from what the speaker is saying now. Sometimes, when a speaker is obviously struggling, an audience seeks sanctuary within a visual aid. It's more comfortable to give one's attention to a chart than to suffer with a speaker who is having trouble.

3. They allow the speaker to focus on a subject just the way he or she wants to. Because the image is painted in words, one can easily

highlight certain details and leave others in the background. Words are the most flexible material a rhetorical artist can work with.

Verbal aids also have certain weaknesses.

1. They are less credible and authentic than their audio-visual counterparts. Naturally, we believe most readily what we can see and hear ourselves.

2. Verbal aids alone may detract from the variety and action of a speech. The speech that interweaves both audio-visual aids *and* verbal examples is apt to score high in variety and therefore in interest. Visual materials can involve the speaker more readily in movement and action and make the delivery more vital. The speaker must point out the parts of a model or chart under consideration, and such functional gesturing can relax the tense speaker or make the novice speaker less self-conscious. Often the speaker must walk between the lectern and the aid, and such movement can emphasize and punctuate meanings in the speech. Stopping after a sequence of steps, for example, can signal either the end or the beginning of a line of thought. By the way one moves, one can even stress the importance of a point just made.

The combination of verbal and visual aids also lends itself to full use of the principle of *repetition.* Speakers can show their subjects first in words and then in actual representation, boosting the impact of the speech.

Rules for Using Verbal Examples

Examples are such important devices that no one can be an effective speaker who has not learned to use them well. Some of the major rules in the art of using examples follow.

Be selective. One example effectively developed is better than four examples jumbled together. The four will cancel each other's impact and make the speech tedious. Use multiple examples only when the different cases illustrate important differences in the subject matter or when the evidence on which you are basing the speech is hard to establish. A statement such as "Cars are more fuel-efficient now than they were twenty years ago" would require at least one and probably several comparative examples to project its full meaning. In a speech on the possible existence of Unidentified Flying Objects (UFO's), the tentative nature of the scientific evidence might force a speaker to use a large number of specific examples. In this case, numerous convincing examples should authenticate as well as animate the speech.

Be representative. Draw your example from the center of your subject matter, not from around the edges. Do not present the rare as though it were the usual. If audience members are already acquainted with your subject, they may well accuse you of carelessness, ignorance, or even dishonesty. If they are not yet acquainted with the subject, but discover the distortion later, they will resent the false impression you gave them.

Be vivid and brief. Let your example work to bring the subject into sharp focus, but don't drag it out. Cut out everything that is unnecessary. Be especially careful of arty, self-conscious prose–poetry. Too many adjectives can sap the power of your sentences. Let nouns and verbs do the hard work. If you find yourself launching into a long explanation, look at the example again. It is probably defective.

Be cohesive. There should be a natural and easy flow through the speech as you move from statement to example and back to statement. Transitions are vital to keep the speech moving smoothly.

AUDIO-VISUAL AIDS

The vital work of depicting subjects and informing audiences can be advanced considerably by effective audio-visual materials. Such aids vary from the subject itself to highly symbolic representations in charts and posters.

The Subject Itself

What could be clearer or more striking than the subject itself in its living reality? The speaker who speaks on toxic plants or even poisonous snakes might find a safe way to bring specimens to class. One disadvantage of the actual subject as an aid is that often the subject does not fit the speech situation. It might be very difficult to haul in an anaconda to illustrate a speech; on the other hand, the audience would be straining so hard to see a grass snake that they might not hear your commentary. Nor does the living subject always cooperate. Your copperhead may not want to open its mouth when you are ready to demonstrate fangs.

Film Representations

When subjects don't lend themselves to actual presentation, speakers can often make effective use of film or slide representations. Films

Elizabeth Hamlin 1979

and slides are generally available on loan through school and public libraries or through public and private agencies that have a vital stake in the topic. The camera can reduce the oversized subject or expand the undersized subject, and it can show the subject in action and within its own context or habitat.

Films, however, can be awkward to use with a speech. There is often a period of fumbling while the film is being started and at its conclusion, and these awkward lapses can cause the speech to exceed the time limits set by the instructor. The attention of the audience must be surrendered to the film and may be hard to regain. Direct contact between speaker and audience is lost. Such loss of contact makes it hard to get feedback from the faces of listeners and thus to adjust the presentation to the moment. Often the visual image is more interesting than its verbal counterpart, so listeners really don't hear the speaker. When the film is over, the speaker can seem terribly drab by comparison, making the speech less effective. For all these good reasons, use a film only when an experienced person can help you with the mechanics of starting and stopping the projector. And use a film only when it is directly relevant and only for the brief time required for definition and example. Weave the film into the speech, not the speech into the film. Use it only after you have achieved a confident, vivid delivery that can compete successfully with the visual images you will show. When in doubt about whether to use a film, ask your instructor's advice.

SLIDES OR TRANSPARENCIES Slides or transparencies, though less engrossing than the film, may be more appropriate as illustrations for public
speeches. For one thing, they allow the speaker more control over the
presentation. It is much easier to integrate the slide or transparency
into the flow of the speech. If you construct your own transparency,
you can include just that information you wish to stress in just the way
you wish to stress it. Because the equipment is simpler to use, you can
minimize awkward lapses of time before and after the visual aid is
presented. Moreover, the slide or transparency gives you greater flexibility. You can pause to emphasize and interpret an especially interesting illustration and to show its particular application to the speech
and audience. Moreover, you do not have to surrender the attention
of the audience to another fascinating communication medium. The
very dullness of slides (compared to films) can be an advantage; they
don't overpower the speaker and the speech. For instructions on how
to develop slides and transparencies for presentation, consult the
specialized readings at the end of this chapter. Ask your instructor
whether there is an audio-visual media center on campus that could
help you.

PHOTOGRAPHS Photographs might seem a happy medium between the
film and the transparency, permitting the vividness of the one and the
flexibility of the other. But the photograph can easily overload the
viewer with irrelevant information. And though pictures can make
words come alive, they can also create two additional problems for
novice speakers. First, the speaker can lean too heavily on them,
forgetting that he or she must create word-pictures that make the
precise point of the speech and invite the proper response. Language
can easily go flat in a speech that depends on photographs. Second,
beginning speakers sometimes make the fatal mistake of giving the
audience pictures to pass around during the speech. The exchange
of pictures creates a constant distraction, and the pictures themselves
become visual competition rather than visual aids.

Other Visual Aids

If you should give a speech explaining the construction principles of
the Cathedral of Notre Dame in Paris, you might find it very useful
to have a three-dimensional scale model to clarify your account. The
model would represent the cathedral and would thus be symbolic.
(For information on the construction of models, see the readings at
the end of this chapter, especially Brown, Lewis, and Harcleroad,

Chapter 11). Even more symbolic would be two-dimensional charts, graphs, maps, and drawings constructed on a blackboard or on poster paper. Such visual aids allow the speaker to render in a concrete manner subjects that are often quite abstract. The gross national product, for example, is an abstraction that can be given tangible form in a chart or graph.

THE BLACKBOARD   The blackboard is useful when the speaker wants to offer a step by step demonstration. This procedure has a built-in element of suspense ("What is the speaker going to draw next?") and is a real attention-holding device. One disadvantage is that the blackboard offers such an easy out that it can tempt careless speakers into not planning very well. Unless such an aid is carefully thought through and its construction rehearsed during every practice of the speech, it can look terribly sloppy and reflect unfavorably on the speech. One answer to this problem is to rough out blackboard designs in advance of the speech, drawing light chalk lines that you can trace over while speaking. This "spontaneous" visual aid gives you the advantage of both suspense and neatness. You enjoy the additional benefit of seeming highly competent and resourceful. Hence the carefully arranged blackboard visual can become a positive factor in speaker credibility.

Another problem is that speakers can get so caught up in drawing the aid that they turn their backs on the audience, lose contact with them, and deliver their speech to the blackboard. Remember, you are risking loss of contact whenever you look away from an audience, and the longer you remain away from them, the greater the risk. Unless your chart is very simple, you should prepare it in advance of the speech so that you can concentrate on the job at hand—effective speaking!

GRAPHS   The prepared visual aid—graph, chart, or map—hasn't the suspense of the on-the-spot happening, but it permits a much more sophisticated and complex visual aid. It makes possible the use of color for reinforcing a mood or underscoring contrasts. Graphs are especially useful for presenting large and complex numerical relationships. The *circle graph*, or *pie graph*, is ideal for presenting the whole picture of a subject and the size of its parts in relation to each other. Figure 9.1 is a circle graph.

The *bar graph* permits dramatic comparisons and contrasts and is highly action-oriented. It is especially effective in persuasive speaking. Figure 9.2 presents such a graph, which could be used to reinforce a speech setting long-range membership goals in a professional association.

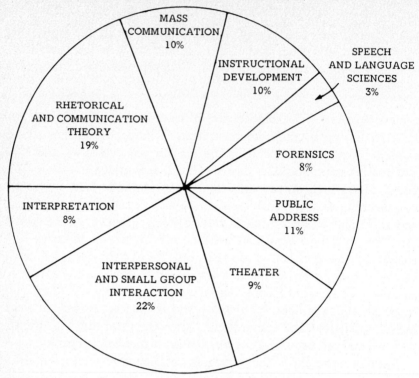

Figure 9.1 CIRCLE GRAPH

Note that this kind of graph makes a connection with our symbolic nature by depicting the goal *above* the level of the present, suggesting the greater power that realizing the goal will bring.

The *line graph* shows tendencies across time. It indicates direction and invites causal explanations and predictions. Figure 9.3 is a line graph.

CHARTS Charts are useful as visual representations of concepts or structures. The *flow chart* depicts a process or a line of responsibility in an organization. The *tree chart* shows the genealogy or the diffusion of a family, language, or invention. By contrast, the *stream chart* shows how many sources come together to produce a person, language, or product. Finally, *sequence charts,* often presented as a series of charts, show different stages of a process. Sequence charts can create interest and even suspense in a speech, as the audience waits to see what the next chart in a series will reveal. Figure 9.4 is a sequence chart.

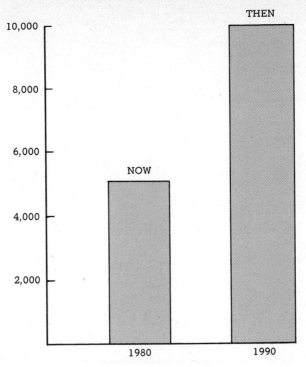

Membership in the Speech Communication Association:
Our Goal for Growth

Figure 9.2 BAR GRAPH

MAPS Maps are also an important kind of visual graphic, and you may want to refresh yourself on their considerable variety (see the discussion in Chapter 6). If you decide that a map will help clarify and define your subject, you must consider how to transform what you find in the library into an aid that will be effective in a speech. Most often, maps have to be adjusted and redrawn to meet the needs of a particular oral presentation. Most of the time this means making the map larger and simpler, leaving out all extraneous details and making relevant details more prominent. Otherwise, the map will be like the photograph that floods the viewer with too much visual information.[4] For example, a speech detailing crop damage in Arkansas from the hot, dry summer of 1980 might use an enlarged outline map showing least affected areas in green, moderately damaged areas in yellow, and severely afflicted areas in brown. (Color here would be a kind of visual *onomatopoeia*, a technique by which the symbol resembles its subject. See Chapter 11.)

4. Robert M. W. Travers, "The Transmission of Information to Human Receivers," *Audio-Visual Communication Review*, 12 (Winter 1964), 373–385.

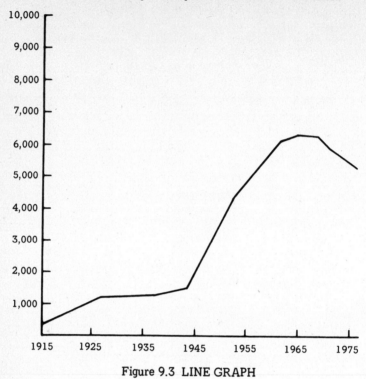

Figure 9.3 LINE GRAPH

Designing Visual Aids

Every good poster or chart should begin with a layout, a rough sketch that allows you to see how the aid will develop before you commit it to final form. As you plan the aid, strive for one consistent underlying *form,* just as you carefully select the basic design principle of the speech itself. The aid should seem balanced to the eye, with the focal point either at the center (formal design) or in one of the corner quadrants (informal design). If, for example, the sequence chart shown in Figure 9.4 were used as a single chart, the lettering in the lower right quadrant would illustrate informal design. If the poster were redesigned in an overall circular pattern, with the lettering placed in the center of the circle of circles, the chart would illustrate formal design.

Be sure that the more important and the less important elements in the poster receive proper *emphasis;* give special attention to the size of illustrations and lettering and to the heaviness (weight) of line. As a rule, you should draw the chart with an eye toward *simplicity*—no complexity for its own sake that an audience can get lost in. Another

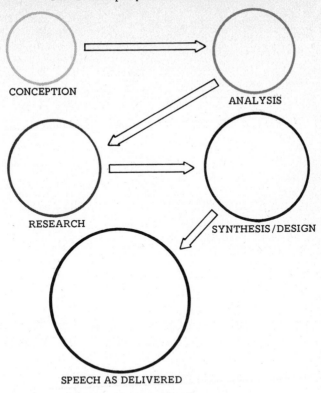

CONCEPTION

ANALYSIS

RESEARCH

SYNTHESIS/DESIGN

SPEECH AS DELIVERED

Figure 9.4 SEQUENCE CHART

vital quality is proper *adjustment* of the overall size of the poster to the dimensions of the room where the speech will be presented and to the size of the audience. Be sure to draw all the features large enough for someone in the back of the room to read them comfortably.

USE OF COLOR Strive for effective *contrast* and *harmony*, especially in the use of colors. Colors themselves can reinforce certain moods and impressions. For example, it would seem quite natural to select the color blue for the sequence chart shown in Figure 9.4. This color suggests power and authority ("blue chip," "blue ribbon," "royal blue,"), connoting here the power of an idea. Red, associated with emotion and action, may be more useful in persuasive speeches. In Figure 9.2, for example, using the color red for the present level in the bar graph might suggest that there is a problem or even a crisis in the present membership level of the Speech Communication Association. Used to represent the future goal, the contrasting color blue would suggest achievement

Patricia Hollander Gross

and reinforce the impression of power conveyed by the greater elevation of the goal. Green, a more restful color, could be used effectively
to impart information.

Colors become most significant in communication when they are
used in certain styles and patterns. One interesting effect, *monochromatic* color, is made up of tints and shades of a single color such as
blue or green or violet. Monochromatic color suggests unity, with
subtle variations within the whole. If Figure 9.4 were in monochromatic color, we might see how the gradual deepening or intensifying
of the color blue can (along with size variation) indicate growth and
development. Another interesting effect is *analogous* color, which uses
colors such as yellow, yellow-green, and green, all neighbors on the
color wheel. While this form suggests the difference or individuality
of components represented, it also expresses their compatibility or
close relationship. The circle graph shown in Figure 9.1 could illustrate
the principle of analogous color if we used colors ranging from orange
to green to symbolize both the relatedness and the individuality of
the divisions of the Speech Communication Association. A third kind
of color effect is *complementary* colors, those that are opposites on the
color wheel. Dark blue and orange, purple and yellow, or red and green
stand out strikingly against each other. Complementary color schemes
emphasize clash and conflict, tension and opposition. They lend themselves to bold, action-oriented speeches.

METHOD OF DISPLAY Along with choosing the kind of chart or graph to use and planning its features, you should plan how and when to display it. Your best bet may be to use a display stand on which you can place your chart when you are ready. Or you may prefer to put the chart up before the speech, concealed by a cover that you can remove easily at the right moment. An uncovered chart tacked up ahead of your speech can become a competing stimulus and a distraction. The audience may gaze aimlessly at it instead of listening to you. While you are using the chart, stand well to the side of it and, as much as possible, face the audience. When you refer to the aid, point precisely to what you are talking about; don't leave your audience searching for the reference you have just made while you are forging ahead to something else. Remember again to maintain eye contact with your listeners and to control their inspection of the chart.

A visual aid is not an unmixed blessing. But if it can help you define key points, if it can bring your subject into sharp, engaging focus for your audience, then it is well worth the trouble and risk involved.

Summary of Major Ideas

Informative speaking often spells out the audience's options for dealing with situations.

Informative speaking tells us what we need to know but did not know about a situation.

Informative speech is characterized by "is" statements, persuasive speaking by "ought to" statements.

Informative speaking transforms the speaker's view of reality into a rhetorical depiction intended to control the perceptions of listeners.

Effective informative speaking begins with a clear realization of purpose and theme.

Design options for informative speaking include developing a subject in terms of time, space, or the categories appropriate to its nature.

A fourth design option focuses on our vital interests, developing a subject according to the universal human needs that it reflects.

Other designs are to consider a subject in terms of cause and consequence or to amplify a subject through a series of repetitions that cumulatively reveal its nature.

A seventh design option is to present unfamiliar subjects by relating them to subjects we do understand, thus applying the principle of analogy.

Other options for design of the informative speech are to present a subject by contrast, showing us what a thing *is* by explaining what it is *not,* or to present the speech as an answer to a series of vital questions.

An effective beginning gains attention, clarifies the purpose of the speech, establishes the speaker's credibility, and motivates the audience to listen.

Examples both clarify and authenticate their subjects. They are central to the development of an informative speech.

Examples should be carefully selected, representative, vivid, and woven cohesively into the speech.

Nonverbal illustrations include the subject itself and various kinds of films, models, and charts.

Nonverbal illustrations can add color, clarity, and credibility to an informative speech. It is important, however, to plan their use carefully and not allow them to distract the audience from the speech itself.

Exercises and Discussion Questions

1. Look in advertising and government news releases for examples of persuasion cloaked as information. What tips you off to the persuasive motive? In what respects does the pseudo-information possess the characteristics of information discussed in this chapter? In what respects does it *not* possess these characteristics?

2. Look in *Vital Speeches of the Day* for examples of informative speeches developed along each of the patterns of organization (design options) described in this chapter. Can you discover any patterns *not* discussed here?

3. In the speeches you studied in Exercise 2, what methods of introduction, development, and conclusion were used? Are the speeches clearly structured around statement of purpose, theme, and primary statements? Can you find cases in which the speaker's purpose is implicit or even disguised?

4. Prepare a speech that defines a subject, using a variety of verbal and audio-visual illustrations. Explain why you used these particular techniques.

5. Write a critique of an informative speech you have attended. Consider the quality of its adaptation, its principle of organization, and the techniques and strategies used in its introduction, body, and conclusion.

6. Scan the morning newspaper for examples of analogy used to explain complex processes. Be especially alert for articles reporting scientific discoveries. How effective are these analogies in making the topic easier to understand?

For Further Reading

A number of excellent works specialize in how to prepare and use visual aids. Among them are James W. Brown, Richard B. Lewis, and Fred F. Harcleroad, *AV Instruction: Technology, Media and Methods* (New York: McGraw-Hill, 1973) and Ed Minor and Harvey R. Frye, *Techniques for Producing Visual Instructional Media* (New York: McGraw-Hill, 1970).

For more on the power of the example in public speaking, see Scott Consigny, "The Rhetorical Example," *Southern Speech Communication Journal*, 41 (1976), 121-134.

10
OUTLINING THE INFORMATIVE SPEECH

Speech is civilization itself. The word, even the most
contradictory word, preserves contact—it is
silence which isolates.

THOMAS MANN, *The Magic Mountain*

```
┌─────────────────────────────────────────┐
│                                         │
│       WHAT TO LOOK FOR IN               │
│          THIS CHAPTER                   │
│  ─────────────────────────────────────  │
│                                         │
│      The experience of outlining        │
│                                         │
│     Developing the formal outline       │
│                                         │
│      Rules for effective outlining      │
│                                         │
└─────────────────────────────────────────┘
```

Throughout the business of designing and developing the informative speech, you have no doubt been outlining your thoughts in search of the best possible pattern of organization. Now it is time to complete a formal outline that represents the final product of such thinking and commits you to a definite speech plan.

Chapter 10 traces a hypothetical experience in developing an outline for informative speaking and identifies the major elements of such outlines and the rules that govern them. Completing the formal outline in the manner suggested will tell you a great deal about the effectiveness of your preparation.

The formal outline lists the major points you want to make in the order in which you want to make them. The outline also indicates the relationship of these points to each other and their relative importance in the speech. Finally, the outline indicates the nature and placement of the important facts, interpretations, and illustrations you will use to clarify and develop these points and to establish them securely in the minds of your listeners. The resulting pattern provides what psychologists call a *gestalt*—a view of the overall form the speaker imposes on the speech. Without such an outline, the resulting speech may ramble and lack discipline. With it, the speech moves decisively toward its destination.

A good outline shows that the speaker has a thorough understanding of the whole subject, a clear perception of its parts, and a grasp of the value of these parts in relation to each other. Some points are important because of the nature of the subject matter. Other points may be prominent in the outline because they are important for this particular audience. Suppose one were outlining a speech on the nature of public financing. These considerations could lead one to emphasize the income tax, a topic of general importance, and revenues from horse racing, a topic of special importance because of intense local interest.

THE EXPERIENCE OF OUTLINING

At the initial stage of outline preparation, you may not need to develop complete sentences—just clear phrases that capture the major thrust of your points. Referring to an example mentioned in Chapter 9, we can imagine the first, rough outline prepared by the speaker who wished "to introduce my listeners to the typical structure of a local political campaign."

I. Financing the candidate (Finance Committee)
II. Informing the candidate (Issues Committee)
III. Presenting the candidate
    A. Direct Voter Contact (Ward and Precinct Committee)
    B. TV and media exposure (Publicity Committee)
IV. ? ? ?

Why has the speaker stopped in confusion? For very good reason. He or she has realized that it is going to be impossible to develop such an extensive subject in any meaningful depth within the six to eight minutes allotted for the speech. The subject is just too ambitious for the scope of such a speech. This discovery affects substantially the research phase of the speech preparation plan. Speakers should be thinking in terms of overall speech outlines *throughout* speech preparation, even as they are analyzing their topics and planning how to research the speech.

The speaker decides now to focus the speech on an interesting *part* of the original topic: the financing of political campaigns. He or she will set out to answer the question "How do political candidates finance their campaigns?" The purpose will be to bring funding practices to light, and the theme of the speech will be that corruption breeds in the darkness of public ignorance.

As our mythical speaker focuses on this new subject, some important new connections are already being made in his or her mind. Not only has the topic been limited and concentrated, but the new purpose and message have suggested a symbolic form, the contrast of light and darkness. As the speaker experiences this discovery, the image sharpens into a contrast between a dark forest and a lighted clearing. The speaker's new informative purpose will be to illuminate this darkness and to drag certain notorious practices into the clearing where all can see them. Now the speech is acquiring dramatic value and a script to fit the light and darkness scene. So the speaker returns to preparing the outline.

I. The cost of local campaigns.

II. Who pays the bills?
   A. Public-spirited citizens.
   B. Candidates themselves and friends.
   C. Various others with axes to grind.
      1. Ideological groups, liberal and conservative.
      2. Labor unions.
      3. Business and manufacturing interests.
      4. Those who anticipate specific favors.
      5. Those who are "grateful" for favors already provided.
III. As we develop this list, the deeper grows the darkness, the more dense the jungle of politics (specific abuses of these various sources can now be developed).
IV. Can we clear this jungle, light this darkness? (Discussion of various options for reform can follow.)

Now the speaker feels confident that he or she is on the right track. And why not? A design has coalesced that should engage much interest and attention. This complex design harmoniously combines categorical considerations with cause and consequence, question and answer, and the contrast provided by symbolic forms. The outline already promises a colorful speech. The first primary statement should lead to some startling and provocative facts. The second primary statement *could* be interesting, especially if the speaker can discover some factual breakdown of the average percentage of campaign funding that is provided by each source. The third primary statement introduces the dramatizing image and should provide some vital examples. And the fourth primary question/statement should allow the audience to ponder its choices. If the speaker can only find the evidence to flesh out such a promising outline!

Simulating the Outline and Research Experience

Well, this *might* have been the early outline for a provocative speech. What happened instead was this. When the author reached this point, he decided to simulate the process he had been describing under the severe time pressures often experienced by a student. What I did (to lift the mask of the third-person pronoun) was to imagine myself as a student who would have no more than three half-days (or nine hours) for the whole process of speech preparation—from analysis through oral practice. With the foregoing initial outline in hand, I went to the library and, following the advice in Chapter 6, first visited the reference

Barbara Alper/Stock, Boston

room. There I consulted the librarian and confirmed that the P.A.I.S. (Public Affairs Information Service) would be an appropriate index with which to begin my search for substance. The previous year's issues alone provided about ten possible articles and speeches on the subject. I picked out the most promising of these and began reading.

This phase of research extended through that morning and into the next. Rather than taking formal research notes, such as I suggested in Chapter 5, I made xerographic copies of the most helpful materials and developed my own index to these copied materials over several sheets of a legal pad. Hence an entry such as "New law threatens to create 'new aristocracy' (*CQ* 1244)" was enough to cue me quickly to a major argument capped by a particularly startling phrase developed in the *Congressional Quarterly Weekly Report,* 36 (May 20, 1978), p. 1244. During the second morning I consulted a professor in the Political Science Department, asked a few vital questions, and ended up reading an extremely helpful chapter in a book that he recommended. There was much more research that could have been done, but I realized that it was time to do a final outline of the speech.

Now a new problem arose. The planning outline that had sent me to the library with such high hopes had turned out, in the light of research, to be nothing more than an elaborate projection of the commonplaces and stereotypes in terms of which I approached the subject before I began my research. The research had given sharper focus to the purpose and re-direction to the theme. It was clear that the experience of outlining is not so much one of building later versions upon earlier versions as a *discarding* process, in which only threads of ideas often survive from the earliest to the final form.

Building a Foundation for the Speech

After surveying my research index, notes, and copied materials, I restated the purpose and theme of this hypothetical speech.

Purpose: *To introduce my listeners to the nature, problems, and regulation of political campaign financing in America.*
Theme: *The movement to curb abuses in political campaign fund raising has solved some old problems but has also created some new ones.*

But now I realized that this would be an incomplete foundation for my speech. I would also need to spell out the response I desired from my listeners.

Response Desired: *New alertness on the part of my audience to some potentially vast political problems and an awakening from that apathy which is the traditional curse of American politics.*

Developing Orienting Material and Initial Focus

So now I considered the form of the outline itself. Some writers advise actually dividing the formal outline itself into introduction, body, and conclusion, but I rejected this procedure on two grounds: (1) It merely states the obvious. (2) It has a tendency to create somewhat artificial divisions in a speech when all should flow together—forming a natural, cohesive unit—from the first words one utters to the last. Good art should conceal itself, not intrude on the speech.

I decided two steps would be essential in getting off to a good start:

Orienting material, which would alert the audience to the main issues and significance of the speech. Such material sets the stage on which the speech will develop.
Initial focus, which concentrates audience attention on my purpose, on the speech theme, and on what my listeners might expect to receive for the attention they would be asked to pay. Here I would give my listeners a program for the speech to come and implant in their minds the framework on which it would develop.

I devised the following outline:

I. *Orienting Material* (contrasting metaphorical quotations)
   A. Jesse Unruh: "Money is the mother's milk of politics."
   B. Hubert Humphrey: "Campaign financing is a curse. It's the most disgusting, demeaning, disenchanting, debilitating experience of a politician's life."
II. *Initial Focus:* Politics makes the American system fly, and money gets politics off the ground. We have to be concerned with the laws that protect us from abuse and contamination of the political money supply. My purpose today is to introduce you to this problem and to the laws presently dealing with it.

Note that I have written out my initial focus word for word. Instinctively, I realized that this focus establishes an absolutely vital understanding and that it must be worked out precisely. The focus will be rehearsed and practiced until it is virtually memorized, unlike the more open, flexible, and extemporaneous style of presentation that is appropriate for other sections of the speech. The more open style invites a closer interaction between speaker and listener, but there are moments in the speech—at the beginning, in the conclusion (final focus), and at primary statements in between—when the closed system of memorized wording may be necessary.

Developing Primary Statements and the Body

Having established my beginning, I moved on to the body and decided right away to bring my listeners directly into the speech and put them on the spot. I would achieve this effect by identifying them as the ultimate cause of campaign abuses, following the causation principle of design. The outline proceeded:

III. The problem begins with us.
   A. Money is a necessity in politics, but people don't want to face up to this fact of life.
   B. Frank J. Sorauf, author of the authoritative textbook *Party Politics in America,* concludes drily: "One can only suppose that large numbers of Americans think that a political stork brings campaign funds."

The direct quotation would support and substantiate the speech and enhance my own credibility. At this point I weighed the desirability of probing the causes of public ignorance about campaign funding, but I decided such an excursion would be off the main route and would draw the speech out to undesirable length.

C. Because of such apathy and ignorance, we *invite* the very corruption that prevents many of us from associating with politics in the first place.
   1. We force the candidate into the kind of demeaning fund raising that Hubert Humphrey once described:

      "I've had to break off in the middle of trying to make a decent, honorable campaign and go up to somebody's parlor or to a room and say, 'Gentlemen and ladies, I'm desperate. You've got to help me. My campaign chairman is here and I'm going to step out of the room.'

      ". . . You just have to grovel around in the dirt. And you see people there—a lot of them you don't want to see. And they look at you, and you sit there and you talk to them and tell them what you're for and you need help and, out of the twenty-five who have gathered, four will contribute. And most likely one of them is in trouble and is somebody you shouldn't have had a contribution from. . . ."

   2. We discourage the bright, idealistic person from entering politics: What decent person would want to be subjected to such humiliation?
   3. We make the candidate dependent on the special interests and on the power-players—on such men as Clement Stone, who gave over $2 million to Nixon's 1972 campaign, or Stewart Mott, who gave over $1 million to McCarthy and McGovern.
   4. Or we make politics a game of the wealthy, those who can pump their own money into a campaign and are beholden to no one but themselves and perhaps a few friends.
D. The political melon broke open during the Watergate investigations, when the public could at last see through to the rotten core.
   1. Money—up to $68 million in the 1972 Nixon campaign—seemed to be at the heart of the corruption.
   2. The people asked, "Is this what politics in America is supposed to be?"

At this point the causation design had clearly emerged. I would place the fundamental blame for the problem right on my audience and would then expose the sordid effects. Because I wanted to avoid irrelevant partisan reactions or the appearance of bias, my reference to "power-players" would balance a Republican with a Democrat.

The real muscle in the demonstration would be provided by the facts and by the strong personal testimony from HHH. The "political melon" image should serve as a dramatic device to restate the point colorfully and vividly near the end of the demonstration. Moreover, a little color would offset the rather technical explanation to follow. Note that the final subpoint in this section also serves as a transition to introduce the next primary statement.

IV. The answer came in the Federal Election Campaign Act of 1972, which was further strengthened in 1974 and 1976.
  A. The law applies to all candidates for federal office and to all committees and individuals who contribute to such candidates.
    1. It requires candidates to file detailed, timely reports that make political contributions a matter of public record.
    2. It establishes certain limitations on contributions and expenditures.
      a. It has discouraged large contributions by individuals.
      b. It has encouraged the formation of Political Action Committees (PACs), which become funnels for union and corporate contributions.
  B. Perhaps most important, the law has established what could prove to be a monumental precedent through its public financing of presidential elections.
V. There have been criticisms of the new law. Has the solution become the problem?
  A. Many feel the cure for corruption has introduced the disease of elitism.
    1. The Supreme Court has ruled (1976) that an individual cannot be limited in contributing to his or her own campaign.
    2. This decision reinforces the advantage enjoyed by wealthy people and PACs.
    3. In 1976 Pennsylvania Senator H. John Heinz, III, pumped more than $2.6 million of his personal fortune into his winning campaign.
    4. Carl Levin, former president of the Detroit City Council and senatorial hopeful in 1978, commented that the Supreme Court decision could "create a new aristocracy" of officeholders who are able to finance their own campaigns.
    5. Common Cause Vice President Fred Wertheimer agrees that, if the present system continues, in less than a decade "two kinds of people will be elected—candidates who represent PACs . . . and very, very wealthy individuals."

B. The new critics are not asking for a return to the old ways but rather for an extension of public financing into other state and federal elections.
   1. Lynn Hellebust, executive director of the Kansas Governmental Ethics Commission, has said, "Public funding sufficient to provide a substantial monetary floor for all major candidates at the national and state level is necessary in order to wage vigorous, effective campaigns."
   2. Our own Professor Mahood of the Political Science Department agrees: "Public financing is the only answer," he told me in an interview last week.
C. Is public financing likely to happen as a general practice?
   1. Not if we leave it up to incumbents and major challengers.
      a. Incumbents don't like it, because it would give instant significance to weak or minor challengers who otherwise might never get off the ground.
      b. Major challengers don't like it, because it imposes spending limitations, which normally have to be enormous in order to topple an incumbent.
   2. Therefore, public financing won't happen unless *we* force it to happen.

Section V focuses primarily on expert opinion and interpretation of the facts developed in IV. It hints at the possibility of a specific solution (public financing) but does not strongly advocate such a solution or discuss it in much detail. Instead, the door is left open to develop such lines of thought in a companion persuasive speech. In its last stages, this section returns to the audience and sets up the final focus.

Developing the Final Focus

VI. *Final Focus:* So we have come full circle—back to ourselves and to the original problem of apathy. As long as we think the stork provides campaign funding, then the 'mother's milk' that Jesse Unruh spoke of will often flow from corrupting sources. It all comes back to us, and how involved we want to become in protecting the system that protects our political freedom. Until we become involved, we might well heed the following paraphrase from Shakespeare's *Julius Caesar:* "The fault, dear voters, lies not in our political stars, but in ourselves."

This final phase of the speech presents an overview and creates a sense of completion. The major technique is to tie the conclusion back in with an image that launched the speech. The final focus should also involve the audience with the speech they have just experienced by suggesting an appropriate general response. The last sentence is a final effort to make listeners remember the dramatic message of the speech. Any final focus must survey the ground covered, summarize the points made, provide a satisfying sense of completion, assist the audience in making a response consistent with the purpose of the speech, and conclude the speech with some memorable statement.

Out of this experience of simulating the preparation of an outline emerged what might have become the plan for a decent informative speech. When I practiced the hypothetical speech, I timed it right at seven minutes. Were I to rehearse further, I would look for places to trim and compress. The secret of presenting information effectively is to provide just those facts necessary to give the speech authority and to educate the audience, without descending into a dull, pedantic recital of figures that no one will remember.

Completing a Bibliography

To complete this full and formal outline, which I shall assume my instructor has asked me to submit before I deliver the actual speech, I might well provide a bibliography. The following format includes a number of sample entries. Note that the bibliography appears at the end of the outline and that it cites books, then articles, and then miscellaneous citations in a descending order of priority.

BIBLIOGRAPHY

BOOKS Sorauf, Frank J., *Party Politics in America* (Boston: Little, Brown, 1976). [The order of citation is author's name; title of book, underlined; and then (in parentheses) place of publication, publisher, and date of publication. For such information see the title page, front and back. Always cite the latest revision of any book, unless there is some special reason to refer to an earlier edition. For articles in collections, cite in order the author; title of his or her essay, in quotations; book title, underlined; name of editor; place, publisher, and date, in parentheses; and page numbers. For example: John Samuelson, "Raising Campaign Funds," *The Art of Politics,* ed. Martha Jordan (New York: Century, 1975), pp. 280–306.]

ARTICLES Lynn Hellebust, "The Limitations of Campaign Finance Disclosure," *National Civic Review,* 67 (May 1978), 223–227.[1] [Note that "67" here indicates the volume number, and that the "pp." is

---

1. Your instructor may prefer that you add a brief account to each citation, indicating how the source was useful in preparing your speech.

omitted before the page numbers as a matter of form when a volume number appears.]

"How It Was for Mr. Humphrey," *The New York Times* (October 13, 1974), Sec. 4, p. 18. [from an unsigned column in a newspaper]

MISCELLANEOUS CITATIONS   During the summer of 1977 I worked in George Thompson's race for Mayor of Jonesville and observed campaign finance practices at close hand. [personal observation]

On December 1, 1978, I interviewed Professor Richard Mahood of Memphis State University's Department of Political Science for his evaluation of public financing of political campaigns. [interview]

The FEC and the Federal Campaign Finance Law, Federal Election Commission (Washington, D.C., 1978). [pamphlet]

On December 5, 1978, I conducted a poll between noon and 1 P.M. in front of the Administration Building, MSU campus. The conclusions I cite are based on a sample of 37 undergraduate students contacted during this period of time. [If you use poll results in your speech, include such background—and additional information about questions asked and sampling techniques—in the speech itself. Your audience is bound to be curious and may be critical if you omit any important information about your procedure.]

A SKELETAL OUTLINE FOR INFORMATIVE SPEECHES

It is possible to abstract from this extended demonstration a model for the formal, complete-sentence outlines of informative speeches.

THE INFORMATIVE SPEECH OUTLINE

Foundation of the Speech

Purpose: _____

Central Message: _____

Response Desired: _____

Superstructure of the Speech

Title (optional)

I. Orienting Material: _____

II. Initial Focus: _____

III. Primary Statement 1 _____

    A. _____

    B. _____

        1. _____

        2. _____

IV. Primary Statement 2 _____

    A. _____

        1. _____

        2. _____

            a. _____

            b. _____

    B. _____

V. Primary Statement 3 _____

    A. _____

    B. _____

        1. _____

        2. _____

            a. _____

            b. _____

                1) _____

                2) _____

                    a) _____

                    b) _____

IV. Final Focus: _____

Bibliography

Books:

Articles:

Miscellaneous Citations:

Sometimes speakers like to carry the process of outlining one step further to the *key-word outline*. This speech plan represents the formal outline in miniature, reduced to the few key words that trace the sequence of major points throughout the speech. Such an outline serves as a prompter solely for the use of the speaker during the speech. It especially helps those who would otherwise fall into the trap of reading from the complete-sentence, formal outline. When the speaker relies on the key-word outline, it's sink or speak! There is no full outline to hide behind, so one is forced to talk directly *with* the audience and to let the speech happen naturally, as an act shared by speaker and listeners. It may take some experimenting for you to discover which (if any) kind of outline works best for you during the actual speech, but outright reading is anathema for speakers in most situations. If you can carry the overall pattern of the speech in your head, to be developed in a spontaneous way during actual delivery, so much the better.

RULES FOR OUTLINING

In the process of simulating the outline experience, a number of rules and procedures have been demonstrated.

Control Coordination and Subordination

Statements that carry approximately the same weight and importance and exhibit the same level of abstraction should be placed on the same level in the outline. I's and II's, A's and B's, 1's and 2's, and so on should all seem to belong together in kind and significance, if a speech is to develop in proper proportions. The grouping of statements together implies that they are *coordinate* in kind and importance. Similarly, the principle of *subordination* requires that statements ascend in orderly levels of significance, magnitude, and abstraction from the (a)'s through the I's. Viewed from the top of the hierarchic structure, such statements should descend in the same order, each level being logically inclusive of the next. As a test of proper subordination, ask the following question about your outline: "Does each subordinate idea or each bit of subordinate material make the idea to which it is subordinate understandable or believable or compelling or enjoyable (depending on the purpose)?"[2]

2. Robert T. Oliver, Harold P. Zelko, and Paul D. Holtzman, *Communicative Speaking and Listening* (New York: Holt, 1968), p. 125.

Michael Crawford

Mastery of coordination and subordination implies that the numbering and lettering systems will be consistent throughout the outline and that statements will be indented in a manner that indicates their relative significance. If you turned the outline on its side, a horizon of priorities, indicating primary statements as the peaks, should be clearly revealed. Finally, proper coordination and subordination are tests of judgment. They indicate whether a speaker has command of a subject.

Perhaps the best way to illustrate the importance of coordination and subordination is through an example in which these principles are horribly violated. Consider this specimen:

I. Political campaigns are necessary.
II. Political campaigns are increasingly expensive.
III. Political campaigns are less expensive in Cleveland than they used to be.
    A. Across the nation they are increasingly corrupt.
    B. Across the world they are increasingly rare.

In this example, I and II may be properly coordinated, but III does not belong on their level. Perhaps III is more properly subordinate to II as a kind of exception to the claim made there. On the other hand, A and B are both unrelated to III. A might more properly have the place of III. B might have some business in the speech as a reflection useful in the final focus, where one might conclude that, as expensive and corrupt as campaigns are becoming, we should at least be thankful that the democratic process remains alive in this country.

Build on Properly Worded Primary Statements

Primary statements should be properly stated. They must be concise and vivid, framed in such a way that they touch audience motivations effectively. Very often they can be expressed *in parallel:*

I. We need reform at the national level.
II. We need reform at the state level.
III. We need reform at the local level.
IV. But first we need to reform outselves!

The many advantages of such parallel structure are obvious. Each statement both leads to a major section of speech development and prepares the way for a dramatic summary in the final focus. Because each sentence has the same basic structure, the variations in each sentence are highlighted. The parallel structure develops useful contrast effects and serves as a device of repetition, imprinting its form deep in the minds of the audience. In this case the structure also emphasizes the unity of the speech and clarifies its basic spatial design. The reverberation of primary statements allows the speech to build a crescendo effect, important in maintaining interest among listeners. Thus we have the appeal of *pure form,* of form in and of itself.

Finally, it is important that primary statements in outlines be framed as *simple, independent clauses.* Avoid complex, elaborate, prolonged structures. A sentence that starts developing more than a single unit of information is a clear indication of the need for a further subdivision of the thought in the outline.

Accordingly, do *not* write:

I. Obesity endangers health and our feelings of self-worth, causing us to lose years off our lives and unnecessary anguish in the time we do have.

Instead, write:

I. Obesity is a threat to our well-being.
   A. It endangers health.
      1. Some studies indicate increased heart disease.
      2. Other studies show definite curtailment of life span.
   B. It also damages our self-image.
      1. Obese people often dislike themselves.
      2. They feel they have nothing of worth to give others.

Obviously, the very discipline of breaking a complex statement down into outline form forces us to consider those details that further develop the thought. In the process of simplifying the form, we actually elaborate the substance.

Limit the Number of Primary Statements

In a short speech it is quite difficult to develop more than four primary statements. Indeed, most such speeches will build on two or three such statements. (The three-statement design adds to speech effectiveness the basic symbolic appeal of the number "three".) Among the designs that may depend on three units of development for their effectiveness are space (national–state–local), time (past–present–future), categories, and topics. Among the two-statement designs are cause–consequence, question–answer, analogy, and contrast. Many of the symbolic forms, especially such image combinations as disease–cure, darkness–light, and war–peace, encourage the two-statement pattern. The main consideration is limiting the subject so that it allows time for adequate development.

Support Primary Statements Adequately

No primary statement that is at all controversial or subject to any doubt should ever be offered without supporting facts, testimony, or demonstration. Stripped of such support, informative speech becomes merely *assertive* speech, and communication is reduced to mere projections of ego and emotion or, even worse, to exchanges of prejudice and ignorance. Such speech obviously has no claim to the attention of any group of people for any length of time.

Focus on the Intended Audience

"How will they react to this?" is a test the speaker must apply constantly. That question may call for several examples in one section of the design, hard facts and argument in another, and vivid images in a third. In some places the speaker may have to plan repetitions and in other places definitions. Other sections may call for stories that motivate. At times the speaker may seek to establish identity and at other times to rebuke his or her listeners. All such moments can be legitimate parts of a speech, and their flow and connectedness are never absent from the speaker's mind during preparation of the outline. "What service am I performing for my listeners with this speech (example, image, demonstration, visual aid)?" is another audience-oriented test speakers can apply as they outline. The adaptation check list developed at the end of Chapters 7 and 8 should be especially useful during outlining.

Summary of Major Ideas

Statements in an outline will be superior or inferior to each other in terms of their natural importance to a subject and in terms of their special application to the audience anticipated for the speech.

The foundation of outlining for informative speaking is one's purpose in delivering a speech, the theme one wishes to communicate, and the response one wishes to stimulate in listeners.

Major divisions within the superstructure of informative speeches include orienting material, initial focus, primary statements and their development, and final focus.

Orienting material alerts the audience to the significance of the speech and creates the atmosphere in which it can develop.

The *initial focus* concentrates audience attention on the purpose, theme, and possible benefits to be derived from the speech.

Primary statements form the basic structure of the body of the speech.

The *final focus* concentrates the message that has been developed into a succinct and memorable completing statement.

Exercises and Discussion Questions

1. From a recent issue of *Vital Speeches of the Day*, select a speech on a topic that interests you. Reconstruct the formal outline from which the speech might have been developed. Does the speech seem effective to you? Can you explain such effectiveness (or ineffectiveness) in terms of the reconstructed outline?

2. Practice delivering your next assigned speech first from the formal outline, second from a key-word outline, and third from no outline at all. Which method seems to work best for you?

For Further Reading

For an extensive discussion of "Outlining and Patterns of Arrangement," see Glen E. Mills, *Message Preparation: Analysis and Structure* (New York: Bobbs-Merrill, 1966). John Angus Campbell also has an excellent discussion of arrangement in *An Overview of Speech Preparation* (Chicago, Ill.: SRA, 1976). John L. Vohs and G. P. Mohrmann offer a fresh approach to structuring and outlining in Chapters 8 and 9 of *Audiences, Messages, Speakers* (New York: Harcourt, 1975).

WORDING AND PRESENTING THE INFORMATIVE SPEECH

Language, taken as a whole, becomes the gateway
to a new world. All progress here opens a new
perspective and widens and enriches our concrete
experience. Eagerness and enthusiasm to talk do
not originate in a mere desire for learning or using
names; they mark the desire for the detection and
conquest of an objective world.

ERNST CASSIRER, *An Essay on Man*

> ### WHAT TO LOOK FOR IN
> ### THIS CHAPTER
>
> ---
>
> Learning the goals and techniques of style
>
> Using the voice effectively
>
> Developing facial and gestural expressiveness

Any speech, no matter how well designed and structured, must express itself through language and through the speaker's presentation. Therefore, choosing words to communicate one's ideas and feelings to listeners is a vital consideration. So also must be the physical channel—the voice, face, and body of the speaker—through which these words flow. Chapter 11 discusses these two vital aspects of expression.

THE ART OF STYLE

The art of language selection for speaking in public comes under the traditional subject of *style*. The special way in which we express ourselves through words constitutes our own speaking style.

Desirable Qualities of Style

Language should be *colorful*, so that it gains and holds our attention. For example, as Malcolm X criticized the ineffectiveness of Civil Rights protests, he might have simply said, "The March on Washington did not do its job." But that conclusion gained both color and a kind of mordant humor as his rhetorical genius expressed itself.

What can the white man use now to fool us? After he put down that march on Washington, and you see all through that now. He tricked you. Had you marchin' down to Washington. Yeah. Had you marchin' back and forth between the feet of a dead man named Lincoln and another dead man named George Washington singin' "We Shall Overcome." He made a chump out of you. He made a

Malcolm X speaking to Black Muslims at a rally in New York City, 1963.
Wide World Photos

fool out of you. He made you think you were goin' somewhere and you ended up going nowhere but between Lincoln and Washington.[1]

Language should also be *personal*, so that it reveals the speaker and expresses his or her personality. The views expressed by the speaker should seem objective, in the sense that they reflect accurate observations and express a balanced, informed intelligence. But the speaker's language is also richly subjective, in the sense that his or her character and identity emerge in the speech. Instead of merely saying, "The citizens of this country must not be intimidated by the present economic situation," Franklin Roosevelt expressed his personal confidence and strength of character in the simple phrase "The only thing we have to fear is fear itself."[2]

Good language should be *vivacious*; it should sparkle with life and energy. Malcolm X, one of the pre-eminent stylists of our time, might have said, "Nonviolent protest is weak but force gets results." Instead, he achieved vivacity.

Any time you're livin' in the twentieth century and you're walkin' around here singin' "We Shall Overcome," the government has failed

1. From a transcription of "The Ballot or the Bullet," delivered on April 3, 1964, in Cleveland, Ohio.
2. "First Inaugural Address," March 4, 1933.

*you. This is part of what's wrong with you. You do too much singin'.
Today it's time to stop singin' and start swingin'.... You can't
sing up on freedom, but you can swing up on freedom.*[3]

As this example shows, Malcolm's style had an idiomatic, folk flavor
that gave it unusual pungency and liveliness.

The language of public speech should also be *precise*, giving us
sharply defined pictures of its subjects and of the exact qualities and
issues under discussion. Precision can be critical not only to the transfer
of information but also to persuasion. This is especially true when a
controversy arises at an abstract level—when, for example, we discuss
war, abortion, hunger, or crime as though they were subjects detached
from life for our intellectual consideration. Recently I heard a speech
against abortion that was quite persuasive simply because it described,
as precisely and clinically as possible, how abortions are performed.
Precision eliminates the artificial distance that can loom between a
subject and an audience when discussion occurs at too high a level of
abstraction. George Orwell, author of *Animal Farm* and *1984*, described the consequences of imprecise language as follows:

*In our time, political speech and writing are largely the defence of
the indefensible.... Thus political language has to consist largely
of euphemism, question-begging and sheer cloudy vagueness. Defence-
less villages are bombarded from the air, the inhabitants driven out
into the countryside, the cattle machine-gunned, the huts set on fire
with incendiary bullets: this is called pacification.... People are
imprisoned for years without trial or shot in the back of the neck
or sent to die of scurvy in Arctic lumber camps: this is called elimination of unreliable elements. Such phraseology is needed if one
wants to name things without calling up mental pictures of them....
A mass of Latin words falls upon the facts like soft snow, blurring
the outlines and covering up all the details.*[4]

The language of the speaker is as *simple* as it can be: Why risk losing
one's audience through an unnecessarily complex manner of expression? Kurt Vonnegut, author of *Slaughterhouse-Five* and *Cat's Cradle*,
makes the case for stylistic simplicity this way: "Our audience requires
us to be sympathetic and patient teachers, ever willing to simplify and
clarify—whereas we would rather soar high above the crowd, singing

---

3. From a transcription of "The Ballot or the Bullet."
4. "Politics and the English Language," *Shooting an Elephant and Other Essays* (London:
Secker and Warburg, 1950), pp. 96–97.

like nightingales."[5] The simple manner is usually more honest, direct, and accurate, and it is grounded as much as possible in the concrete. Sojourner Truth reduced the argument over alleged intellectual inferiority among blacks and women to a simple moral issue, using a concrete analogy drawn from everyday life: "If my cup won't hold but a pint, and yours holds a quart, wouldn't you be mean not to let me have a little half-measure full?"[6]

It follows also that such language applies the principle of *economy*: Brevity increases impact. An inflated, extended, artificial style of formal speech is not often effective. It is economy that makes the maxim—the short but memorable statement—so effective. Susan B. Anthony used to good effect an old revolutionary maxim: "Resistance to tyranny is obedience to God."[7]

Finally, and perhaps most important, style should be *appropriate* to the speaker, audience, occasion, and subject. As a rule, the language you generally use will be best for speaking in public too. The effect of "trying on" language that belongs to another time and person is usually ludicrous. This is especially true when young people try to talk like sage octogenarians and when older people parrot what they think is "cool" talk, trying to drink from some semantic fountain of youth.

Many audiences constrain word selection, although a college audience is relatively tolerant with respect to language usage. Good taste is always in season, because any audience resents unnecessarily gross or vulgar language. Make your words as tough and honest as your subject seems to require. Some audiences, of course, are highly sensitive to certain words, which are like land mines for the unwary speaker. Once while speaking to an audience of conservative businessmen, I noticed that the atmosphere had suddenly grown chilly. After the speech my host commented, "You were doin' fine until you said 'labor union.'" For that audience, those words were a devil-term, and the author had committed an unforgivable sin!

Occasions can obviously constrain the choice of words. The language appropriate for a funeral address will not be suited to an after-dinner speech. The classroom occasion, however, is more neutral and flexible; the speaker must create the occasion for the speech within the speech itself. Possibly the academic occasion imposes stricter standards of correct grammar and pronunciation and command of vocabulary.

5. "How to Write with Style," *Newsweek*, Sept. 15, 1980, p. 91.
6. "Ain't I a Woman?", *Feminism: The Essential Historical Writings*, ed. Miriam Schneir (New York: Random House, 1972), p. 95.
7. "The United States of America vs. Susan B. Anthony," *Feminism*, p. 136.

Finally, language should be appropriate to the subject itself. Inappropriate language works only when irony and sarcasm are intended, and here the manner of utterance should immediately make clear what the speaker actually means.

Color, personality, vivacity, precision, simplicity, economy, and appropriateness—all these qualities of style characterize the ideal informative speech.

Techniques of Informative Style

The resources of language reach deep into the symbolic nature of humankind. We can draw on powerful dramatic images (such as light and darkness, sickness and healing, war and peace) that appeal to all people. Or we can use symbolic forms that belong specifically to our society and language that expresses our sense of the present time. This section deals with some of the techniques that make effective use of charismatic language. Many such techniques belong to persuasion and will be discussed in a later chapter. However, at least four major stylistic techniques are as useful in informing as they are in persuading.

COMPARISON AND SIMILE One of the pioneers of modern speech education, A. E. Phillips, wrote near the turn of the twentieth century that speech effectiveness often depends on the speaker's ability to relate the unknown to the known. Phillips called this principle "reference to experience."[8] To use the principle well, you must first understand thoroughly the experience of your listeners so that you know what they are familiar with. Second, you must thoroughly understand your subject. With these understandings you are in position to relate listeners to subject. Such a rhetorical principle seems to depend on contiguity and analogy, which we discussed in Chapter 10. The principle applies when a speaker, anticipating that his or her audience will have difficulty understanding, switches into this manner of expression: "It is like a . . ." or "It's as though it were . . ." The speaker is using the technique of comparison or simile.

The difference between these two subspecies is simply this: When the "like" objects belong to the same category of experience, the technique is a *comparison*. (For example, a speaker might explain to an audience of Bostonians that "The crime problem in Philadelphia is very much like what we have to endure, in that . . ." Here the com-

8. *Effective Speaking* (Chicago, Ill.: Newton, 1908), p. 33.

parison links two cities, members of the same category.) When the link is drawn *across* categories, however, the relationship becomes *figurative,* resulting in a *simile.* (A speaker might say, "The movement swept across this campus like a hurricane, leaving all rules and procedures scattered in its path.") This example shows why a speaker might prefer simile. A simile can create a more dramatic image of a subject, just as a comparison yields more precise, technically accurate relationships. Elizabeth Cady Stanton dramatized inequities in the law concerning women via the following simile: "How like feudal barons you freemen hold your women."[9]

The very word "figurative" suggests that similes and other such forms of expression can stimulate the minds of listeners to create graphic, colorful word pictures of subjects. These images can linger long after the speech occasion itself is forgotten. Clearly these "flowers of language," as they were once called, can also be practical, effective devices of communication.

CONTRAST AND IRONY Closely related to comparison and simile is stylistic contrast. Instead of drawing two subjects close together through comparison, we set them deliberately apart for the sake of sharper definition. Actually the two techniques can work together. "Our crime problem is quite like that of Chicago, quite unlike that of Tokyo" is a joint use of comparison and contrast.

Irony exists when, for the sake of effect, the speaker asserts a similarity or a relationship that is obviously not true. The audience takes delight in discovering the opposite meaning for itself, congratulates itself on its perceptiveness, and feels well disposed toward the speaker, with whom it shares something like a secret.[10] Just as comparison and contrast can work together, irony can cooperate with simile. "He seems like a true encyclopedia on his subject," spoken of someone who had just revealed total ignorance, is an example.

Irony often depends on the speaker's delivery to make its intention clear. Two different ways of saying "That's a fine way to begin the semester" can make for entirely different meanings. One manner of speech simply *confirms* the sense of the words, whereas the other *contradicts* and overrules the simple surface meaning. This violation of normal expectations makes the second usage ironic.

9. "Address to the New York State Legislature, 1854." *Feminism,* p. 115.
10. See Wayne Booth, *A Rhetoric of Irony* (Chicago, Ill.: University of Chicago Press, 1975) and his essay "The Pleasures and Pitfalls of Irony: or, Why Don't You Say What You Mean?" *Rhetoric, Philosophy, and Literature: An Exploration* (West Lafayette, Ind.: Purdue University Press, 1978), pp. 1–13.

METAPHOR Just like its first cousin simile, metaphor crosses the categories by which we sort and make sense of the world. But unlike simile, metaphor issues no warnings, gives us no turn signals in the form of "like" or "as." Rather, metaphor vaults suddenly over categories to present us with an often radical and totally surprising way of seeing and saying things. Thus metaphor can startle us into sharing a perception and experiencing a depiction that is strange to us. Let us assume a rhetorical situation in which the speaker wanted to communicate the idea that sharing knowledge has a religious quality in that (1) it exercises and satisfies a deep and ancient urge in us and (2) it encourages us to grow in wisdom and mental stature. "Sharing knowledge is our Communion," the speaker might conclude, "and the true priests of our time are the teachers." While these metaphors might possibly offend someone in the audience, they should make a clear and memorable impression on most listeners.

Obviously, metaphor can help us see a situation in a new or vivid way. It can give us perspective on a situation. It almost always contains the seed of an attitude. Once implanted in our minds, that seed can grow into a fully developed orientation that influences our statements and actions. Thus metaphor can be both informative and persuasive. It is the most popular and the most potentially powerful tool of rhetorical language available to the speaker.

ONOMATOPOEIA We have already noted how a strategic example can focus perceptions precisely on a subject, especially when the subject is vast and abstract. Onomatopoeia is a quality sometimes achieved in the wording of an example that can add authenticity and graphic realism to the effect created. This ancient Greek term describes the tendency of certain words to imitate what they represent. Words like "buzz," "crawl," "trudge," "bark," "murmur," and "whisper" all offer the special quality of onomatopoeia as they depict. Look for chances to enliven your own speech with onomatopoeia.

PREPARING FOR DELIVERY

After the formal outline is completed and the final wording has been carefully considered, there is only one thing left in speech preparation—rehearsal for presentation. Yet many speeches come to grief on these rocks! Hours can be invested in research and planning, yet the speaker fails to add the vital minutes of practice that would ensure success. During oral practice you actually *hear* what you have been preparing.

"That was very nice, dear, but don't you think you should begin to address yourself to a broader constituency?"

As you rehearse, imagining your audience in front of you, it is amazing how some techniques that looked effective on paper can *sound* dismal and how other excellent ideas for wording and arranging can come to you spontaneously. Here also you must *time* your speech, discovering what must go and what can stay in order to satisfy the time limit set for the assignment. Don't forget that most speeches have a tendency to run longer than planned in rehearsal, as the speaker adjusts to feedback from listeners. Leave yourself some leeway.

Rehearsal is a time for gradually freeing yourself from the detailed written outline and transferring the speech from paper to your head. The following seven steps can be useful in achieving this transfer.

1. Read the entire outline over silently, trying to fix the primary statements in your head.
2. Read the entire outline aloud, looking up from it at appropriate moments to establish eye contact with the imaginary audience.
3. Repeat step 2 several times, trying with each repetition to increase the time spent in eye contact with the audience.

4. Read the outline again silently and slowly, fixing in your mind the orienting material, the initial focus, the final focus, and the sub-points under the primary statements. Do not try to memorize the speech word for word, but do fix the progression of ideas firmly in your mind.
5. Practice the speech aloud, trying not to look at the written outline and reading only quoted material.
6. Check the outline to see what points you may have omitted or placed in improper order.
7. Repeat steps 5 and 6 until you are comfortable delivering the speech.

As much as you try to avoid it, you must often read some quoted material. Deal with this problem in the following ways:

1. Keep the quoted material as brief as possible.
2. Punctuate your reading by looking at your audience frequently so that you maintain contact with them.
3. Place the verbatim material high on the lectern and step back from it, or hold it up near eye level, so that you reduce the angle of departure from direct contact as much as possible. *Do not hold verbatim material down near your waist or at the base of the lectern.* Such positions make the angle of departure from eye contact too radical.
4. Remember that reading lacks the vitality and color of direct communication, and compensate by making your voice and movement as interesting and vigorous as possible.

Don't forget that the rehearsal is a simulation and that the conditions for practice ought to resemble as closely as possible those of the actual speech. Try to obtain access to your classroom to practice your speech.

The instrument of delivery, of course, is your own body. We shall discuss its effective use in terms of *voice* and *movement.*

Voice

Nature has endowed us with the basic working machinery for effective sound production. But, as one book puts it, "Though speech is a human endowment, how well we speak is an individual achievement."[11] If nature has cheated you a bit and left you with a speech impairment, by all means consult the speech pathology clinic on your campus or in your neighborhood. And remember that some of the most effective

11. Jon Eisenson, *Voice and Diction: A Program for Improvement* (New York: Macmillan, 1974), p. vii.

speakers in history have been so-called "speech defectives," who developed a distinctive manner of delivery around the supposed disadvantage.

As you consider the adequacy of your voice for communication, the first thing you will need is a good tape recording of your own normal speech patterns. Don't be surprised at your first reaction: "Is that me?" Then ask yourself the following questions:

1. Does my voice convey my meaning?
2. Would I listen to this voice if I were in the audience?
3. If this voice were not my own, what would I like to change in it?
4. Does this voice present me at my best?

This section considers the speaker's voice in terms of a number of specific vocal qualities, so that you may seek to improve if your answers to the foregoing questions were not altogether satisfactory. If extensive work is needed, consult the readings at the end of the chapter. Here we will discuss pitch, pace, volume, variety, pronunciation, and expressiveness.

PITCH Pitch is the natural placement of the voice on a scale from high to low. Each of us has what is often called an *optimum pitch* or *natural pitch*, the level at which our voices operate with greatest ease and efficiency. Unless we place quite high or quite low on that scale, pitch is not something we should worry about.

The problem some of us encounter with pitch is that our voices can be quite sensitive to our emotional state. The kind of fright experienced by the acutely anxious speakers described in Chapter 2 can force the voice out of its natural range and reveal emotional strain. Normally this problem disappears as one grows better accustomed to the speech situation. A well-prepared speech that has been carefully rehearsed will do much to boost one's confidence and alleviate this problem. Ideally, one attains what might be described as a vocal state of "animated relaxation." A relaxed but animated voice is also more rich and mellow, pleasing us by its quality and timbre. Remember in the meantime that what you hear as strain in your own voice may be overlooked entirely by the audience, which is concentrating more on what you are saying. *Speech-consciousness rather than self-consciousness may be the key to solving most problems of delivery, including the vocal problem of unnatural pitch.* Concentrate on getting your message across as effectively as possible, and let your voice take care of itself.

PACE Many of the vocal problems of novice speakers involve the pace of a speech. One such problem arises when a speaker, intimidated by the speech situation, produces slow, hesitant, faltering speech. A second problem (the opposite of the first) occurs when speakers, nervously wishing to end the ordeal and stimulated further by a massive dose of adrenalin, fire away at such a pace that the audience feels verbally assaulted. Under these conditions, listeners are more concerned with erecting barriers against the verbal barrage than with actually listening. A third problem, frozen or mechanical cadence, is also due to the fear response. Here the speaker becomes rigid and inexpressive. The jaws clatter and sounds are emitted, but they fall into such a dull, singsong pattern that the audience soon withdraws its attention. Perhaps the speaker has made an unconscious decision to evade the threatening faces by lulling them to sleep. He or she has decided to reveal nothing, to risk nothing, and thus to escape from the situation.

You should try to establish a comfortable pace, perhaps a little more deliberate than your normal conversation. You should be flexible enough and relaxed enough to vary the pace, and you should practice the art of pausing for the sake of emphasis and as a transition device. Whether you achieve proper pacing usually depends on whether you have practiced the speech adequately in advance.

VOLUME One of the basic principles of delivery is that a speech must be loud enough to be heard. Yet many speakers ignore this obvious requirement. Perhaps they get involved with the faces nearest them, forgetting that those in the back of a room also have to hear. Or perhaps they are afraid that loudness may be mistaken for assertiveness (a quality they painfully lack). There is no need to blast audience members out of their seats, but clearly one should speak loudly enough to reach the most distant listeners. When you are rehearsing the speech, try speaking louder than you think will be necessary. Exaggeration of both voice and gesture during rehearsal can be a good exercise for public speakers in the early stages of development. Try shouting the following statements:

"They're not going to get away with it!"
"How long will this go on?"
"We can stop them—are you with me?"
"We can find a better way!"
"We can live better lives!"

The following exercises may also be helpful:

1. Count from one to five, gradually increasing the volume of each number. Begin with a barely audible "one" and build to a "five" that would be heard easily across a meeting hall.

2. Repeat this exercise, except that, after you reach "five," count backwards to "one," gradually decreasing your volume until the "one" is barely audible.

Such practice can make you a more flexible speaker with a range of volume adaptable to different rhetorical situations.

VARIETY   Vocal variety suggests an interesting and enthusiastic person who is sensitive and open to the often complex play of meanings in things and who wants to share such awareness with others. Thus vocal variety can add to a speaker's attractiveness, encourage identification, and reinforce credibility. Surveying the sometimes inconsistent evidence, Eisenson concludes that "effective speakers and male speakers considered to have good voices tend to use both greater variability and a wider range of pitch than do less effective speakers."[12]

Some of the most effective kinds of variety are changes of pitch, the sudden softness or loudness that expresses intense feeling, and the dramatic pause that calls attention to something the speaker has just said. The pause provides variety by the way it interrupts the pace of a speech. To develop such variety, practice reading aloud, as expressively as you can, favorite poems and dramatic moments from novels or plays. Try practicing the death scene of the revolutionary bandit Sordo, from Hemingway's *For Whom the Bell Tolls:*

> *Whether one has fear of it or not, one's death is difficult to accept. Sordo had accepted it but there was no sweetness in its acceptance even at fifty-two, with three wounds and him surrounded on a hill.*
>
> *He joked about it to himself but he looked at the sky and at the far mountains and he swallowed the wine and he did not want it. If one must die, he thought, and clearly one must, I can die. But I hate it.*
>
> *Dying was nothing and he had no picture of it nor fear of it in his mind. But living was a field of grain blowing in the wind on the side of a hill. Living was a hawk in the sky. Living was an earthen jar of water in the dust of the threshing with the grain flailed out and the chaff blowing. Living was a horse between your legs and a carbine under one leg and a hill and a valley and a stream with trees along it and the far side of the valley and the hills beyond.*
>
> *Sordo passed the wine bottle back and nodded his head in thanks.*[13]

12. *Voice and Diction: A Program for Improvement,* p. 92.
13. Ernest Hemingway, *For Whom the Bell Tolls* (New York: Scribner, 1945), pp. 312-313.

PRONUNCIATION There are no absolute standards of right and wrong in pronunciation. Rather, such standards are established over time by actual use in a speech community. Especially influential in this natural process are those who lead the community and represent its ideals of sophistication and education. Speakers who depart from such practice, who pronounce words "incorrectly," can seem very foolish and even untrustworthy. Indeed, credibility can suffer instantly and irreparably from a mispronounced word.

If you are in doubt about how to pronounce a word, consult the latest dictionary for current, acceptable practice in your speech community. An especially useful reference work is John S. Kenyon and Thomas R. Knott's *A Pronouncing Dictionary of American English* (Springfield, Mass.: Merriam, 1953), which indicates how the three major dialect regions, Eastern, Southern, and General American, vary in standard pronunciations of words. Also useful is W. Cabell Greet's *World Words: Recommended Pronunciations* (New York: Columbia University Press, 1948), which suggests how 25,000 words from foreign languages might be presented in oral English. A third very useful book is the *NBC Handbook of Pronunciation*, 3rd ed. (New York: T. Y. Crowell, 1964), which is especially easy to use.

Insofar as dialect is concerned, there is again no absolute right or wrong, and all standards derive from the relative manners and customs of various social groups. No one dialect is innately superior to another. There certainly are times, occasions, and audiences for which certain distinct dialects are an advantage or a disadvantage, either encouraging or discouraging identification and credibility. If your dialect reflects the best standards of your own community, you shouldn't rush to tamper with your speech and to obliterate what may represent a valuable association with a cultural group. If, however, the dialect would create barriers to understanding for significant portions of the audience, then you have real cause for concern. Part of adaptation to the public speaking situation may be intense developmental work in establishing habits of pronunciation that both preserve your identity, protecting authentic ties to culture, and at the same time open the door of communication to others from other social groups. Good pronunciation can both confirm and transcend the speech habits developed in our youth.

Absolutely unacceptable by any standards are two common faults: (1) lazy vocal patterns that mumble out words as though the speaker's mouth were full of mush and (2) pompous, inflated, pretentious vocal patterns in which the speaker affects language that he or she thinks is stylish. Your own public speaking manner should simply represent your best verbal behavior within your normal style of conversational speech.

EXPRESSION A final consideration is how the voice can reveal the speaker. As you practice your speech, let your voice say that you are enthusiastic about your subject and that you want to communicate it. Moreover, your voice should register the emphasis you give to things. Emphasis emerges within each sentence and among all the sentences of a speech. It gives a kind of "third dimension" to oral communication that is denied to writing.

Speakers should also practice to achieve the effect of intensity, which can make one eloquent. Such speech is humanistic because it *realizes* the speaker as well as the speech during significant moments of utterance.

Movement

Much of what we have said about voice applies as well to movement. Faults in voice often carry over into faults in movement, and vice versa: A frozen face usually accompanies a frozen voice. The same close ties occur when the speaker is able and accomplished. Vivacity of voice and movement usually go together. Movement will be discussed with respect to *face* and *gesture*.

FACIAL EXPRESSION Facial expressiveness is a major communication resource for all primates. We engage each other's attention through our eyes. The face is best thought of as a mirror for the meanings of the speech. Indeed, the face can even overrule and reverse the surface meanings of words. This is especially true when the speaker intends irony or sarcasm.

Because the speaker's face contains many and subtle cues, the frozen-face–frozen-voice syndrome can be a serious barrier to communication. Usually this problem is a clear sign of fear. Communication implies risk and vulnerability, so the speaker decides not to risk exposure—not to communicate. The frozen face represents not a mirror but a mask behind which the speaker hides. The only solution is hard practice, experience, and growing confidence. Concentrate on developing a responsive face, especially as you practice the opening of your speech.

For an appropriate exercise, try to communicate with facial expressions only (no words) the feelings of fear, anger, hatred, love, inspiration, reverence, pity, joy, mirth, doubt, sorrow, uncertainty, confidence, and determination. If you don't develop more flexibility, at least you'll give your facial muscles a good workout!

GESTURE Gesture includes movement of the hands, walking, and general stance and bearing. *The goal of effective gesture is full, free, purposeful action that supports and advances the thought of the speech.* The body becomes a secondary system of communication to reinforce the primary symbolic medium of words. The time to be conscious of gesture is during practice and rehearsal. During the actual speech, your attention is devoted entirely to your ideas and to the faces in front of you. Even during rehearsal you are never concerned with how a certain movement will look in itself, but rather with how it can punctuate, underscore, or clarify the ideas you are trying to get across.

Basic to any effective movement is a concept we can call the *gestural circle*. The major arcs of this circle are readiness, preparation, execution, and return. As Figure 11.1 suggests, all movement in a speech revolves around the idea being expressed. No gesture or sound is included for its own sake; All are held in orbit by the speech purpose and theme. The gestural circle begins with *readiness*. In order to move in response to your ideas, your hands and body must be in positions that invite (or at least do not inhibit) responsive movement. The *preparation* phase of gesturing, especially pertinent to hand gestures, comes as the hand "cocks" itself to deliver a gesture. In emphasizing strongly an expression such as "I don't know," one can raise one's hand in preparation for the gesture stroke itself, which falls as an emphatic accompaniment to the word "know." The *execution* phase of gesturing is the actual performance of the movement. *The return* phase carries the face, hand, or foot back to a position of alert readiness for the next gesturing movement.

Achieving Purposeful Movement

When you are introduced as the next speaker, you should move quickly to the front of the room, arrange your notes on the table or lectern, and take a proper stance for speaking. Such a stance is any comfortable, alert position near your listeners from which you can move easily in response to your own thoughts. Most speakers prefer a position off to the side or even in front of the lectern, so that the audience has a full view of them. Such a position seems to release one to walk in response to the speech. As you engage a certain person in eye contact, you can

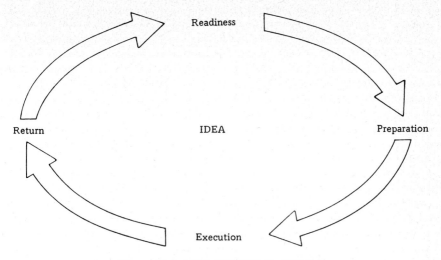

Figure 11.1 THE GESTURAL CIRCLE

step toward that person, perhaps coming to a stop as you complete the thought and as your hand completes an accompanying gesture. Then, as you begin a new thought, you can engage eye contact with another person in another part of the room and step in that direction.

Try the following exercise. Take a position frontal to an imaginary audience with your feet spread slightly (not crossed or locked together). The stance should be *open* in the sense that one foot is advanced slightly beyond the other, the heels closer together and the toes pointing in directions that form about a 45° angle. From this position, speak *without movement or gesture* the following sequence of phrases as though they formed the final focus for an informative speech.

1. So now you see where we stand.
2. Some tell us that the problem will go away, that in the meantime we just have to learn to live with it.
3. Others urge a vigorous attack on causes and effects. "We just can't wait," they say, "for time to heal this sickness."
4. Still others say there is no solution. "Let's be realistic," these people advise, "and accept this problem as part of life. Why beat our heads on a stone wall?"
5. So how do you feel about it? I've shown you the facts and outlined what different experts advise us to do. The choice is yours.

Now try the same sequence again, imagining an audience in front of you. Present sentence 1 to the back center of this audience. For

Ellis Herwig 1980

sentence 2, find a face near the front left and take three or four steps toward that person, coming to a stop as you approach the end of the sentence, especially the emphatic "live with it." As you begin sentence 3, turn to a face near the front center and take several steps toward that person, coming to a stop with the word "effects." Present the second sentence in 3 directly to that face without moving further. With the sentences in 4, move on to another face front right, coming to a stop after several steps on the word "solution." As you go into the concluding sentences in 5, take several steps back so that you are once again addressing the group as a whole. Come to a final resting position before beginning the second sentence in 5.

This exercise should indicate how movement can punctuate and dramatize a speech, adding interest and color. But if your body is "captured" behind a lectern, it is very difficult to make purposeful movements. Such a position does not establish readiness. Now repeat the same exercise, this time adding expressive hand gestures. Try especially to emphasize with gestures such words as "now" in sentence 1 (note how the voice rises in congruence with the execution of the gesture) and such verbs as "live" in sentence 2 and "wait" in sentence 3. As these gestures add another dimension of life and color, observe how they also animate the voice and face. Indeed, the entire body becomes a self-reinforcing instrument for the thought being expressed, in which all sources of movement interanimate each other. Only when these sources somehow work out of phase, or fail to contribute to the total message, should we single them out for special attention.

One quite common gestural fault is associated with the readiness phase. Speakers, wondering what to do with their hands, may decide to lock them behind their backs. This is another unconscious effort to escape communication. As soon as the hands clasp each other behind, other movements become stilted, the faces become wooden, the voices lose animation. As such speakers proceed, an observant listener may notice telltale twitches in the arms and shoulders, signs of frustrated impulses to gesture. If these hands would only release each other, soon one would see them hanging at the speaker's sides, and then rising in response to the thought, preparing and executing gestures quite spontaneously. Often this is exactly what one sees during the first speeches in a public speaking class. When the hands finally struggle through to gesture, the results are sometimes as dramatic as if someone had just plugged in a Christmas tree. What was dull suddenly sparkles. What was listless is suddenly full of life.

A SAMPLE INFORMATIVE SPEECH

Thressia Taylor emerged as one of the most popular students in her public speaking class. Possessed of a radiant personality, she delivered her speeches with considerable warmth and power. Because she built a reputation early as a speaker who did careful research, she enjoyed high credibility. At the time she presented this speech, Taylor, a nurse at a city hospital, had lost over forty pounds in her own weight-reduction program. The class was aware of her courage as a dieter and of her profession. Therefore, they had many reasons to listen with respect to her views on nutrition.

Because she enjoyed such credibility, she did not feel it necessary to cite respected authorities and publications in order to affirm her conclusions and advice. Normally, such citations would be required to establish an informative speech as worthy of serious attention and respect. Had her analysis and advice departed from that usually heard by her listeners, even she would have been compelled to introduce experts to testify in support of her claims. As it is, her major rhetorical problem is to build on, enliven, and dramatize what many of her listeners already know but perhaps would prefer to forget.

As she meets this challenge, observe how she anticipates a general class interest in the care of fine cars and how she builds much of her informative speech on the basic design of a sustained analogy, the metaphor of the human body as machine. As the audience became conscious of this device and curious about how she would maintain the figurative comparison throughout the speech, interest remained high and favorable attention was assured for what otherwise might have been a fairly commonplace message.

If you had a new diesel-fuel Mercedes Benz, would you use regular gas in it? "I would hardly be that dumb," you may be thinking. But many of us do abuse—every day and far more stupidly— a much more valuable machine, the most valuable we will ever possess. I am talking about our own bodies.

Perhaps we need a plate hanging from the ends of our noses that would read: "Feed this body nourishing food only." Because many of us don't think anything about eating junk foods. We skip meals and never eat breakfast. We think we are getting plenty to eat, when often we are sadly undernourished.

What is nutrition and how important is it? Unfortunately, when a part of the body wears out, there are no parts stores around the corner. How long you will last depends a great deal on what you eat. Nutrition starts with the food you eat and how your body uses that fuel to live, to grow, to have energy for the many things you do, and to support your health.

Good nutrition not only helps you feel good—it also helps you look good. And it all starts with food that not only tastes good but is good for you.

Food is made up of basic chemical substances called nutrients. These nutrients include protein, carbohydrate, fat, vitamins and minerals, and water. Nutrients serve three major functions. First, they supply energy for your activity and warmth. Second, they provide for growth and repair of your body tissues. Third, they help regulate the many complex processes of your body.

Protein, the first nutrient we shall consider, must build, maintain, and repair all tissues of your body, as well as assist in many other bodily functions. Protein is made up of substances called amino acids. There are two types of amino acids: the essential ones, which your body cannot make, and the nonessential ones, which your body can produce. While all the amino acids are necessary, proteins with the essential amino acids in the proportions needed by your body have superior nutritional quality. These essential amino acids come from animal sources such as meat, fish, eggs, cheese, and milk. Nonessential amino acids are found in vegetables like dry beans, peanuts, and cereal. A serving of protein would be from one and a half to two and a half ounces of meat. You must have two servings or more each day to keep this body builder on the job.

The second nutrient we shall consider is carbohydrate, or starch and sugar. This nutrient is important not only because it is our least expensive source of energy but also because it helps our bodies use fat efficiently. We should get most of our carbohydrate from whole grain, enriched or fortified breads and cereals, and fruits and vegetables, because these foods also supply important vitamins and minerals. You should have four or more servings a day to keep your machine well tuned and running smoothly.

The third nutrient on our list is fat, our most concentrated source of energy. Doctors tell us that we eat too much of it and recommend that we limit our intake of calories from fat. Otherwise, we may get sluggish and carry too heavy a load for our engines.

Vitamins and minerals, which make up our fourth nutrient category, regulate the body. Some minerals are also necessary for building bones, teeth, and red blood cells, but neither vitamins nor minerals supply energy. You can't take them in little pills and expect them to take the place of good fuel.

Finally we come to water, a nutrient absolutely essential for life. You can live longer without food than without water. It is an important part of every cell in your body, and it constitutes about one-half of your body weight. Water carries nutrients to and waste from cells in the body, aids in the digestion and absorption of food, and helps regulate body temperature. Drink plenty of it, and keep the rust out of your radiator!

You know that most cars last only until you make the final payment. Perhaps we can't do much about that, but we can prolong the life of this other, more precious machine we've been talking about. Providing it with quality fuel in the right quantity is the first step in preserving and protecting this great marvel of natural technology.

Summary of Major Ideas

Style is the art and strategy of language selection.

Good language for speech is colorful, personal, vivacious, precise, simple, economical, and appropriate.

Comparison relates items within the same category; *simile* forges links between items in different categories. Comparison is more precise, simile more dramatic.

Contrast sets items apart for the sake of sharper definition. Irony, by asserting a close relationship between items, actually emphasizes their distance from each other.

Metaphor can startle us into new awareness by relating subjects that are not usually associated.

Onomatopoeia is the tendency of certain words (such as "hum") to imitate their subjects, thereby achieving unusual authenticity of depiction.

Speech-consciousness rather than self-consciousness is the key to remedying most kinds of faulty delivery.

One's pronunciation in public speaking should reflect the best standards of one's own community and should be comprehensible to others outside the community but within the same language system.

An expressive voice registers enthusiasm, emphasis, and intensity.

The goal of effective gesture is full, free, purposeful action that supports and advances the thought of the speech. Basic to any effective movement is the gestural circle: readiness, preparation, execution, and return.

Exercises and Discussion Questions

1. Scan the morning newspaper, your favorite magazine, or the nightly news on television for examples of comparison, simile, contrast, irony, metaphor, and onomatopoeia. Bring these specimens to class for discussion. How effective were they in context, and what tasks did they perform?

2. "Charades" is an excellent game for developing expressiveness of gesture. Divide the class into two sections. Each person in each section then attempts *by movement only* to suggest a commonly known title from categories such as books, plays, motion pictures, television series, poems, or speeches, however extensive the class may wish to make the list of such categories. The communicator announces the category, and the others in his or her section then try to guess the title from the visual cues given. Proceed by alternating sections until everyone has "communicated." A time limit can be imposed. The game is won by the section that guesses its titles in the shortest time. In order to play most effectively, develop a common "vocabulary" of gesture—predetermined signs for such useful meanings as number of words (perhaps indicated by the number of fingers held up), "little word" (hands close together), "sounds like" (perhaps a cupped hand by the ear), "looks like" (per-

haps hands rounded at eyes), and "you're on the right track, keep going" (gestures of encouragement) in addition to the standard head shakes indicating "yes" and "no."

For Further Reading

For classic treatments on the subject of style, see Aristotle's *Rhetoric*, Book III, and Longinus's *On the Sublime*. Of more recent vintage are Jane Blankenship, *A Sense of Style: An Introduction to Style for the Public Speaker* (Belmont, Calif., Dickenson, 1968); G. P. Mohrmann, *Composition and Style in the Writing of Speeches* (Dubuque, Iowa: William C. Brown, 1970); Michael Osborn, *Orientations to Rhetorical Style* (Chicago, Ill.: SRA, 1976); and Kenneth Burke's sensitive approach to the power of language in *Language as Symbolic Action* (Berkeley, Calif.: University of California Press, 1966).

Among the useful works for developing your voice are Jon Eisenson, *Voice and Diction: A Program for Improvement*, 3rd ed. (New York: Macmillan, 1974); Elise Hahn, *Basic Voice Training for Speech*, 2nd ed. (New York: McGraw-Hill, 1956); John A. Gasham and Glenn G. Gooder, *Improving Your Speech* (New York: Harcourt, 1960); and Paul Heinberg, *Voice Training for Speaking and Reading Aloud* (New York: Ronald Press, 1964).

IV
THE PERSUASIVE SPEECH

Though it is desirable to study informative and persuasive speaking separately, informative and persuasive elements often intertwine in actual communication as intimately as the chord progressions in a Bach fugue or the vines on an ancient Greek vase. At the very least, persuasion and information assist each other over the barriers that can block communication. This section first considers the challenge and design of persuasive speeches. It then takes up the relationship between argument and persuasion and discusses the arts of outlining and expressing the persuasive speech.

Persuasion may well be the most important single theme in the study of rhetoric. Aristotle observed that persuasion is necessary to make the truth effective. It is not enough simply to *know* what is true and to want to share that truth with others. One must also recognize the obstacles that stand in the way of their receiving that truth and know how to overcome those barriers. Isocrates's thoughts gleam as brightly today as they did twenty-five hundred years ago when the great Greek educator first recorded them:

> Because there has been implanted in us the power to persuade each other and to make clear to each other whatever we desire, not only have we escaped the life of the wild beasts, but we have come together and founded cities and made laws and invented arts; and, generally speaking, there is no institution devised by man which the power of speech has not helped us to establish.[1]

1. *Antidosis.* 254. *Isocrates*, trans. George Norlin (New York: Putnam, 1929), 11:327.

12
THE CHALLENGE AND
DESIGN OF PERSUASION

There is a weird power in a spoken word. . . .
JOSEPH CONRAD, *Lord Jim*

The purpose of this chapter is to introduce the nature of persuasion, to define the challenge you will face as a persuader, and to identify the basic designs that lend themselves to persuasive speeches.

CHARACTERISTICS OF PERSUASIVE SPEAKING

We can define the nature of persuasive speaking by contrasting it with the six essential qualities of informative speaking developed in Chapter 9.

1. Whereas informative speaking tends to clarify our options in choice situations, persuasive speaking urges us to *make a choice*. It tends to reduce our options until only one choice seems to remain. Thus one of the basic strategies of persuasive speech is the systematic elimination of alternatives. Here informing and persuading can function together as alternating phases within an overall process of communication. Information expands our awareness of options; then persuasion directs our attention to the most desirable option. For example, one phase of a public discussion of the energy crisis is to let us know our alternatives. The second phase is to secure our commitment to the best course of action. Information illuminates, and persuasion evaluates.

2. Whereas informative speaking focuses on its subject, persuasive speaking turns more to the audience and concentrates on controlling *audience response*. The speaker–listener relationship becomes even more vital in persuasive speaking.

3. As the speaker–audience relationship grows more significant, leading and following roles also assume greater importance. The traditional part for the speaker is that of leader, although Plato argued in his

Gorgias that speakers tend to follow the crowd rather than lead them. At the very least, however, speakers must articulate the needs and desires of those who hear them. There is no question that the roles of public speaking and leadership naturally go together. Speakers must function well as leaders if listeners are to play their part as followers. Any audience instinctively inspects a speaker for leadership qualities, and speaker credibility is crucial in the persuasive context.

4. Whereas informative speech asks little commitment from its listeners, persuasive speech typically asks a great deal. The low tension of informative speaking gives way to the *high tension* of persuasive speaking. And the minimal risk involved in attending to information gives way to the considerable risk of exposing oneself to persuasion. What if the speaker should betray your trust? What if the courses of action proposed turn out to be disasters? At its most extreme, persuasion may ask audience members to assume a new identity: to become a Marxist or feminist or Buddhist. Jesus warned His followers that, if they would be truly persuaded by His message, they must be born again.

5. Whereas informative speech stresses clarity and interest, persuasive speech often emphasizes the arousal of *powerful feelings*. Such feeling may be required to overcome human inertia and to set a group marching together toward the goal.

6. Persuasive speaking begins where informative speaking ends—with the strategic depiction of reality. Beyond depiction and arousal, in which audience emotions are stimulated and engaged, is group identification, in which listeners discover a relationship with each other and with the speaker as leader. This phase invites a *plan of action*, a vision that reveals the way to a better future.

Beyond the selling of a plan of action is persuasion that helps the group remember what it is and how it came about. The speaker's intent is to prevent lethargy and loss of enthusiasm from undermining group identity. Such persuasion often occurs on special occasions, such as presidential inaugural addresses or Memorial Day proclamations. It can also occur within a single speech, as the speaker reminds us of the importance of some value before applying that value to an immediate problem. One speech may exhibit several or even all of these persuasive functions, but it usually emphasizes one of them. For example, it may challenge a depiction, stimulate emotions, invite group identity, propose a plan of action, or celebrate group values. The greater the challenge of the speech and the more risk it asks its audience to take, the more comprehensive it will be. Martin Luther King's final speech, which called for a total commitment to the sanitation strike in Memphis, placed that single moment of time at the center of the vast sweep of history. Listeners could *see* the world that called for their commitment, could *feel* the pain of oppressed people, could sense their *role* in a clear group identity affirming King as leader and the Memphis mayor as villain, could resolve on new *action* along the lines indicated by King, and could feel themselves exalted in a triumphant *renewal* of the spirit behind their cause.

THE CHALLENGE OF PERSUASION: ADAPTING TO THE AUDIENCE

Audience and situation determine the need for persuasion. Informative speakers generally assume an audience that is at least neutral if not favorable to their message. Listeners will receive what they say, once they gain undivided interest and attention. The rhetorical world they assume is one in which competing speakers do not usually enter the picture. Therefore, speakers are free to concentrate on communicating the features of a subject as effectively as possible. The only enemies are distraction, boredom, and detachment.

Persuasion, however, begins with a vision of the world as filled with forces contending for our concern and commitment. This world provides barriers that you as a persuader must overcome if you are to be successful. Many of these barriers arise from the nature of listeners:

1. Their comfort with a way of life that you would ask them to change

2. Their reluctance to listen to arguments that call for risk and sacrifice

3. Their belief in values that your position might change or endanger

4. Their previous commitment to other, competing ways of thinking and courses of action

5. Their previous perception of you as (perhaps) someone less than an expert on the issue at hand

You may even confront hostile listeners or opponents who are alert for any possible flaw in the speech you present. Little wonder, then, that so much can go wrong in persuasion. Sometimes even effective persuasive efforts see few immediate results, as the good words slowly erode opposition.

Clearly, the persuasive speaker must prepare with an anticipated audience in mind. To the audience analysis checklists at the conclusions of Chapters 7 and 8, the following questions must be added.

Fidel Castro, president of Cuba, speaking to the United Nations General Assembly, 1979.

Wide World Photos

1. Can you show that the situation you would bring about is worth its cost in comfort and risk?

2. Can you prove that the attitude or action you urge is compatible with and even affirms audience values?

3. Can you cope with previous audience loyalties and commitments?

Justifying the Cost

You must prove that the situation you would bring about is worth the price your listeners must pay. This task is threefold.

Counteract the tendency of listeners to exaggerate this cost. In order to justify *not* acting, we often exaggerate the difficulty of the action proposed. You must be able to *show us to ourselves* undertaking action effectively. "We can do it, and here's the way we're going to do it" should be your theme.

Prove that compelling reasons justify the cost. You must present vivid images of the need for action and evidence to establish that these images are authentic and reliable. You must have command of the facts, must reason correctly from these facts, and often must cite experts who support your conclusions. The greater the cost required, the more compelling must be these reasons to act. The more surprising and shocking the images of need, the more conclusive and reliable the evidence must seem.

Indicate that the new world to be created will be more satisfying. You must offer a vision of the future which shows the better life we are working to create. "I may not get there with you," said Martin Luther King, "but I can see the Promised Land." The speaker must share that vision with his or her listeners.

Affirming Values

You must satisfy listeners that the attitude or plan of action you urge is compatible with accepted values, or you must show that other and greater values will be served. This issue is all-important, because the values people hold become the premises from which they reason on fundamental issues. For example, if listeners are wary of your new welfare program because "people ought to take care of themselves," then you may have to style your program as "a hand up, not a handout." You must show how people will be able to take care of themselves, once this program goes into effect. And moreover, other great values, such as education for one's children and a healthy, secure, and comfortable life, will be served by your program.

You cannot convince us by ignoring or scoffing at our values. As you respect them, you honor us. By your skill at depiction you must help us *see* how our values will be served by your program. And as you reason from our values, using them as premises for your argument, you create the grounds for true identification between us and yourself.

Coping with Previous Audience Commitment

You must adjust to the loyalties and commitments you discover already existing among your listeners. The *set* of the "audience mind" as it first encounters the persuasive message is crucial to the reception of a message. The set of that mind also weighs heavily in your selection of the tone, style, and form of the message. Let us assume a situation in which I am campaigning for the Tennessee Valley Authority, a once hotly contested issue in the Southeast. In a given day I must make three speeches. In the morning I address a group of opponents, in the afternoon a group that has yet to make up its mind, and in the evening a group of supporters.

As I arrive at my morning meeting, I encounter a chilly and distrustful atmosphere. *In the speech I give to opponents, the beginning is probably the most crucial phase of the speech,* because, if I cannot dispel any of this suspicion and hostility, my message will never be heard. So I decide on an approach that will acknowledge right away what my listeners already know, that I am not in agreement with many of them. My hope is that such candor will establish the beginnings of trust, if not identification. If they cannot see me as a friend, they may at least see me as an honest opponent, and that could start a thaw.

So I say, "Some of you may wonder why a person like me should be in favor of the TVA. After all, this is my home. I was born in these hills, went to church here at the Shady Mountain Methodist Church, attended Shady Mountain elementary school . . ." So I am off, building a little family history that I hope will remove the horns they had expected to find on me. After a story or two that will confirm the authenticity of my background, I will discuss the values that they and I together hold dear. Then I will connect those values to my position, using evidence they should respect. Throughout, my language must never be inflammatory or excitable, for I do *not* wish to arouse these listeners—not yet. Until I can get them to consider my point of view, I cannot hope to win their emotional commitment. Today I simply want to secure a favorable beachhead in their awareness. My purpose is to take away some of the sting of their opposition and, among the thoughtful opponents especially, to raise a question or two in their minds and send them away wondering whether there might not be another legitimate point of view.

At the afternoon meeting I anticipate people who are interested in the issues but are withholding their commitments. The question is why they have not yet committed themselves to my side. Perhaps they lack vital information. Perhaps they need reassurance on one or two important points. Or perhaps they have not yet been motivated to the point of commitment: They may need to be aroused in favor of my side. I have just described the major challenge to my speech, and (probably) the order in which it will develop. After establishing common ground and shared heritage at the beginning, I will offer vital information, then provide reassurance on the points that are blocking commitment, and finally add motivating material. *The major challenge for the persuasive speech to undecided listeners comes in the body of the speech.* I want to convert them into supporters, and I see a real chance to do so.

My evening audience is made up of people who are presumably already committed to my position. Why are they there, and why am I speaking to them? Perhaps some of them have lost a little enthusiasm and need to be reminded of the issues at stake. They simply need to be inspired: to review the reasons that bring us together, to feel again the emotional ties that connect us, to celebrate our common values and heroes, and to renew our commitment against the forces that oppose us. These listeners may have to be reminded of the soundness of our plan and sustained and encouraged for the struggle ahead. Some may need fresh direction and explanation of recent events in our campaign. *The most crucial phase of the persuasive speech to supporters is the conclusion.* It usually determines whether listeners leave with a new spirit and a clear purpose.

Often, of course, the speaker does not know the prior position of the audience on the issue at hand. Or listeners may represent the entire spectrum of possible opinion. Before such unknown or mixed audiences, you would be wise to aim at the center of the target, assuming that a good number of the listeners are willing to reserve judgment, prepared to listen to vital facts and arguments, in need of reassurance upon certain important points, and open to motivational appeals. Such a speech should not overly antagonize opponents, should hearten supporters, and may well secure commitments from those "undecideds" in the center.

It is clear from this analysis that the challenge of persuasion is considerable. The persuasive situation is charged with risk; speakers may not succeed, and their efforts may even backfire. The audience risks the cost of commitment, the possible disaster of a wrong commitment, and at best the inconvenience of change. Indeed, so much is at stake in most persuasive situations that speakers must be utterly convinced of the ethical soundness of the attitudes and actions they are advocating. Whatever persuasive strategy you employ before hostile, undecided, or supportive listeners, no persuasion is justified unless you can give affirmative answers to these questions:

1. Have I done all I can do to put together a responsible speech that squares with the facts as I know them and unfolds its reasoning correctly?

2. Am I myself willing to accept the course of action or the attitude I am recommending to others? If I have reservations, do I confess them honestly in the speech?

INFORMATIVE/PERSUASIVE DESIGNS

The design for a persuasive speech reflects the general strategy of that speech. This strategy is selected in light of the subject, the anticipated

Ellis Herwig 1980

set of audience mind, the intention of the speaker, and whatever other special circumstances apply at the moment of speaking.

Chapter 9 noted in passing how certain designs for informative speech can also be used persuasively. Now we shall examine this usefulness in greater detail.

Time

The *historical pattern* becomes persuasive when you are trying to rearrange your listeners' view of the past so that they see the present and the future in a different light. For example, British and American speakers before the American Revolution saw the past relationships between their countries quite differently. In their speeches, the British typically remembered an extensive sequence of generous acts performed by the Mother Country for one of its more ungrateful colonies. American speakers, on the other hand, recalled a history full of exploitation and abuse inflicted on a long-suffering people by an arbitrary and tyrannical power far removed from their shores. The one view called for firm discipline of the rebellious colony; the other called for the colony's protest and defiance. Out of this clash between discipline and defiance came revolution.

If the historical pattern seems appropriate to your speech, remember that the more you depart from the image of the past we already accept, and the more important that prior image is to our orientation, the greater your need to present compelling evidence to back up your claims. Your case for a rhetorical reconstruction of the past must be so convincing that no reasonable person could deny it.

Hypothetical time allows you to show the audience an image of themselves undertaking some action urged by you. The dramatic appeal of such an image influences audience members to undertake the action. Likewise, *predictive time* becomes a design strategy for persuasion when you contrast the bleak future that will befall listeners *unless* they undertake some action and the bright future that awaits them *if* they do.

Space

The kind of contrasting spatial design that gives us the view of war first from the general on the hill and then from the soldier in the trenches below can be persuasive as well as informative. Elevation suggests superiority, but it can also mean arrogance, an unjustified pre-eminence over others, and even a loss of touch with reality. In the example mentioned, you could steer the persuasive message either way. You might conclude that the soldier in the trenches lacks perspective and that only the general can really see what's going on. Let the generals conduct the war, while the rest of us stay in line. Or you might argue that the general on the hill has an unrealistic view. Only the soldier in the trenches truly experiences the catastrophe of war. All war is evil, and those who would urge it on others should be made to come down from the hill and learn what it really means to engage in battle.

Obviously, how you position your subjects in space projects your values about them. If your listeners accept your sense of vertical arrangement, they are likely to accept your values too, and that may well be your ultimate intent.

Figurative space (Chapter 8) can be a very potent symbol for the overall design of persuasion. To picture us throughout a speech as climbing toward the speaker's solution, with occasional glimpses downward into the pit that awaits us if we falter, is to provide a powerful inducement. Often the tone of the speech and even the voice of the speaker rise as the persuasive argument reaches its conclusion.

Categories

Categories reflect our habits of thinking. Persuaders, for example, recognizing our attraction to the number three, may develop three main reasons for our accepting their argument or may divide their presentation in terms of (1) the need for a change, (2) principles to guide change, and (3) a proposed solution. When the categories the audience is accustomed to are substantive and deeply ingrained ("Men belong at work, women in the home." "Caucasians are the superior race." "The American way of life is best."), the persuader who finds these categories to be obstacles must confront them by presenting vivid, authenticated word-pictures to show that the old ways of thinking are out of touch with reality and to offer a new way of looking at the world.

Categories, then, offer two options for design. You can use them to provide a conventional approach to your subject, or you can confront them if they pose an ethical and practical barrier to your purpose.

Motivational Topics

Speeches that touch human motives are often persuasive, and the appeal to motives can become an overall principle of design in a persuasive speech. Thus you could design arguments that show progressively how a proposed course of action would satisfy basic human needs; ensure safety and security; make possible an affiliation with new, desirable groups; develop group esteem and pride; and open the doors to advancement and self-realization. Or you might pick the one universal human need that seems most relevant in the situation and bring all of your speech to bear on it alone. Thus a speech urging handgun control might deal strictly with the issue of safety, whereas a speech urging an educational program might concentrate on our desire to make something better of ourselves.

Causation

Most people believe that all effects have causes, and our curiosity for information makes us want to know how and why things come about. It is just one further step to conclude that we can *control* effects by controlling causes. The persuasive speaker can design a speech that (1) identifies some effect and defines it as a problem, (2) isolates the cause of this problem, (3) proposes a plan that will change or remove this underlying cause, and (4) points to the new and desirable effects such a change will bring about. When Susan B. Anthony used the causation design in one of her favorite speeches, she (1) described the economic injustices suffered by women, (2) identified the cause of those problems as the lack of political power, (3) advocated voting rights for women to provide such power, and (4) argued ingeniously that political rights for women would also aid working men, because exploited women lower the wage base for the entire working class.[1]

Never pass up the chance to show probable opponents how they too might benefit from your proposal. You may not convert them, but you can take some of the steam out of their opposition.

Repetition

Often thought of as a stylistic device, repetition can become a principle of organization in persuasion. You can design a speech so that the audience is exposed repeatedly to an idea until it is driven deep into their minds.

One way of achieving this effect is to accumulate examples, one after the other, each one more compelling than the last, until the conclusion you draw seems inescapable. This mode of repetition is actually the rhetorical use of *induction*. Inductive thinking draws its conclusions from an inspection of reality. In persuasive induction, the speaker's artful accumulation of examples creates the impression of such an investigation. You might ask, for example, "Is there hunger in this city? Let me tell you the story of Mary Jane, age 1, and of Rose Wilson, age 81, and of Marie Smith, who will soon give birth to still another malnourished child." Your speech would then proceed to depiction, letting each of these three cases represent a large class of affected persons. Each example would be calculated to touch off a different, reinforcing response in listeners.

Such a design is especially useful when the idea being advanced is somewhat novel or radical. Repeated exposure in various artful ways can make the idea seem more familiar and less disturbing by the end of the speech.

Analogy

The use of analogy as a design option for informative speaking is the strategy of relating the unknown to the known, so that comprehension crosses from one to the other. But more than comprehension and understanding can cross in analogy. We form powerful attitudes that become attached to certain subjects, and to relate them to other subjects is to invite a crossing of attitudes. This is the basis for the use of analogy as a design option in persuasion. Knowing your audience's

1. "Woman Wants Bread, Not the Ballot!" *Feminism: The Essential Historical Writings*, ed. Miriam Schneir (New York: Random House, 1972), pp. 137–142.

favorable attitude toward governmental administration in Sweden, you point out how your tax proposal is similar to the successful procedure followed in that country, and you expand this analogy into a point-by-point comparison. Or, if you want to use figurative analogy, you sell your tax proposal by relating it to the overall structure of our government. "This is no new or radical proposal," you might say. "Its foundations were laid long ago in Constitutional practice. It is simply one more column in the vast edifice of freedom that our people are constantly building. It raises that structure just a bit further toward the stars." Now if you can fill this symbolic design with appropriate argument and proofs, you should have fashioned a most appealing persuasive speech.

Contrast

Contrast defines and thus can inform. But contrast can also serve the aims of persuasion. If you feel that your listeners despise Russian taxation policies, you can show how your proposal is a point-by-point *opposite* of those policies. Or, if you can picture the situation you would like to change as a sickness, you can offer your taxation proposal as a cure and develop an entire speech within that overall frame of reference. Thus literal contrast and figurative contrast drawing on symbolic forms can both be useful in persuasion.

Question–Answer

The repeated use of questions at important points in persuasive speeches can be quite effective. Using the rhetorical question as a principle of design, you can organize an entire speech around certain key questions, which are posed at important moments in the speech:

What has happened to us?
Why has it happened?
Who is responsible?
Where is the problem most acute?
When can we look for relief?
How can we change this situation?

Rudyard Kipling's "serving-men," who provided the base of the system of analysis described in Chapter 5, serve again as a principle of design in persuasion.

PERSUASIVE DESIGNS

Certain speech designs belong exclusively to persuasion. The most useful such patterns are *problem solution*, *syllogism*, and *dialectic*.

Problem Solution

Your first task may be to convince listeners that they really do have a problem. This is sometimes not easy, because people often bury their heads in the sand until some crisis looms over them. You may have to telescope the problem so that people can see it *as it will become* unless they act now. Patrick Henry painted a picture of future slavery for those who wanted to deny the need for revolution:

> They tell us, sir, that we are weak; unable to cope with so formidable an adversary. But when shall we be stronger? Will it be the next week, or the next year? Will it be when we are totally disarmed, and when a British guard shall be stationed in every house?[2]

Effective imagery, which builds on and brings to life convincing evidence, is important in this pattern. Francis Bacon, the great Renaissance scholar, was sensitive to this rhetorical function and indeed made it central to his definition of the work of rhetoric. The speaker's task, he said, is to "apply reason to imagination for the better moving of the will."[3]

One of the most interesting action words associated with the problem-solution pattern in our time is "crisis." This word underscores for listeners the seriousness of the problem described in the speech.[4] To speak of an energy crisis, a credibility crisis, or an inflation crisis is to signal listeners that they must pay special attention to the problem at hand.

When developing the problem-solution pattern, do not overwhelm the audience with too many aspects of the problem. Rather, select the most important features and show how the proposed solution might resolve or improve them. Once you convince your listeners that they

2. "Liberty or Death," *American Speeches*, ed. Wayland Maxfield Parrish and Marie Hochmuth (New York: Longmans, Green, 1954), p. 94.
3. *The Advancement of Learning*, in *Great Books of the Western World*, Vol. 30 (Chicago, Ill.: Benton, 1952), p. 66 (Second Book, XVIII, 2).
4. For an analysis of the semantic power of "crisis," see Lyda Eugenia Twitty McGee, "Crisis and the Making of American Foreign Policy: A Rhetorical Analysis of the 1947 Greco-Turkish Crisis," (Unpublished Master's thesis, Memphis State University, 1976).

"Are you ready for leadership?"

Drawing by C. Barsotti; © 1979 The New Yorker Magazine, Inc.

do have a problem, they will be strongly motivated to consider your solution seriously. To focus on the solution you advocate you may well have to discuss other available options, showing why these alternatives are less desirable. As the range of options gradually narrows to this one choice, you must show that this solution is practical and within the power of your auditors to enact. In "Liberty or Death," Patrick Henry follows the section previously quoted with this assurance:

> Sir, we are not weak, if we make a proper use of those means which the God of nature hath placed in our power. Three millions of people, armed in the holy cause of liberty, and in such a country as that which we possess, are invincible by any force which our enemy can send against us.

Beyond showing that the solution can work and indicating how it can work, persuasive speakers must often reveal the better future that their solutions will lead to. Much of the function of Martin Luther King's most famous speech, aptly titled "I Have a Dream," was to communicate his vision of such a future:

I have a dream that one day on the red hills of Georgia the sons of former slaves and the sons of former slaveowners will be able to sit down together at the table of brotherhood.

I have a dream that one day even the state of Mississippi . . . will be transformed into an oasis of freedom and justice.

I have a dream that my four little children will one day live in a nation where they will not be judged by the color of their skin but by the content of their character.

I have a dream today.

I have a dream that one day, down in Alabama, . . . little black boys and little black girls will be able to join hands with little white boys and white girls as sisters and brothers.

I have a dream today.[5]

Such visions of the future serve a vital telescoping function. According to Francis Bacon, the rationale behind their usefulness is as follows: We are normally moved most by objects that are near us and appeal to our senses. This means that, when immediate pleasure and pain come into conflict with our long-range good, which is a distant abstraction, we are more apt to choose in accordance with our immediate interests. But if you can telescope the future so that it seems close to us and can create the illusion of its actual presence, then we may commit to a long-range solution even if it means we must give up some immediate pleasure or suffer some momentary pain. Through the orator's vision we can be induced to do what is in our best interest.

Finally, it is often important that you indicate the first step or two that must be taken, in order to carry listeners to the threshold of action. It is vital that you secure commitment to undertake this action, even if the commitment be only to sign a statement or to respond to a question: "Now, who will march with me tomorrow?" You may have to coax your audience, for important commitments are not undertaken lightly. People know they are assuming risks when they put their names on the line. They may look around to see whether others are responding. If some of those present are already strongly in favor of your proposal, such people can step forward and break the ice.

Our various examples confirm that problem-solution designs are often enhanced by powerful symbols. Such patterns become more dramatic when presented in terms of such images as light and darkness or disease and cure. The problem, of course, is cast in terms of darkness and sickness, whereas the solution is transformed symbolically into light and healing.

5. From a transcription of "I Have a Dream," delivered on August 28, 1963, in Washington, D.C.

The rhythm of problem and solution is central to the adjustments that people are constantly making to their environment. Thus persuasion becomes central to the quality of our survival in a world of our own making.

Syllogism

Persuasive designs may sometimes seem to have little to do with rational processes, but often they borrow the basic form of logic. In these instances, the underlying form of the persuasive speech can look like a large-scale projection of a syllogism, the basic model of all deductive thinking. The syllogism begins with a *major premise*, which asserts some general claim: "Americans are wasteful" (categorical premise), "If we don't stop poisoning our waters, we will destroy the food chain" (hypothetical premise), or "Either we stop waste or we increase the chances for famine and war" (disjunctive premise). When used in public speaking, major premises purport to express commonly held beliefs. Such premises represent shared generalizations that speakers can draw on to build specific chains of reasoning for their purposes.

In a syllogism the major premise is followed by a *minor premise*, which focuses on the rhetorical situation relevant to the speech. Thus "We are Americans," "But last year we continued poisoning our waters at an alarming rate," and "But we have launched a significant effort to stop waste" would be minor premises that might be used in connection with the foregoing examples. The function of the minor premise is to relate a specific situation to the folk wisdom expressed in the major premise.

From this interaction of specific and general, minor and major, emerges the *conclusion* of the syllogism: "Therefore, we are wasteful," "Therefore (unless we change quickly and significantly), we shall destroy the food chain," and "Therefore, we are trying not to increase the chance of famine and war." The conclusion obviously represents the point or thrust of the entire reasoning process.

As we look at this simple but profound pattern of major premise, minor premise, and conclusion, it is easy to see how it might become the overall framework for a persuasive speech. This framework extends from a general reaffirmation of beliefs through the description of a specific situation to the conclusion you wish to draw from this interaction of situation and belief. Syllogism can be a particularly dramatic pattern for persuasion, catching its auditors up in an intense struggle over ethical issues, the oughts and ought-nots of human conduct. Because commitment involves risk (and even danger), listeners often try to resist and escape the web of moral obligation that the syllogistic form weaves. Thus the speaker omits no steps in the process—indeed, will even dwell on and reinforce all the turns of thought.[6] The speaker's aim is to *capture* his or her listeners and to allow no possibility of their evading the ethical imperative to act.

You might begin a speech, for example, by asserting that Americans have always believed we should recognize each other as human beings with basic rights. You might turn to history for some powerful examples, forcing your listeners to grant the truth of this major premise, heightening its importance and its personal value to them. They grant the major premise, knowing even as they do that you are setting the stage and that they have just taken the first risk. Now the speech shifts to a specific subject, the American Indian. "Are they not human?" you ask rhetorically. You then describe the courage, morality, and sensitivity of American Indians until no reasonable person could deny that premise.

But such affirmation of the minor premise establishes another link in the chain of commitment. Audience members can feel your persuasion pulling them through the syllogistic pattern toward a conclusion. For now you turn to a description of the fate of native Americans at our hands. In effect you are contrasting the logical and moral conclusion ("These people should certainly enjoy rights and recognition as human") with their actual experience. Action and belief are out of harmony, and morality and reality have drifted apart. The audience listens, trying perhaps to find some way out of the growing sense of ethical obligation. You anticipate these evasions and parry them in your speech: "You may not have been there then, but you are here now. You may not have been guilty before, but you will be guilty if you do not act now, *now that you know.*"

All Americans, you conclude, must become involved in vindicating the national honor. We must raise justice and our own principles out of the dirt. It all begins, you conclude, in the here-and-now and with the quality of the commitment your listeners make to the plan of action you set before them. Thus the syllogistic form confronts audience members with a dramatic decision, points them in a certain direction, and makes clear the consequences of their acting or not acting.

6. In his *Rhetoric,* Aristotle asserts that the rhetorical syllogism or *enthymeme* is often characterized by its omission of or assumption of a premise. He suggests that such omission can be a good strategy, especially when the audience itself supplies the missing link. His observation could be true under certain conditions, but only when listeners are already favorably disposed to the speaker and when belaboring all the steps of the reasoning involved would weary them. In a speech that asks for commitment and risk, the omission of any step is not wise strategy.

Such design can call on symbols to heighten even further its urgency and impact. Symbolic space could be invoked: "Our treatment of the Indians was a retreat from basic principles. We must regain the high moral ground we abandoned." Sin-redemption could also prove useful: "We have sinned against our own principles. We must redeem ourselves before we can recover them." Similarly, the syllogistic design could call on the charismatic language of our society: "Progress" and "freedom," for example, might be cited in the premises to push us toward a conclusion.

Dialectic

Dialectic involves the clash of opposed positions in argument. The nature of dialectic suggests three possible designs for persuasive speeches.

REFUTATIVE   In the refutative dialectical design, the persuader sets out to confront an opposing position directly. The intent is to destroy or at least damage that position by pointing out its absurdities, irrelevancies, and inconsistencies. The speaker often attacks the most vulnerable points first, hoping to cast doubt on the credibility of the entire opposed position. The point of attack may be illogical reasoning, flimsy or insufficient evidence, or even the character of an opposing persuader when credibility is a real issue. The persuader has little hope of convincing the opponent. His or her aim is to persuade an audience of neutrals or to reinforce an audience of supporters.

Refutative design can generate rather bitter and highly partisan speeches. It acknowledges a world of "us" and "them," a world divided along hard attitudinal lines. Often the design is useful during the early stages of social and political movements, when speakers want to create an identity for their followers sharply separate from the perceived oppressors. Emmeline Pankhurst saw no possibility of compromise or negotiation with the male establishment of Great Britain. Her rhetoric envisioned a state of actual as well as psychological warfare between the sexes until the male oppressors surrendered their master roles.

If you live in a world of such strongly entrenched and opposed positions on the issues that are most meaningful to you, you may find this design useful, if not inevitable.

CONVERSIONARY   The conversionary form of dialectical design can be useful when you are addressing hostile or opposed listeners with some hope of either converting them or taking the sting out of their opposition. As illustrated earlier in this chapter, the speaker often seeks first to establish common ground and addresses less controversial issues before turning to the difficult issues on which people truly divide. The speaker is understanding and conciliatory. His or her attitude is not that of representing the superior side in a dispute, but rather that of wanting to share some vital information that might affect your listeners' point of view. The basic conversionary strategy is to soften the sense of dialectical opposition, rather than to emphasize and exploit it.

Lucy Stone used this kind of persuasive design in a speech she delivered at a National Woman's Rights Conference in Cincinnati in 1855:

> The present condition of woman causes a horrible perversion of the marriage relation. It is asked of a lady, "Has she married well?" "Oh, yes, her husband is rich." Woman must marry for a home, and you men are the sufferers by this; for a woman who loathes you may marry you because you have the means to get money which she can not have. But when woman can enter the lists with you and make money for herself, she will marry you only for deep and earnest affection.[7]

Though no design for persuasion is inherently more or less moral than another, the ethics of humanism would seem to suggest that you explore the possibility of converting your opponents through conversionary persuasion before resorting to the bitterness and division that the refutative approach so often entails.

TRANSCENDENT The transcendent design is a dialectical form that seeks a position above or beyond opposed positions. Essentially, the persuader's aim is to relocate the dispute on a level where opponents might agree or at least come together in a new understanding. Such transcendent rhetoric characterized the persuasive speeches by United States leaders aimed at producing an agreement between Egypt and Israel in 1978. The conference at Camp David was itself symbolic of such persuasion, lifting the scene of that long and acrid dispute out of the Middle East and placing it on a peaceful mountain in Virginia.

Following the transcendent design of persuasion, speakers often (1) praise the leadership and integrity of all sides involved in the dispute, (2) emphasize strengths as well as weaknesses of the various positions, and (3) show how the vital interests of all sides can be protected and strengthened by a new, transcending resolution. In such persuasion the speaker appears in the attractive symbolic role of peace maker. The audience for such persuasion is complex. It includes the

7. "Disappointment Is the Lot of Woman," *Feminism*, p. 108.

various groups of opponents, whom the speaker hopes to convert to the new resolution, as well as those who are not directly involved in the dispute. This latter, often larger group of noncombatants is often crucial to the persuader's success. The tension caused by disputes may threaten and disturb a community, and such general audiences welcome relief from the tension. Thus, if they are convinced that the speaker has an attractive and sound proposal, they can create enormous pressure on opposed sides to accept the speaker's recommendations.

Clearly, persuasion that transcends disputes can be quite attractive to audiences, and you would be well advised to explore the possibilities of such design. Your speech can heighten its dramatic appeal by drawing on symbolism, as President Sadat demonstrated in his characterization of the Camp David Accords: "The foundations of the peace structure have been placed already and they are far from the swamps of no-war, no-peace. Only the upper stories remain to be built."[8] At other moments we might expect speeches built on the transcendent pattern to emphasize the "human family" theme, as they urge opponents to join together in starting anew.

Summary of Major Ideas

Whereas informative speaking outlines the range of our options, persuasive speaking urges us to make a choice.

Persuasive speaking concentrates on controlling audience response.

Leading and following dynamics are more vital to the persuasive speech situation than to informative speech.

Persuasive speaking asks for commitment, which often involves some risk on the part of listeners.

The major challenge of persuasion is to overcome barriers within listeners.

In persuasion addressed to opponents, the beginning of the speech is likely to be the most crucial moment. In persuasion addressed to undecided listeners, the body of the speech should be most critical to its success. In persuasive speeches intended for supporters, the conclusion may be most vital to rhetorical success.

Persuasion shares with information the use of time, space, categorical thinking, motives, causation, repetition, analogy, contrast, and question–answer patterns in the overall design of speeches.

8. From a United Press International dispatch, *Memphis Commercial Appeal* (December 26, 1978), p. 1.

Problem solution, syllogism, and dialectical designs belong exclusively to the province of persuasion.

The ability to "telescope" the future, bringing its image close to listeners, is vital to persuasion.

The syllogistic form of persuasion proceeds from a reaffirmation of beliefs held in common (major premise), through the description of a specific situation (minor premise), to the recommendation the speaker draws from this interaction of situation and belief (conclusion).

In refutative dialectical design, the persuader confronts an opposed position directly with the intent of destroying it.

In conversionary dialectical design, the persuader hopes to either convert or "soften" opponents.

In transcendent dialectical design, the speaker seeks to find a new basis on which to resolve a dispute to the satisfaction of all parties.

Exercises and Discussion Questions

1. Analyze the speeches made on the subject of a recent controversy. How is the challenge of persuasion met by the contending parties? What overall designs of persuasion can you identify in their speeches?

2. The "Letters to the Editor" section of the Sunday newspaper is a sometimes rich source for the study of persuasion in the raw. On any given Sunday, consider the specimens available. Did the writers select their approaches to the audience wisely? Which letters are most persuasive? Why?

3. Under which conditions might it be wise *not* to refute an opposing position through a refutative approach to persuasion?

4. Consider Plato's view that popular speakers tend to follow the crowd more than to lead. Do you agree? What evidence would you present in support of your view? Even if true, is this tendency necessarily bad?

5. Study the speeches delivered in celebration of some recent occasion. What values are reinforced by these speeches?

For Further Reading

Among the books that deal with persuasion are the classic treatise by Machiavelli, *The Prince,* and two more recent works: Saul Alinsky, *Rules for Radicals, A Practical Primer for Realistic Radicals* (New York: Random House, 1971) and Eric Hoffer, *The True Believer, Thoughts on the Nature of Mass Movements* (New York: Harper,

1951). The Hoffer work is especially interesting in that it studies the behavior of people caught up in social and revolutionary movements and the forces that move and persuade them. The book has special implications for the study of conversionary rhetoric.

Within the field of speech communication, other significant books have begun to probe persuasion's many mysteries. Among them are:

John Waite Bowers and Donovan J. Ocks, *The Rhetoric of Agitation and Control* (Reading, Mass.: Addison-Wesley, 1971)

Gary Cronkhite, *Persuasion: Speech and Behavioral Change* (New York: Bobbs-Merrill, 1969)

Perspectives on Communication in Social Conflict, ed. Gerald R. Miller and Herbert W. Simons (Englewood Cliffs, N.J., Prentice-Hall, 1974)

Herbert W. Simons, *Persuasion: Understanding, Practice, and Analysis* (Reading, Mass.: Addison-Wesley, 1976)

13

DEVELOPING, OUTLINING, AND WORDING THE PERSUASIVE SPEECH

If men were not apart from one another, there would be no need for the rhetorician to proclaim their unity. . . . Rhetoric is concerned with the state of Babel after the Fall. . . . Rhetoric . . . is rooted in an essential function of language itself, a function that is wholly realistic, and is continually born anew; the use of language as a symbolic means of inducing cooperation in beings that by nature respond to symbols.

KENNETH BURKE, *A Rhetoric of Motives*

WHAT TO LOOK FOR IN
THIS CHAPTER

The need for argument in persuasion

Forms of argument

Defective argumentation

Outlining the persuasive speech

The language of persuasion

If we think of persuasion in its broadest sense as the use of symbols to influence ourselves or others, there are two primary modes of persuading. *We can condition, or we can convince.* Persuading by conditioning most often means repeating a message until it comes to be accepted as true. Almost all effective persuasion depends to some extent on conditioning. Taking a patient approach to the problem of persuading opponents is, in effect, mounting a long-range campaign that allows the audience to become accustomed to a position as it is artfully repeated through many speeches. So there is no ethical problem with conditioning as such.

The problem with such persuasion arises when manipulators decide to make it the primary means of influence. These persuaders take a simple message and simply drum it into our heads. There is little substance in that message and little justification for accepting what it recommends. It aims not at the mind but at the conditioned response. Indeed, the art of such manipulation can be to disguise products or political candidates instead of revealing them. Conditioned persuasion can be quite dehumanizing: It views us more as laboratory animals than as free men and women whose assent must be earned in open argument.

"Argument," indeed, is the key word here. Argument is that process by which we give to others reasons for accepting our recommendations. In argument, we explain to others how we came to our conclusions and recommendations, revealing the premises from which we argue, the facts we find relevant and how we came by them, and the inferences we have drawn from these facts. Argument addresses its appeal primarily to the conscious mind, to which it opens its processes for inspection. It invites reflection, seeking not just a reaction but a *decision* in its favor. It wants not just a response but an act of will, a commitment that will have lasting value.

Clearly, then, argument is at the heart of ethical persuasion. Just as clearly, argument itself can be defective and dishonest. Assumptions can be disguised, facts can be invented, and the speaker can exploit arousal for the sake of immediate impact, regardless of the consequences. Nevertheless, the basic impulse of argument—to reveal all the reasoning that supports one's conclusions—is sound.

Without argument there is no real reason for selecting one depiction of reality over another, nor can arousal be justified. Without argument groups have no real basis for their identity, nor are plans of action deliberated and options considered. We become simply dancers to music that we don't really understand, creatures who obey another's will. Our society has no real meaning to be celebrated, for it has never been justified. *The legitimacy of the entire rhetorical process depends on the primacy of argument in persuasion.*

Just as the illustration (verbal and nonverbal) is the major technique of informative speaking, so is the *unit of proof* central to that persuasion which works by argument. Any well-developed argumentative speech contains many such units of proof woven into a complex fabric of appeals. Thus, just as Chapter 12 surveyed the overall design of persuasion, this chapter examines the fine texture of argument, beginning with this concept of the unit of proof. It then identifies various forms of argument that build upon the unit of proof and exposes the fallacies and flaws that can plague argument. The final section of the chapter discusses outlining and wording the persuasive speech. It completes the basic plan of speech preparation that has been evolving since Chapter 5.

UNIT OF PROOF

Chapter 12 revealed that persuasion can develop in a pattern that follows the classic model of the syllogism, which consists of a major premise, a minor premise, and a conclusion. That special design lends itself to an indirect approach to persuasion: first by affirming and reviving common values (major premise), second by establishing the existence of some situation or condition (minor premise), and only then by drawing the persuasive conclusion. Usually, however, proof in a persuasive speech begins with establishing the existence of some *situation.*

The pressure exerted on the persuader who is establishing the existence of a situation may vary dramatically. The audience may grant outright that the situation exists; in this case no controversy arises about the facts. But it may not be so simple. For example, you may accept without difficulty that the world is round and that the earth is not at the center of the universe, but for Columbus the first "fact" was somewhat more speculative, and for Galileo the second "fact" was downright heresy. If you are presenting the picture of a situation that runs counter to what your audience expects, you may have to introduce many experts as witnesses to the truth of what you say, and the task of presenting what may seem a strange new world will call on all your powers of depiction.

Once a situation is presented and accepted, the persuader must introduce warrants that advance his or her purpose. *Warrants* are another way of describing the major premise, emphasizing the work performed by the major premise in popular argument.[1] Warrants are drawn from the general values that society, represented concretely in the speaker's audience, has created and sustained as its identity. These values provide a storehouse of potential warrants from which speakers may draw as necessary and appropriate. Warrants permit interpretations of facts: It is in light of them that situations gain meaning and argumentative thrust.

The stark fact that a student was sexually assaulted on campus last week may not in itself point in any particular persuasive direction nor lead to any conclusion. But such an act of violence has the potential for supplying the minor premise in an as-yet-unformed syllogism. Only in light of a cluster of warrants invoked by a speaker ("Our sexual identity is precious to our personhood." "No person should have to submit to physical violation." "The campus especially should be a haven for safe and secure living.") does the entire meaning of such an act emerge, pointing us toward certain conclusions and actions.

Thus speakers must know the value premises dear to their audiences. They must know how to bring emerging premises into conscious awareness and how to awaken dormant premises into vivid realization so that they can be used to interpret events. Especially useful in this process can be *image* ("Rape is the nightmare you cannot awake from"), *example* ("Last year two victims on this campus attempted suicide, while others had to leave and seek psychiatric help"), and *authority* ("Dr. Johnson has said that there is no species of brutality more destructive of personhood than rape").

1. The concept of the warrant is developed in Stephen Toulmin's *The Uses of Argument* (Cambridge, England: Cambridge University Press, 1958). See also the application of this concept in Chapter 15, where the use of argument in debate is considered.

Often premises may seem in conflict and must be reconciled before the speaker can interpret the meaning of some event. If you would invoke a campus curfew, you may have to argue that the premise involving safety from sexual assault must take precedence over a conflicting premise involving the freedom of movement on campus. Whatever the challenge of the particular speech, persuasion cannot occur until some base for ethical interpretation has been carefully laid in the speech.

Combining a certain situation with a certain warrant or warrants produces a *claim* on listeners, which corresponds to the conclusion of the formal syllogism. The claim is indeed a conclusion that the speaker draws about a situation in light of a premise or cluster of premises. In a persuasive speech, claims should connect with each other in an overall chain of argument leading toward some recommended action or orientation. Thus a speaker might develop the following chain of conclusions, each of which represents the thrust of a particular argumentative structure and all of which move toward a recommended action:

This campus no longer safeguards us against brutal crime.
Campus security forces are woefully understaffed.
Students themselves must organize security patrols on campus.
Come to a planning meeting tonight at the campus union.

Thus we can see how three elements—situation, warrants, and claim—constitute the major elements of the unit of proof,[2] illustrated in Figure 13.1. It is interesting that, unlike the model of formal logic (the syllogism), persuasive argument often begins, not with the affirmation of some major premise, but with the urgency of some specific situation that functions as the minor premise. Thus the order of the formal model may be rearranged when it is used in practical persuasive discourse.

FORMS OF ARGUMENT

As you develop units of proof within the persuasive designs you select, there are many forms of argument available to you. Often these forms are miniature versions of the overall principles of design discussed in Chapter 12. For example, arguments based on cause–effect premises are common throughout persuasive speeches. Arguments that assume

2. For another view of the unit of proof, see Douglas Ehninger and Wayne Brockriede, *Decision by Debate* (New York: Dodd, Mead, 1963).

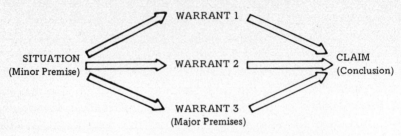

Figure 13.1 MODEL OF THE UNIT OF PROOF

the relevance of motives or appeal to the sense of past and future are often useful. Likewise, arguments based on analogy and contrast abound in persuasion.

Any extended inspection of persuasive speeches will reveal the rich variety of argumentative forms, a few of which are outlined here.

Definition

Clarifying and establishing the reality of a situation—(in effect, the minor premise) is argument by definition. This "death" that the speaker is depicting—is it natural and inevitable, or the price some must pay for progress, or suicide, or self-defense and justifiable homicide, or mass murder and genocide? The same bare fact of death takes on different meanings and qualities as the speaker defines it.

Emmeline Pankhurst realized how the question of definition could be vital in adjusting audience vision. Consider, for example, the sensitivity to definition she reveals in the following argument. "We women, in trying to make our case clear, always have to make a part of our argument, and urge upon men in our audience the fact—a very simple fact—that women are human beings. It is quite evident you do not all realize we are human beings or it would not be necessary to argue with you that women may, suffering from intolerable injustice, be driven to adopt revolutionary methods."[3]

Definition is associated closely with the rhetorical function of identification, for which it becomes a major technique. It you can help audience members define themselves in common terms, you will have set the stage for them to act in common as well.

Perspective

Closely related to definition is argument that seeks to liberate an audience from the constraints of a previous way of seeing things so that

3. "When Civil War Is Waged by Women," *Feminism*, pp. 297-298.

they can perceive the reality of the minor premise. Elizabeth Cady Stanton had to bring in an imaginary visitor from outer space to make audience members confront the inconsistency between their laws and their public professions of sentiment:

> *Just imagine an inhabitant of another planet entertaining himself some pleasant evening in searching over our great national compact, our Declaration of Independence, our Constitutions, or some of our statute-books; what would he think of those "women and negroes" that must be so fenced in, so guarded against? Why, he would certainly suppose we were monsters, like those fabulous giants or Brobdingnagians of olden times, so dangerous to civilized man, from our size, ferocity, and power. Then let him take up our poets, from Pope down to Dana; let him listen to our Fourth of July toasts, and some of the sentimental adulations of social life, and no logic could convince him that this creature of the law, and this angel of the family altar, could be one and the same being.*[4]

Kenneth Burke has pointed out that speakers sometimes have to administer verbal shock treatment before an audience can *see* a subject in the manner intended.[5] Often we have been conditioned *not* to see subjects in certain ways. Hence all members of a social group may have a kind of institutionalized blindness when it comes to certain sensitive subjects. New views may seem incongruous with our expectations. It may require daring on the speaker's part to free listeners from the constraints of these perspectives.

One sensible pattern for developing such argumentation is to present evidence that gradually undermines any previous, contrary expectations. Then you might present a living example that contradicts the images that had previously been accepted. You might seal the speech with some final statement of a new perspective: "The liberty bell still rings in this country. It rings for all who want to be free. Some of us in the South need to take the cotton out of our ears so that we can hear it."

Malcolm X used such "perspective by incongruity" to counter what he saw as a dangerous complacency in the civil rights movement. To those who took comfort in the limited legal gains achieved early in the movement, he offered a harsh new view of themselves. "You're a twentieth century slave!" he said, and went on to confess, "I don't see an American dream. I see an American nightmare."[6]

4. Address to the New York State Legislature, 1860," *Feminism*, pp. 119-120.
5. See his discussion in *Permanence and Change: An Anatomy of Purpose* (New York: New Republic, 1935), pp. 118-164.
6. From a transcription of "The Ballot or the Bullet," delivered in Cleveland on April 3, 1964.

Concreteness

Sometimes controversies evolve onto a level of abstraction far removed from reality, and the real urgency of a situation may be forgotten. A kind of blindness to actual fact may even develop, and fantasy may take over. Argument rooted in the concrete reality of the case may be useful to restore an accurate realization of the minor premise.

In a recent speech on abortion, one student speaker strengthened her case against legalized abortion by describing in graphic detail how abortions are actually performed. She did not violate canons of good taste, but her depictions were sufficiently vivid to create revulsion in her audience over induced prenatal death. By returning an abstraction to concrete reality, she had forced her listeners to confront reality from her point of view. Such argument is especially useful when listeners wish to avoid facing up to certain aspects of the issue before them.

Characterization

Some arguments base their appeal on the perceived character of people involved in the persuasive situation. The images of speakers themselves, we have noted, may play a powerful role in the fate of persuasion. So also, however, do the characters they create in the persuasive dramas of their speeches. Edward M. Kennedy, speaking before the Democratic Convention of 1980, idealized "the common man and the common woman" and urged that those images function as the "foundation" of the Democratic Party. In effect Kennedy argued for the development of major premises consistent with the values implied in those images. An important theme of Ronald Reagan's "Inaugural Address" was its effort to revive the characterization of the American "hero," which Reagan connected with the "We the People" theme drawn from the American tradition. The president was attempting to revitalize an image that could function in the role of a major premise to authorize his point of view.

Through the stylistic device of *personification*, characterization can even enter arguments about abstract subjects. This device operates when we speak of an abstraction (such as a government or a nation) as though it were a living creature with a personality and feelings. One often hears political and patriotic talk about the motherland or about Uncle Sam. Apparently, it is easier for audiences to relate to such subjects when they can think of them as exhibiting human characteristics. Personification thus becomes a device for encouraging identification and for awakening audiences to the importance of premises.

Personification can incite hatred and revulsion as well as patriotism. Consider how Malcolm X aroused his audience against the hypocrisy of the United States during a crucial time in the civil and human rights movement:

> There he is, standing up in front of other people, Uncle Sam, with the blood of your and my mothers and fathers on his hands, with the blood dripping down his jaws like a bloody-jawed wolf, and still got the nerve to point his finger at other countries. You can't even get civil rights legislation, and this man has got the nerve to stand up and talk about South Africa, or talk about Nazi Germany, or talk about Portugal—No! No more days like those![7]

Audience Challenge

This especially interesting kind of argumentation challenges an audience that may be reluctant to form a conclusion. Listeners may be willing to grant the major premise and even the minor premise, but for some reason they refuse to draw the obvious conclusion. Perhaps that final recognition would necessitate action that these listeners really don't want to take or would create such inner conflict that they prefer to repress the entire persuasive experience. At such moments the speaker must goad the audience into granting the obvious conclusion. Ronald Reagan, accepting the Republican nomination for President, challenged alienated supporters of Jimmy Carter with a series of questions.

> Can anyone look at the record of this Administration and say, "Well done"? Can anyone compare the state of our economy when the Carter Administration took office with where we are today and say, "Keep up the good work"? Can anyone look at our reduced standing in the world today and say, "Let's have four more years of this"?[8]

This sampling of argumentative forms, which gives you only an introduction to the many that are possible in human communication, confirms that depiction, the control of images of reality, is basic to the persuasive enterprise. The usual struggle in rhetoric is over who will shape our perceptions and thereby control our formation of the minor premise.

7. From "The Ballot or the Bullet."
8. See the speech reprinted in the Appendix.

© 1956 United Features Syndicate, Inc.

DEFECTIVE ARGUMENTATION

The persuasive speaker must make a fine fabric out of the many argumentative forms available. Above all, the speech must be free of flaws of composition that would ruin such careful design. For this reason we turn now to some of the more common defects of reasoning, which you should be sure to avoid in your own argumentation.

Errors of Induction

The characteristic method of scientific reasoning, *induction*, occurs when we draw our conclusions from direct observations of fact. "Eighty percent of our students favor abolition of all foreign language requirements" purports to be an induction. To determine how accurate it is, we would have to inquire into the conditions of observation. *How many examples* did the speaker consider? If the speaker questioned ten people while on the way to class, we might well challenge the adequacy of the sample. *How well distributed* was the sample? It makes considerable difference whether one's sample included seniors and graduate students as well as freshmen.

Along with quantity and distribution of sample, time and place of sampling can be important factors, especially when the opinion tested might be somewhat variable. If you sampled views on the foreign language requirement at "drop" time, for example, when consciousness of grades and the relative difficulty of courses peaks, you might register an unusually negative group opinion. And interviewing students near the "drop" office might considerably compound the degree of distortion.

We should also inspect the generalization drawn from the induction. "Eighty percent of the immature students on this campus prefer abolishing the language requirement" would be both ambiguous and improper. Does the speaker mean that the statement holds *only* for immature students and that mature students have a different opinion? Does the speaker imply that these groups might be separated that clearly? Or does the statement suggest that students as a whole on this campus are immature, their general bias against the language requirement being a sign of that immaturity? The meaning of the statement is uncertain at best. From another point of view, the statement represents *premise contamination*, the intrusion of an improper word into the generalization. The inclusion of "immature" is not just a case of vagrant emotionalism disturbing the purity of an intellectual operation. The word actually "begs the question" by presupposing a judgment that has not yet been justified or proved by argument. For more on such problems and the way to avoid them, see the discussion of polling techniques in Chapter 6.

Emotion can be a problem in itself if you are in such an overwrought state that the audience questions your ability to register a dispassionate observation. Desperate speakers will see what they want to see in a situation. Unless listeners share their desperation, they will hesitate to accept such observations.

Errors of Deduction

Deduction is the process of coming to conclusions about supposed states of reality, which function as minor premises, in the light of general beliefs and values, which function as warrants or major premises. One measure of the quality of deductive reasoning is *categorical precision*. Consider the proposition "College athletes are dumb." As a simple expression venting someone's mindless prejudice, this statement is probably no worse than others of its kind. But trouble begins the minute you treat it as a major premise—as the foundation for a line of reasoning in a speech. How do you define "athletes"? Do you include table tennis players and swimmers as well as basketball and football players? And what do you mean by "dumb"? Do you have the evidence that would support such an unqualified premise, even if the major terms are quite precisely defined? If you can't meet the challenge of such questions, your audience may react somewhat differently than you had hoped. "It's not the jocks who are dumb," they may sniff. "It's the orators."

A second kind of technical fault mars deductive reasoning when the speaker treats what are at best probable premises and conclusions as though they were certain. If the premise "X's are Y's" holds about 90 percent of the time, and if I am about 90 percent certain that "Z is an X," my conclusion that "Z is a Y" must be considerably qualified by the compounded *uncertainty factor* of both major and minor premises. Any public persuader who asserts such conclusions as though they were graven in stone is ignoring the uncertainty factor that lurks in most public controversy. It is better to point out to listeners that uncertainty exists. Then you will not lose their trust when your line of reasoning does not hold in a particular case.

A third kind of technical flaw occurs when faulty cause–effect and oversimplified two-valued forms of reasoning contaminate the deductive pattern. The *hypothetical* and *disjunctive* syllogisms especially invite such problems. The hypothetical ("if–then") pattern of reasoning sometimes confuses simple association with causation, perceiving one event as generating another when actually the first simply went before the second in time. The same people who always wear their lucky boots and ties before the big game might also argue that we ought to have a tax cut, because the last time we had one we avoided war, increased employment, and reduced crime. In formal logic this kind of reasoning is known as the *post hoc ergo propter hoc* fallacy (after the event and therefore because of it). Similarly, disjunctive ("either–or") reasoning can box us into a manner of thinking that offers us only two choices, one of which is presented as ultimately desirable, the other as drastically undesirable. If our minds are dazzled by rhetorical images of these options, we may be blinded to many other choices that are available in the situation. We may be unable to make those fine distinctions that would show us the relative advantages and disadvantages of each of these various options. Thus what may seem only technical faults or fallacies in syllogistic form may actually be deep rhetorical problems in human reasoning. Our choices may not be between liberty and death, but rather among various kinds and degrees of freedom and enslavement. If we reject your heaven we may have something other than hell to choose. The two-valued option urges immediate commitment, but patience may be more appropriate, as audiences seek other and better options.

Statistical Fallacies

Technical fallacies can also rob complex forms of inductive reasoning of their validity. This is especially true when the speaker creates *statistical illusions* to which modern audiences, who are often intimidated by mathematical and scientific language, are so vulnerable. Conclusions built on averages, for example, can be quite deceptive. If I tell you not to worry about poverty in our city because the *average* income is above the poverty line, my figures may actually indicate a situation in which numerous families are quite well off but numerous others are desperately poor. The average creates an illusion of general well-being not at all reflective of reality. Another kind of statistical illusion can occur in comparative reasoning using percentages, when the bases of the comparison are unequal. In a certain college debate, a speaker developed the following argument: "Because the Gross National Product of the United States is growing at an annual rate of only 6 percent, while that of the Soviet Union is growing at a rate of 14 percent, the Russians are rapidly overtaking us." The effect was devastating when his opponent pointed out that a 6 percent rise in the American GNP represented more actual growth than a 14 percent rise in the Russian GNP. (In approximate figures, 6 percent of 500 billion is greater than 14 percent of 200 billion.)

Avoidance of Argument

Another abuse of reasoning is the practice of avoiding argument. This practice tries to deflect audience attention from the issue by raising another issue on which the speaker feels safer. In political debate this practice is often called the *red herring*, indicating that the speaker raises some sensational charge and drags it across the track of the argument, hoping to draw the attention of the audience and even the opposition along the false trail.

> *"Why should I deal with these alleged facts when everyone here knows you are a Communist?"*
> *"Don't avoid the issue—"*
> *"Communist!"*
> *"I am not a Communist!"*
> *"Then why did you attend Communist meetings at the university?"*

In terms of logic, this particular "red herring" would be termed an *ad hominem* attack; it turns from the issue at hand to defame the character of the opponent.

OUTLINING THE PERSUASIVE SPEECH

The design of the persuasive speech, in terms of both selecting the overall form and weaving the fine texture of the argument, reaches the stage of final preparation in the outline. Much of what has been said about outlining the informative speech applies as well to persuasion. The informative speech outline, for example, depends upon clear realizations of *purpose*, *theme*, and *response desired*. The persuasive speech outline both conforms to and transforms this pattern.

Persuasive Proposal, Rationale, and Assumptions

In persuasive speaking the statement of the theme becomes the *proposal*, which introduces a course of action or response desired from the speech. Thus

> Theme: *The movement spawned by Watergate to curb abuses in political campaign fund raising has solved some old problems, but it had also created some new ones.*

becomes

> Proposal: *We ought to adopt a national system for the public financing of political campaigns.*

Every proposal must have a *rationale*, either implicit or explicit, in the speech. The rationale is the essential reason that justifies the proposal and synthesizes the argumentation in the speech. In this instance,

> Rationale: *Public financing of American political campaigns is the only sure cure for corruption and elitism.*

Supporting this rationale is a foundation of *assumptions*, which are the vital warrants for the speech. Speakers should usually bring them out in the speech for inspection by listeners. In this instance the assumptions might include the following:

1. Corruption and elitism in the political system are undesirable.
2. Corruption and elitism are *more* undesirable than any possible waste or even unfairness that might result from the administration of public financing.
3. As a priority for expenditure of public funds, public financing of political campaigns is more important than other claims on the public treasury.
4. A sound and workable plan for public financing is available.

If the assumptions can be supported adequately, the rationale will be sound and the proposal may well be accepted.

Orienting Material, Initial Focus, and Primary Statements

As you design the superstructure of the speech, you will come first to the *orienting material*. Just as in informative speaking, you will want to arouse real interest in your subject with some striking opening that promises to develop a topic of real consequence. The only difference is that the persuasive speaker penetrates closer to audience motivations. The orienting material may paint some disturbing picture or some scene of promise and plenty. We expect to learn what the problem is or what program can create such well-being. The persuasive speaker's orienting material, then, foreshadows the subject to come. It has already begun the job of convincing and preparing the audience.

Likewise, the *initial focus* identifies the essential problem or promise of the speech. The wording is likely to be more strongly charged than that of the informative statement. But, as we have noted, the degree of strength and color in this wording may well depend on where the audience stands initially with respect to the subject.

The arrangement of primary statements reflects the design you have selected and your persuasive strategy. With the *problem-solution* pattern, for example, the primary statements develop realization of the problem and appreciation for a solution. In the *syllogism* design, they trace the major steps in the overall logical movement.

Across the centuries two major ideas about patterning primary statements in persuasion have emerged in rhetorical theory. The first such conception was developed long ago by the classical writers and was primarily *forensic* in nature.[9] That is, it was suited to persuasion in courts of law and was, therefore, closely related to our refutative variation on the dialectical design. It told speakers both how to fortify their own positions and how to attack the opposition. The classical writers varied somewhat in approach, but the fact that they were preoccupied with one rather narrow form of persuasion assured much uniformity among them. Most often they advised that speakers begin by *conciliating* the audience, winning the sympathy and goodwill of listeners, and establishing common ground. Speakers would then proceed to a *narration* of the event or events that caused the dispute. This phase would obviously provide much room for what we have called the art of *depiction*. The audience no doubt would anticipate bias in these supposed reflections of reality, but by their credibility and art, speakers must make listeners abandon their wariness. The images created during narration must seem entirely credible and entirely authentic, and they must establish themselves in the minds of auditors as truth.

Having established such a base of narration, speakers could move on to *argument*. The argument was mainly an interpretation of the narrative, drawing out its implications and guiding the audience to certain

---

9. See the discussion in George Kennedy, *The Art of Persuasion in Greece* (Princeton, N.J.: Princeton University Press, 1963).

inferences. The argument was built for the most part on the topic or principle of *probability*. Was it not probable, given the "facts" described in the narration, that the defendant was innocent (or guilty)? Of course, the power of such probability rested on the assumption that human behavior is consistent, predictable, and accountable. Only by making this assumption can one talk meaningfully about what is or is not probable in specific cases. Read any great Roman forensic oration (such as *Pro Caelius*, Cicero's defense of a young nobleman against a woman of questionable virtue), and you will see how artful such a narrative and how skillful such an argument can be.

According to the classical writers on persuasion, speakers, having developed a powerful argument, could then turn to *refutation*, pointing out that the opposition's claims are unfounded. Having obliterated the opposition position and removed all lingering doubt from the minds of listeners, speakers could move powerfully to the *conclusion*, painting vividly the consequences of audience commitment both for and against the position being advocated. The speech would typically end in a statement of faith in the wisdom and fairness of auditors.

Though it is profoundly insightful into human nature, the classical pattern for persuasive speaking is also narrow in scope. It applies to just that form of persuasive speaking—courtroom orations of attack and defense—that the ancients found most crucial in public life. A second major pattern for the key statements of persuasive speaking emerged in this century with Alan Monroe's formulation of the "motivated sequence."[10] Monroe thought five steps were necessary in any complete persuasive effort.

1. *Attention:* Creating a state favoring alertness on the part of listeners to the speech subject
2. *Need:* Showing the audience that the state of affairs under discussion is not entirely helpful to (and indeed may be endangering) their interests
3. *Satisfaction:* Revealing a program of attitude and action that could correct this problematic state of affairs
4. *Visualization:* Painting effective word-pictures of what will happen if we do (or do not) put this program into action
5. *Action:* Asking for audience commitment to the program, preferably for immediate action on its first phase.

Monroe's motivated sequence reminds speakers during outline preparation of the need to stimulate the listeners they will face. Therefore,

10. The concept was introduced in his *Principles and Types of Speech* (New York: Scott, Foresman, 1935).

it is an excellent persuasive pattern for keeping the importance of audience adaptation directly before us. It is especially useful for implementing the problem-solution persuasive speech.

Final Focus

Artful persuasion leaves its audience with a clear *final focus*, which heightens the persuasion to its ultimate intensity and points directly to the attitude or action desired. Without such final focus, audience members feel frustrated and are unable to see how to express their aroused feelings in constructive efforts. Only with a hostile audience, whose hostility has been gradually softened during the speech, might a speaker leave this final focus unstated, to be discovered by listeners as they ponder the implications in their own minds. If a speaker can lead an audience to the threshold of such self-discovery, the rhetoric has been superbly artful and successful. When listeners think that the conclusion is their own, the experience is profoundly persuasive.

A Skeletal Outline for Persuasive Speeches

It is possible to abstract from our discussion a model for outlining persuasive speeches. We recommend full-sentence outlines, which encourage clear thinking, at this decisive stage of speech preparation.

THE PERSUASIVE SPEECH OUTLINE
Foundation of the Speech

Purpose: _____

Proposal: _____

Rationale: _____

Assumptions: _____

Response Desired: _____

Superstructure of the Speech

Title (optional)

I. Orienting Material: _____

II. Initial Focus: _____

III. Primary Statement 1: _____

    A. _____

    B. _____

        1. _____

        2. _____

IV. Primary Statement 2: _____

    A. _____

        1. _____

        2. _____

            a. _____

            b. _____

    B. _____

V. Primary Statement 3: _____

    A. _____

    B. _____

        1. _____

        2. _____

            a. _____

            b. _____

                (1) _____

                (2) _____

                    (a) _____

                    (b) _____

VI. Final Focus: _____

Bibliography

Books:

Articles:

Miscellaneous Citations:

Nick Sapieha/Stock, Boston

WORDING THE PERSUASIVE SPEECH

After the persuasive speech has been designed, developed, and committed to outline, speakers must still discover the most effective wording for their efforts and must rehearse the actual presentation. Persuasive language is not something *other than* informative language; rather, it is *more than* informative language.

The Language of Persuasive Depiction

COMPARISON AND SIMILE   These techniques are as useful in persuasive speaking as they are in informative speaking. But now the subject brought in for the sake of comparison or figurative association *makes a comment* on the speech subject—over and above whatever illustrative value it may have. This "more than" principle becomes clear when we consider the example used in our discussion of simile in the language of information: "The movement swept across this campus like a hurricane, leaving all rules and procedures scattered in its path." The persuasive equivalent might be: "The movement tore across this campus like a hurricane, destroying all rules and procedures, leaving us at the mercy of the new barbarians who preach love and practice hatred." Here the simile has become more expressive of the speaker's feelings, more direct and personal in tone, more accusatory in effect. The context of this image is clearly and unmistakably a persuasive speech.

CONTRAST AND IRONY These techniques are also right at home in persuasion. In addition to the informative purpose of clear definition, stylistic *contrast* serves the persuasive purpose of compelling an audience to face a choice. An informative speaker might say, "What is freedom of speech? It is a right enjoyed only in societies that are confident in their basic social and political systems. It is *not* enjoyed in insecure societies that discourage any nonconformity and therefore make a virtue out of sameness." The persuasive counterpart of such contrast might be the following: "In the final analysis we have but two choices. Shall we follow the example of those societies that censor and control all discussion? Or shall we endure the discomforts of freedom, committing ourselves to protecting even those who may seem obnoxious or foolish? Freedom has always come at a price, and we had better decide now whether we're willing to pay it." Here the contrast sharpens the choice and heightens the drama of choosing.

The nature of *irony* may lend itself more to informative speech. Irony helps us contemplate in a detached and sometimes comic way the foibles and inconsistencies that beset the human condition. "Locked in time, we dream of the timeless." Irony can elevate us above the struggle, and often becomes somewhat philosophical in tone.

Place irony in a persuasive context and it rapidly changes coloration. Persuasive irony tends to be transformed into *sarcasm* and even *invective.* The kind of bite it can have is well illustrated in a sermon by the fifteenth-century Italian church reformer, Savonarola. As he considers all the wealth, pomp, and corruption of the Church of his time, Savonarola recalls the earlier days of a simpler faith and produces a memorable statement of the ironic contrast: "But do you comprehend what I wish to say to you? In the primitive church the chalices were of wood and the prelates were of gold; today the prelates are of wood and the chalices are of gold."[11] Such sentiments led Savonarola to be tortured and finally hanged. In like manner, the great Greek orator Demosthenes used ironic sarcasm to try to goad Athenians into making preparations against their formidable foe, Philip of Macedonia, father of Alexander the Great: "You are each more successful in that to which your time and your interest is given—he in actions, yourselves in words."[12]

11. "On the Degeneration of the Church," ed. Chauncey M. Depew, *The Library of Oratory,* Vol. 1 (New York: The Globe Publishing Co., 1902), 386–393.
12. "The Second Philippic," *Demosthenes' Public Orations* trans. A. W. Pickard-Cambridge (New York: Dutton, 1963), p. 134.

Clearly then, irony is used in persuasion to sting and shame an audience or to ridicule an opponent. It is not without risk as a persuasive technique.

METAPHOR This means of expression can be persuasive as well as illuminating, because it offers us perspective, a way of looking at our world. Such perspective predetermines what we shall accept and reject in terms of depiction. If I begin by thinking of you as a swine, then all my subsequent thinking about you must be influenced by that depiction. Consider a statement by a hypothetical feminist: "This class is nothing but a pen for all you male chauvinists, but don't expect to wallow in us any more!" In the first clause of the sentence, this graphic metaphor hints that it is going to make a somewhat conventional figurative association between pigs and men. The word "pen" in combination with "male chauvinist" is a rather broad and obvious suggestion. We have seen this kind of metaphorical leap made before, and we spot the clue quickly. However, the second clause of the sentence both artfully confirms and *surpasses* our expectation. The verb "wallows" confirms the metaphor, but it makes the figurative leap in a novel way. It not only echoes and completes the metaphor, but also suggests the place of women in the ugly world depicted. As it develops, the metaphor becomes an entire orientation, a way of seeing complete in itself and consistent with itself.

Metaphor can be a hidden persuader of considerable importance. It can extend its influence over time and have great social impact. This was true of the thematic metaphor for working humanity built up during the early days of the Industrial Revolution: "The worker is a machine" or sometimes even "The worker is a cog in *my* machine." This image, nurtured and propagated in editorials, political speeches, and even sermons and popular fiction, had the effect of dehumanizing labor and justifying low wages and long hours.[13] Once implanted, such an image can be very hard to dislodge.

Experiments have indicated that one critical factor in the success of persuasion is the presence or absence of powerful metaphors in the conclusions of speeches.[14] Such metaphors, moreover, can boost the speaker's credibility.

13. See Emery Neff, *Carlyle and Mill: An Introduction to Victorian Thought* (New York: Columbia University Press, 1926), pp. 144–158.
14. See John Bowers and Michael Osborn, "Attitudinal Effects of Selected Types of Concluding Metaphors in Persuasive Speeches," *Speech Monographs*, 33 (1966), 148–155. This study was followed by others, which confirmed that metaphor can be a critical factor in persuasion. See J. C. McCroskey and W. H. Combs, "The Effects of the Use of Analogy on Attitude Change and Source Credibility," *Journal of Communication*, 19 (1969), 333–339; and N. Lamar Reinsch, Jr., "An Investigation of the Effects of the Metaphor and Simile in Persuasive Discourse," *Speech Monographs*, 38 (1971), 142–145.

ONOMATOPOEIA   The miming of a subject by the very sound of the word used to describe it can serve the special needs of the persuader. When speakers talk of *"groaning* under the yoke of oppression" or of *"striking* a *blow* for freedom," the words themselves reflect the urgency of the subject. They suggest that the speaker is someone who has been close to the experience depicted. Therefore such language should have a favorable effect on credibility.

SYNECDOCHE AND METONYMY   Synecdoche and metonymy are focusing devices: semantic spotlights to search out just those features of subjects that serve the speaker's purpose. In *synecdoche* that feature is some part or action *of* the subject. For example, one energy-conservation strategy used to make large cars seem unattractive is to spotlight them negatively as "gas-guzzlers." Various campaigns of reform in our time have used the name "movement" to identify their cause. This synecdoche is rooted in the actual marching, demonstrating, and other forms of direct action that often are a part of such campaigns. The semantic strategy of focusing on the whole campaign as "movement" emphasizes the potency of such causes. It suggests purpose, direction, and action. As Eric Hoffer has pointed out, many who become involved in such campaigns are seeking just these qualities in their own lives.[15] Thus the synecdoche itself becomes a powerful magnet for drawing recruits to the cause and helps reassure those who are already involved. Against enemies of the campaign, the name can work as intimidation.

These examples illustrate that synecdoche makes a part of the subject represent its whole. It gives us a selected, restricted view. Its rhetorical function, rooted in the Law of Priority, is to make a certain feature prominent in our minds just as it thrusts other features into the background.

In *metonymy* the feature spotlighted is some closely related thing— not so much *of* the subject as *associated with* the subject. Political uses, such as George McGovern's "Come *home,* America!" during the 1972 presidential campaign, can serve to spotlight features that are charged with emotional and symbolic importance. Metonymy can help remind us of our roots, values, and goals by focusing attention on concrete symbols that represent those abstractions. Log cabins, apple pie, and fires on the hearth can mean much more than shelter, food, and sources of physical warmth. Such metonymy can vibrate with many rich meanings for those listening to a speech.

15. See his discussion in *The True Believer: Thoughts on the Nature of Mass Movements* (New York: Harper, 1951).

T. C. Fitzgerald

The Language of Arousal

We have already noted how personification can help create feeling for abstractions by lending them human form and personality. Also vital to arousal is the use of examples, which Chapter 9 discusses extensively as an informative device. For a specific, representative case, we can develop feelings that we might not readily develop about generalizations or abstractions.

Another stylistic device of arousal is *hyperbole.* The language of arousal lends itself to exaggeration, and rhetorical exaggeration is what we mean by hyperbole. Audiences often hestitate before making a commitment, knowing that much may be asked of them. In order to overcome their hesitation, persuaders have a natural tendency to overstate their cases. Be wary of this tendency in your own persuasion, for hyperbole quickly becomes distortion and dishonesty. Especially before undecided listeners and opponents, you can lose a great deal of vital credibility when your exaggeration is exposed.

The Language of Identification

The language of group identity is full of "we" and "our," the court-ship language that draws speakers and listeners closer together in the common cause. Such pronouns are a clear invitation to identification.

The value of group identification is clearest when the group is endangered. As Abraham Lincoln closed his "First Inaugural Address" on the eve of a war that would divide the nation, he tried to counter the forces of division by appealing directly to the powerful sentiments of group identification:

> I am loth to close. We are not enemies, but friends. We must not be enemies. Though passion may have strained, it must not break our bonds of affection. The mystic chords of memory, stretching from every battle-field, and patriot grave, to every living heart and hearth-stone, all over this broad land, will yet swell the chorus of the Union, when again touched, as surely they will be, by the better angels of our nature.[16]

The Language of Renewal

Persuasion in its renewal phase celebrates the group identity and argues for its continuation and growth. The language of renewal is often highly *ritualistic*, such that the language itself builds up a certain tradition of usage that the audience comes to enjoy. Thus we anticipate that Fourth of July orations, presidential proclamations on Thanksgiving, and Christmas sermons will be cast in much the same language from year to year. It is this *sameness* that we come to expect and enjoy, perhaps because it reassures us of stability and the continuation of a way of life we value.

PRESENTING THE PERSUASIVE SPEECH

Presentation skills in persuasion build on qualities discussed in Chapter 10. Your face should not only help you express the speech, but it should also attest to your earnestness and conviction. Gestures may become more intense, more animated, and more frequent as you make a point that is vital to your argument.

Among the qualities of effective persuasive delivery, genuiness and sincerity are the most important. The audience should sense in you a "personal witness" to your message. In effective persuasion the speaker seems to *grow* during the speech, just as the audience awakens to a greater sense of possibility.

---

16. *American Speeches,* ed. Wayland Maxfield Parrish and Marie Hochmuth (New York: Longmans, Green, 1954), p. 43.

SAMPLE PERSUASIVE SPEECHES

Tim Adams, a grain inspector on the Mississippi River, took a night course in public speaking at a state university. Tim had no experience speaking in public, and he had to overcome some initial discomfort. Quickly, however, he established himself both as a first-rate critic of speeches and as a person who had something to say. His speeches possessed that essential quality discussed in Chapter 4, *substance*. He also revealed an ability to make precise distinctions and draw tightly reasoned inferences.

Tim was sensitive to what he considered unjust social conditions, so persuasive speaking became his most effective means of expression. Two of his speeches follow. One concerns capital punishment; the other considers the right of public employees to go out on strike.

Valerie spoke to us about what I'm sure she would consider legalized murder: abortion. That term is a sort of paradox—legalized murder—since murder is defined by Webster's dictionary as "unlawful killing." What I want to talk about contains many such paradoxes, and it is, I think, one more form of legalized murder, one not just paid for by the government, but actually executed by the government. And it is murder in the first degree; it is premeditated, willful, and coldly carried out. I would like to talk tonight about capital punishment.

The death penalty has no place in the law books of a civilized society, yet it remains there in many of our states. Since it is no longer often invoked, it is hard for a public outcry against it to develop. But the fact remains that people are still deprived of their lives under this statute. Witness Gilmore and Spenkelink. We must not allow ourselves to settle into complacency until this law is stricken from the books, for it brutalizes society and is both futile and immoral.

Historically, according to Richard McGee, correctional administrator, criminal justice has been based on serving three needs: rehabilitation, retribution, and deterrence. Obviously the death penalty cannot serve the first, unless stated in a negative sense: that those incapable of rehabilitation are only a burden to the state and society and are best dealt with by execution. This reminds me of Hitler's reasoning that mental defectives are useless to society, cannot be rehabilitated, and should therefore be killed.

I can't agree with this argument at all. For one thing, it is totally impossible to judge who is able to be rehabilitated and who isn't. In fact, according to Hugo Bedau in his book Death Penalty in America, murderers have generally a lower rate of recidivism after parole than other parollees. And when they do return to prison, it is seldom for as serious a crime as murder.

Capital punishment also undermines the rehabilitation of the prison population as a whole. We have often heard of the condemned bravely facing the gallows, accepting his fate with dignity—in fact, made a hero for it. The feeling is especially strong among his fellow inmates. As a result, they identify with him and curse the system that would treat him so badly, creating another obstacle to their rehabilitation.

The second need fulfilled by the criminal justice system is retribution. To many, this is the fundamental aim of justice, making the criminal pay for his crime for the sake of vengeance. But should revenge be involved in society's treatment of criminals? It is certainly true that desire for revenge is a natural human instinct, but should society encourage this instinct? Shouldn't we try to suppress it instead?

Revenge is by no means universally effective. Only a few of those who commit murder are executed. Some are never even caught. Some are acquitted because of a skilled defense, through inequities in the system, or for some other reason unrelated to their guilt. Still others don't receive the maximum sentence or are granted a reprieve. So only those unlucky enough to receive none of the breaks ever suffer the death penalty. It is therefore a very arbitrary kind of revenge, one that is based not so much on the crime as on the caprice of fate.

But even if retribution is a just basis for our treatment of crime, why is it best served by execution? We don't treat other crimes by taking an eye for an eye: We don't steal from the thief or rape the rapist. Why then, when we consider the taking of life to be the most heinous of crimes, do we repay it by committing the same heinous crime?

Consider this case of retribution and "justice," recounted by Lewis E. Lawes, a warden at Sing Sing prison in New York.

In the Canadian Arctic, 600 miles from Dawson City, two Eskimos were hanged on the gallows by Canadian Mounted Police, pursuant to a sentence of death duly and legally pronounced according to the law of the Dominion Government. The men who were executed had been themselves the executioners, according to due tribal form and ceremony (to them as legal and binding as any white man's laws), of an Eskimo murderer. But because their assumption of the function of executioners was sanctioned only by tribal law, they paid the identical penalty which a few months before they had meted out.

Who should execute the Canadians for killing the Eskimos? And where does it all end?

There is a third aim of criminal justice, that of deterrence. The death penalty is meant to deter the act of murder. Does it? On the face of it, one would think so. Certainly we would answer that we would be more effectively deterred by the fear of death; but then we don't possess the criminal mind. Obviously it is not an absolute deterrent, or it would never have to be invoked. I think its ability as even a partial deterrent is greatly exaggerated. There is a mountain of evidence to show that it is not an effective deterrent. One study of crime rates in California, reported by Dr. William F. Graves in the journal Medical Arts and Sciences, showed an increase in murders on the days of execution. Rather than teach us the horror of killing and the sanctity of life, capital punishment brutalizes society and makes killing more justifiable.

So I can't see that any of the three aims of justice is properly served by capital punishment. It is therefore futile. But there are still other reasons for opposing it. One is that it is so final; there is no possibility of correcting a mistake. Don't believe that a lot haven't been made. Mistakes have been discovered countless times, both before and after the execution has taken place. Probably countless other mistakes have been made and never discovered.

Another argument against capital punishment, touched on by the Supreme Court, is its discriminatory nature, both intentional and unintentional. It is an indisputable fact that the rich, who can afford the best lawyers, are seldom executed. The poor and the friendless are the most frequent victims of the law. It is impossible for a judge or jury not to bring their own prejudices into the courtroom. And these prejudices are reinforced by the sensational press coverage surrounding a capital trial.

In some cases, the death penalty has been used almost exclusively to punish nonwhites. According to the Greenberg and Himmelstein study in the authoritative series Crime and Delinquency, the death penalty for rape is rarely enforced against a white man or against a black man convicted of raping a black woman. But it has been frequently used, especially in the South, in cases of black men raping white women.

You might ask yourselves, "Why be concerned with the death penalty when it is so rarely used today?" The answer is that, as long as the law allows it, there will be executions, however infrequently. Their very infrequency points out the arbitrariness of the sentence.

Caryl Chessman wrote this letter to his lawyer on the day he was executed:

Dear George,

Now my long struggle is over. Yours isn't. This barbarous, senseless practice, capital punishment, will continue. In our society other men will go on taking that last walk to death until . . . when? Until the citizens of this State and this land are made aware of its futility. Until they realize that retributive justice is not justice at all.

I die with the burning hope that my case and my death will contribute to this awareness, this realization. I know that you will personally do all in your power, as citizen and lawyer, to convince your fellows that justice is not served, but confounded, by vengeance and executioners.

Good luck.

My best,

Caryl

Tim begins his speech by adapting nicely to a previous effective speech on abortion. (One might possibly question the wisdom of connecting his cause, which is controversial enough in its own right, with another volatile issue.) He strikes the position of his speech in very sharp value terms at the beginning: Capital punishment is a law that should be "stricken from the books, for it brutalizes society and is both futile and immoral." Should he have presented a vivid instance of injustice under capital punishment before stating such a strong position?

He divides his speech very nicely at the outset in terms of the three traditional functions of the criminal justice system. Note how he connects the mentality that defends capital punishment with the reasoning of Hitler, an association that could have been below the belt but in the context of this speech is not offensive. As he develops the refutative design, observe how he talks *with* his audience, anticipating their responses and answering them. He works close to his listeners through direct, conversational language ("you and I") and the language of identification ("we" and "us").

Once he cuts capital punishment off from its justifying premises in the criminal justice system, he attacks it on its own terms as unfair and arbitrary. He argues powerfully that its mistakes are fatal and beyond correction. An effective example at this point might have made the point even more devastating.

Tim ends his speech with an effective quotation from Caryl Chessman. In a different context, perhaps with an execution pending on the local scene, he might have wanted some specific action from his listeners. Here he is content to ask them for a commitment of attitude.

At 7 o'clock on the Saturday morning of July 1, 1978, employees of the Memphis Fire Department went on strike. During the next 3 days over 200 fires were reported, over a dozen of them resulting in extensive damage.

One such fire destroyed the Vance Avenue branch of the Memphis Public Library. Striking firefighters were on the scene already when a single pumper truck arrived, manned by captains and assistant fire chiefs, and the strikers taunted those trying to battle the blaze. "Let it burn," yelled one of them. Another striker said, "We could have put it out in 15 minutes, before the flames even reached the library."

This library was in one of the more economically depressed areas of the city, where educational opportunities are scarce to begin with. As one area resident said, "That's the worst thing that could have happened to this neighborhood. They've been having a little school up there for the children. Now they'll have to catch the bus to go to the library."

I had a friend who taught school a few blocks from there, who said it was the only place his students could go to read or study. Its loss severely affected his ability to teach and theirs to learn.

Downtown, a group of strikers outside Fire Department Headquarters were jubilant at the news of another fire at Chelsea and Stonewall. "The brass just lost a two-story frame," one of them yelled, as reported in The Commercial Appeal.

Mr. and Mrs. Howard L. Payne lost their nearly completed $85,000 Whitehaven home to fire, even though it was right down the street from a fire station. The trucks that answered the call had to come all the way from downtown and were too late.

"I don't know if I'm really bitter," said Mr. Payne, "but it's disappointing because one of the things about building it here was that a fire station is just down the street. I understand some of their labor problems, but there ought to be a better way to work it out."

How does the community get put in a situation like this? Fire and police strikes are a relatively new event. Though the Boston Police Department went on strike shortly after World War I, fire and police strikes didn't really catch on until the late 60s. In most states, such strikes are illegal and should remain so. In order to understand why public employees must not have the legal power to strike, even though the private labor community is allowed that option, we must first look at the basic differences between public and private employees.

One difference obviously is <u>their employer</u>. When public employers strike, they are not striking against a company; they are striking against the government and therefore against all society. As Franklin Roosevelt said, "Particularly, I want to emphasize my conviction that militant tactics have no place in the functions of any organization of government employees."

A strike against a private company in essence affects only that company and the strikers, because the public can always more or less take its business elsewhere. But this is impossible in a public employee strike—which brings us to a second difference.

<u>The uniqueness of their services.</u> When fire or police protection is cut off by a strike, we have nowhere else to go. This gives the strikers unlimited power and is one of the chief attractions of striking. But such strikes can be drastic and dangerous. This is a third difference between public and private employees, especially police officers and firefighters: <u>the essentialness of their services.</u> A community cannot survive long without such protection. And if it is true that a tax-paying community has a fundamental right to such protection, then it must also be true that those who provide it have no right to withhold it and therefore no right to strike.

Another difference between public and private employees is the source of their wages. Private business is profit-oriented; public business is not. In a strike of private employees, the affected company can always raise prices to cover the costs, leaving the consumer the option of paying the higher prices or not buying the product. The only means the government has of financing its operations, however, is through taxes. Therefore we have no options. The public employee has no monetary productivity, so increased productivity can't cover the costs. We must all shoulder the costs, willingly or not. The Connecticut Supreme Court in 1951 said:

> Under our system, the government is established by and run for all of the people, not for the benefit of any person or group. The profit motive, inherent in the principle of free enterprise, is absent [in government agencies].
>
> It should be the aim of every employee of the government to do his or her part to make it function as efficiently and economically as possible. The drastic remedy of the organized strike to enforce the demands of unions of government employees is in direct contravention [contradiction] of this principle.

When those who have sworn to protect our lives and property suddenly stop doing so, they hold a gun to our heads. They become the most important political body in the community, usurping the powers we have given to our elected officials. The U.S. District Court for the District of Columbia has offered its opinion:

> In the private sphere, the strike is used to equalize bargaining power, but this has universally been held not to be appropriate when its object and purpose can only be to influence the essentially political decisions of government in the allocations of its resources.

> The basic question here is: Who serves whom? We pay for the public services so we should receive them. When we pay and don't receive them, what is our recourse? What happens to respect for government when it cannot produce what we have paid for and are entitled to? Illegal strikes by public employees must remain illegal, or we will lose—not just money, but also the credibility of our institutions.

Tim's speech is notable for its excellent beginning. The listener is immediately thrust *into* the situation Tim finds objectionable and is caught up in several interesting narratives. The design and strategy of the speech are two-fold. First, use the repetitive design by accumulating effective examples to show the human consequences of public employee strikes. Second, develop an effective contrast design to separate the public employee strike from its counterpart in the private sector. The effect of such separation, accomplished here by well-reasoned distinctions, is to deny the former the legitimacy of the latter. An opposing speaker would have to confront and refute Tim's reasoning before using the analogy to private sector strikes as a warrant to justify the public employee strike. Having depicted the human consequences well and having denied any legal and moral justification, Tim hopes his audience will join in his repudiation of the public employee strike.

Special strengths here are Tim's narrative ability in making the opening examples come to life. He followed the advice of Chapter 2 to use direct quotations, and he selected his examples ingeniously to create an overall image of violated society, which in this case crossed race and class lines. His arguments in separating the public employee strike from the private sector strike are well documented and elegantly drawn.

If he had had more time, Tim might well have presented the arguments of the striking workers for the sake of refuting them. Such a two-sided approach to persuasion might have developed at the end of his initial examples, at the point of his hasty historical account of the public employee strike. The speech ends abstractly, and, in view of the beginning, rather weakly. If Tim could have returned his listeners to the local scene, through one more concrete example, he might have ended on a more powerful note.

Summary of Major Ideas

Ethical persuasion puts the emphasis on convincing rather than conditioning.

Argument, which is at the heart of ethical persuasion, is that process by which we give others reasons for accepting our recommendations.

Basic to argumentative persuasion is the unit of proof, which includes situation, warrant, and claim. Situation in argument establishes some vital reality. The warrant is a value that gives a situation its meaning.

Argument can proceed by definition, which adjusts audience vision and establishes the reality of a situation.

Argument can develop by creating new perspectives for listeners, which bring the minor premise into focus for them.

Argument can also proceed by taking controversy from the abstract level to the concrete level, restoring a sense of reality.

Argument can develop from the characters of those involved in controversy and can be assisted by the artificial characterization provided by personification.

Correct induction in argument depends on the adequacy and distribution of the sample, on timing, and on how generalizations are worded.

Deductions can be flawed by categorical vagueness, treating probable conclusions as though they were certain, and by oversimplifying in the hypothetical and disjunctive syllogisms.

In the persuasive speech outline, the theme becomes the proposal. The persuasive speech outline should spell out the major assumptions of the speech.

The classical forensic pattern and Monroe's motivated sequence are two approaches to the arrangement of primary statements in the persuasive outline.

In persuasion, comparison and simile comment on their subjects as well as illuminate them.

Stylistic contrast in persuasion confronts the audience with a choice, whereas irony tends to become sarcasm and invective.

Using a metaphor establishes perspective, which is vital to persuasive depiction.

Synecdoche and metonymy are focusing devices that can direct our attention to just those features of a subject that are vital to a persuasive effort.

The language of persuasive arousal has a tendency to exaggerate through the use of hyperbole.

Persuasive presentations should emphasize the speaker's sincerity and conviction.

Exercises and Discussion Questions

1. Find examples of persuasion that emphasize conditioning. What would it take to make these examples emphasize convincing instead? Would their ethical nature be improved?

2. Many people have objected to 30-second radio and television political advertisements, arguing that such persuasion must emphasize conditioning over convincing in vital choice situations. What do you think about this issue? Research the question for an open class discussion.

3. See whether you can detect the interplay of units of proof in a recent persuasive speech in *Vital Speeches of the Day*. By what argumentative forms does the speech proceed? Do you detect any flaws in the reasoning?

4. For the speech you studied in Exercise 3, develop a complete outline that goes through the steps discussed in this chapter. Are the assumptions made clear in the speech, and does it develop a coherent rationale for its proposal?

5. Look for examples of the stylistic techniques discussed here. Bring them to class for discussion of their effectiveness.

6. Name some important social and political metaphors of our time, and give the reasons for their importance.

For Further Reading

An excellent collection of essays on the nature of argument has been provided in *Perspectives on Argumentation,* ed. Gerald R. Miller and Thomas R. Nilsen (Chicago, Ill.: Scott, Foresman, 1966). Douglas Ehninger and Wayne Brockriede, *Decision by Debate* (Chicago, Ill.: Dodd, Mead, 1963) is a modern classic that establishes a practical bridge between the theory and the practice of argumentation. The book develops the essential ethical quality of argument in persuasion. Another modern classic on argumentative persuasion is Karl R. Wallace, "The Substance of Rhetoric: Good Reasons," *Quarterly Journal of Speech*, 49 (1963), 239–249.

Still quite useful and enjoyable as an investigation of the flaws of statistical inductive reasoning is Darrell Huff, *How to Lie With Statistics* (New York: Norton, 1954).

V

PUBLIC SPEAKING IN THE MANAGEMENT OF PUBLIC PROBLEMS

In *Origins*, Richard Leakey and Roger Lewin develop the argument that humans are by nature cooperating beings.[1] Speech serves the needs of cooperation in two fundamental ways. It offers a means of managing conflict that otherwise would drive people apart from each other. And it provides rituals of identification that draw people closer together.

On almost every issue that comes up, people support different programs. Their persuasions compete with each other in the market place of ideas. Managing the conflict that can develop becomes a vital concern for the well-being of society. How can we harness conflict so that some productive good comes of it? Can we arrange matters so that the most intelligent and enlightened view has the greatest chance to influence human affairs? These questions pose a challenge to the ethical and constructive public speaker. They suggest specialized roles, formats, and situations for which the speaker must develop special skills.

One such format is the small group discussion, an organized probe into the nature of some disturbing or problematic situation. Group discussion helps keep the focus on the facts in a controversy, and it often takes the steam out of conflict by revealing that fears are not really justified. The group discussion often discovers new options and helps opponents recognize each other as human beings rather than as the two-dimensional stereotypes they are apt to form of each other before they have actually met. Such an informal setting can also draw out agreements that might not be reached in large-scale rhetorical confrontations, where positions must often be struck more rigidly and dramatically.

As the small group grows, arrives at particularly difficult problems, or becomes vested with great responsibility for resolving conflict, the speaker must acquire the skills of *parliamentary procedure*. Parliamentary procedure helps to regulate and control discussion when it is

---

1. *Origins* (New York: Dutton, 1977).

heated by passion. It is codified fairness that also contains a built-in impulse toward careful deliberation and toward commitment to a decision. Thus it is both conservative and action-oriented at the same time. It helps to prevent the curse of talking about it but not doing anything about it.

The parliamentary assembly often provides the appropriate setting for that last great peaceable resolver of human conflict, formal debate. Debate is often useful when group discussion bogs down and disagreement continues over competing courses of action. Whereas discussion promotes the informal convergence or coming together of different positions, debate deliberately holds these positions apart from each other and at some distance from the audience, so that listeners can inspect them more closely and dispassionately before coming to a decision.

Thus there is a kind of natural connection among these speech formats and skills. Taken all together, they give us some civilized control over what could otherwise become a jungle of conflict. They are mechanisms to harness the forces of human symbolic behavior. As such, they have been vital to the emergence of culture and civilization as we know them today.

Chapter 14 introduces group discussion and parliamentary procedure, and Chapter 15 treats the management of conflict through debate.

14

CONFLICT MANAGEMENT THROUGH GROUP DISCUSSION AND PARLIAMENTARY PROCEDURE

Liberty, as a principle, has no application to any state
of things anterior to the time when mankind have become
capable of being improved by free and equal discussion.

JOHN STUART MILL, *On Liberty*

Group discussion: nature, process, and functions

Participation in group discussion

Planning for group discussion

Use of parliamentary procedure

When we speak of group discussion, we have in mind collective efforts to analyze and understand problems and to decide on common actions. Each person in the group contributes—or should *feel* that he or she contributes—to the group decisions and accepts responsibility for implementing those decisions. Normally five to nine people function most effectively in small group decision making, depending on the cohesiveness of the group.

THE FUNCTIONS OF GROUP DISCUSSION

Successful discussion depends on the quality of group investigation and the management of conflict, and both of these functions require certain skills and a knowledge of procedures.

Investigating Problems

The motive that brings a group together for discussion is the urgency of some felt difficulty. Most often, the nature of this problem is quite clear: It has not rained recently, or interest rates threaten to impede the growth of the economy. Occasionally, however, the nature of the problem is *not* clear, and you hear groups asking themselves such questions as "We are not doing well, not nearly as well as we expected. What's wrong with us?" For such groups, problem identification is a vital first step. Every possible point of view must be explored, because the entire direction of discussion and subsequent action will depend on the answer to the question *What is the nature of our problem?*

Once a group has defined its problem, the focus of investigation can turn to causes: *Why has the problem come about?* This question sometimes leads to a crucial stage of group inquiry. Much depends on the kinds of questions members ask and what are considered legitimate and productive points of inquiry. If the problem is drought, for example, it makes a great deal of difference which of the following two questions we ask.

Have atmospheric conditions not been conducive to rain?
Have we angered the gods?

Such first questions about causation can determine whether we eventually wind up seeding clouds or sacrificing humans.

Therefore we should not assume too much at this early stage and should encourage even questions that seem wild or irrelevant. Group members must realize that they can ask such questions without embarrassment, humiliation, or punishment. It is a special responsibility of the group leader to encourage tolerance. When we feel we can no longer ask bold questions without reprisal, conformity sets in, group thinking stagnates, and the discussion becomes sterile and unproductive.

The group should also take its time on the question of causation. Only when the question of causes is thoroughly considered can long-range solutions be discovered. Otherwise we may end up with programs of action that treat only superficial symptoms of the deeper problem.

Causation often invites exploration into the history of the problem. *How has the problem evolved up to the present time?* This inquiry helps us spot trends and predict consequences. If the crime rate has been rising steadily at 5 percent each year for the past 5 years, with the emphasis on crimes against persons, we can predict the magnitude of the crime problem in the immediate future. We can also determine how drastic a remedy we must apply or, given the nature of the crime problem, *which* causative factors we must concentrate on to reverse the trend.

Discussion must then turn to the size and scope of the problem: *Whom does this problem affect, and how does it affect them?* Obviously, the precision of our information becomes an important consideration here. Nothing is more frustrating to constructive action than a group of people responding to what they think are the facts, when actually they are reacting only to the shadows of their own fears and fantasies. The people who once hanged witches were absolutely convinced they were reacting rationally to an objective set of circumstances.

Having pinpointed the problem, traced it to its roots, and measured its impact, we now turn to possible solutions. *What are the options available to the group?* Discussion needs to illuminate fully their comparative advantages and disadvantages. Comparative costs, measured in human as well as material terms, are certainly a major consideration. Each option's relative likelihood of success needs to be weighed, as well as the capacity of the group to implement the various options. Some choices may represent short-term copings and others long-range solutions. Certain options may promise new and additional benefits, and this potential needs to be weighed in making a decision. The group may not reach unanimous agreement in deliberating these matters, but it can usually come to a majority decision. Indeed, it must make a commitment if the discussion is to end successfully. Thus the leader must finally confront the group with this vital question: *To which of these options or combinations of options are we willing to make a commitment?* And once that vital matter is resolved, *What is our plan of implementation?*

Before the group completes its work, it must decide on a method of evaluation. No commitment to a plan of action should be irrevocable. *What concrete expectations does the group have of this solution? When will the group expect results and how will it assess them?* The answers to these questions will determine whether the group will remain committed to the course of action it has selected.

Such is the process of investigation in group discussion; this procedure is summarized below.

THE PROCESS OF INVESTIGATION IN GROUP DISCUSSION

1. What is the nature of the problem?
2. Why has the problem occurred?
3. How has the problem occurred, and what is the history of its development?
4. Who is affected by this problem, and how much?
5. What are the options available for dealing with this problem?
   a. How costly are they?
   b. How likely are they to be successful?
   c. How difficult will they be to execute?
   d. How completely should they resolve the problem—both now and in the future?
   e. What new and special benefits are they likely to bring about?
6. Which option or combination of options will the group commit itself to? How will it implement this commitment?

Bettye Lane/Photo Researchers

7. How will the group measure the success of this solution?
   a. What are the expectations?
   b. When should these results have happened?
   c. At what point will the group decide to reaffirm or revise its strategy?

Managing Conflict

On almost all vital questions that affect a group, one can expect to find disagreement and conflict over definition, causes, consequences, and options. Hence management of conflict becomes a basic challenge for group discussion. Management of conflict implies two vital processes: minimizing conflict as much as possible and transforming conflict into a positive force working in favor of the group. The small group can manage conflict in several ways.

1. It can build on common ground that does exist. In the very act of joining together for discussion, participants imply that they share some common interest. To the extent that the group can remind itself of its shared interest and common background of experience, conflict can be reduced. Small group sessions should begin with individuals introducing themselves and explaining their interest in the question at hand. As

members become acquainted with each other, it becomes easier to build a base of understanding and even sympathy. As the group develops its work, leaders especially should look for opportunities to reinforce this sense of shared experience, in order to counteract the natural stresses that accompany any important inquiry.

2. The small group format draws out information that often takes the steam out of uninformed or misinformed disputes. Nothing can be more passionate than an argument between two group members over a fact possessed by neither. The verification and introduction of that fact will often cool the atmosphere.

3. The small group approach prevents minds from closing prematurely on controversial subjects. When people discover an area of disagreement on a subject, one of their most typical (and destructive) tendencies is to dig themselves into entrenched positions. Stubborn and full of pride, they generate the kind of conflict that usually only clouds an issue. The small group atmosphere, however, discourages the hardening of attitudes into rigid positions until investigation has been pursued and accomplished. Of course no one can prevent the strongly opinionated person, locked into a position from the outset, from entering a discussion. Such people, who usually violate both the principles and procedures of group discussion, are only likely to hurt the position they represent. The group must struggle to overcome their negative influence.

4. Ideally, the small group format impresses on people's minds the importance of deeper values to which conflict is a threat. An effective group leader helps group members focus on more lasting considerations than the agitation of the moment. A group may disagree, for example, on the means of effective medical care, but they agree on the need for such care. A group may disagree on which is *more* important, education or medical care, but members agree that both *are* important. The leader must see that group members never lose sight of such wider horizons and of the deeper values that hold the group together.

5. The small group discussion creates an atmosphere of deliberation that moderates emotion and discourages self-interest among participants. At its best, the group steers an even course through any conflicts that arise between individual members. Members can check their personal reactions by submitting them to group judgment. The collective view is not always right, nor is it always calm and sensible. But a skillfully conducted group discussion makes rational decisions on most issues more likely.

6. The small group format seeks the compromises that are vital to civilized society and respectful of those caught up in conflict.

Sometimes right and wrong may be difficult to determine, and different people may present claims that seem legitimate but in conflict with each other. When these opposed interests and claims stand in the way of group process, then the group, especially through its leader, must search for compromise. Nothing is more admirable than the ability to find that small crack in what had seemed an impregnable wall of conflict.

7. At the very least, the small group can work to clarify and place in proper proportion those issues on which parties intelligently disagree. Once these issues have been identified, they can be submitted via debate to an audience authorized to make a decision. As we have seen, there can be a progression in the forms of public address that we are studying. The informative speech often raises questions that become the contentions of the persuasive speech; the persuasive speech may seem to invite the investigation so characteristic of group discussion; the group discussion often focuses on issues that can be resolved only by formal debate before larger audiences. This is not to say that the group itself cannot argue and come to decisions—often such a group may be authorized to make decisions. But when crucial policy issues arise in a society accustomed to democratic participation, it is usually wise for formal debate to be conducted before the larger constituency. On such issues the small group may recommend, but the larger group should rule on such recommendations at the conclusion of debate, either ratifying or rejecting them. The techniques of such debate are the subject of the next chapter.

PARTICIPATING IN GROUP DISCUSSION

An important indication of the success of a group in investigating problems and managing conflict is the degree to which members of the group feel responsible collectively for decisions that are reached. Those whose views are *not* adopted must nevertheless find the group identity so satisfying, its procedures so fair, that they too are willing to endorse group decisions. *Do the dissenters also participate?* That is the vital question.

The Responsibilities of Group Members

Our understanding of the goals and functions of group discussion suggests a composite picture of ideal *discussants*. Such people come to discussions primarily to learn, not to advocate prefabricated positions. They seek the truth wherever the search may take them.

Bettye Lane/Photo Researchers

Ideal discussants are also lovers of the human community. They recognize the vital functions of groups and subscribe to the ethics of group belonging. They find fulfillment in the cooperative search for truth, so they come prepared to discuss the questions they think might arise. They have learned all they can about these questions, and they are concerned, not with how much they can dominate, but with how and how much they can contribute to the collective search. They have high tolerance for the quirks of other people; indeed, they value individuality. They seek to build on the strengths of others and to compensate for their weaknesses. They intuitively respect the humanity in others, such that it is really difficult for them not to enjoy others or to nurse grudges and resentments over time.

Ideal discussants, moreover, are psychologically strong. They need not be preoccupied with protecting fragile egos and are able to open their eyes to the truth. They have a well-defined point of view, which contributes distinctly to the collective perspective. This same stability means they are able to make small surrenders for the sake of larger, long-term gains. They are able, for example, to concede a point when they are wrong or for the sake of helping the group survive a confrontation. They are not afraid to compromise, because, having closely examined the issues, they know when and how much they can compromise. Of course, what we are painting here *is* an ideal, and most of us fall short of it most of the time.

On a more concrete level, it is important to realize when *not* to speak. Good discussants are so respectful of the group and its purpose that they speak only when they can make an important contribution to the deliberative process. Therefore, they are listened to respectfully when they do speak. Their contributions are not limited to new and helpful bits of information. Sometimes a restatement and summary of a long line of inquiry—offered with the preface "Let me see if I understand what we are saying"—can focus a discussion and put it back on track. At other times the ability to ask the right question is absolutely vital. At still other times an intelligent interpretation of a confused situation, persuasive in its impact on collective thinking, can advance group consciousness and the achievement of consensus. Effective group participation can mean any and all of these specific contributions.

The Responsibilities of Group Leaders

Among the participants in a group discussion, the *group leader* should have special qualities in addition to those of effective discussants.

One school of thought much heard in recent years maintains that formal leadership in a group is both unnecessary and corrupting. All group members should be equal, it would say, whereas leadership immediately sets up a hierarchy in which one or several are "more equal than others." All should participate in a natural process of decision making. Let the judgment rise from the group. If we are patient, something beautiful will emerge from the group unadulterated by leadership.[1]

How pleasant it would be if this dream of directionless group discussion could be made to work! However, experience indicates that supposedly leaderless groups often decline into either anarchy or tyranny. For practical reasons, there has to be some leadership in a group. Someone must be there to orchestrate the lines of investigation. Such a person enjoys a measure of power either delegated by the group itself or conferred by some other authority. At best, leaders are genuinely admired, liked, and respected by the groups they lead. The authority they exercise is natural insofar as it rises from recognition of the leader's unusual ability.

What is this ability? What are the special traits of leadership? Good leaders are blessed with a certain largeness of spirit, for which the best word is "magnanimity." They are patient, not petty, people. They realize that a group must often grope its way out of a quandary without being rushed or pushed too hard. They are also sensitive to the need for all to have their chance to be heard. This same fairness leads them

1. See, for example, the penetrating discussion and readings suggested in Karlyn Kohrs Campbell, "The Rhetoric of Women's Liberation: An Oxymoron," *Quarterly Journal of Speech*, 59 (1973), 74–86.

to exercise discipline when it must be exercised for the sake of the group: They will restrain those who would monopolize discussion and calm those whose tempers flare. Essentially, however, they are positive people who accept discipline as an occasional necessity of leadership.

They are curious and open, eager to see what some new line of investigation may reveal, open to the new ideas that may result. They are dedicated to achievement of the group goal and keep the group moving in the direction of its destination. As they cajole and encourage and guide, they are able to avoid stepping unnecessarily on sensitive toes. They are knowledgeable of the subject under discussion and well versed in the rules of discussion itself. Good leaders impose these rules gracefully and appropriately, so that they serve the group rather than warping the direction of its inquiry.

Throughout the discussion, leaders demonstrate a keen sense of orchestration. They know when to pursue a point, and how far. Finally, good leaders are charged with an energy that ignites the group and impels it in constructive directions.

PLANNING FOR GROUP DISCUSSION

Leadership does not consist only in character traits, although such traits may be of primary importance. It also involves the small but vital arrangements that any good leader must make. The first major step is to create the proper setting for discussion.

Setting

The atmosphere for discussion should encourage relaxation and enjoyable interaction among participants when they are not concentrating on the task at hand. For this reason industries and organizations often prefer resort sites, or places far removed from the normal grind of daily business, for discussion settings. Good leadership also means planning for the small things—such as coffee breaks, blackboard and chalk, and pens and notepaper for participants. Effective planning of such details can help create an atmosphere of efficiency in which good discussion can flourish. The room selected for discussion should be both comfortable and businesslike, and it should permit uninterrupted concentration on the problem at hand. Usually the group meets around a table to reduce distance among participants, to facilitate note taking, and to encourage a sense of teamwork.

The selection of the table can have important consequences for discussion. (Perhaps this explains why the negotiations in Paris to end the Vietnam War foundered for months over the size and shape of the conference table.) A round table tends to produce more democratic discussions, because all positions on the circumference of a circle are equally imposing. Such a table usually encourages balanced, face-to-face interaction among all participants. On the other hand, a long, rectangular table promotes more authority-conscious group discussions. The positions at either end of the table are conspicuously those of the leaders or challengers to leadership. Physical proximity to the leader at such a table can be important to those competing for prominence. Then again, people often discuss matters differently, and more informally, when they are addressing people directly across from them at a table. Their style may change as they turn to speak to those who sit at a distance along the table. The arrangement can lend itself to the formation of cliques and even to divisiveness in the group.

For these many reasons, leaders must plan carefully the *arrangement* of the room in which discussion will occur and must select a table or compensate for the table available, taking into account the effects we have mentioned, the purpose of the discussion, and the nature of those participating.

Agenda

After the leader has planned the setting for discussion, he or she must set the agenda. The agenda should be distributed to all members in advance of the meeting so that they can reflect on it and bring well-considered thoughts to the discussion. The agenda reflects the leader's belief in how the discussion may most profitably proceed, but it may be altered as a result of discoveries made during discussion. Indeed, in some situations, the leader may wish to let the group itself set its own agenda out of common consent and may offer only advice, guidance, and occasional encouragement. When mistrust is especially high, such participatory agenda setting is most appropriate, because it allays fears that the order of discussion is being stacked in favor of one interest or another.

Whether recommended by the leader or resolved by common consent, agenda setting is normally not difficult—indeed, it can follow the natural process of investigation described on page 324. Of course each problem has its own special character, and the topics posed for the agenda must be adjusted accordingly. The history phase of inquiry, for example, may be vital to some problems but of small importance to others. This is why leaders must be knowledgeable about the problem *before* the discussion. They must know *which* questions to ask, *how* to ask them, *how long* to dwell on them, and *in what order* these questions may most profitably be considered.

Finally, leaders should show good judgment in projecting the number, progression, and timing of meetings to deal with a problem. Many problems are complex, and to force the entire process of investigation and resolution into a single meeting might yield only fatigue and bad decisions. Sometimes, too, a group must be allowed to back away from a particular controversy that arises during inquiry. Often a night's sleep miraculously clears away what had seemed insuperable difficulties. On the other hand, scheduling too much time between meetings can cause the discussion to grow stale and may delay a solution to death. Thus a sense of proper pace and timing is vital to leadership.

USING PARLIAMENTARY PROCEDURE

Throughout this chapter we have stressed the importance of *fairness* in managing conflict and preserving respect for leadership. Parliamentary procedure codifies the rules of fairness. If followed scrupulously, parliamentary procedure locks the group into a formal order of conducting business. This promotes deliberation, assures a hearing for all sides, and gives weight and importance to group decisions. As Bryant and Wallace have said, "Parliamentary procedures are good to the extent that they make a meeting fair and orderly. They are intended to make the will of the majority prevail, at the same time protecting the right of the minority to voice its opinion and to prevent hasty action."[2] Parliamentary procedure also makes the group commit itself to some kind of formal conclusion to a line of inquiry, even if that decision be to make no formal decision at the time.

Proceeding by parliamentary rule can help promote precision in group undertaking. When you say, "I move that . . . ," attention is directed to the motion and its exact meaning. Such proceeding is deliberate—sometimes even slow—but it has a marvelous way of stabilizing and regulating the discussion of complex or controversial issues. Parliamentary procedure should be invoked at the following times:

2. Donald C. Bryant and Karl R. Wallace, *Fundamentals of Public Speaking*, 3rd ed. (New York: Appleton-Century-Crofts, 1960), p. 441.

1. At the beginning of discussion when the leader anticipates controversy on an issue.
2. Whenever the group runs into substantial disagreement in the course of discussion.
3. When the group is vested with formal responsibilities and is expected to reach decisions concerning policy.
4. As the group grows larger, making informal discussion less useful and more awkward. At some point in its expansion, such a group evolves into the parliamentary assembly.

It is impossible to provide an exhaustive survey of parliamentary custom here, but the following sections spotlight some of its most useful features and the general wisdom and good sense that support them. Consult the readings at the end of the chapter for more comprehensive works on parliamentary law.

Order of Business

When an organization meets regularly by parliamentary law, a certain pattern of business provides overall structure to the proceedings.

1. Chair calls meeting to order.
2. Secretary reads minutes, which are corrected if necessary and then approved (minutes may be distributed in advance of the meeting to save time).
3. Committees and officers make reports.
4. Unfinished business.
5. New business.
6. Announcements.
7. Adjournment.

As helpful as such a routine may be, the danger is that it can stagnate into exactly that—just a routine. One of the special arts of chairing is to spotlight important items of business on the agenda in all advance announcements of meetings. Meetings should be called only to do business, and members should leave feeling that worthwhile business has been accomplished or at least attempted. Otherwise, meetings become hollow rituals and the group may begin to decline.

Main Motions

Strictly speaking, meaningful discussion of any item on the agenda does not begin and cannot be initiated until a main motion proposes to

"All in favor of putting __everything__ on the back burner, say 'Aye.'"

Drawing by Stevenson; © 1977 The New Yorker Magazine, Inc.

commit the group to some action or some official point of view. The motion normally states some *positive* action to be taken, even when the group sentiment seems negative: "I move that we go on record in favor of the recent action by the Student Senate with respect to campus traffic violations." The only exception to such procedure occurs when the group wishes to express itself very strongly: "I move that we go on record in opposition to the recent action by the Student Senate regarding traffic regulation on this campus." Observe that the motion itself does not contain "color" words such as "despicable action" or "irresponsible Student Senate." The group statement itself, expressed in the passage of the motion, is regarded as a strong repudiation. Such deliberate understatement expresses the group's confidence in the expression of its will. Overstatement is undignified, in bad form, and conveys a sense of desperation. It is as though a weak, insecure group must reinforce the expression of its will with loaded language. Too often such loaded language merely types the group—perhaps undeservedly—as irresponsible in its deliberations.

Main motions must be precise expressions of group will. To achieve this precision, and to test group opinion before the framing of a motion, many groups conduct informal exploratory discussions before formal action begins. Such initial exploration can become part of the formal proceedings of a group when a member offers the following resolution: "I move informal consideration of. . . ." Such consideration then holds until the group has fashioned a motion that appears to enjoy a good chance of approval. To reinforce the possibility of good resolutions, a particularly ingenious requirement of parliamentary procedure is that the main and all subsidiary motions require a *second*. If a motion is offered of such little consequence that no one else wishes to see it considered, the chair will say, "The motion dies for lack of a second," and the table is again open for a main motion.

Once a main motion is made, it claims all the attention of the group. Until it is properly disposed, any other main motion and all other extraneous discussion are "out of order" (unless the group approves a motion "to suspend the rules"). How are such motions made in the first place? Often the chair invites them, saying in effect, "The floor is open for a motion." In response, a participant might say: "I move that . . ." or "I offer the following resolution: Resolved, that. . . ." After the motion has been stated, either the chair asks for a second or a second is simply offered: "I second the motion." The chair then says, "The floor is open for discussion."

The fate of a motion obviously depends on its merits and its survival of the close scrutiny that characterizes any healthy discussion group. But its fate also depends on some common-sense rules of fairness and decorum.

1. Remarks should be addressed to the chair. Keep personalities out of the picture as much as possible, and avoid referring to people by name. "How can you say that, Kerry?" is not the kind of contribution that lends itself to an illuminating discussion.

2. The chair should encourage the statement of all possible views on an issue. For this reason the chair may ask for possible dissent from a view that seems to be emerging in strength. Sometimes the chair must contend with a strong-willed person who tends to monopolize the discussion and to intimidate others. Both firmness and supreme tact are vital qualities in such situations. A simple "Thank you, but can we hear now from others?" may serve to divert attention from such individuals. Invoking parliamentary procedure places the chair, who has presumably been the leader of the discussion group, under a special obligation to be objective. As discussion grows more formal, the chair should refrain from voicing any personal opinion. Only when the expression of his or her point of view seems desired by the group during a stalemate, or when a valuable consideration is being neglected, should the chair

inject personal views into the discussion. Leaders who really wish to play advocate's roles should relinquish the chair by appointing a surrogate who serves during the remainder of discussion on that motion.

3. Group members who have not yet spoken on an issue should take precedence. It may even be necessary occasionally to regulate the length and frequency of statements (for example, to limit everyone to one statement no more than five minutes long). Such limitations are neither healthy nor desirable, and they create additional control problems for the chair. Discussion must be as free as possible, so advance limitations should be invoked sparingly and reluctantly.

Subsidiary Motions

Main motions can present formidable problems in discussion, and a group often struggles to come to some decision on them. Among the coping mechanisms at the group's disposal are a number of subsidiary motions, all of which are in order during consideration of a main motion. They provide means to shape and modify motions so that they are more acceptable, to discipline discussion, or to delay consideration until some better time. They can help overcome obstacles to group progress; unfortunately, they can also be abused in such a way as to establish such obstacles.

Subsidiary motions themselves act on and are subject to other motions, as noted in the discussion that follows. In the order that we discuss them here, each takes precedence over those that go before it. The order of precedence, of course, is not an order of importance; no motion is more important than a main motion. The order of precedence simply establishes the sequence in which motions will be considered. The motion to amend would be considered before a motion to postpone indefinitely, but it must give way to a motion to refer to committee. The motion to "lay on the table" enjoys the most precedence among the subsidiary motions.

POSTPONE INDEFINITELY   This motion is debatable, and the main motion to which it applies also remains debatable. Somewhat rarely used, it is a way of avoiding action on a motion, so it could be useful in sensitive situations. It cannot be amended, because to affix any time would be to render the postponement no longer indefinite.

AMEND   Amendments may be offered to strike, substitute, or add words to a motion. The motion to amend is the creative motion of group discussion. It allows the main motion to change and evolve and improve during discussion. The motion to amend is debatable only to the extent that the motion to which it refers is debatable. For example, a subsidiary motion to postpone consideration of a main motion to a certain time is debatable only on the propriety (advisability) of such postponement, and a motion to amend the postponement to another time is debatable only on the change of time proposed. I might say, "I move that we substitute Thursday for Tuesday in the motion to postpone consideration." If my motion to amend were seconded, I would proceed to show why Thursday would be preferable to Tuesday as a time for considering the question. If my motion to amend were approved, a vote would still be necessary on the original motion to postpone consideration of the main motion.

The motion to amend can itself be amended, but the process ought not to extend beyond that level. The line must be drawn somewhere, or the group would lock itself into infinite regress on an issue, debating amendments to amendments to amendments until only confusion remained. Such a result would obviously defeat the basic reason for having a discussion. The need for complex amendments to amendments may call, instead, for a motion to refer to committee, so that a better main motion can be provided to begin with.

Amendments must relate clearly to the motion on the floor, or they are subject to an out-of-order ruling by the chair. They must not reverse the intention of the main motion. (If the group wishes to escape an undesirable motion, it should defeat that motion and present a more desirable alternative as an independent main motion.) Once a main motion is passed, it may still be amended. But in this case the motion to amend assumes the status of a main motion.

REFER TO A COMMITTEE Sometimes a group gets snarled over quite specific but highly complex questions of fact. Because it cannot see the situation clearly, the group is not aware of the range of its options and cannot predict the consequences of any one course of action. In such situations the motion to "refer to a committee" can be helpful. The motion is both debatable and amendable, and the primary issue is often: Do circumstances require a decision now, even if we have less than complete information? Such a committee is instructed to investigate the situation and to return with a full report, often with recommendations. The motion should specify the size of the committee, how it is to be chosen, when it should report, and whether the report should include recommendations as well as findings on facts. "I move that a committee of five, chosen by the chair, be charged with the task of investigating this problem and returning recommendations to the group one week from today." Or the motion might specify nominations from the floor as the method of selecting the committee, in which case a successful vote on the motion would lead directly to the election of the committee.

Leaving the selection of the committee to the chair can present that esteemed person with a delicate political problem. Often several groups have advanced sharply opposed views. The chair must decide whether it is wise to include leaders of these groups on the committee, or whether such a move would only create a stalemate. If the dispute has been bitter and personal, the chair may decide to select more neutral members for the committee. In general, however, it is better to have leaders of the contending factions (if any have developed) on the investigating committee. The chair might strive, say, to include two such leaders, plus three other people who are respected for their good judgment and impartiality. Such a committee might well produce, not just a better-informed judgment, but a consensus that heals conflict.

When the committee returns with its recommendations, the question is still on the main motion. In light of the recommendations, the group may accept or reject the motion. Or the committee may recommend amendments to make the motion more acceptable. In such cases, the vote is taken first on the amendments themselves and then on the main motion if and as amended.

POSTPONE TO A CERTAIN TIME   Sometimes an issue may seem to arise prematurely or near the end of a session. In such cases, someone may move to postpone consideration either to the next meeting or to the proper time. For example, the Student Government Association may be considering a request to fund the university debating team. A member points out that the team will be sponsoring and leading a public debate the next week and that members may wish to watch the debaters in action before voting. Such a motion is debatable only on the propriety of postponement and may be amended only as to time.

LIMIT OR EXTEND THE LIMITS OF DEBATE   It is truly unfortunate when a group has to place limitations on speech. The practical problems of enforcing time limits can in themselves add to the divisiveness surrounding an issue. Such a motion should be offered only as a last resort for regulating a truly difficult deliberation or as an absolutely necessary discipline for controlling a large group. For these reasons, the motion to limit debate is made difficult to pass; it requires a two-thirds vote. A group should especially tolerate a full expression of feeling from a minority before deciding to limit the number of speeches a member can make and the length of those speeches. It is better even to tolerate some delaying tactics than to set the precedent for limiting freedom of expression in the future, when one may suddenly find oneself in the minority, battling for the right to speak.

When it must be offered, this motion is not debatable. It may be amended in terms of the number of times someone may speak and the permissible length of statements. Other subsidiary motions to limit debate include motions limiting the total time of debate on an issue and motions setting a definite time for a vote. These variations have both advantages and disadvantages. They control indefinite discussion, but they rely on the assumption that the group can come to an intelligent decision within the time stipulated in advance.

The motion to extend the limits of debate may offer some relief from such limitations, and is useful especially when a majority feels that deliberation must proceed further on a difficult issue.

PREVIOUS QUESTION   As discussion ripens on an issue, there comes a moment when everything pertinent and worthwhile seems to have been said. That is the moment to "move the previous question," a motion which closes discussion and moves directly to a vote. Ideally, the floor should be held open until all who wish to speak have spoken fully. The motion requires a two-thirds vote for passage (reflecting again the reluctance in parliamentary rule to abridge expression). The form for such a motion becomes "I move the previous question on the immediately pending question (or on all pending questions)." Such a motion is itself not debatable or amendable. If carried, this motion requires an immediate vote on all questions to which it applies.

LAY ON THE TABLE   The motion to "lay on the table" is another one of those often used and sometimes abused techniques of parliamentary procedure. Technically, it seems innocent enough. When this motion is passed, the issue is set aside temporarily while some higher-priority item of business is considered. Discussion on the tabled motion can be reopened, usually at the next meeting of the group, by a motion to "take from the table," which has the status of a main motion. The motion to "lay on the table" is neither debatable nor amendable, but the motion to "take from the table," once seconded, can itself reopen debate on the desirability of further consideration. If such a motion is passed, the motion to which it applies must still be acted on, and further debate on the merits of the question is in order. If a motion is not removed from the table before the end of the next regular meeting of the group, it ceases to exist as a motion. The question may be opened again, however, by a fresh motion at a later time.

The trouble with this motion is that it can become simply a back-door dismissal of the business at hand. Of course there may be good reason for such a move. Discussion may have produced only heat and no light, with no promise of anything more than further wrangling. A direct vote on the motion might serve only to divide the group further into bitter factions. Or a motion may simply emerge as defective and not worthy of further deliberation or even the dignity of a vote. In such cases the motion "to lay on the table" becomes a kind of consignment to the oblivion of lost causes. The motion becomes morally questionable, however, when it is used to escape responsibility for a difficult but necessary choice.

Incidental Motions

As discussion proceeds on a main motion, technical problems having to do with procedure itself occasionally arise. A number of incidental motions are available to help groups deal with these problems as they occur. In their timeliness, these motions take precedence over main or subsidiary motions. There is no particular order of precedence among them, and some of them do not require a second.

INFORMATION AND INQUIRY "Request for information" may indicate an individual's uncertainty, confusion, or lack of knowledge about some aspect of the business before the committee. You might interrupt a speaker to say, "Request for information." The chair would say, "State your request." You might then ask, "does Ms. Jordan know the cost of her proposal?" The speaker may respond to the request, although she is not obligated to give you the information you desire at that moment. Parliamentary inquiry can concern procedure itself and can affect the manner in which an issue is pursued. You might rise to say, "Point of inquiry." Once recognized, you might continue, "Could we entertain a motion to refer to committee at this time?" The question might become a parliamentary trial balloon leading to an actual motion.

POINT OF ORDER This motion is appropriate when a participant feels that the rules of order have been violated in some important way. You might say, "Point of order. Did we have a second for this motion?" The chair will then either grant your point, correct your misunderstanding, or explain the reasons for the deviation from the order of business.

APPEAL FROM THE DECISION OF THE CHAIR If you feel the chair has made a mistaken ruling, you can say, "I appeal from the decision of the chair that. . . ." If your appeal is seconded, the chair must submit the ruling to majority vote for support or denial: "The decision to . . . has been appealed. All in favor of sustaining the opinion of the chair say aye (or rise or hold up their hands). All opposed?" Needless to say, such appeals can try the patience of the group and should be made judiciously. No one should want to acquire a reputation for being obnoxious or for delaying business.

DIVISION OF THE HOUSE   A member may call for "division" whenever the chair makes a judgment on a voice vote that the member feels may be erroneous. Thereupon, the chair must call for either a show of hands or a standing vote.

OBJECT TO CONSIDERATION   This motion is intended to save the group the labor of considering obviously defective or frivolous main motions. It must be made immediately after the statement of such a motion. The chair then calls for an immediate vote on whether the motion should be considered. Here again, because sensitive issues of the rights of a minority may be involved, a two-thirds vote is required in order for the group *not* to consider a motion.

SUSPEND THE RULES   As groups become larger and more formal in procedure, they usually follow agendas of business that have been agreed on well in advance of a meeting. Occasionally, however, matters arise that may call for a suspension of such procedure. Events occurring right before or even during the meeting may thrust issues rather suddenly into prominence. Or a group may wish to suspend the rules in order to pay conspicuous honor to members or constituents who have rendered some great and unusual service. The motion to suspend the rules should state the reason for the suspension. The motion cannot be amended or debated, and it requires a two-thirds vote for approval. When the special purpose described by the motion has been served, the normal order of business resumes.

WITHDRAWAL OF A MOTION   Sometimes discussion reveals conclusively to the satisfaction of everyone—including the person who originally offered the motion—that it is defective. At that point, a request may be entertained to withdraw the motion. The chair should ask whether there is any objection to withdrawal; if there is none, the motion ceases to exist. If there is any objection, the chair should ask immediately for a majority vote either to withdraw or to retain the motion.

A common misunderstanding of this motion is that, if the original mover and second desire to withdraw, the motion ceases to exist. Of course, it is no doubt rhetorically powerful when movers and seconders repudiate their own motions, but the fate of motions remains with the larger group before which they have been introduced.

"Second-Chance" Motions

No group is above making mistakes, and time can erode the value of previous decisions. Two special "second-chance" motions permit a group to reverse actions it has previously sanctioned.

MOTION TO RECONSIDER   If carried, this motion opens a previously re-solved question once again to full discussion. The motion is in order during the same meeting in which the original motion was passed or no later than the next meeting. The motion to reconsider has merit when action has been hasty, when key members have not been heard, or when evidence and information have surfaced and put the situation in a new light. Under the rules of parliamentary law, this motion can be offered only by a member who voted *with* the prevailing side when the motion was originally considered. The switch of a vote toward the defeated side indicates a possible reversal of opinion.

MOTION TO RESCIND OR REPEAL   The more powerful negative motion, be-cause it is a direct denial and nullification of the original motion, is the motion to repeal. It requires a two-thirds vote, unless notice of the motion has been given at a previous meeting. This provision is meant to give seriousness and stability to the conduct of group business.

Privileged Motions

Certain motions are called "privileged," because they are intended to protect individual members and the integrity of the group. For this reason these motions take precedence over all others. Whenever there is reason to raise them, they must be given immediate attention.

CALL FOR THE ORDERS OF THE DAY   A "call for the orders of the day" can interrupt a speaker or a line of discussion that has wandered from the agenda. The chair yields to this motion, when it is raised appropri-ately, and restores the meeting to its established order of business. A member may then move "to suspend the rules" in order to consider a special motion, if such special action seems warranted.

QUESTION OF PRIVILEGE   A member may interrupt any speaker to raise a question of privilege. This motion is meant to protect personal interests of a member. It may range from a request to control excessive loudness in the room to a formal complaint about offensive remarks a speaker may have just made. The chair rules on the question of privilege, and the chair's decision stands unless it is challenged and reversed on an appeal.

MOTIONS TO RECESS AND ADJOURN   The motion to recess is privileged when other motions are being considered and at such times is not debatable and is amendable only as to time of recess. The motion can be very useful when the recess allows tempers to cool and minds to clear on a hotly contested subject. The recess may also permit some vital lobbying among members or provide a chance to find some badly needed information. The motion to adjourn, which requires a second and majority approval, brings the parliamentary meeting to a formal and orderly conclusion.

The table on pages 346–349 lists all these various motions, indicates how they are handled, and describes the functions they perform.

Summary of Major Ideas

Successful group discussion depends on the quality of investigation of the problem and the skill of conflict management.

Discussion should be venturesome and free, especially during the early stages of identifying a problem and probing for its causes.

Discussion must often probe the history of a problem in order to determine how it might be controlled in the future.

Discussion must identify the population affected by a problem and its impact on them.

A group must weigh its options in terms of comparative cost, likelihood of success, practicality, comprehensiveness, and special advantages and disadvantages.

A successful group must come to a decision and develop plans for implementing it and evaluating the results.

The management of conflict in group discussion depends on the leader's ability to minimize friction and to transform conflict into positive energy. Minimizing conflict often depends on emphasizing common ground and shared interests and on finding information that is in dispute.

PARLIAMENTARY PROCEDURE

Motions (in descending order of precedence)	Requires second	Can be debated	Can be amended	Vote required	Functions
1. Main	Yes	Yes	Yes	Majority	Proposes to commit group to a specific action or point of view.
2. Postpone indefinitely	Yes	Yes	No	Majority	Can dispose of a motion without coming to vote directly on a sensitive issue.
3. Amend	Yes	When motion to which it applies is debatable	Yes	Majority	Can shape and improve a pending motion.
4. Refer to committee	Yes	Yes	Yes	Majority	Allows further study of a complex issue and careful development of recommendations.
5. Postpone to a certain time	Yes	Yes	Yes	Majority	Allows for more timely consideration.
6. Limit debate	Yes	No	Yes	Two-thirds	Imposes discipline. Useful when the group is large, the agenda is crowded, the issues are controversial, and time is limited.

Subsidiary motions

	Motion				Vote required	Purpose
Subsidiary motions (continued)	7. Previous question	Yes	No	No	Two-thirds	Closes discussion and moves to vote on pending motion.
	8. Lay on the table	Yes	No	No	Majority	A convenient way to dispatch a troublesome motion without voting directly on its merits. Motion to "take from the table" is in order until the end of the next scheduled meeting.
Incidental motions (no particular order of precedence among them)	9. Request for information	No	No	No	Depends on response by person to whom request is directed.	Can provide specific information at critical points in deliberation.
	10. Point of order	No	No	No	Chair resolves	Helps keep discussion on track.
	11. Appeal from decision of chair	Yes	Yes (on merits of decision—chair can explain rationale)	No	Majority	Regulates power of chair and prevents human error.
	12. Division of house (call for specific count of votes)	No	No	No	Chair resolves	Satisfies member of the losing side of a close voice vote. Can make members commit themselves personally to their votes by show of hands.

PARLIAMENTARY PROCEDURE

Motions (in descending order of precedence)	Requires second	Can be debated	Can be amended	Vote required	Functions
Incidental motions (no particular order of precedence among them) (continued)					
13. Object to consideration	No	No	No	Two-thirds	Can prevent loss of time and dignity in considering frivolous and defective main motions.
14. Suspend the rules	Yes	No	No	Two-thirds	Allows a group to change its own agenda to consider a timely motion or a motion conferring special honor on a member.
15. Withdrawal of motion	No	No	No	Majority	Allows disposal of an obviously flawed motion without further deliberation. Often clears the way for a substitute motion.
"Second-chance" motions					
16. Reconsider	Yes	When original motion is debatable	No	Majority	Effective when new information has emerged or when members were absent for original vote. Must be offered by a member who voted on the prevailing side.
17. Rescind and repeal	Yes	Yes	Yes	Majority or two-thirds	Allows correction of serious mistakes and repudiation of previous position. Majority vote suffices when notice has been given at the previous meeting of intent to offer a motion of repeal.

18. Call for orders of day	No	No	No	None required	Points out error in handling order of business. May be reversed by motion to suspend the rules.
19. Question of privilege	No	No	No	Chair resolves	Protects members from discomfort or from intemperate personal remarks.
20. Recess	Yes	Only as to time	Yes	Majority	Provides some rest and relief from a controversial issue and a busy agenda.
21. Adjourn	Yes	No	No	Majority	Draws meeting to a formal close.
22. Fix time of next meeting	Yes	No (when another motion is pending)	Yes	Majority	Generally raised in connection with the motion to adjourn, this motion can assure orderly continuation of the group when meetings are not regularly scheduled, or it can revise that schedule in light of special needs.

Privileged motions

A successful group creates an atmosphere of deliberation, which promotes civility and rational decision making and works against premature commitment.

Group discussion seeks compromise where possible and helps clarify those issues that must be submitted to debate.

The setting for discussion can be critical to its success or failure.

Parliamentary procedure promotes fairness, encourages an atmosphere of deliberation, assures a hearing for all sides, and gives formality and weight to group decisions.

The chair should refrain from taking sides in a controversy and should encourage the expression of all opinions on an issue.

The main motion, the foundation of parliamentary procedure, proposes to commit the group to some action.

Subsidiary motions provide means for improving and successfully concluding the discussion of main motions. Precedence in parliamentary law establishes the order in which motions should be considered.

Incidental motions deal with technical problems that can arise during the discussion.

A group can correct and clear away defective decisions via the "second-chance" motions: the motion to reconsider and the motion to repeal.

Privileged motions protect the rights of members and the integrity of the group.

The motion to amend allows the group to change a main motion in accordance with discoveries and decisions made during discussion.

Exercises and Discussion Questions

In order to appreciate the possible interplay among forms of problem resolution in public controversy, the public speaking class should choose some vital question for in-depth consideration. On three successive meetings of the class, conduct on this issue a group discussion, a formal debate, and a parliamentary assembly of the entire class. The assembly should emphasize using a wide variety of subsidiary, incidental, and privileged motions.

The group discussion begins with a question for inquiry, the debate considers the major recommendation of this group as a proposition for action, and the parliamentary assembly seeks general group consensus on what should actually be done. This consensus should be expressed in a main motion approved by a majority of the class. Repeat as time permits on other issues, involving as many people as possible in key roles in the process.

For Further Reading

The nature of group discussion and small group communication is developed in a number of specialized books. Among them are the following:

Ronald L. Applebaum, *Fundamentals of Group Discussion* (Chicago, Ill.: SRA, 1976).

Ernest G. Bormann, *Discussion and Group Methods: Theory and Practice* (New York: Harper & Row, 1975).

Robert S. Cathcart and Larry A. Samovar, *Small Group Communication; A Reader* (Dubuque, Iowa: William C. Brown, 1974).

Gerald M. Phillips, *Communication and the Small Group* (Indianapolis, Ind.: Bobbs-Merrill, 1973).

For more detailed discussions of parliamentary procedure, see:

John Jeffrey Auer, *Essentials of Parlimentary Procedure* (New York: Appleton-Century-Crofts, 1969).

Henry L. Ewbank, Jr., *Meeting Management* (Dubuque, Iowa: William C. Brown, 1968).

Ray E. Keesey, *Modern Parliamentary Procedure* (Boston: Houghton Mifflin, 1974).

Henry M. Robert, *Parliamentary Practice: An Introduction to Parliamentary Law,* bicentennial ed. (New York: Irvington, 1975).

15

CONFLICT MANAGEMENT
THROUGH DEBATE

A debater is not a propagator who seeks to win
unqualified acceptance for a predetermined point
of view while defeating an opposing view. Rather,
when he places himself in the highest tradition of
debate, he is an investigator who cooperates with
fellow investigators in searching out the truth or in
selecting that course of common action which seems
best for all concerned, debaters and public alike.

DOUGLAS EHNINGER AND WAYNE BROCKRIEDE
Decision by Debate

Imagine an evening many millenia ago, long before recorded history, when a band of our hominid ancestors gathered around a campfire on the savannahs of Africa. If you could have visited that faraway scene, you might have recorded the following observations.

There are about twenty-five of them—men, women, and children— and they huddle close to the fire for warmth and safety from the open veldt that lies beyond the circle of light. The men are planning a hunt, and their conversation, with the help of many gestures and much miming of action, sounds very much like human symbolic speech. Apparently an argument has broken out, because two of the men are screaming at each other and appear ready to fight. Their rage is interrupted by the voice of an old man, who apparently enjoys much respect:

"Each of you must give the other a chance to speak uninterrupted. After you both have spoken, you shall have another chance to answer each other. Then the rest of us may ask you questions. After we hear your answers we shall decide who is right, and you must honor our decision."

What we have imagined here—the roots of the modern practice of debate—must have happened time and again and more and more proficiently, as these early humans, who lived and died according to how well they could cooperate and reach consensus, discovered the values of deliberation and debate.

Formal debate as we have come to know it occurs when two sides in a controversy meet to present opposing views on a question. Even in the conflict of debate there is cooperation, for the two sides must (1) agree that there is a question worth debating, (2) agree to engage in debate on it, and (3) accept the audience as fit and proper to hear the debate and decide on its merits. Of course any exchange of symbols shared in common is a cooperative act. But debate as we shall describe it goes further in promoting the power of reason and people's right to decide their destinies in the full light of their options.

This chapter investigates the rationale, structure, and strategy of debating.

RATIONALE FOR DEBATE

Debate is a valuable practice for three major reasons:

1. It regulates certain tendencies of communication that, without regulation, could be very damaging.
2. It counters other communication tendencies that could create irrational and harmful conditions.
3. It promotes certain principles and values that are vital to any positive, humanistic orientation.

Understanding these values will also help us understand the power and usefulness of debate.

Debate as Regulator

Debate regulates the natural tendency of communication to simplify issues in order to push us toward decisions, such as rhetoric that reduces all situations and options to black-and-white, two-sided choices. Speakers manage to discover all goodness and virtue on one side (their own!), all evil and wickedness on the other. Whenever we hear just one side of an important and far-reaching issue, we run the risk of hasty and unwise decisions and actions.

What debate does is to invite opposing sides into each other's presence, where they must justify themselves as they confront each other. Moreover, each counters the other's tendency to oversimplify and distort the issue. Their confrontation exposes the audience to different views and prevents hasty, shallow identification between speaker and audience. The audience can see speakers performing spontaneously and under intense pressure, a view not permitted when speakers are able to arrange and orchestrate how they will appear. There is more honesty in the ethos, and audiences can better judge whether speakers truly deserve a personal identification. Debate also *discourages premature commitments* to courses of action. An audience is not often swept away by persuasion when one speech is immediately followed by

Abraham Lincoln challenged Stephen A. Douglas to a series of seven debates during the Illinois senatorial campaign of 1858.

The Bettmann Archive

another that reveals its shortcomings. Thus debate teaches us to delay making a commitment until we have given an issue full, rational consideration. Then our commitments to action will have more meaning and value. Competing debaters owe much to each other, in the sense that the conflict selects and sharpens their arguments. The audience hears a finer rhetoric and makes better decisions. Rare is the decision that cannot be improved by debate.

In its tendency to prevent haste and to make public decision making more deliberate, debate performs a second great regulative function. It helps *stabilize* public opinion. Think of how uncertain matters would be if we were constantly changing our minds in response to this or that persuasion. When we are exposed to debate, we make our decisions in the full light of all the options available to us. Such decisions are more intelligent, and they promote a more stable social order. They make possible long-range planning for difficult but desirable objectives.

Debate as Protector

Debate can guard us from other important abuses of the communication process, such as those that follow.

1. Related to the oversimplifying tendency we have just discussed is a kind of characterization known as *stereotyping*. All of us use stereotypes in our everyday thinking, but the practice does lend itself to

unfair portrayals. Stereotyping reduces someone's rich and complex humanity to just a few, often irrelevant traits that we think characterize a type of person. "Well, what can you expect of a black!" (or man or redneck or professor or student or whatever the stereotyping demon in us has established as a predictable category). Debate fights this unfair tendency. It invites the person or position being stereotyped to speak for itself and establish its own character.

2. A second kind of abuse is *jargon*, communication that pretends to be saying something when it is actually saying nothing at all. Such communication is really countercommunication, because it hides the truth behind a cloud of words. It has never been described better than by George Orwell. In an essay entitled "Politics and the English Language," written after World War II, Orwell observed:

> *Things like the continuance of British rule in India, the Russian purges and deportations, the dropping of the atom bombs on Japan, can indeed be defended, but only by arguments which are too brutal for most people to face, and which do not square with the professed aims of political parties. Thus political language has to consist largely of euphemism, question-begging and sheer cloudy vagueness. Defenceless villages are bombarded from the air, the inhabitants driven out into the countryside, the cattle machine-gunned, the huts set on fire with incendiary bullets: this is called* pacification. *Millions of peasants are robbed of their farms and sent trudging along the roads with no more than they can carry: this is called* transfer of population *or* rectification of frontiers. *People are imprisoned for years without trial or shot in the back of the neck or sent to die of scurvy in Arctic lumber camps: this is called* elimination of unreliable elements. *Such phraseology is needed if one wants to name things without calling up mental pictures of them. . . . The inflated style is itself a kind of euphemism. A mass of Latin words falls upon the facts like soft snow, blurring the outlines and covering up all the details.*[1]

Concerning our own official governmental communication during the Vietnam conflict, Henry Fairlie observed: "The war was conducted not in secret, but in jargon."[2]

Fortunately, both in Great Britain and this country, we have the salutary custom of debate on public issues. Debate makes such vague and sugarcoated language account for itself. In the direct confrontation of positions, it is hard for language to avoid depiction. Under the

---

1. *Shooting an Elephant and Other Essays* (London: Secker and Warburg, 1950), pp. 96–97.
2. "The Language of Politics," *Atlantic Monthly*, 235 (January 1975), 31.

pressure of relentless attack and rebuttal, either you speak the facts as they are or your silence becomes eloquent testimony to deceit.

3. A third abuse of communication is an unhealthy over-reliance on emotion and image. An effective communicator must engage the feelings of listeners, of course, and must help them *see* the subject vividly and colorfully. But when emotion and image operate in the absence of logic and evidence, or in outright defiance of the rational and actual structure of things, then communication has been turned to perverse ends. One of the interesting special features of this problem occurs when powerful image patterns such as darkness and light, sin and redemption, or war and peace are put to inappropriate uses. It is one thing to dramatize a problem situation as darkness and to offer one's solution as a lovely dawn when one can back up the vivid metaphors with plain fact and hard reasoning; it is quite another when the metaphors take over the job of persuasion on their own, and image starts masquerading as argument.

When Hitler became enamoured of picturing himself as an Aryan saint come to save Germany from the sin of self-betrayal, then fact and reason—indeed rationality itself—were no longer important. Similarly, a self-proclaimed savior, caught up in the hypnotic power of his own language, could convince 900 people that their only salvation was mass suicide at Guyana. These were situations in which debate was proscribed. No tyrant can afford to sanction its balancing of views, its prudent circumspection, its deliberate sanity.

One effect of debate is to maintain a healthy connection between image and fact, between emotion and reason.

4. A fourth abuse of communication relevant to debate occurs when speakers arouse strong feelings in an audience without providing clear, constructive outlets for those feelings. Such misguided rhetoric is self-defeating even if well intentioned, for once we are aroused by rhetoric that does not offer a plan of action, it will be hard to engage our feelings again. Such rhetoric desensitizes us.

Once again, the discipline of debate helps us avoid the mistake of arousing our audience prematurely. We know that, if we launch a debate by attacking some present policy or institution, we had better have a well-considered alternative to offer, or our opponents will expose our inadequacy for all to see.

Debate as Promoter

A great virtue of debate is that it exercises some of our most fundamental and cherished principles. Freedom of speech, for example, would hardly be very meaningful if the principle were not expressed in free and open debate. Debate helps us develop a tolerance for hearing and considering other opinions, without which free speech could be only an illusion and a "paper right" without social consequence. Moreover, debate keeps the blood pumping through our beliefs by exposing them to their opposition. Without debate we would forget *why* we believe as we do, and living conviction would harden into dogma.

Debate also promotes respect for the audience. Much mass communication today pictures us as *targets* of persuasion; we may even be considered *victims* ripe for exploitation. The television rating system simply assigns us all numbers and lumps us into viewing categories, without identity or humanity. We are then sold in the mass to the highest advertising bidders, who pander to what they think is our general taste. In the face of such dehumanizing views, debate elevates the audience to the role of *judge*. As we weigh opposed arguments, we become the architects of our own destiny. We can even design policies that combine the best elements of both arguments. Thus we can go beyond judging and *create* new possibilities for attitude and action.

Finally, debate provides a last alternative to violence and affirms our faith in the word over the fist for resolving humanity's disputes. If debate ever dies in our society, then much that is worthwhile in us will have died also.

The Enemy of Debate

If debate has such clear regulative, protective, and promotional value, why don't we see more of it? Why aren't debates going on constantly on every subject on every street corner? Perhaps there is more informal debate going on than we think, and perhaps the process of debate is very much alive in this subterranean sense. But there is a great enemy of debate, and that enemy is ourselves. As soon as anyone challenges our views, our natural impulse is to hush the irritating and obnoxious voice. We can talk freedom while—without realizing it—we suppress the views of others.

Another of our antidebate tendencies is the group intolerance we can develop for any kind of deviation or show of independence. When a group is in a militant mood, or when it feels threatened, not many members will be able to stand and argue successfully against the imposing group attitude or practice. The deep divisions and conflicts over free speech in American society during the Vietnam War indicated what a difficult and fragile thing debate can be. To listen to someone whose views we find abhorrent demands all of our civility and tolerance.

And when positions are so rigidly struck that the parties involved refuse to accept an unfavorable decision or even a compromise, and when they view any mediating effort suspiciously, then the value of debate crumbles and the darker forces in our nature come forth. To protect debate in such times, we have to guard against our own impulses.

THE STRUCTURE OF DEBATE

In any formal debate there are always three major structural elements: a *proposition*, the *affirmation* of that proposition, and its *negation*.

Proposition

Debate always presupposes that initial investigation and discussion have already gone into some topic of public concern. Debate occurs when the process of deliberation reaches a critical stage of disagreement over some specific question. For example, "What shall we do about the problem of energy?" is much too broad and vague for debate. Such a question is an invitation to group discussion. But let us suppose that further investigation of this question develops a specific area of controversy. Cast in terms appropriate to debate, a proposition emerges along the following lines: "Resolved, that nuclear energy is receiving too much emphasis in our research efforts to develop new sources of energy." This proposition should set the scene for a specific confrontation between those who would affirm it and those who would deny it.

The debate *proposition*, therefore, is a statement that identifies a specific area of controversy and proposes a response to that controversy which invites affirmation and negation. The purpose of debate is to subject the proposition to a trial-by-combat of ideas, the most searching and severe kind of intellectual scrutiny, so that whatever response the audience makes will be enlightened.

Debate propositions fall into the three general categories of fact, value, and policy.

FACT Some questions of fact really don't belong to debate. If a disagreement can be solved by finding the answer through research, debate is indeed inappropriate. But other questions of fact do invite debate. One such question occurs in judicial argumentation: Did the accused actually commit a certain crime? Here the question is one of *past fact*. We cannot invite the jury to verify the event now one way or the other, for it has already occurred and has faded from perception. Debate concerns the *probability* that the accused committed the act. If the prosecution can build an overwhelming sense of probability in its favor, it should win the guilty verdict. On the other hand, if the defense can establish reasonable doubt that the defendant committed the act, then (in our system of law) the defense should win. To establish the cases, prosecution and defense both call on witnesses to the actions and motives of the defendant and to features of the alleged crime that are relevant to the question. Is it probable, an attorney for the defense might argue, that my client—old and weak as he is—could have strangled the victim? In almost all instances, except perhaps when eyewitness accounts are so convincing that they simply cannot be controverted, the issue of past fact is resolved, not by the senses, but by argumentation on such probabilities.

Questions of *future fact* are also appropriate for debate, especially when we are concerned with predicting the consequences of actions. "Resolved, that atomic energy will prove more practical and useful than solar energy" implies a policy question in the present ("Should we emphasize nuclear research over solar research?"). By featuring an issue of future fact, the proposition invites debaters to focus on that specific dimension of the controversy. Debates on future fact obviously can be useful as preliminaries to policy debates, because we must project a future before we can prepare for it.

Debate can indeed deal legitimately with questions of fact. But debate normally is most helpful in resolving questions of value and policy.

VALUE   A debate proposition can invite us to inspect the morality of an issue. Is our policy toward X "nothing but genocide" or is it "motivated by the highest principles?" Often such propositions bring emotion into the cool arena of debate, because values are often highly personal. Logic and evidence may not necessarily lead to a resolution of the conflict between opposed moral positions.

However, debate can be useful in the conflict of values. Because they see the world from different perspectives, the opposing sides discover different facts for an audience. Upon these facts they raise different structures of reasoning. For an audience, exposure to sharply differing sets of fact and arguments can be quite enlightening. Such debating may not lead to a public resolution of conflict, but it can help listeners see more clearly through the murky depths of an emotional issue. If we can see more clearly and completely, the personal choices and commitments we make should be better informed.

POLICY   Most formal debates concern questions of policy, personal as well as social. Should I smoke marijuana? Ought the sale of marijuana to be legalized? Should I smoke cigarettes? Should the government stop subsidizing tobacco farmers? Controversy over policy can range across the spectrum from the most private to the most public decision making.

The policy debate is the most complex and crucial form of forensic engagement. A single policy controversy can include disputes over fact and value as well as over the wisdom of action. Thus the successful policy debater must be able to depict effectively, must possess ethical sensitivity, and must have the creative gift of designing better policy or of repairing and defending present policy. Add to these requirements the pressure of a direct confrontation, and you can see how policy debates push speakers to the limits of their abilities. But only under such pressure can we become better communicators.

Requirements for Propositions

Whether the controversy concerns fact, value, or policy, propositions for debate must satisfy certain basic requirements.

CLARITY The debate proposition must be clearly stated, or debaters may well go off in different directions, arguing issues irrelevant to each other. A resolution such as "We ought to stop contaminating the environment" is much too ambiguous for debate. On the other hand, "We ought to ban the use of DDT for pesticide control" should launch a clear debate. Obviously, much depends on how debaters themselves interpret the question.

It is also possible to frame a debate proposition too narrowly, which creates a problem opposite that of ambiguity. A resolution such as "Resolved, that we should break diplomatic relations with Russia unless they cease persecution of Jews and dissidents" could serve as a main motion for a parliamentary assembly. But as a debate proposition, it would probably be too confining a statement. It predetermines the main line of argument for the affirmation, and robs the debate of its creative potential for the *discovery* of responses possible within this controversy. In the example given, "Resolved, that this government should respond more meaningfully to Russian violations of human rights" would be a more appropriate statement of the proposition. It would facilitate exploration and not predetermine an exact focal point and outcome. It would leave the affirmation with more creative latitude for building a case, just as it would increase the burden of preparation and enlarge the learning experience for the negation.

The statement of the proposition should be as simple as possible without qualifying dependent clauses or complex sentence construction. The more turns and byways there are in this statement, the more wrong directions the subsequent debate can take.

LEGITIMACY   A good debate proposition lays the groundwork for a legitimate, reasonable clash between affirming and negating views. An earlier example, "We ought to stop contaminating the environment" is defective by this criterion. Who in their right minds would argue that we should contaminate the environment? As stated, the resolution creates an untenable position for the negation. A legitimate proposition makes it possible for reasonable people to appear either in support or in opposition.

A further aspect of a properly worded question is that it should place the affirmative in a challenging, attacking position and the negation in a defending posture. It is said that the negative enjoys the *presumption,* whereas the affirmative must carry the *burden of proof.* The negative appears on the side of some pre-existing policy, prevailing value position, or generally accepted construction of past or future events. The affirmative challenges present policy, attacks what presumes to be the established value position, or offers a view that would alter the usually accepted depiction of the past and anticipation of the future. The presumption is that the position taken by the negative will prevail unless the affirmative can successfully carry the burden of proof.

In terms of debate structure, this relationship between the contending parties explains why the affirmative must always initiate the debate encounter. The status quo prevails until significantly challenged. Thus the proposition is stated so that it reflects the sentiment of the affirmative side and invites the debate encounter. In affirming the resolution, the proper side opens the debate. For example, "Resolved, that our system of public welfare should not be changed" is a faulty proposition, because it places the side enjoying the presumption in the position of opening the debate. In this awkward situation, the negative, if it said anything at all, could offer only general praise of the present system. Beyond this it could venture only a risky and hazardous effort to anticipate arguments that would not even be raised until the affirmative took the floor. On the other hand, "Resolved, that our present system of public welfare should be abandoned" is in a form appropriate for debate.

FAIRNESS   The whole intention of debate is subverted if the proposition is biased from the beginning. We ought to be especially wary of loaded, question-begging words that can slip so easily into the statement of propositions. In "Resolved, that the United States should stop its imperialistic blockade of Cuba," the term "imperialistic" obviously begs the question. We ought to conclude that sort of thing at the end of a successful affirmative presentation, not assume it at the outset. Vivid, persuasive language belongs in the presentations on both sides of a proposition, but not within the proposition itself.

INTEREST   Finally, any good debate proposition focuses on an area of controversy that greatly interests the audience. Some topics are so timely and divisive that it is difficult not to have an exciting debate on them. Therefore, it is good if a class can discuss well in advance of scheduled debates the topics that members would prefer to have investigated. Opponents can then negotiate in advance a good statement of the proposition in light of the requirements we have discussed. After all, in classroom debate it is more desirable that *both* sides do well than that one side decisively defeat the other.

Affirmation

The challenge of the affirmative must be so effective that, unless the negative can blunt its thrust, the presumption will be lost. When the affirmative mounts such a challenge, it can be said to have established a *prima facie* case. If the negative feels it can ignore the challenge, the debate does not proceed. In academic debate, of course, this is only a theoretical reservation, because negatives always stand to refute even the most illogical and insubstantial attack. But in the rough and tumble of real-life debating, those representing the negative often try to ignore the affirmative attack and thereby avoid the risk of debate. They maintain this low-profile protection of the status quo *unless and until they feel the audience requires them to answer.* For example, an incumbent in a political race usually does not respond to or even acknowledge the existence of an opponent unless and until the challenger gains enough support to constitute a real threat. Therefore, to develop an effective debate case in the public arena is to build the intrinsic power of a sound case and the appeal of that case to many people or to people in power. As the negative sees the power and the appeal of the affirmative case growing and spreading, it will feel compelled to answer, and the debate proceeds.

The affirmative should begin with some statement that highlights the importance of the debate, perhaps some specific example indicating the need for a change in perception, value, or policy. This opening should be followed by a statement of the proposition for debate. The affirmative should then define whatever troublesome or vague terms may lurk within the proposition. For example, in a resolution calling for "substantial change" in some existing policy, the affirmative might say, "By 'substantial change' we mean a total

Ellis Herwig 1980

renovation of the present structure, as we shall indicate in the affirmative plan." It is good, especially in classroom debate, for affirmative and negative to negotiate an agreement about definitions before the actual encounter. If the negative has to dispute the definitions as being unfair, inaccurate, and so on, the debate may never get off the ground. The debaters may well spend all their time arguing before an exasperated audience over what it is that they are going to argue.

When the proposition has been stated and the foundation of definitions established, the affirmative is ready to proceed to the heart of its case. This procedure will vary according to the kind of debate.

FACT   In a debate over the nature of past fact, the affirmative has the problem of gradually weakening some previously accepted version of past events. Thus the affirmative presents witnesses, constructions of motives, and interpretations of circumstance that cumulatively weaken the credibility of the established view, just as they build the validity of a new perspective. In the final section of the speech, the debater should be in a position to complete this new depiction impressively.

The affirmation in debates over future fact should follow approximately the same pattern, adjusted of course to the problems of prediction. The debater should make use especially of present trends and expert testimony and should be attentive to the impact of the predicted future on the motive interests of the audience. The speech should end with a vivid and credible projection of that future.

VALUE The affirmative case on questions of value depends on drawing convincing connections between the specific moral problem of the debate and the underlying pattern of values that is presumably accepted by a majority of the audience. One sensible strategy might be to reawaken first an appreciation for pertinent portions of this basic moral fabric:

> All of us say that we believe in fair play. Our very Constitution says that we shall not discriminate on grounds of race, or religion, or national origin. The Constitution in effect forbids us to set up any artificial barriers to the advancement of any human being. Each person shall be judged on his or her own merit, and no one shall suffer by being tossed into a category. Unfortunately, the Constitution forgot to mention homosexuals.

Having renewed our sense of a fundamental moral value, the debater is prepared to relate the specific to the general. Evidence can now be introduced to build and heighten the sense of injustice. Viewed against the backdrop of the underlying moral code, such specific evidence should move the audience toward accepting the proposition: Resolved, that laws discriminating against homosexuals are unfair.

POLICY In debates concerning policy, the affirmative must prove there is a *need* for the kind of change proposed in the resolution. To establish this need, the debater must answer the question *Why should the audience want to change existing conditions?* The debater can meet this challenge by showing that fundamental flaws in the present system demand a new approach. Or again, especially in so-called "comparative advantage" cases, the debater can emphasize how much better things could be with a new approach. Usually a debater combines these two appeals, pointing up problems within the present system and developing the advantages of a new system. And, because some people are moved more by moral needs and others by material and practical considerations, wise affirmative debaters develop both kinds of arguments in building their cases.

The second great imperative for constructing affirmative cases on policy questions is to show *how the action can be undertaken.* This plan for change should be developed in enough detail so that a credible procedure is at least outlined. The plan should be consistent with the definition of terms and should remedy the weaknesses attacked in the present system. The debater should also point up any additional benefits that the plan will bring about. The structure of the affirmative case varies from debate to debate, but one common and sensible pattern is to stress first the need to change the present system, then to indicate the nature of the plan proposed, to show how the plan will meet that need, and to paint a glowing picture of additional advantages the audience will receive upon adopting the affirmative proposal.

REBUTTAL   After the affirmation has presented its case for the proposition and the negation has developed a position against the proposition, both sides have an opportunity to answer each other's argumentation. This chance to attack and defend is called the *rebuttal*. The rebuttal calls on the debater's ability to respond spontaneously to the presentation of an opposing position. In a debate over fact, one can assume that the negative will have smudged one's depictions of the past or future and that these images will have to be renewed and strengthened. In a value debate, the negative will have tried to drive a wedge between general value structure and the specific case at hand. One must restore that vital sense of connection so that the audience feels confronted by a moral imperative. In a good policy debate, the negative will have developed a damaging attack on both the need and the plan by the time the affirmation stands for rebuttal. Therefore, it is essential to rebuild the major portions of the case, the *why* and *how* of the debate resolution. Moreover, this vital repair work must be accomplished within a limited time and executed in such a way that the affirmative remains on the offensive.

To accomplish these difficult tasks, affirmative rebutters should have available fresh evidence to shore up their positions. They should inspect negative argumentation closely to see what evidence or reasoning they can appropriate for their own use. Turning the tables on the opposition can make the difference in a close debate.

The pattern for a successful rebuttal usually develops this way: Pick some especially weak and important argument to refute first, so that you cast doubt from the outset on the credibility of the entire attack. Then review the major negative argumentation on need and plan, showing how the reasoning or evidence is flawed, invalid, or contradictory. If the negative has ignored major portions of the affirmative case, be sure to emphasize such omission as an important concession. Go on the attack against the negative's argumentation, ending with some especially strong point and with a final plea for adoption of the proposition.

Negation

The negative always begins by offering its own view of the significance of the debate. If there is an important question concerning the fairness and adequacy of any definition, now is the time to raise it, along with the reason for such concern. A weak definition, especially one that does not square with the later development of the affirmative plan, could become a major issue in the debate and should be highlighted especially during the rebuttal period.

FACT The negative approach to propositions of fact is similar to that of the affirmative. But the negative enjoys a special advantage at the outset, what one might call the *authority of popular concurrence*. Simply stated, this advantage is the presumption that what most people accept as an authentic depiction of past or future is likely to be correct—or is more likely to be correct than the alternatives. This presumption is not always justified, of course, but the burden of overturning it may seem heavy indeed on the affirmative.

Building on the authority of popular concurrence, the negative can attack the credibility of affirmative witnesses, introduce its own witnesses, develop countermotives, and establish contrary signs, trends, and circumstances. Accepted judgments about the past and future can be confirmed and reinvigorated. Indeed, the negative strategy must always be, not simply to ward off a particular affirmative attack, but to strengthen the presumption for future debate encounters. The aim is to make the presumption seem so unassailable that any future opponent will be discouraged. One sign of a presumption in trouble is the frequency of debate on it.

VALUE The negative can take either one of two fundamental approaches in debating questions of value. One option is to meet the affirmative directly on the vital connection claimed between the specific issue being debated and the underlying fabric of social values. The negative can drive a wedge between the specific and the general by showing how the fundamental values invoked by the affirmative do not justify the specific application claimed. Indeed, the negative will argue, such values suggest a totally opposite conclusion. For example, to an affirmative case asking for tolerance of a certain extremist group on grounds of freedom of expression, the negative might respond that the only way to preserve freedom is to suppress those who would destroy it.

Another option open to the negative is to argue that, whereas one social value may justify the specific application urged, an even more fundamental value denies that application. The debate then turns to the hierarchy and structure of values that ought to govern our lives. Civil rights activists in the 1960s, for instance, answered charges that their demonstrations were unlawful by pointing to the deeper Constitutional bedrock of the law. Such debating can become philosophical and profound, as is demonstrated beautifully in the classic Greek drama *Antigone*. Antigone admits that, by human law (embodied in Creon, the king) she ought not to bury the reeking carcass of her slain brother, but she insists that she must follow first the law of God. In a similar kind of value conflict, opponents of the Equal Rights Amendment to the Constitution sometimes argue that nature or the process of evolutionary development has created sexual differences between men and women that make it impossible to assure equal treatment under the law. Such advocates invoke the law of nature as superior to the laws of humanity.

POLICY The negative stance in a policy debate follows a natural pattern of attack and defense. It is often good, however, to reverse the order of this pattern, opening the first negative speech with a constructive view that heightens appreciation for the present beleaguered policy, institution, or procedure. The most positive image is needed to counteract the picture painted by the affirmative. Moreover, it introduces a number of virtues that, the negative can argue, stand to be sacrificed under the changes proposed by the affirmative.

But is there any real justification for a change, anyway? The negative now goes on the offensive, training its guns on the affirmative's *need* case. Its best approach is to argue that an asserted weakness in present policy is actually a strength. Or, the negative may say, the affirmative has not *proved* that a weakness exists (and thus has not successfully carried the burden of proof). This line of approach invites a close inspection of the evidence supporting the affirmative contentions. Perhaps the authorities cited are actually unqualified. Perhaps the evidence is obsolete. The evidence may also be insufficient to justify the sweeping conclusions drawn by the affirmative. Or there may be no logical connection between evidence and conclusion. Such a logically defective conclusion is called a *non sequitur* ("it does not follow").

Still another strategy is to grant that there is indeed a problem but to insist that the affirmative has exaggerated it. Moreover, present policy is not responsible for the problem; certainly the affirmative has not been able to prove that it is. Furthermore, the problem would actually become worse if the affirmative proposal were adopted. Finally, the affirmative plan would create other difficulties of such massive proportions that the present problem would look small by comparison.

These are some of the major lines of argumentation open to the negative as it targets the affirmative's need case. The negative should try to destroy or at least substantially weaken the major contentions that support the need portion of the case. If the need crumbles, the affirmative plan that rests on the need must also settle into the dust.

As the negative turns finally to the *how* portion of the case—that is, to the plan itself—*relevance, adequacy,* and *practicality* should be the key words. Does the plan really fit the needs presented (is it relevant?)?

"Protocol or no, if he doesn't stop talking soon, I'm gonna eat him."

Mort Gerberg/© Oct. 7, 1967 Saturday Evening Post

Is the plan presented in enough detail, or is the affirmative asking us to buy a pig in a poke (is it adequate?)? And finally, does the plan offer a workable, reasonable, and affordable procedure, or does it project pie-in-the-sky idealism about a world that never could be, or a world so costly that one would not *want* it to be (is it practical?)? The negative can use these questions to good advantage. It should also be attentive to such matters as whether the plan has ever been tried. If it has not, it is unproven. If it has, its weaknesses should stand exposed. These defects, the negative can argue, will become all the more serious and numerous in the new application.

REBUTTAL   For a successful negative, the rebuttal is a time to demolish affirmative efforts to rebuild the need and restore the plan. Often the main negative speech or speeches create such a large job of reconstruction that little time remains in the affirmative rebuttal for a counterattack on the constructive portion of the negative case. If only glancing blows have been struck in that direction, or if that part of the case has been substantially ignored, then the negative rebutter has a very nice option. The speaker might choose to begin the rebuttal by emphasizing the importance of this omission, holding it as only typical of the futility of affirmative argumentation. Thus the debater could use the omission as a device to discredit the affirmative case in general and to enhance the effectiveness of other points that will follow. Or the debater might save this point for last, concluding that the affirmative apparently admits by its silence that we do enjoy benefits under the present system. As the negative concludes its part in the debate, it can praise existing procedures and ask us not to throw away advantages that all concede.

Otherwise, the main themes of the negative rebuttal are fairly obvious: There is no need, the plan is defective, and adoption of the proposition would be disastrous.

THE DEBATE FORMAT

Although debate can be quite spontaneous and informal, the discipline that debate imposes on opponents has led to the development of highly structured formats that assure equal access to audiences and encourage penetrating discussions that illuminate the issues in controversy. Most useful among these formats are the following.

Team Approach

Most traditional forms of academic debate require a team approach. Perhaps the most basic form of academic debate assigns two speakers to each side and gives each speaker a ten-minute main ("constructive") speech and a five-minute rebuttal. The order of speaking is as follows:

Constructive speeches: 1st affirmative, 1st negative, 2nd affirmative, 2nd negative
Rebuttals: 1st negative, 1st affirmative, 2nd negative, 2nd affirmative

Thus the affirmative both initiates and completes the debate encounter. The affirmative enjoys the final position in team-debate rebuttals, because this position is supposed to be a favored one. The structure of the rebuttal speeches helps to balance the real advantage enjoyed by the negative in terms of presumption—the understanding that present procedures will continue unless a compelling rationale for change can be developed.[3]

3. There is a school of thought that sees presumption as only a technical or legal advantage. Such an interpretation was popularized by Bishop Whately in his classic *Elements of Rhetoric* (1828) and persists in such modern works as Douglas Ehninger and Wayne Brockriede, *Decision by Debate* (New York: Dodd, Mead, 1962). I prefer to interpret presumption as an advantage based in human nature. We have a natural tendency to prefer the continuation of policies, institutions, and political incumbents as long as they are working reasonably well and until some dramatically better alternative presents itself. Thus presumption is a *real* advantage in most debating.

One-on-One Debate

In intraclass debating, it is often desirable to drop the team approach in favor of a one-on-one format. There simply may not be time to develop a team approach, with the division of labor that such an approach suggests. And it may be educationally preferable for each speaker to be responsible for developing an entire case on one side or the other of a question. As much as possible, debaters should contend for a side they actually believe in, and the confrontation should be a natural one between disputants. The 10-minute-5-minute pattern may run too long for such novice debates. An 8-4 pattern or even a 6-3 arrangement may be adequate for the first experiences with formal debate. The pattern of one-on-one debate proceeds in simple alternation: affirmative constructive, negative constructive, affirmative rebuttal, negative rebuttal.

Cross Examination

An interesting variation on these formats is to add a time for direct cross examination. The 8-4, one-on-one arrangement, for example, can become a 7-2-3 format, allowing debaters 2 minutes to question their opponents. Thus the debate flow would proceed: affirmative constructive, negative cross examination of affirmative, negative constructive, affirmative cross examination of negative, affirmative rebuttal, negative rebuttal.

Direct cross examination sharpens the debate clash, builds suspense, and generally makes debating more interesting and enjoyable for an audience. Moreover, cross examination practice in class helps the speaker develop skills of immediate adjustment and composure under pressure. The purpose of cross examination is to clarify uncertain or obscure points, to expose questionable assertions, slipshod research, or faulty reasoning, or to force the opponent into such a corner that he or she can escape only by making a damaging admission. Cross examination should not, however, become a time for personal attack. Debaters should appear confident and courteous with each other and should ask and answer questions promptly. They should maintain eye contact with the audience as they pose and respond to questions.

The questioner controls the time and may interrupt if the responder seems launched on some long-winded or irrelevant answer. However, the questioner must stick to questions and not make statements or browbeat the responder. The questions should seem fair and relevant: "When did you first develop these Communist sympathies?" is the sort of question one should avoid. Nor can the questioner insist on "yes" or "no" answers when the questions themselves are quite complex.

The questioner should phrase questions in a positive, neutral manner: "Did you know . . ." rather than "Didn't you know . . ." phraseology is appropriate. The questions should not scatter all over the case, but should develop in a sequence that leads to some important clarification, exposure, or admission. This sequence should begin with common ground on which agreement can be expected and should move from that concurrence into a series of follow-up probes:

Q. "Now, you have used Professor Thornton as support for your argument concerning need, have you not?
A. "Yes, I have.
Q. "Are you aware that Professor Thornton has a new statement on this controversy in the latest issue of Atlantic Monthly?
A. "I haven't had a chance . . .
Q. "I see. You are not aware, then, I suppose, that Professor Thornton completely reverses her position in this new statement?
A. "Well, I don't know that I would agree . . .
Q. "Thank you. Now let's move to another claim you make . . ."

Questioners cannot launch a series of questions for opponents to answer in later rebuttal time, nor should responders consult with colleagues or defer answers until later. Either practice is a sign of weakness and inexperience.

For their part, responders can refuse to answer unfair questions if they can give a good reason why the question is unfair. They should refuse to be boxed into yes–no answers, when the question clearly invites a thoughtful, considered response. Responders should not, however, dilly-dally with straightforward questions. Answers should be to the point of the question. However, responders should establish qualifications when appropriate:

Q. "Do you believe in equal treatment for everyone?
A. "I strongly believe in equal treatment under the law. We could hardly begin, however, to govern the complex personal and social interactions people have with each other. Nor ought we to try."

If responders feel they are being browbeaten and hurried, they can deliberately slow the pace of their answers and perhaps register a good-humored protest: "If you will allow me time to answer," you will discover that I can put together an entire sentence!" Or if the questioner fumbles uncertainly, the responder can answer very quickly, thus pointing up the opponent's ineptitude.

MONITORING THE DEBATE
AND AUDIENCE REACTION

A timekeeper should be appointed and time cards prepared large enough for debaters to see easily. These cards should be on constant display during the debate to indicate to debaters at any given moment how many minutes remain in a speech. For a 10-minute debate speech, the timekeeper begins by displaying a "10" card and changes cards in descending order to indicate the passage of the allotted time. Often there is a "1/2" card for use when half a minute remains, so that debaters know when to conclude, and a "stop" card held high by the timekeeper to indicate to all present that the legitimate time for the speech has expired. To continue beyond this time could well damage the speaker's case.

Two kinds of decisions can be reached by the audience to the debate. Listeners can record their positions before and after the debate on shift-of-opinion ballots and can record a separate judgment about which side prevailed in the encounter. See Figure 15.1 for the form of such a ballot.

A teller can be appointed to quantify the number and magnitude of the opinion shifts and can total audience judgments concerning debater effectiveness. The teller might record that three persons shifted four attitudinal spaces in favor of the affirmative, which would mean that one person experienced a substantial change of opinion. In the same debate, the negative may have influenced two auditors to the extent of two attitudinal spaces but could conceivably prevail on the question of who has done the better job of debating. Such a result would offer consolation for both sides.

Obviously, shift-of-opinion balloting is too crude to record with any precision the dynamics of audience affect during a debate. It does not tell us how stable or valuable the changes that result may be. A slight impact on the position of an opinion leader may have more far-reaching influence than other, more obvious changes in the opposite direction. Such balloting also presumes equal difficulty in producing shifts on both sides of a question. There are some propositions in which the difficulty factor is so great that any shift in your favor could be a triumph! Nevertheless, such balloting is enjoyable as a part of the drama of debate—so long as we do not take the results too seriously.

DEBATE STRATEGY

Most debates are won or lost on the basis of the quality and extent of the research preparation that goes before them. The first phase of

```
On the proposition, _____
_____,
my position is:

PRE-DEBATE        9      8      7      6      5      4      3      2      1
                Intensely        Favor        Neutral        Oppose        Intensely
                Favor                                                       Oppose

POST-DEBATE       9      8      7      6      5      4      3      2      1
                Intensely        Favor        Neutral        Oppose        Intensely
                Favor                                                       Oppose

In my judgment the better job of debating was done by the

                    _____ Affirmative.

                    _____ Negative.
```

Figure 15.1 SHIFT-OF-OPINION BALLOT

research for a well-prepared debater is to anticipate as many as possible of the issues that might arise in the debate. Phase two is to accumulate critical information bearing on these issues.

Because the affirmative enjoys the advantage of surprise, the negative must be broadly prepared so that it can meet the affirmative attack from whatever direction it may come. Think of this surprise advantage as balancing to some extent the advantage of presumption enjoyed by the negative.

However, in intraclass debates, where the intention is less to achieve victory at all costs and more to have a healthy clash of views in which both sides appear at their best, affirmative and negative may well confer before the debate on the approaches they intend to take. This pre-debate conference allows for the best use of the limited research time available, and makes for a higher-quality confrontation that probes more deeply into the basic issues in the controversy.

The Use of Testimony

Effective research should provide you with important opinions and quotations from experts in the field of the controversy you are debating. Without expert testimony, debate would become simply a heated exchange of assertions. When we introduce testimony, we are in effect calling up witnesses to testify for our side in the debate. Thus we borrow credibility from those who have earned it by their distinguished and widely recognized expertise.

Such witnesses are especially vital when you can connect them directly to your most important lines of argument. Be sure to introduce them properly, as in the following manner: "Now, why is this such an important need? Professor Anderson can tell us why. George Anderson is a distinguished scientist at Yale University, a person recognized internationally for his research in this area. Writing just last month in the *Current Anthropology*, Dr. Anderson says . . . ." This hypothetical use of testimony illustrates many important rules for the effective use of testimony.

1. Point up the qualifications of the source.
2. Don't overlook the charisma of words such as "scientist" and "Dr." nor the opportunity to associate with distinguished seats of learning like Yale University. Such terms and institutions carry their own intrinsic presumption of merit.
3. Emphasize the recency of the material.
4. Emphasize the additional authority of distinguished journals, books, and newspapers in which the expert's remarks were published.
5. When possible, quote experts directly. This is like summoning them into the presence of your listeners to make some vital statement.
6. The more controversial and important the point at issue, the more careful, elaborate, and precise must be your use of testimony. Therefore, be sure to record important statements accurately during research, and include all details about the publication of these statements. Have a good acquaintance with the experts you quote. You may need such information in the heat and pressure of debate, especially if your opponent should charge: "Just who are they to make such statements?"

Beyond such rules implicit in the illustration, two additional cautions are in order.

7. Look for sources who are not tainted by obvious bias. A biased source invites refutation. On the other hand, a source your audience might expect to be biased *against* your position, but who actually makes statements that seem favorable, provides the strongest possible testimony. When people testify against their own apparent self-interest, the assumption is that they are telling the hard truth.
8. Avoid over-reliance on a single source. You have too much to lose, should the opposition successfully attack its credibility. If the issue involved is crucial, a single source can seem terribly thin and can raise damaging questions in the minds of listeners about the extent of your research and the validity of your position.

Chapter 13 noted how a persuasive speech is a complex pattern woven from many smaller argumentative designs, all of which develop in terms of the unit of proof. Because of the intense pressure of debate encounters, the making of these designs and the manner of their combination take on a distinctive character and come under close scrutiny.

The development of an argument in debate tends to follow a certain procedure. First, there is often an attempt to establish the *relevance* of the argument: "Now, my opponent claims . . . ." It is clear that what follows will have refutative relevance. This expectation is immediately satisfied by a statement indicating the debater's *position:* "But clearly this belief is mistaken. What is true is . . . ." But now this statement of position requires *proof,* both substantiating data and concurring opinion: "How do we know this is true? Because *The New York Times* of Aug. 15, 1982, reports . . . . What do these facts mean? Dr. Carl Sagan tells us that . . . ." Having established relevance, position, and proof, the debater must finally point up the *significance* of the argument to the overall debate. "Now what does all this mean? It means that the affirmative can no longer claim that a need exists. Until they can show a need, there is no real reason to even consider making a change." Thus the debate moves through relevance, position, proof, and significance. But to assure a sense of ongoing flow, each argument in the overall pattern of a case must also have a transitional *coupler,* a statement joining it to the relevance element of the next argumentative design within the pattern. Thus we might say, "But even if there were a need, that would hardly justify the plan of action they have proposed. Let us consider some of its more glaring defects . . . ." The debate case develops through many such designs until it achieves its overall effect: a powerful, cumulative appeal for a favorable decision and a firm commitment from the audience.

Another view of argument in debate shows us the impact of intense confrontation on the unit of proof, which tends to expand under the pressure. Remember that the concept of the unit of proof includes the critical elements of situation, warrant, and claim.[4] The warrant, which authorizes or justifies the movement from situation to claim, can be offered explicitly, or it can lie beneath the surface of an argument. In persuasion, speakers sometimes simply assert a claim in

---

4. The concept was developed in Stephen Toulmin, *The Uses of Argument* (Cambridge, England: Cambridge University Press, 1958), and modified in Ehninger and Brockriede, *Decision by Debate.* It is further modified in this discussion.

response to a situation. They rely on the audience to supply the warrant without being coaxed or convinced. In other words, the warrant is a relevant principle of behavior, and speakers proceed on the assumption that it is automatically activated whenever certain situations are described. But the pressure of debate tends to bring warrants to the surface for closer inspection, where they themselves may be contested.

When warrants or major premises are called into question, the speaker must produce *backing,* or justification for the warrant. You can call on testimony, induction, or self-evident maxims, as illustrated in Figure 15.2.

Some major kinds of backing that are *not* shown in Figure 15.2 are the specific example, appeals to historical tradition ("Our forefathers died for this idea"), credibility appeals by speakers to their own experience ("I saw it—that's why I know it's true!"), and direct appeals to audience sympathy ("You wouldn't want to work if all your money went to the government. That would be nothing but modern slavery!").

As Chapter 13 revealed, the real struggle in persuasion may take place, not over major premises, but over the true nature of the situation. Backing may also be demanded in debate for the speaker's descriptions of reality. This is especially true if what the speaker describes is something different from what listeners feel they have seen. Another great area of struggle in debate may develop over which major premises apply to the situation in contention. Hence the confrontation may not be over the validity of a warrant but over its appropriateness within an argumentative structure. For example, you may not deny that freedom of speech is precious, but you may well argue that it does not apply to expression that promotes violence and destruction of other people's property. Often, arguments over the relationships between situation and warrant focus on the *quality* and definition of the situation described, on the *intent* of the warrant as a social value, and on the *consequences* of either applying it or withholding it in the particular case.

Justified by the warrant and reassured by the strength of the backing, we progress toward a claim until we come to the *qualifier.* The qualifier adjusts the force of the claim by recognizing conditions under which it might not hold (see Figure 15.3). Such conditions may be said to comprise one or more *reservations.* Normally, the opposition in a debate does the job of reminding an audience of reservations. Indeed, opponents may assert that such qualifying conditions actually *do* exist and that the claim either cannot be drawn at all or, at best, can be drawn weakly. For this reason, it is sometimes good to anticipate such an attack by bringing up the reservation yourself, recognizing its power *if* it could be shown to exist in the present situation, but showing

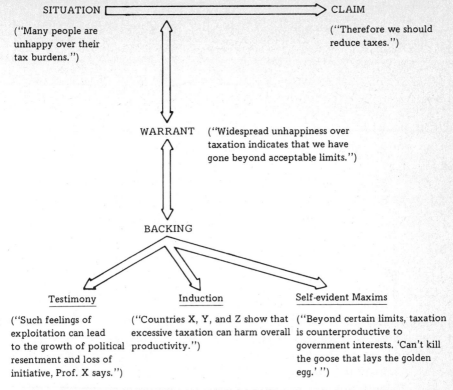

SITUATION ⟶ CLAIM

("Many people are
unhappy over their
tax burdens.")

("Therefore we should
reduce taxes.")

WARRANT ("Widespread unhappiness over
taxation indicates that we have
gone beyond acceptable limits.")

BACKING

Testimony

("Such feelings of
exploitation can lead
to the growth of political
resentment and loss of
initiative, Prof. X says.")

Induction

("Countries X, Y, and Z show that
excessive taxation can harm overall
productivity.")

Self-evident Maxims

("Beyond certain limits, taxation
is counterproductive to
government interests. 'Can't kill
the goose that lays the golden
egg.' ")

Figure 15.2   USE OF BACKING TO JUSTIFY THE WARRANT

conclusively that it is irrelevant under existing circumstances. If you can anticipate a refutation without appearing overly defensive about it, you can often disarm an argument before your opponent has a chance to use it.

Adaptation in Debate

Debate requires an ability to think clearly and effectively in a pressurized situation, especially during the rebuttal. One skill that will help you develop this ability is effective note taking.

You should have available several pens or pencils and a legal pad. For the simplest possible technique of note taking, draw a line down the middle of a page on the legal pad, as shown in Figure 15.4. Figure 15.4 is an example of notes taken for a hypothetical debate. The proposition for this hypothetical debate is: Resolved, that capital punishment should be abolished. The notes, those of a negative debater, indicate the order and nature of intended refutation. Notice the decision to develop

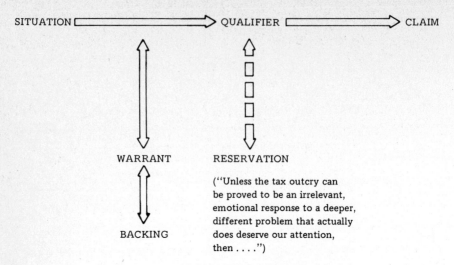

Figure 15.3 ANTICIPATING A RESERVATION

the constructive portion of the speech during its final section and the intention to tie artistically the final remarks—"Don't forget image of the victim!"—to the opening remarks of the affirmative.

If you are on the affirmative, take notes in the right column on negative argumentation as it develops. If you are on the negative, outline the affirmative case in the left column. The opposite column is for your own brief notes indicating the direction your refutation will take during rebuttal. As the opposing speaker nears the end of his or her presentation, glance back over your outlined case. Place large stars—large enough to catch your eye easily as you stand at the lectern—by the arguments you wish to develop. By each star place a number, (1, 2, 3, 4, and so on) indicating the order in which you will mention these points during refutation. Next collect the research cards you will need to develop your answers, and arrange them in the order of this planned sequence of refutation.

During all these rapid preparations as your opponent is concluding, keep one ear open for the final remarks he or she is making. If you have a partner, discourage any whispered advice during these final vital moments when you need all your powers of concentration.

The Debater's Attitude

Just as a debate automatically creates tension between opposing positions, it also creates stress for the people arguing those positions. Thus you should keep in mind certain basic rules of conduct.

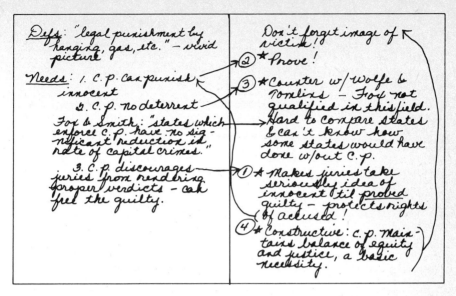

Figure 15.4   NOTE TAKING DURING DEBATE

1. Never appear flustered. If your opponent surprises you with an argument, try not to show it. Assume that any argument can be answered and that you will find the answer.

2. Never look at your opponent(s) while you are debating. You are not likely to convince the opposition, so keep your attention where it belongs—on the audience. Moreover, avoiding such eye contact makes it easier to keep the debate focused on issues instead of personalities. You should maintain a courteous relationship with opponents. Be especially careful to avoid bitterness and sarcasm.

3. Be ready and eager to go when it is your time to speak. Don't look as though you'd rather be anywhere else as you come to the speaker's stand. Your manner should indicate that you are confident as you approach an important communication experience.

4. Maintain appropriate conduct when you are not speaking. Distracting behavior while opponents are speaking will only win them sympathy and you disfavor. It is difficult, however, especially during a final rebuttal, to sit quietly without a chance to respond, while an opponent makes false claims or unfair interpretations. In such moments, you simply have to rely on your audience to spot such tactics. Sometimes you can signal your displeasure and alert the audience by shaking your head in disapproval.

5. Certain special rules of fairness characterize rebuttals of high quality argued by debaters of good character. Rebuttal is a time for developing

answers to issues that were introduced within the constructive speeches. It is not the time for inserting new topics of discussion; such procedure can only be taken as a sign of disorganization and weakness. It suggests that you may be abandoning the issues you first chose to develop and that you are now desperately seeking some new ground to stand on. During the final rebuttal, moreover, introduction of new issues is absolutely unfair. Obviously, the last rebuttal is highly sensitive from the standpoint of debate ethics, but it does give you the considerable advantage of being the last voice heard. Use this advantage fairly and well.

Summary of Major Ideas

The fundamental nature of debate is cooperative conflict—the agreement to disagree in a formal, regulated manner on a certain proposition before a certain audience.

Debate counteracts the rhetorical tendency to oversimplify situations and dehumanize opponents. It adds stability and direction to public decision making and encourages well-considered commitments.

Debate helps expose overblown jargon that is actually designed to inhibit communication. And it helps prevent over-reliance on emotion and image.

Debate promotes some of our most cherished principles: freedom of speech, tolerance for other views, a preference for conviction over dogma, and respect for the rights of listeners to come to judgment and control their own destiny.

A great enemy of debate is our impulse to stifle people whose views we find disagreeable and obnoxious. A second great enemy of debate is the tendency of groups to discourage any kind of independent or deviant thinking and speaking.

The debate proposition is a statement that identifies a specific area of controversy within public deliberation and invites affirmation and negation of some response to that controversy.

Debate resolutions can focus on past or future fact, on values, or on policies.

The affirmative challenges present policy, attacks what is presumed to be the established value position, or offers a new view of the past or future.

The affirmative initiates the debate by presenting and defining the resolution, explaining why it should be accepted, and (in policy debates) showing how it can be put into effect.

The negative defends an established interpretation of facts, a prevailing value judgment, or an existing policy or procedure.

The negative enjoys the presumption in debate; the affirmative must carry the burden of proof.

In a debate on past or future fact, the negative enjoys the *authority of popular concurrence,* the presumption that what most people accept as an authentic depiction is likely to be correct.

The use of expert testimony in debate has the effect of calling witnesses in support of one's position.

Each link in an effective overall argument must show its relevance, establish its position, develop its proof, and point up its significance to the debate.

Argument travels from situation to claim by virtue of some warrant. The warrant must seem adequately backed, and the claim takes into account any reservations that might qualify it.

Rebuttals should develop issues that have already been introduced. They should not open new topics of discussion.

Exercises and Discussion Questions

1. Study the Kennedy–Nixon, Carter–Ford, and Reagan–Carter presidential campaign debates. In what senses were they true debates? In what senses were they not true debates? What were the critical points of gain and loss in these debates? Is such debating useful to the public? Should candidates be required to debate in order to qualify for federal campaign support funds? What suggestions would you make about debate format in a presidential campaign?

2. Can you find any flagrant examples of jargon or bureaucratic "officialese" that actually hide the truth? How might a good debater expose such tactics? Illustrate in terms of the examples you find.

3. Can you think of public or private controversies that never really come into focus because the opposing sides are actually arguing different resolutions? Or of arguments in which the opposing sides pass each other in the fog because they are using totally different definitions of the same terms?

4. For a research project, trace the evolution of a cultural controversy that continues over long periods of time, such as the debate over women's rights.

5. Times of war do not normally encourage open debate between people espousing different points of view. Why is this so? Can you think of exceptions to this rule? Can you account for them?

6. Develop three propositions for debate that satisfy the criteria of clarity, legitimacy, fairness, and interest. Present and defend them in class, where the best propositions can be selected for class debate assignments.

7. Analyze the structure of an argumentative speech, using the models presented here. How compelling are the warrants? Is the backing sufficient? Are the claims appropriately qualified? Is there a clear and coherent pattern of establishing relevance, position, proof, and significance?

For Further Reading

Appreciation for the power and value of debate in society may well begin with John Stuart Mill's classic treatise *On Liberty*, especially Chapter II, "Of the Liberty of Thought and Discussion." Walter Bagehot's "The Age of Discussion," *Physics and Politics* (1873; reprint New York: A. A. Knopf, 1948), discusses the significance of free debate in the development of cultural institutions. Michael Osborn's *Orientations to Rhetorical Style* (Chicago, Ill.: SRA, 1976) recommends debate as a corrective for many of the ills and abuses of rhetorical language.

The technical features of debate theory are developed systematically in Richard Whately's classic work, *Elements of Rhetoric*, ed. Douglas Ehninger (1828; reprint Carbondale, Ill.: Southern Illinois University Press, 1963). This theory is updated in Douglas Ehninger and Wayne Brockriede *Decision by Debate* (New York: Dodd, Mead, 1962). Significant philosophical development occurs in Stephen Toulmin's *The Uses of Argument* (Cambridge, England: Cambridge University Press, 1958).

Appendix

WHO SHALL GUIDE AMERICA? THE ONGOING POLITICAL DEBATE

Three speeches of recent times symbolize the ongoing struggle in this country over which of the major parties will provide its political direction. Therefore, even though the speakers were not meeting in direct confrontation, these speeches may be studied as a kind of extended debate. The speeches also represent the *systemic* use of communication we discussed in Chapter 1; they attempt to organize our behavior and attitudes on a large scale. They illustrate especially the rhetoric of persuasive *renewal* in that they attempt to revive and apply fundamental social values.

We shall study these speeches for their use of communication techniques. Also we hope to learn something more from them about our political options. Our assumption is that significant political speakers delivering significant speeches tend to mirror the souls of their respective parties.

Barbara Jordan, congresswoman from Texas, presented a keynote address that "electrified" the Democratic National Convention of 1976 and received a "thunderous reception."[1] The traditional role of the convention keynote speech is precisely that of renewal: to remind delegates and the unseen millions watching on television or listening on radio of what the party stands for and to arouse their enthusiasm for the convention and campaign ahead. Representative Jordan, a black woman, was hardly a keynote speaker in the traditional mode, but her speech performs the traditional functions. Note that she uses the novelty of her being keynoter in the opening of her speech and that she discusses her rhetorical strategy with the audience in order to dramatize her final selection of a speech theme.

Her dream of "building a national community" is certainly a transcendent vision, and Jordan is clearly attempting to practice herself the advice she is giving to others. It is also a partisan vision in that she

---

1. *New York Times*, July 13, 1976, p. 24, and Oct. 3, 1976, p. 42. See also an analysis of the rhetorical challenge she overcame in Wayne N. Thompson, "Barbara Jordan's Keynote Address: Fulfilling Dual and Conflicting Purposes," *Central States Speech Journal*, 30 (Fall 1979), 272–277.

wishes to undertake such reconstruction on the "bedrock" or "foundations" of Democratic Party principles. She summarizes these principles in a somewhat abstract manner, giving prominence to equality and inclusiveness, to innovation, and to the authority of "the people." She also identifies an impulse that works against national community, the tendency of Americans to fragment into special interest groups. To counteract this impulse, she advises that we cultivate generosity and affection, and she admonishes political leadership on its special responsibility. Note how she echoes and sets off each completed thought with a short declarative sentence or phrase. This distinctive stylistic practice reinforces not only the idea but also her personal image as someone of strong convictions. She *commits* to her thoughts by repeating them. Her powerful pattern of vocal delivery further strengthened this sense of commitment as the speech was presented.

Her conclusion balances her introductory focus on her own uniqueness by underscoring another unusual practice, quoting a Republican president. The prominence she gives to Lincoln's "As I would not be a slave, so I would not be a master" reaffirms the pre-eminence of equality among the values she recommends for the Democratic Party.

It appears, therefore, that Barbara Jordan both fulfilled the ritualistic function of the keynote speaker and avoided the triteness that sometimes goes with rhetorical rituals. The nature of speeches of renewal is to reveal the speaker as an oracle or prophet, a person of vision to whom the entire context of the present moment—in all its historical, social, and spiritual depth and meaning—has been revealed. Such speech, Aristotle observed, emphasizes the skill of the orator. It also emphasizes his or her insight, character, and leadership qualities. It functions to help us celebrate leadership and to renew our appreciation of our social identity.

DEMOCRATIC CONVENTION KEYNOTE ADDRESS[2]
By Barbara Jordan

One hundred and forty-four years ago, members of the Democratic Party first met in convention to select a Presidential candidate. Since that time, Democrats have continued to convene once every four years and draft a party platform and nominate a Presidential candidate. And our meeting this week is a continuation of that tradition.

2. Delivered July 12, 1976, at the Democratic Party convention in New York. Printed in *Vital Speeches of the Day*, 42 (August 15, 1976), 645–646.

But there is something different about tonight. There is something special about tonight. What is different? What is special? I, Barbara Jordan, am a keynote speaker.

A lot of years passed since 1832, and during that time it would have been most unusual for any national political party to ask that a Barbara Jordan deliver a keynote address . . . but tonight here I am. And I feel that notwithstanding the past that my presence here is one additional bit of evidence that the American Dream need not forever be deferred.

Now that I have this grand distinction what in the world am I supposed to say?

I could easily spend this time praising the accomplishments of this party and attacking the Republicans but I don't choose to do that.

I could list the many problems which Americans have. I could list the problems which cause people to feel cynical, angry, frustrated: problems which include lack of integrity in government; the feeling that the individual no longer counts; the reality of material and spiritual poverty; the feeling that the grand American experiment is failing or has failed. I could recite these problems and then I could sit down and offer no solutions. But I don't choose to do that either.

The citizens of America expect more. They deserve and they want more than a recital of problems.

We are a people in a quandary about the present. We are a people in search of our future. We are a people in search of a national community.

We are a people trying not only to solve the problems of the present: unemployment, inflation . . . but we are attempting on a larger scale to fulfill the promise of America. We are attempting to fulfill our national purpose; to create and sustain a society in which all of us are equal.

Throughout our history, when people have looked for new ways to solve their problems, and to uphold the principles of this nation, many times they have turned to political parties. They have often turned to the Democratic Party.

What is it, what is it about the Democratic Party that makes it the instrument that people use when they search for ways to shape their future? Well I believe the answer to that question lies in our concept of governing. Our concept of governing is derived from our view of people. It is a concept deeply rooted in a set of beliefs firmly etched in the national conscience, of all of us.

Now what are these beliefs?

First, we believe in equality for all and privileges for none. This is a belief that each American regardless of background has equal standing in the public forum, all of us. Because we believe this idea so firmly, we are an inclusive rather than an exclusive party. Let everybody come.

I think it no accident that most of those emigrating to America in the 19th century identified with the Democratic Party. We are a heterogeneous party made up of Americans of diverse backgrounds.

We believe that the people are the source of all governmental power, that the authority of the people is to be extended, not restricted. This can be accomplished only by providing each citizen with every opportunity to participate in the management of the government. They must have that.

We believe that the government which represents the authority of all the people, not just one interest group, but all the people, has an obligation to actively underscore, actively seek to remove those obstacles which would block individual achievement . . . obstacles emanating from race, sex, economic condition. The government must seek to remove them.

We are a party of innovation. We do not reject our traditions, but we are willing to adapt to changing circumstances, when change we must. We are willing to suffer the discomfort of change in order to achieve a better future.

We have a positive vision of the future founded on the belief that the gap between the promise and reality of America can one day be finally closed. We believe that.

This, my friends, is the bedrock of our concept of governing. This is a part of the reason why Americans have turned to the Democratic Party. These are the foundations upon which a national community can be built.

Let's all understand that these guiding principles cannot be discarded for short-term political gains. They represent what this country is all about. They are indigenous to the American idea. And these are principles which are not negotiable.

In other times, I could stand here and give this kind of exposition of the beliefs of the Democratic Party and that would be enough. But today that is not enough. People want more. That is not sufficient reason for the majority of the people of this country to vote Democratic. We have made mistakes. In our haste to do all things for all people, we did not foresee the full consequences of our actions. And when the people raised their voices, we didn't hear. But our deafness was only a temporary condition, and not an irreversible condition.

Even as I stand here and admit that we have made mistakes I still believe that as the people of America sit in judgment on each party, they will recognize that our mistakes were mistakes of the heart. They'll recognize that.

And now we must look to the future. Let us heed the voice of the people and recognize their common sense. If we do not, we not only blaspheme our political heritage, we ignore the common ties that bind all Americans.

Many fear the future. Many are distrustful of their leaders, and believe that their voices are never heard. Many seek only to satisfy their private work wants. To satisfy private interests.

But this is the great danger America faces. That we will cease to be one nation and become instead a collection of interest groups; city against suburb, region against region, individual against individual. Each seeking to satisfy private wants.

If that happens, who then will speak for America?

Who then will speak for the common good?

This is the question which must be answered in 1976.

Are we to be one people bound together by common spirit sharing in a common endeavor or will we become a divided nation?

For all of its uncertainty, we cannot flee the future. We must not become the new puritans and reject our society. We must address and master the future together. It can be done if we restore the belief that we share a sense of national community, that we share a common national endeavor. It can be done.

There is no executive order; there is no law that can require the American people to form a national community. This we must do as individuals and if we do it as individuals, there is no President of the United States who can veto that decision.

As a first step, we must restore our belief in ourselves. We are a generous people so why can't we be generous with each other? We need to take to heart the words spoken by Thomas Jefferson:

Let us restore to social intercourse that harmony and that affection without which liberty and even life are but dreary things.

A nation is formed by the willingness of each of us to share in the responsibility for upholding the common good.

A government is invigorated when each of us is willing to participate in shaping the future of this nation.

In this election year we must define the common good and begin again to shape a common good and begin again to shape a common future. Let each person do his or her part. If one citizen is unwilling to participate, all of us are going to suffer. For the American idea, though it is shared by all of us, is realized in each one of us.

And now, what are those of us who are elected public officials supposed to do? We call ourselves public servants but I'll tell you this: we as public servants must set an example for the rest of the nation. It is hypocritical for the public official to admonish and exhort the people to uphold the common good if we are derelict in upholding the common good. More is required of public officials than slogans and handshakes and press releases. More is required. We must hold ourselves strictly accountable. We must provide the people with a vision of the future.

If we promise as public officials, we must deliver. If we as public officials propose, we must produce. If we say to the American people it is time for you to be sacrificial; sacrifice. If the public official says that, we (public officials) must be the first to give. We must be. And again, if we make mistakes, we must be willing to admit them. We have to do that. What we have to do is strike a balance between the idea that government should do everything and the idea, the belief, that government ought to do nothing. Strike a balance.

Let there be no illusions about the difficulty of forming this kind of a national community. It's tough, difficult, not easy. But a spirit of harmony will survive in America only if each of us remembers that we share a common destiny. If each of us remembers when self-interest and bitterness seem to prevail, that we share a common destiny.

I have confidence that the Democratic Party can lead the way. I have that confidence. We cannot improve on the system of government handed down to us by the founders of the Republic, there is no way to improve upon that. But what we can do is to find new ways to implement that system and realize our destiny.

Now, I began this speech by commenting to you on the uniqueness of a Barbara Jordan making the keynote address. Well I am going to close my speech by quoting a Republican President and I ask you that as you listen to these words of Abraham Lincoln, relate them to the concept of a national community in which every last one of us participates: As I would not be a slave, so I would not be a master. This expresses my idea of Democracy. Whatever differs from this, to the extent of the difference is no Democracy.

Four years after Representative Jordan's speech, Ronald Reagan stood in triumph at the Republican National Convention to accept his party's nomination for president. His speech on that occasion was described as the most important of his life, and it was "performed with a skill that surprised even his admirers and dismayed his foes. . . ."[3] Though much in Reagan's speech differs from Jordan's vision of America, he begins with the same concern: building or rebuilding the American sense of community. The principles and values emphasized in these two visions of community, however, are quite different. By contrast with Jordan's emphasis on equality, inclusiveness, innovation, and the authority of "the people," Reagan offers "family, work, neighborhood, peace, and freedom" as the order within his "community of shared values." This selection of values and the order in which they appear are deliberate, for Reagan repeats them both at the beginning and near the end of his speech, and he nurtures a sense of their importance throughout.

The implications of these two lists of values may tell us much about the speakers and the parties they represent. Jordan emphasizes concern for people who have not been treated as equals and favors social change to achieve such equality. Beyond respect for this value, the grounds for membership in Jordan's national community are not explicitly stated. Perhaps this is deliberate; if the value requirements for communal membership are left vague, the society can remain open and "inclusive," as she puts it. People can come together and then develop social values that justify their shared membership in the community. Reagan, on the other hand, emphasizes social stability and security, themes of order and not of change. The word "equality" is never heard in his speech, and his invitation to community is limited to those who already share his clearly defined hierarchy of values.

Both speakers and both parties lay claim to "the people," but the depictions they offer differ in striking ways. Whereas the Democrats develop a romantic notion of "giving a voice to the voiceless," the Republicans offer an equally romantic notion of the people as descended from patriots and pioneers. In Ronald Reagan's view of history, no American fought the Revolutionary War without honor. He seems to glorify small-town America, Norman Rockwell's America, where the people and their virtues remain uncomplicated. It is significant that the hero of Reagan's Inaugural Address, Martin Treptow, was a small-town barber. Work and family are repeated again and again as the most persistent themes among these virtues. At one point in his speech, Reagan offers a vision that seems to express these values most concretely: "It's time to put America back to work, to make our cities and towns resound with the confident voices of men and women of all

3. *Time*, 116 (July 28, 1980), 29.

races, nationalities and faiths bringing home to their families a paycheck they can cash for honest money."

Because Americans are already in possession of great virtues derived from the American heritage, Republicans see little need for social change, and their ideal government is one that does not interfere with the natural exercise of these virtues. One very legitimate stage for federal government action, however, is national defense, for this "island of freedom" with all its God-given blessings of liberty and abundance exists in a threatening world and must be protected. Translated into terms of practical policy, Reagan would have the federal government interfere as little as possible with domestic concerns, except to provide a healthy climate for business enterprise. But he would have the government exercise a dominant, activist role on the international scene as "leader of the free world."

In his speech Reagan criticizes the Carter administration for having created a hydra-headed monster of economic disaster, defense weakness, and energy shortage. As he develops these lines of attack, observe his effective use of a number of rhetorical techniques. At several points he uses the rhetorical question to great advantage, as when he asks, "Can anyone look at the record of this Administration and say, 'Well done'?" He employs several food-related metaphors, first accusing the Carter administration of having concocted an "economic stew that has turned the national stomach," then returning to the notion that the federal government is overweight and needs to go on a diet. One of the most important of Reagan's metaphors, the "safety net" theory of public welfare, is mentioned only briefly. This image, important because it has developed as a basic conception in the Reagan approach to welfare reform, appears to mean that the purpose of welfare is to protect the most helpless among us against the worst disasters. Though it legitimizes such a limited function, the metaphor may also have reduced the sense of public obligation to provide welfare support.

Such symbols may indeed express the essential differences between the major parties. The Republicans generally appear to favor constrained government at home and an activist role abroad; the Democrats often favor just the opposite. Lest we simplify too much, however, there is surely a certain dynamism in Reagan's conception of American society. He thinks, for example, in aggressive horizontal metaphors, speaking (in a manner faintly reminiscent of John Kennedy) about getting the country moving again and promising to leave no one behind in this new march into the future. Perhaps we can take some comfort in the values that seem to persist in the rhetoric of both parties.

REPUBLICAN PRESIDENTIAL NOMINATION[4]

Acceptance Address

By Ronald Reagan

Thank you very much. We're using up prime time. Thank you very much. You're singing our song. Well, the first thrill tonight was to find myself for the first time in a long time in a movie on prime time.

But this, as you can imagine, is the second big thrill.

Mr. Chairman, Mr. Vice President-to-be, this convention, my fellow citizens of this great nation:

With a deep awareness of the responsibility conferred by your trust, I accept your nomination for the Presidency of the United States. I do so with deep gratitude. And I think also I might interject on behalf of all of us our thanks to Detroit and the people of Michigan and to this city for the warm hospitality we've enjoyed.

And I thank you for your wholehearted response to my recommendation in regard to George Bush as the candidate for Vice President.

I'm very proud of our party tonight. This convention has shown to all America a party united, with positive programs for solving the nation's problems; a party ready to build a new consensus with all those across the land who share a community of values embodied in these words: family, work, neighborhood, peace and freedom.

Now I know we've had a quarrel or two but only as to the method of attaining a goal. There was no argument here about the goal. As President, I will establish a liaison with the 50 Governors to encourage them to eliminate, wherever it exists, discrimination against women. I will monitor Federal laws to insure their implementation and to add statutes if they are needed.

More than anything else, I want my candidacy to unify our country; to renew the American spirit and sense of purpose. I want to carry our message to every American, regardless of party affiliation, who is a member of the community of shared values.

Never before in our history have Americans been called upon to face three grave threats to our very existence, any one of which could destroy us. We face a disintegrating economy, a weakened defense and an energy policy based on the sharing of scarcity.

The major issue of this campaign is the direct political, personal, and moral responsibility of Democratic Party leadership—in the White

4. Delivered July 17, 1980, at the Republican Party convention in Detroit, Michigan. Printed in *Vital Speeches of the Day*, 46 (August 15, 1980), 642–646.

House and in the Congress—for this unprecedented calamity which has befallen us. They tell us they've done the most that humanly could be done. They say that the United States has had its day in the sun, that our nation has passed its zenith. They expect you to tell your children that the American people no longer have the will to cope with their problems; that the future will be one of sacrifice and few opportunities.

My fellow citizens, I utterly reject that view. The American people, the most generous on earth, who created the highest standard of living, are not going to accept the notion that we can only make a better world for others by moving backward ourselves. And those who believe we can have no business leading this nation.

I will not stand by and watch this great country destroy itself under mediocre leadership that drifts from one crisis to the next, eroding our national will and purpose. We have come together here because the American people deserve better from those to whom they entrust our nation's highest offices, and we stand united in our resolve to do something about it.

We need a rebirth of the American tradition of leadership at every level of government and in private life as well. The United States of America is unique in world history because it has a genius for leaders— many leaders—on many levels.

But back in 1976, Mr. Carter said, "Trust me." And a lot of people did. And now, many of those people are out of work. Many have seen their savings eaten away by inflation. Many others on fixed incomes, especially the elderly, have watched helplessly as the cruel tax of inflation wasted away their purchasing power. And, today, a great many who trusted Mr. Carter wonder if we can survive the Carter policies of national defense.

"Trust me" government asks that we concentrate our hopes and dreams on one man; that we trust him to do what's best for us. But my view of government places trust not in one person or one party, but in those values that transcend persons and parties. The trust is where it belongs—in the people. The responsibility to live up to that trust is where it belongs, in their elected leaders. That kind of relationship, between the people and their elected leaders, is a special kind of compact.

Three-hundred-and-sixty years ago, in 1620, a group of families dared to cross a mighty ocean to build a future for themselves in a new world. When they arrived at Plymouth, Massachusetts, they formed what they called a "compact," an agreement among themselves to build a community and abide by its laws.

This single act—the voluntary binding together of free people to live under the law—set the pattern for what was to come.

A century and a half later, the descendants of those people pledged their lives, their fortunes and their sacred honor to found this nation. Some forfeited their fortunes and their lives; none sacrificed honor.

Four score and seven years later, Abraham Lincoln called upon the people of all America to renew their dedication and their commitment to a government of, for and by the people.

Isn't it once again time to renew our compact of freedom; to pledge to each other all that is best in our lives; all that gives meaning to them—for the sake of this, our beloved and blessed land?

Together, let us make this a new beginning. Let us make a commitment to care for the needy; to teach our children the virtues handed down to us by our families; to have the courage to defend those values and virtues and the willingness to sacrifice for them.

Let us pledge to restore, in our time, the American spirit of voluntary service, of cooperation, of private and community initiative; a spirit that flows like a deep and mighty river through the history of our nation.

As your nominee, I pledge to you to restore to the Federal Government the capacity to do the people's work without dominating their lives. I pledge to you a Government that will not only work well but wisely, its ability to act tempered by prudence, and its willingness to do good balanced by the knowledge that government is never more dangerous than when our desire to have it help us blinds us to its great power to harm us.

You know, the first Republican President once said, "While the people retain their virtue and their vigilance, no Administration by any extreme of wickedness or folly can seriously injure the Government in the short space of four years."

If Mr. Lincoln could see what's happened in these last three and a half years, he might hedge a little on that statement. But with the virtues that are our legacy as a free people and with the vigilance that sustains liberty, we still have time to use our renewed compact to overcome the injuries that have been done to America these past three and a half years.

First, we must overcome something the present Administration has cooked up: a new and altogether indigestible economic stew, one part inflation, one part high unemployment, one part recession, one part runaway taxes, one part deficit spending seasoned with an energy crisis. It's an economic stew that has turned the national stomach.

Ours are not problems of abstract economic theory. These are problems of flesh and blood; problems that cause pain and destroy the moral fiber of real people who should not suffer the further indignity of being told by the Government that it is all somehow their fault. We do not have inflation because—as Mr. Carter says—we've lived too well.

The head of a Government which has utterly refused to live within its means and which has, in the last few days, told us that this coming year's deficit will be $60 billion, dares to point the finger of blame at business and labor, both of which have been engaged in a losing struggle just trying to stay even.

High taxes, we are told, are somehow good for us, as if, when government spends our money it isn't inflationary, but when we spend it, it is.

Those who preside over the worst energy shortage in our history tell us to use less, so that we will run out of oil, gasoline and natural gas a little more slowly. Well, now, conservation is desirable, of course, but we must not waste energy. But conservation is not the sole answer to our energy needs.

America must get to work producing more energy. The Republican program for solving economic problems is based on growth and productivity.

Large amounts of oil and natural gas lay beneath our land and off our shores, untouched because the present Administration seems to believe the American people would rather see more regulation, more taxes and more controls than more energy.

Coal offers a great potential. So does nuclear energy produced under rigorous safety standards. It could supply electricity for thousands of industries and millions of jobs and homes. It must not be thwarted by a tiny minority opposed to economic growth which often finds friendly ears in regulatory agencies for its obstructionist campaigns.

Now make no mistake. We will not permit the safety of our people or our environmental heritage to be jeopardized, but we are going to reaffirm that the economic prosperity of our people is a fundamental part of our environment.

Our problems are both acute and chronic, yet all we hear from those in positions of leadership are the same tired proposals for more Government tinkering, more meddling and more control—all of which led us to this sorry state in the first place.

Can anyone look at the record of this Administration and say, "Well done"? Can anyone compare the state of our economy when the Carter Administration took office with where we are today and say, "Keep up the good work"? Can anyone look at our reduced standing in the world today and say, "Let's have four more years of this"?

I believe the American people are going to answer these questions, as you've answered them, in the first week of November and their answer will be, "No—we've had enough." And then it will be up to us— beginning next January 20—to offer an Administration and Congressional leadership of competence and more than a little courage.

We must have the clarity of vision to see the difference between what is essential and what is merely desirable; and then the courage to bring our Government back under control.

It is essential that we maintain both the forward momentum of economic growth and the strength of the safety net between those in our society who need help. We also believe it is essential that the integrity of all aspects of Social Security be preserved.

Beyond these essentials, I believe it is clear our Federal Government is overgrown and overweight. Indeed, it is time our Government should go on a diet. Therefore, my first act as chief executive will be to impose an immediate and thorough freeze on Federal hiring. Then, we are going to enlist the very best minds from business, labor and whatever quarter to conduct a detailed review of every department, bureau and agency that lives by Federal appropriation.

And we are also going to enlist the help and ideas of many dedicated and hard-working Government employees at all levels who want a more efficient Government just as much as the rest of us do. I know that many of them are demoralized by the confusion and waste they confront in their work as a result of failed and failing policies.

Our instructions to the groups we enlist will be simple and direct. We will remind them that Government programs exist at the sufferance of the American taxpayer and are paid for with money earned by working men and women and programs that represent a waste of their money—a theft from their pocketbooks—must have that waste eliminated or that program must go. It must go by Executive Order where possible, by Congressional action where necessary.

Everything that can be run more effectively by state and local government we shall turn over to state and local government, along with the funding sources to pay for it. We are going to put an end to the money merry-go-round where our money becomes Washington's money, to be spent by states and cities exactly the way the Federal bureaucrats tell us it has to be spent.

I will not accept the excuse that the Federal Government has grown so big and powerful that it is beyond the control of any President, any administration or Congress. We are going to put an end to the notion that the American taxpayer exists to fund the Federal Government. The Federal Government exists to serve the American people and to be accountable to the American people. On January 20, we are going to reestablish that truth.

Also on that date we are going to initiate action to get substantial relief for our taxpaying citizens and action to put people back to work. None of this will be based on any new form of monetary tinkering or fiscal sleight-of-hand. We will simply apply to government the common sense that we all use in our daily lives.

Work and family are at the center of our lives, the foundation of our dignity as a free people. When we deprive people of what they have earned, or take away their jobs, we destroy their dignity and undermine their families. We can't support families unless there are jobs; and we can't have jobs unless the people have both money to invest and the faith to invest it.

These are concepts that stem from an economic system that for more than 200 years has helped us master a continent, create a previously undreamed-of-prosperity for our people and has fed millions of others around the globe and that system will continue to serve us in the future if our Government will stop ignoring the basic values on which it was built and stop betraying the trust and good will of the American workers who keep it going.

The American people are carrying the heaviest peacetime tax burden in our nation's history—and it will grow even heavier, under present law, next January. We are taxing ourselves into economic exhaustion and stagnation, crushing our ability and incentive to save, invest and produce.

This must stop. We must halt this fiscal self-destruction and restore sanity to our economic system.

I've long advocated a 30 percent reduction in income tax rates over a period of three years. This phased tax reduction would begin with a 10 percent "down payment" tax cut in 1981, which the Republicans in Congress and I have already proposed.

A phased reduction of tax rates would go a long way toward easing the heavy burden on the American people. But we shouldn't stop there.

Within the context of economic conditions and appropriate budget priorities during each fiscal year of my Presidency, I would strive to go further. This would include improvement in business depreciation taxes so we can stimulate investment in order to get plants and equipment replaced, put more Americans back to work and put our nation back on the road to being competitive in world commerce. We will also work to reduce the cost of government as a percentage of our gross national product.

The first task of national leadership is to set realistic and honest priorities in our policies and our budget, and I pledge that my Administration will do that.

When I talk of tax cuts, I am reminded that every major tax cut in this century has strengthened the economy, generated renewed productivity and ended up yielding new revenues for the Government by creating new investment, new jobs and more commerce among our people.

The present Administration has been forced by us Republicans to play follow-the-leader with regard to a tax cut. But in this election year we must take with the proverbial "grain of salt" any tax cut proposed by those who have already given us the greatest tax increase in our nation's history.

When those in leadership give us tax increases and tell us we must also do with less, have they thought about those who've always had less—especially the minorities? This is like telling them that just as they step on the first rung of the ladder of opportunity, the ladder is being pulled out from under them. That may be the Democratic leaderhip's message to the minorities, but it won't be our message. Ours, ours will be: We have to move ahead, but we're not going to leave anyone behind.

Thanks to the economic policies of the Democratic Party, millions of Americans find themselves out of work. Millions more have never even had a fair chance to learn new skills, hold a decent job or secure for themselves and their families a share in the prosperity of this nation.

It's time to put America back to work, to make our cities and towns resound with the confident voices of men and women of all races, nationalities and faiths bringing home to their families a paycheck they can cash for honest money.

For those without skills, we'll find a way to help them get new skills.

For those without job opportunities we'll stimulate new opportunities, particularly in the inner cities where they live.

For those who've abandoned hope, we'll restore hope and we'll welcome them into a great national crusade to make America great again.

When we move from domestic affairs, and cast our eyes abroad, we see an equally sorry chapter in the record of the present Administration:

—A Soviet combat brigade trains in Cuba, just 90 miles from our shores.

—A Soviet army of invasion occupies Afghanistan, further threatening our vital interests in the Middle East.

—America's defense strength is at its lowest ebb in a generation, while the Soviet Union is vastly outspending us in both strategic and conventional arms.

—Our European allies, looking nervously at the growing menace from the East, turn to us for leadership and fail to find it.

—And incredibly, more than 50, as you've been told from this platform so eloquently already, more than 50 of our fellow Americans have been held captive for over eight years—eight months—by a dictatorial foreign power that holds us up to ridicule before the world.

Adversaries large and small test our will and seek to confound our resolve, but we are given weakness when we need strength; vacillation when the times demand firmness.

The Carter Administration lives in the world of make-believe. Every day, drawing up a response to that day's problems, troubles, regardless of what happened yesterday and what'll happen tomorrow.

But you and I live in a real world, where disasters are overtaking our nation without any real response from Washington.

This is make-believe, self-deceit and, above all, transparent hypocrisy.

For example, Mr. Carter says he supports the volunteer Army, but he lets military pay and benefits slip so low that many of our enlisted personnel are actually eligible for food stamps. Re-enlistment rates drop and, just recently, after he fought all week against a proposed pay increase for our men and women in the military, he then helicoptered out to our carrier the U.S.S. Nimitz, which was returning from long months of duty in the Indian Ocean, and told the crew of that ship that he advocated better pay for them and their comrades. Where does he really stand, now that he's back on shore?

Well, I'll tell you where I stand. I do not favor a peacetime draft or registration, but I do favor pay and benefit levels that will attract and keep highly motivated men and women in our volunteer forces and back them up with an active reserve trained and ready for instant call in case of emergency.

You know, there may be a sailor at the helm of the ship of state, but the ship has no rudder. Critical decisions are made at times almost in comic fashion, but who can laugh?

Who was not embarrassed when the Administration handed a major propaganda victory in the United Nations to the enemies of Israel, our staunch Middle East ally for three decades, and then claimed that the American vote was a "mistake," the result of a "failure of communication" between the President, his Secretary of State and his U.N. Ambassador?

Who does not feel a growing sense of unease as our allies, facing repeated instances of an amateurish and confused Administration, reluctantly conclude that America is unwilling or unable to fulfill its obligations as leader of the free world?

Who does not feel rising alarm when the question in any discussion of foreign policy is no longer, "Should we do something?" but "Do we have the capacity to do anything?"

The Administration which has brought us to this state is seeking your endorsement for four more years of weakness, indecision, mediocrity and incompetence. No. No. No American should vote until he or she has asked: Is the United States stronger and more respected now than it was three-and-a-half years ago? Is the world safer, a safer place in which to live.

It is the responsibility of the President of the United States, in working for peace, to insure that the safety of our people cannot successfully be threatened by a hostile foreign power. As President, fulfilling that responsibility will be my No. 1 priority.

We're not a warlike people. Quite the opposite. We always seek to live in peace. We resort to force infrequently and with great reluctance—and only after we've determined that it is absolutely necessary. We are awed—and rightly so—by the forces of destruction at loose in the world in this nuclear era.

But neither can we be naive or foolish. Four times in my lifetime America has gone to war, bleeding the lives of its young men into the sands of island beachheads, the fields of Europe and the jungles and rice paddies of Asia. We know only too well that war comes not when the forces of freedom are strong, it is when they are weak that tyrants are tempted.

We simply cannot learn these lessons the hard way again without risking our destruction.

Of all the objectives we seek, first and foremost is the establishment of lasting world peace. We must always stand ready to negotiate in good faith, ready to pursue any reasonable avenue that holds forth the promise of lessening tensions and furthering the prospects of peace. But let our friends and those who may wish us ill take note: the United States has an obligation to its citizens and to the people of the world never to let those who would destroy freedom dictate the future course of life on this planet. I would regard my election as proof that we have renewed our resolve to preserve world peace and freedom. That this nation will once again be strong enough to do that.

Now this evening marks the last step, save one, of a campaign that has taken Nancy and me from one end of this great nation to the other, over many months and thousands and thousands of miles. There are those who question the way we choose a President, who say that our process imposes difficult and exhausting burdens on those who seek the office. I have not found it so.

It is impossible to capture in words the splendor of this vast continent which God has granted as our portion of His creation. There are no words to express the extraordinary strength and character of this breed of people we call Americans.

Everywhere we've met thousands of Democrats, Independents and Republicans from all economic conditions, walks of life bound together in that community of shared values of family, work, neighborhood, peace and freedom. They are concerned, yes, they're not frightened. They're disturbed, but not dismayed. They are the kind of men and women Tom Paine had in mind when he wrote, during the darkest days of the American Revolution, "We have it in our power to begin the world over again."

Nearly 150 years after Tom Paine wrote those words, an American President told the generation of the Great Depression that it had a "rendezvous with destiny." I believe this generation of Americans today also has a rendezvous with destiny.

Tonight, let us dedicate ourselves to renewing the American compact. I ask you not simply to "trust me," but to trust your values—our values—and to hold me responsible for living up to them. I ask you to trust that American spirit which knows no ethnic, religious, social, political, regional or economic boundaries; the spirit that burned with zeal in the hearts of millions of immigrants from every corner of the earth who came here in search of freedom.

Some say that spirit no longer exists. But I've seen it—I've felt it— all across the land, in the big cities, the small towns and in rural America. It's still there, ready to blaze into life if you and I are willing to do what has to be done; we have to do the practical things, the down-to-earth things, such as creating policies that will stimulate our economy, increase productivity and put America back to work.

The time is now to limit Federal spending; to insist on a stable monetary reform and to free ourselves from imported oil.

The time is now to resolve that the basis of a firm and principled foreign policy is one that takes the world as it is and seeks to change it by leadership and example; not by harangue, harassment or wishful thinking.

The time is now to say that we shall seek new friendships and expand others and improve others, but we shall not do so by breaking our word or casting aside old friends and allies.

And the time is now to redeem promises once made to the American people by another candidate, in another time and another place. He said:

"For three long years I have been going up and down this country preaching that government—Federal, state and local—costs too much.

I shall not stop that preaching. As an immediate program of action, we must abolish useless offices. We must eliminate unnecessary functions of government.

"We must consolidate subdivisions of government and, like the private citizen, give up luxuries which we can no longer afford." And then he said:

"I propose to you my friends, and through you, that government of all kinds, big and little, be made solvent and that the example be set by the President of the United States and his Cabinet."

That was Franklin Delano Roosevelt's words as he accepted the Democratic nomination for President in 1932.

The time is now, my fellow Americans, to recapture our destiny, to take it into our own hands. And to do this it will take many of us, working together. I ask you tonight, all over this land, to volunteer your help in this cause so that we can carry our message throughout the land.

Isn't it time that we, the people, carry out these unkept promises? That we pledge to each other and to all America on this July day 48 years later, that now we intend to do just that.

I have thought of something that's not a part of my speech and worried over whether I should do it. Can we doubt that only a Divine Providence placed this land, this island of freedom, here as a refuge for all those people in the world who yearn to breathe free? Jews and Christians enduring persecution behind the Iron Curtain; the boat people of Southeast Asia, Cuba and of Haiti; the victims of drought and famine in Africa, the freedom fighters in Afghanistan, and our own countrymen held in savage captivity.

I'll confess that I've been a little afraid to suggest what I'm going to suggest. I'm more afraid not to. Can we begin our crusade joined together in a moment of silent prayer?

God bless America.

Thank you.

Scarcely a month later, Senator Edward Kennedy stood before the Democratic National Convention as a defeated candidate for his party's nomination. Kennedy's primary campaign had been an ill-fated disaster, but late in the race he had begun to show real strength, just as the winning incumbent, President Jimmy Carter, had begun to show increasing weakness. Kennedy's appearance before the convention during television prime time would become, Carter forces hoped, an act of reconciliation, unifying the party for the tough campaign against the Republican challenger. In the scenario of the convention, Kennedy's speech was to have been his final, graceful act of retiring from the political wars of that year. Instead, with, as *Newsweek* put it, "one superb speech that was by turns graceful, rousing, poetic, and defiant,"[5] Kennedy thrust his own vivid personality again to the fore, upstaging Carter's acceptance speech of the following evening and making the president seem all the more drab by contrast. Instead of his exit from the 1980 political wars, Kennedy's speech may have signaled his entry into the campaign of 1984. Listening to his opening, "I have come here tonight not to argue for a candidacy, but to affirm a cause," Carter forces may have heard echoes of another famous, artful disclaimer at the opening of Mark Antony's funeral speech in Shakespeare's *Julius Caesar:* "I come to bury Caesar, not to praise him." Just as Antony's speech became, by skillful indirection, an indictment of the assassins who had allowed him to address the Roman throng, so Kennedy's speech, which directly attacked Ronald Reagan, also indirectly criticized the Carter candidacy.

Kennedy, of course, was and is a complex and enigmatic presence on the American political scene. He is the last of the Kennedy brothers, and listeners could hear in his style some of the formal phrasings and cadences of President John Kennedy. They could also hear the passionate social concern of Robert Kennedy. Indeed, the speech can be read and heard now as an anthem, not just to Edward Kennedy's lost candidacy, but to the cause of old liberalism, rehearsing once more its romantic preoccupation with "the common man—and the common woman." For those who might object that his speech was a last hurrah for an old and discredited liberalism, "an empty, if stirring, exercise in liberal nostalgia,"[6] Kennedy answers in anticipation that what he champions are not "outworn views, but . . . old values that will never wear out."

Even the tears evoked by the speech that night might have had a certain complexity. They could have been tears for the fading Kennedy dynasty and all that it meant for our time. Or the tears could have been for lost liberalism, as delegates recalled the passionate conviction of its sociodramas and the reformer roles it once provided. Perhaps there were also tears of tribute for a hard-fought campaign that had not succeeded, mixed with tears of frustration for the flawed hero who, had he not been pursued relentlessly by the furies of Chappaquiddick, might have stood before them as their nominee.

Kennedy's speech is more political than Barbara Jordan's in the sense that it is less philosophical and more concrete. Whereas Jordan talks of "equality and inclusiveness," Kennedy speaks of the Equal Rights

5. *Newsweek,* 96 (August 25, 1980), 31.
6. *Newsweek,* p. 32.

Amendment and of representing "the humble members of society—the farmers, mechanics, and laborers." Whereas Jordan speaks of "innovation," Kennedy advocates national health insurance. Much of the power of Jordan's speech derives from its style and delivery; Kennedy also generates power by taking bold stands on specific issues. But Kennedy is sensitive to style and symbol. He reclaims the god-term of "progress" from the Republicans, saying that "Progress is our heritage, not theirs."

Kennedy's style is also unique. Whereas Jordan relies on the brief confirmatory phrase or sentence to reinforce her commitment to an idea, Kennedy uses stylistic imitation of other great leaders of the Democratic Party to lay claim to a certain symbolic heritage. When Kennedy says, "each generation of Americans has a rendezvous with a different reality," we hear an echo of Franklin Roosevelt's First Inaugural. When Kennedy says, "History only helps those who help themselves. . . . We as a people are ready to give something back to our country in return for all it has given us," we hear again his own brother's Inaugural Address. Through such strategic reverberations, Kennedy stirs in us the memories of patriotic rituals. He renews the memories of heroes and associates himself with those memories. He seems the successor to his brother's Camelot, and he reinforces the sense of legitimate succession by invoking the symbolic themes of New Freedom (Woodrow Wilson), New Deal (Franklin Roosevelt), and New Frontier (John Kennedy) and adding that of "new hope." This theme could become the rallying cry for a run for the presidency in 1984, should Kennedy decide to try again.

Kennedy's quoting Reagan directly in connection with major social issues was probably the most effective attack of the entire campaign. Criticisms of opponents become ritualistic during political campaigns, and they may lose power simply because they are expected. Moreover, direct attacks can be resented if they seem unfair. The method of quoting the opponent directly, however, minimizes the sense of unfairness. When the quotations are outrageous, the technique can be quite effective. Kennedy also counters directly Reagan's attack on "big government," saying "The demand of our people in 1980 is not for smaller government or bigger government, but for better government." But whether intended or not, the speech also contains a subtle indictment of Carter as well. Whereas Carter had tried to lower expectations of the power of the presidency, Kennedy emphasizes that "together a President and the people can make a difference." The very boldness of Kennedy's stand for orthodox liberal ideology—and for specific issues related to it—contrasted sharply with Carter's somewhat vague and even inconsistent positions. So it could well be that

Kennedy was deliberately indicting *both* Carter and Reagan as he concluded, "So let us reject the counsel of retreat and the call to reaction."

Throughout the speech you will find many phrases that moved and excited listeners. Kennedy's criticism of certain tax shelters, such as his description of the business lunch deduction as "food stamps for the rich," and his nautical metaphor for his own campaign ("Often we sailed against the wind but always we kept our rudder true") come to mind as examples. His final quotation from Tennyson's "Ulysses" is fitting—not only excellent and apt in its sentiment, but also useful in placing the final focus of the speech where it needed to be: on Kennedy himself and those who had sailed with him on the great adventure of his campaign. This focus suggests personal growth and strength, and the kind of image Kennedy must build to counteract doubts about his character.

PRINCIPLES OF DEMOCRATIC PARTY[7]
By Edward M. Kennedy

Well, things worked out a little different than I thought, but let me tell you, I still love New York. My fellow Democrats and my fellow Americans: I have come here tonight not to argue for a candidacy, but to affirm a cause.

I am asking you to renew the commitment of the Democratic Party to economic justice. I am asking you to renew our commitment to a fair and lasting prosperity that can put America back to work.

This is the cause that brought me into the campaign and that sustained me for nine months, across a hundred thousand miles, in forty different states. We had our losses; but the pain of our defeats is far, far less than the pain of the people I have met. We have learned that it is important to take issues seriously, but never to take ourselves too seriously.

The serious issue before us tonight is the cause for which the Democratic Party has stood in its finest hours—the cause that keeps our party young—and makes it, in the second century of its age, the largest political party in this Republic and the longest lasting political party on this Planet.

Our cause has been, since the days of Thomas Jefferson, the cause of the common man—and the common woman. Our commitment has been, since the days of Andrew Jackson, to all those he called "the

7. Delivered August 12, 1980, at the Democratic Party convention in New York. Printed in *Vital Speeches of the Day*, 46 (September 15, 1980), 714-716.

humble members of society—the farmers, mechanics, and laborers.'' On this foundation, we have defined our values, refined our policies, and refreshed our faith.

Now I take the unusual step of carrying the cause and the commitment of my campaign personally to our national convention. I speak out of a deep sense of urgency about the anguish and anxiety I have seen across America. I speak out of a deep belief in the ideals of the Democratic Party, and in the potential of that party and of a President to make a difference. I speak out of a deep trust in our capacity to proceed with boldness and a common vision that will feel and heal the suffering of our time—and the division of our party.

The economic plank of this platform on its face concerns only material things; but is also a moral issue that I raise tonight. It has taken many forms over many years. In this campaign, and in this country that we seek to lead, the challenge in 1980 is to give our voice and our vote for these fundamental Democratic principles:

Let us pledge that we will never misuse unemployment, high interest rates, and human misery as false weapons against inflation.

Let us pledge that employment will be the first priority of our economic policy.

Let us pledge that there will be security for all who are now at work. Let us pledge that there will be jobs for all who are out of work—and we will not compromise on the issue of jobs.

These are not simplistic pledges. Simply put, they are the heart of our tradition; they have been the soul of our party across the generations. It is the glory and the greatness of our tradition to speak for those who have no voice, to remember those who are forgotten, to respond to the frustrations and fulfill the aspirations of all Americans seeking a better life in a better land.

We dare not forsake that tradition. We cannot let the great purposes of the Democratic Party become the bygone passages of history. We must not permit the Republicans to seize and run on the slogans of prosperity.

We heard the orators at their convention all trying to talk like Democrats. They proved that even Republican nominees can quote Franklin Roosevelt to their own purpose. The Grand Old Party thinks it has found a great new trick. But forty years ago, an earlier generation of Republicans attempted that same trick. And Franklin Roosevelt himself replied ''Most Republican leaders . . . have bitterly fought and blocked the forward surge of average men and women in their pursuit of happiness. Let us not be deluded that overnight those leaders have suddenly become the friends of average men and women. . . . You know, very few of us are that gullible.''

And four years later, when the Republicans tried that trick again, Franklin Roosevelt asked: "Can the Old Guard pass itself off as the New Deal? I think not. We have all seen many marvelous stunts in the circus—but no performing elephant could turn a handspring without falling flat on its back."

The 1980 Republican convention was awash with crocodile tears for our economic distress but it is by their long record and not their recent words that you shall know them.

The same Republicans who are talking about the crisis of unemployment have nominated a man who once said—and I quote: "Unemployment insurance is a prepaid vacation plan for freeloaders." And that nominee is no friend of labor.

The same Republicans who are talking about the problems of the inner cities have nominated a man who said—and I quote: "I have included in my morning and evening prayers everyday the prayer that the federal government not bail out New York." And that nominee is no friend of this city and of our great urban centers.

The same Republicans who are talking about security for the elderly have nominated a man who said just four years ago that participation in Social Security "should be made voluntary." And that nominee is no friend of the senior citizen.

The same Republicans who are talking about preserving the environment have nominated a man who last year made the preposterous statement, and I quote: "Eighty percent of air pollution comes from plants and trees." And that nominee is no friend of the environment.

And the same Republicans who are invoking Franklin Roosevelt have nominated a man who said in 1976—and these are his exact words: "Fascism was really the basis of the New Deal." And that nominee, whose name is Ronald Reagan, has no right to quote Franklin Delano Roosevelt.

The great adventure which our opponents offer is a voyage into the past. Progress is our heritage, not theirs. What is right for us as Democrats is also the right way for Democrats to win.

The commitment I seek is not to outworn views, but to old values that will never wear out. Programs may sometimes become obsolete, but the ideal of fairness always endures. Circumstances may change, but the work of compassion must continue. It is surely correct that we cannot solve problems by throwing money at them; but it is also correct that we dare not throw our national problems onto a scrap heap of inattention and indifference. The poor may be out of political fashion, but they are not without human needs. The middle-class may be angry, but they have not lost the dream that all Americans can advance together.

The demand of our people in 1980 is not for smaller government or bigger government, but for better government. Some say that government is always bad, and that spending for basic social programs is the root of our economic evils. But we reply: The present inflation and recession cost our economy $200 billion a year. We reply: Inflation and unemployment are the biggest spenders of all.

The task of leadership in 1980 is not to parade scapegoats or to seek refuge in reaction but to match our power to the possibilities of progress.

While others talked of free enterprise, it was the Democratic Party that acted—and we ended excessive regulation in the airline and trucking industry. We restored competition to the marketplace. And I take some satisfaction that this deregulation was legislation that I sponsored and passed in the Congress of the United States.

As Democrats, we recognize that each generation of Americans has a rendezvous with a different reality. The answers of one generation become the questions of the next generation. But there is a guiding star in the American firmament. It is as old as the revolutionary belief that all people are created equal—and as clear as the contemporary condition of Liberty City and the South Bronx. Again and again, Democratic leaders have followed that star—and they have given new meaning to the old values of liberty and justice for all.

We are the party of the New Freedom, the New Deal, and the New Frontier. We have always been the party of hope. So this year, let us offer new hope—new hope to an America uncertain about the present, but unsurpassed in its potential for the future.

To all those who are idle in the cities and industries of America, let us provide new hope for the dignity of useful work. Democrats have always believed that a basic civil right of all Americans is the right to earn their own way. The party of the people must always be the party of full employment.

To all those who doubt the future of our economy, let us provide new hope for the reindustrialization of America. Let our vision reach beyond the next election or the next year to a new generation of prosperity. If we could rebuild Germany and Japan after World War II, then surely we can reindustrialize our own nation and revive our inner cities in the 1980s.

To all those who work hard for a living wage, let us provide new hope that the price of their employment shall not be an unsafe workplace and death at an earlier age.

To all those who inhabit our land, from California to the New York Island, from the Redwood Forest to the Gulfstream waters, let us provide new hope that prosperity shall not be purchased by poisoning the air, the rivers and the natural resources that are the greatest gift of this continent. We must insist that our children and grandchildren shall inherit a land which they can truly call America the beautiful.

To all those who see the worth of their work and their savings taken by inflation, let us offer new hope for a stable economy. We must meet the pressures of the present by invoking the full power of government to master increasing prices. In candor, we must say that the federal budget can be balanced only by policies that bring us to a balanced prosperity of full employment and price restraint.

And to all those overburdened by an unfair tax structure, let us provide new hope for real tax reform. Instead of shutting down class-rooms, let us shut off tax shelters.

Instead of cutting out school lunches, let us cut off tax subsidies for expensive business lunches that are nothing more than food stamps for the rich.

The tax cut of our Republican opponents takes the name of tax reform in vain. It is a wonderfully Republican idea that would redis-tribute income in the wrong direction. It is good news for any of you with incomes over $200,000 a year. For the few of you, it offers a pot of gold worth $14,000. But the Republican tax cut is bad news for middle income families. For the many of you, they plan a pittance of $200 a year. And that is not what the Democratic Party means when we say tax reform.

The vast majority of Americans cannot afford this panacea from a Republican nominee who has denounced the progressive income tax as the invention of Karl Marx. I am afraid he has confused Karl Marx with Theodore Roosevelt, the obscure Republican President who sought and fought for a tax system based on ability to pay. Theodore Roosevelt was not Karl Marx—and the Republican tax scheme is not tax reform.

Finally, we cannot have a fair prosperity in isolation from a fair society.

So I will continue to stand for national health insurance. We must not surrender to the relentless medical inflation that can bankrupt almost anyone—and that may soon break the budgets of government at every level.

Let us insist on real controls over what doctors and hospitals can charge. Let us resolve that the state of a family's health shall never depend on the size of a family's wealth.

The President, the Vice President, and the Members of Congress have a medical plan that meets their needs in full. Whenever Senators and Representatives catch a little cold, the Capitol physician will see them immediately, treat them promptly, and fill a prescription on the spot. We do not get a bill even if we ask for it. And when do you think was the last time a Member of Congress asked for a bill from the federal government?

I say again, as I have said before: if health insurance is good enough for the President, the Vice President, and the Congress of the United States, then it is good enough for all of you and for every family in America.

There were some who said we should be silent about our differences on issues during this convention. But the heritage of the Democratic Party has been a history of democracy. We fight hard because we care deeply about our principles and purposes. We did not flee this struggle. And we welcome this contrast with the empty and expedient spectacle last month in Detroit where no nomination was contested, no question was debated and no one dared to raise any doubt or dissent.

Democrats can be proud that we chose a different course—and a different platform.

We can be proud that our party stands for investment in safe energy instead of a nuclear future that may threaten the future itself. We must not permit the neighborhoods of America to be permanently shadowed by the fear of another Three Mile Island.

We can be proud that our party stands for a fair housing law to unlock the doors of discrimination once and for all. The American house will be divided against itself so long as there is prejudice against any American family buying or renting a home.

And we can be proud that our party stands plainly, publicly, and persistently for the ratification of the Equal Rights Amendment. Women hold their rightful place at our convention; and women must have their rightful place in the Constitution of the United States. On this issue, we will not yield, we will not equivocate, we will not rationalize, explain, or excuse. We will stand for E.R.A. and for the recognition at long last that our nation had not only founding fathers, but founding mothers as well.

A fair prosperity and a just society are within our vision and our grasp. We do not have every answer. There are questions not yet asked, waiting for us in the recesses of the future.

But of this much we can be certain, because it is the lesson of all our history:

Together a President and the people can make a difference. I have found that faith still alive wherever I have traveled across the land. So let us reject the counsel of retreat and the call to reaction. Let us go forward in the knowledge that history only helps those who help themselves.

There will be setbacks and sacrifices in the years ahead. But I am convinced that we as a people are ready to give something back to our country in return for all it has given us. Let this be our commitment. Whatever sacrifices must be made will be shared—and shared fairly. And let this be our confidence: at the end of our journey and always before us shines that ideal of liberty and justice for all.

In closing, let me say a few words to all those I have met and all those who have supported me at this convention and across the country.

There were hard hours on our journey. Often we sailed against the wind, but always we kept our rudder true. There were so many of you who stayed the course and shared our hope. You gave your help; but even more, you gave your hearts. Because of you, this has been a happy campaign. You welcomed Joan and me and our family into your homes and neighborhoods, your churches, your campuses, and your union halls. When I think back on all the miles and all the months and all the memories, I think of you. I recall the poet's words, and I say: "What golden friends I had."

Among you, my golden friends across this land, I have listened and learned.

I have listened to Kenny Dubois, a glassblower in Charleston, West Virginia, who has ten children to support, but has lost his job after 35 years, just three years short of qualifying for his pension.

I have listened to the Trachta family, who farm in Iowa and who wonder whether they can pass the good life and the good earth on to their children.

I have listened to a grandmother in East Oakland, who no longer has a phone to call her grandchildren, because she gave it up to pay the rent on her small apartment.

I have listened to young workers out of work, to students without the tuition for college, and to families without the chance to own a home. I have seen the closed factories and the stalled assembly lines of Anderson, Indiana and South Gate, California. I have seen too many—far too many—idle men and women desperate to work. I have seen too many—far too many—working families desperate to protect the value of their wages from the ravages of inflation.

Yet I have also sensed a yearning for new hope among the people in every state where I have been. I felt it in their handshakes; I saw it in their faces. I shall never forget the mothers who carried children to our rallies. I shall always remember the elderly who have lived in an America of high purpose and who believe it can all happen again.

Tonight, in their name, I have come here to speak for them. For their sake, I ask you to stand with them. On their behalf, I ask you to restate and reaffirm the timeless truth of our party.

I congratulate President Carter on his victory here. I am confident that the Democratic Party will reunite on the basis of Democratic principles—and that together we will march toward a Democratic victory in 1980.

And someday, long after this convention, long after the signs come down, and the crowds stop cheering, and the bands stop playing, may it be said of our campaign that we kept the faith. May it be said of our party in 1980 that we found our faith again.

May it be said of us, both in dark passages and in bright days, in the words of Tennyson that my brothers quoted and loved—and that have special meaning for me now:

I am a part of all that I have met . . .

Though much is taken, much abides . . .

That which we are, we are—

One equal temper of heroic hearts . . . strong in will

To strive, to seek, to find, and not to yield.

For me, a few hours ago, this campaign came to an end. For all those whose cares have been our concern, the work goes on, the cause endures, the hope still lives, and the dream shall never die.

Six months after Kennedy's speech, Ronald Reagan was celebrating victory and preparing to assume the presidency. The ongoing debate had been resolved for a time in favor of the Republican Party. It is likely, however, that the two major political parties will continue to disagree over values and the sense of order and proportion we give to our various concerns. The two parties seem to function as an ongoing dialectical process, in which each periodically assumes the role of thesis to the other's antithesis. Out of this ongoing but apparently productive conflict continues to emerge at least part of the peculiar synthesis that is the American identity: that unique blending of spirit and form that constitutes our collective being. Speaking in public will continue to play a large part in informing this sense of being.

INDEX